Austrian
DESSERTS

Toni Mörwald
Christoph Wagner

Austrian
DESSERTS

OVER 400 CAKES, PASTRIES, STRUDELS, TORTES, AND CANDIES

In Cooperation with Martin Weiler
Photography by Ulrike Köb

Translation by Tobi Haberstroh

SKYHORSE PUBLISHING

Note
The given measurements will make four servings, unless otherwise noted.
Tarts, cakes, cookies, and confections can be portioned as desired.
The given measurements of flour refer to fine white pastry flour unless otherwise specified.

Recipe information:
Toni Mörward, Inn & Restaurant "Zur Traube"
Kleine Zeile 13–17
A-3483 Feuersbrunn
AUSTRIA
Phone: 011-43-2738-2298-0; Fax: 011-43-2738-2298-60
toni@moerwald.at
www.moerwald.at

Bibliographic Information of The German Library
The German Library catalogued this publication in the
German National Bibliography; detailed bibliographic data
can be found on the internet at http://dnb.ddb.de

10 9 8 7 6 5 4 3 2 1

Library of Congress Cataloging-in-Publication Data is available on file.
ISBN: 978-1-61608-434-9

Printed in China

Contents

Dear Readers,

Austria has always been a country where the heavens are filled with sweet temptations. An Austrian kitchen without sweet cooking would be completely unthinkable. Sometimes you get the impression that the meat dishes in Austria were only invented to lengthen the anticipation for dessert.

But actually, dessert is the greatest challenge for every cook, whether amateur or pro. Anyone who has ever hosted dinner knows dessert makes a meal successful.

This volume is concerned with making sure that this sweet climax succeeds every time. It is a fundamental cookbook for creating up-to-date baked goods and desserts. Up-to-date means first and foremost that we have tried to cater to modern dietary habits and, wherever possible, to use lots of fruit, soft dough, and light and airy creams. In a special chapter, we offer you a little basics course on "whole foods baking" according to the newest findings in nutritional physiology.

That admittedly does not change the fact that the words "sweet" and "sinful" are closely connected when it comes to baked goods. A sweet kitchen without sugar, chocolate, puff pastry, strudel, pancakes, whipped cream, brittle, marzipan, and all the other delectable seductions would miss the point, plain and simple.

Nevertheless, true enjoyment lies in moderation. For this reason, we have also placed particular importance on portion size so that the calorie-rich sweets do not leave behind an unnecessary feeling of being too stuffed or heavy. In this way, *Austrian Desserts* differs from older Austrian baked goods cookbooks, which were designed more for the needs of a hardworking rural population than for our modern urban hedonism.

Of course no one will stop anyone who still "really wants to sin" from simply having double the amount. Some of the following five hundred or so desserts are made with cake, cream, ice cream, fruit sauce, and similar ingredients. Of course, all of these components can be prepared separately or combined differently. That, too, separates the modern from the traditional Austrian kitchen: Here, there are no limits on fantasy and creativity.

On the following pages, we want not only to offer you authentic recipes, but also share all kinds of facts about the historical background of the sweet Austrian kitchen. And if you happen to be on a diet currently, you can use this dessert cookbook simply as a culinary reader, even just in anticipation of later sweet indulgences.

Austrian Dessert does not forget good old tradition, but is also a fundamental dessert cookbook that is tailored to the needs of a new generation who do not think of themselves as having a sweet tooth, but who simply want to have "sweet dreams" without regret. This book is the handbook for sweet dreams, and we dedicate it to you personally!

With sweet greetings,

Toni Mörwald

Christoph Wagner

Basics of the Sweet Austrian Kitchen

BASIC DOUGHS, BATTERS, AND GLAZES

BASIC DOUGH

The word "dough" comes from kneading, which says the most important thing about its creation. The basic ingredient is always a grain that has been ground and mixed with liquid, fat, eggs, nuts, sugar, and flavoring and finally baked. Most doughs are also suitable for freezing.

As the Pastry Turns

The invention of puff pastry is the stuff of legends. It is entirely possible that it was Viennese bakers who first got the idea to roll out butter on water-based dough to make it airier. Presumably this technique was brought north by Viennese journeymen and Danish pastry developed from leavened flaky dough in Denmark. It is not a coincidence that the otherwise thoroughly patriotic French call pastries made of this dough "Viennoiserie" even today. Meanwhile in France, the expression "millefeuille," which means "1,000 leaves," was invented for puff pastry or flaky pastry. That is admittedly one of the many little exaggerations that appear so often in the history of Grande Cuisine. In truth, a properly made puff pastry has more than 144 layers—which is still enough for it to be very flaky due to the trapped air and the water content. The important process of rolling out and folding the dough many times is known to pastry chefs as "turning." Traditionally, you need four turns for the puff pastry to turn out perfect.

BASIC DOUGH FOR TARTS

Ingredients for 2 tarts
(10 in (26 cm) diameter)
2 sticks plus 3 tbsp (270 g)
 Butter, room temperature
1 cup plus 1 tbsp (240 g)
 Granulated sugar
2 Eggs
4 cups (500 g) Flour
Zest of 1 lemon
Dash of salt
Flour for the work surface
Butter for the pan
Dried lentils or peas as
 weights

Cream the butter with the granulated sugar. Add the lemon zest and salt and then the eggs. Incorporate the flour and cool the dough for 1 hour in the refrigerator, covered. Preheat the oven to 375 °F (190 °C). On a floured work surface, roll the dough out to the proper size and line a buttered springform with it. Cover with parchment paper and dried lentils or peas. Bake for 12–15 minutes. After baking, remove the parchment paper and lentils or peas and use the tart base as you wish.

Bake Time: 12–15 minutes

Bake Temperature: 375 °F (190 °C)

PUFF PASTRY

Ingredients for the starter
4 cups (500 g) Flour
3½ tbsp (50 g) Butter
1 Egg yolk
1 tsp (5 g) Salt
1 tbsp Rum or vinegar
¾ cup (180 ml) Water

For the butter brick
4 sticks plus 3 tbsp (500 g)
 Butter
⅔ cup (80 g) Flour
Flour for the work surface

For the starter dough, first knead flour with butter, salt, rum or vinegar, water, and egg yolks to an elastic dough. Roll into a ball, cut in half, and let rest for about 30 minutes.

For the butter brick, knead the butter with the flour until smooth and form a brick. Roll out the starter on a floured work surface, lay the butter brick on top, and fold the dough over. From the center, carefully roll out the dough in all directions with a rolling pin without rolling it thinner than ½ inch (10mm). Then come the four turns.

First turn: Fold the dough over in thirds (creating 3 layers) and roll out again.

Second turn: Fold the dough over in quarters (creating 4 layers), cover the dough, and let it rest for about 30 minutes.

Third and fourth turns: Roll out the dough again and repeat the first and second turns. Then the dough will have a total of 144 layers (3x4x3x4). Let the dough rest in the refrigerator. It is best to wait until the next day to work with it further.

DANISH PASTRY

For the butter brick, it is best to grate the cold butter into shavings with a coarse plane or cut into pieces. Mix in the flour and form a brick. Let it sit in a cold place (for several hours if possible).

To make the starter dough, mix yeast into the cold milk and then knead with the remaining ingredients to form a smooth dough. Roll into a ball with the heels of your hands. Cut in half, cover with plastic wrap, and let rest for 10 minutes in the refrigerator. As with the puff pastry (see p. 11), fold in the butter with a simple, a double, and another simple turn. Use dough as you please. Brown Danish pastry at 430 °F (220 °C) and finish baking at 350 °F (180 °C).

Tip: Make sure that Danish pastry dough, which also happens to be called leavened puff pastry, is always kept very cool while working.

To be sure your yeast dough rises properly . . .
. . . it is advised that you always follow these rules:

- Always use room temperature ingredients.
- Avoid capturing air inside the dough as you knead it.
- Make sure that it is above 68 °F (20 °C) in your work room.
- Use butter with the lowest possible salt content.
- Use only fresh yeast and make sure that it has not dried out.
- For the preparation of yeast dough, use only pure wheat flour.
- Always let your starter and yeast dough rise in the warmest spot in your work room.

Ingredients
For the Butter Brick
3 sticks (350 g) Butter
6 tbsp (50 g) Flour

For the Starter Dough
4¾ cups (600 g) Flour
½ cup (60 g) Confectioner's sugar
4¼ tbsp (60 g) Butter
7 tbsp (60 g) Yeast
1¼ cups (300 ml) Milk, cold
1 Egg
1 Egg yolk
1 tsp (6 g) Salt
Dash of vanilla sugar
Zest of 1 lemon

LEAVENED DOUGH

Ingredients
3 cups (375 g) Flour
1⅔ cup (375 g) Flour, coarse
3 Eggs
½ cup (12 cl) Oil
Dash of salt
1½ cups (375 ml) Milk,
   lukewarm
5 tbsp (45 g) Yeast
⅔ cup (75 g) Confectioner's
   sugar
1 stick plus 2½ tbsp (150 g)
   Butter, melted

Mix smooth and coarse flour together. Crumble the yeast in a second bowl and mix with lukewarm milk. Mix in half the flour, dust the top with flour, and cover the starter dough with a towel (the towel should not touch the dough). Let rise in a warm spot for about 30 minutes. Beat in the salt, eggs, sugar, remaining flour, liquid butter, and oil with a cooking spoon until the dough separates from the side of the bowl. Cover and let rise another 20 minutes in a warm spot. Continue according to the recipe, but always bake in a closed oven from 430 °F down to 350 °F (220 °C to 180 °C).

BRIOCHE DOUGH

Ingredients
6 tbsp Milk
5 tbsp (45 g) Yeast
8 cups (1 kg) Flour
8 tbsp Sugar
Dash of salt
5 sticks plus 2½ tbsp (600 g)
   Butter, room temperature
12 Eggs

Warm the milk, mix in the yeast, mix in some of the flour to create a starter, and let rise in a warm spot until the volume has doubled. Mix the rest of the ingredients into the risen starter and beat the dough until bubbles form. Cover the bowl with a towel (the towel should not touch the dough) and let rise again in a warm spot. Repeat this process two more times. Finally, let the dough sit in a cold place for 1 hour and then fill the appropriate pan or make braids or buns according to the recipe. Bake for about 20 minutes in a preheated oven at 430 °F (220 °C).

Bake Time: 20 minutes

Bake Temperature: 430 °F (220 °C)

What is Brie Doing in Brioche?

Culinary historians know a few things about the word "brioche." For example, that this leavened bread, originally made without a starter, appeared for the first time in 1404 in a recipe manuscript. Alexandre Dumas, creator of the Three Musketeers and author of a large culinary dictionary, claimed that brioche was so called because in classic brioche, some brie used to be mixed into the dough. This theory is considered to have been disproven, because brioche can be traced back to the Norman root broyer/brier, which means nothing other than pounded/combined. So, no cheese in breakfast brioche. And cross my heart: marmalade goes much better. (See recipe on page 13.)

Pâte Brisée (Linzer Dough)

Cut the butter into small pieces and let soften to room temperature. Sift the flour into a bowl, add confectioner's sugar, salt, vanilla sugar, lemon zest, and egg yolks, and knead with fingertips. Quickly knead in the butter (don't take too long!), form a ball, and let sit for an hour in a cool place. Preheat the oven to 350°F (180°C). Roll the dough out thin and lay it on a baking pan or in the tart pan, stipple with a fork (poke several holes), and bake until golden brown. Let cool and then continue as desired.

Bake Time: about 8 minutes

Bake Temperature: 350°F (180°C)

Ingredients for 2 tortes (10in (26 cm) diameter) or 1 cake
base (12x18in (30x45 cm))
3⅔ cups (450 g) Flour
2 sticks plus 5 tbsp (300 g) Butter
1¼ cup (150 g) Confectioner's sugar
1 Egg yolk
Lemon zest
2 tsp (10 g) Vanilla sugar
Dash of salt

One, Two, Three from Linz

Long before the invention of the Linzer Torte, the "pretty Linzers" were already known as outstanding bakers. In many old cookbooks, Linzer dough is named after them, even though in reality it is nothing but a classic pâte brisée. Because the sugar, butter, and flour are used in a ratio of 1:2:3, this dough was sometimes called a one-two-three dough in Austrian vernacular.

STRUDEL DOUGH

Sift the flour onto a work surface, make an indent in the middle, and add in the oil and salt. Add the water little by little and knead all the ingredients to a smooth dough that does not stick to your hands. Place the dough in a bowl and spread oil on top so that a skin will not form. Cover with a damp towel that does not touch the dough and let rest at room temperature for half an hour. Then use as you please.

Use: as apple, pear, or apricot strudel, or as decoration, such as strudel leaves

Ingredients for 10 Servings
2⅔ cups (300 g) Wheat flour
2 tbsp (25 ml) Oil
1 tsp (5 g) Salt
⅔ cup (150 ml) Water,
   lukewarm
Oil for spreading

10 Golden Rules for Successful Strudel Dough

Many housewives hesitate to make strudel dough themselves and instead reach for simpler premade products. Those who can say that they made their strudel themselves will get even more attention from guests. It is not as complicated as it looks by far. If you follow these "golden housewife rules" you need have no worries about the quality of your strudel:

1. *Practice makes perfect. The second strudel dough will be better than the first. By the tenth, you will have the routine down. And by number twenty, at the latest, strudel will be as easy as the proverbial pie.*
2. *Make sure that the water is tempered well. Too hot is better than too cold.*
3. *Allow the dough an adequate rest before using it. Let it rest in a slightly warmed container that holds warmth well. Strudel dough does not like being cooled.*
4. *The strudel dough should always rest in a container covered with a towel or plate.*
5. *Roll the dough out with a rolling pin as evenly as possible and lay it on a sufficiently floured, warmed(!) cloth.*
6. *Remove all rings before working on this dough, because they can easily tear the dough during kneading.*

7. *Reach between the dough and the cloth with both hands. Make sure that the backs of your hands face up and are bent, and spread your fingers as much as possible.*
8. *As soon as the dough is on your two hands, you only need to move the dough back and forth in a steady rhythm, gently and without haste. The dough is elastic enough that it adjusts to this movement and gets thinner evenly without tearing.*
9. *As soon as the dough is as thin as newspaper (or, as they used to say, as translucent as a poppy petal), all bumps and thick edges must be cut off or pressed thin between your thumb and forefinger.*
10. *After adding the filling, move the dough only with the help of the cloth lying underneath. You only need to hold it tautly from the left and right and lift it slowly. Then the dough will practically roll itself together.*

BUTTER STREUSEL

Ingredients for
the Covering of a Tart
⅔ cup (80 g) Flour
4¼ tbsp (60 g) Butter
½ cup (60 g) Confectioner's
  sugar
Dash of cinnamon
Dash of salt
1 tsp (5 g) Vanilla sugar

Mix the flour with room temperature butter, confectioner's sugar, cinnamon, salt, and vanilla sugar and roll the mixture into crumbs between your hands. Use as you please or line a baking sheet with parchment paper, spread out the streusel, and bake at 340 °F (170 °C) until golden brown. Spread on a fruit tart or fruit waffle.

Tip: If you spread some melted butter on the streusel before baking, it will get crispier and be a prettier color.

Bake Time: about 5 minutes

Bake Temperature: 340 °F (170 °C)

PALATSCHINKEN (AUSTRIAN CRÊPE) DOUGH

Mix milk with eggs, granulated sugar, and salt. Mix in the flour last. Heat oil in a pan, pour in a thin layer of dough, and tilt the pan so that the dough can even out. Cook the palatschinken until golden brown, turning once.

Tip: The classic Viennese way to eat palatschinken is filled with apricot marmalade. But they also taste excellent with fillings of various other marmalades, ground nuts, creamy quark, and ice cream, or garnished with chocolate sauce.

It All Depends on the Filling
The most important thing for pancakes is the consistency and fullness of the dough, but palatschinken, which originated in Romania and Hungary, are about delicateness. Palatschinken should be so fine and thin that the filling can shine and not be battered by dough that is too opulent or even soggy.

Ingredients for
8 Palatschinken
1 cup (250 ml) Milk
1 cup plus 1 tbsp (140 g)
   Flour
2 Eggs
1 tsp Granulated sugar
Dash of salt
Oil for cooking

QUARK DOUGH FOR FILLED DUMPLINGS

Cream the butter with the confectioner's sugar. Stir in the quark, then the eggs, and season with lemon zest, rum, and salt. Mix in the breadcrumbs and let set for 2 hours. Use as you please.

Tip: This dough works very well for fruit, poppy, nut, or chocolate dumplings.

Ingredients for 15 × 20
Dumplings
1¾ tbsp (25 g) Butter
2 tbsp Confectioner's sugar
2 Eggs
12 oz (350 g) Quark
Lemon zest
Splash of rum
Dash of salt
3½ oz (100 g) White bread
   crumbs

Quark from the Pot

Topfen is the Austrian name for the type of cheese that is called quark in Germany. "Topf" means "pot" and topfen is simply cream cheese that comes from the same pot as the sour milk that made it. The technique of curdling skimmed milk with fermented milk cultures and rennet and then separating the whey from the fresh cheese was known to Mongolian pastoral people. The technique is around 9,000 years old. The watery, low-fat topfen has been popular since then. It is indispensible in the sweet Austrian kitchen for making "sinful" creams and fillings as well as lower calorie doughs and batters that are easy to digest. Topfen is also rich in vitamins and micronutrients and provides three times as much protein as milk, making it more filling.

Precisely because of these advantages, topfen is a sensitive raw product and should be looked after appropriately, especially in dessert cooking. That is why you should always be aware of the following rules:

> Make sure that topfen is always white to creamy yellow, tastes mildly sour, is not secreting whey, and is not exhibiting any effects of going bad, such as mold, discoloration, or similar. Bitter tones in the taste are a sign that it is going bad.

> Topfen should always be stored in a cool place, protected from light. At room temperature it will go bad quicker, become sour, and have a change in taste.

> Caution: Topfen is very susceptible to strange smells. Thus, it should be kept in a tightly sealed container and never stored near strongly aromatic ingredients and food.

> The more sour cream that topfen contains, the softer, smoother, and more spreadable it will be, yet also the higher calorie it will be. There are similar cheeses of varying fat content available.

CHOUX PASTRY

Bring water, butter, sugar, and salt to boil in a saucepan. Remove from heat as soon as the mixture begins to boil and stir in the sifted flour. Stir smooth with a cooking spoon. Place the pan back on the heat and stir until the dough separates from the pan. Remove from the heat again and now slowly mix in one egg after another (ideally with a hand mixer). The dough should absorb the eggs well and should not become greasy. Bake the choux pastry as directed in a preheated oven at 350–430 °F (180–220 °C) for 15–20 minutes.

Bake Time: 15–20 minutes (according to size)

Bake Temperature: about 350–430 °F (180–220 °C)

Ingredients
For about 30 Profiteroles
1 cup (250 ml) Water
1 tbsp Sugar
4½ tbsp (65 g) Butter
Dash of salt
1 cup (125 g) Flour
3 Eggs

1
Bring water, butter, sugar, and salt to boil.

2
Remove from heat and stir in the sifted flour. Sit smooth with a cooking spoon.

3
Place the saucepan back on the heat and stir until "burnt," until the dough separates from the pan. Remove from heat and stir in the eggs bit by bit.

4
Put the batter in a pastry bag with a star tip and squeeze out puffs.

5
Put the profiteroles in the oven.

6
Remove from the oven, let cool briefly, then remove from sheet.

BASIC BATTERS

Next to dough, batter is the most important foundation of baked goods and confectionary art. Its hallmark is a high proportion of eggs, which are used either together or separated into white and yolk. By using particular ingredients, such as chocolate, almonds, nuts, cocoa, or poppy, the flavor of batters can be varied in many ways.

COLD SPONGE CAKE
FOR ROULADES

Preheat the oven to 400 °F (200 °C). Mix the egg yolks in with ⅕ of the granulated sugar, a dash of vanilla sugar, salt, and lemon zest. In a separate bowl, beat the egg whites lightly, add the rest of the granulated sugar, and then beat the egg whites to stiff peaks. Fold the two mixtures together, but not completely. Sift the flour in and carefully fold in. Line a baking sheet with parchment paper and spread out the batter on it. Bake for 15–20 minutes. After baking, overturn onto parchment paper sprinkled with granulated sugar and carefully pull the parchment paper from the cake.

Bake Time: 15–20 minutes

Bake Temperature: 400 °F (200 °C)

Ingredients for 1 Roulade
Yields 12× 18in (30× 45 cm)
10 Egg yolks
1 cup less 2 tbsp (200 g)
  Granulated sugar
Dash of vanilla sugar
Dash of salt
Lemon zest
8 Egg whites
1¼ cups (160 g) Flour
Granulated sugar for sprin-
  kling

COLD SPONGE CAKE FOR SCHNITTEN

Ingredients for 1 Sponge Cake Base Yields 12× 18in (30×45 cm)
5 Egg yolks
3 tbsp (20 g) Confectioner's sugar
Dash of vanilla sugar
Dash of salt
Lemon zest
5 Egg whites
7 tbsp (100 g) Granulated sugar
1 cup (125 g) Flour
Granulated sugar for sprinkling

Preheat the oven to 400 °F (200 °C). Cream the egg yolks with the confectioner's sugar, vanilla sugar, salt, and lemon zest. Beat the egg whites slightly, add the granulated sugar, and beat to stiff peaks. Fold the two mixtures together, but not completely. Sift in the flour and carefully fold in. Line a baking sheet with parchment paper and spread out the batter on it. Bake for about 10 minutes. After baking, overturn onto parchment paper sprinkled with granulated sugar and carefully pull the parchment paper from the cake.

Bake Time: 10 minutes

Bake Temperature: 400 °F (200 °C)

COLD SPONGE CAKE FOR TORTES

Ingredients for 1 Torte (10in (26 cm) diameter)
5 Eggs
1 Egg yolk
⅔ cup (150 g) Granulated sugar
Dash of vanilla sugar
Dash of salt
Lemon zest
1 cup plus 3 tbsp (150 g) Flour
3½ tbsp (50 g) Clarified butter, melted
Granulated sugar for sprinkling

Preheat the oven to 350 °F (180 °C). Beat the eggs, egg yolks, granulated sugar, vanilla sugar, salt, and lemon zest until creamy. Beat until the batter stops growing in volume. Carefully fold in the flour, and then stir in the hot clarified butter. Line a cake ring with parchment paper, fill with batter and bake for 35 minutes. After baking, overturn onto parchment paper sprinkled with granulated sugar. Carefully pull the parchment paper from the cake and remove from the cake ring.

Bake Time: about 35 minutes

Bake Temperature: 350 °F (180 °C)

Warm Sponge Cake

Preheat oven to 350°F (180°C). Beat the eggs with the granulated sugar in a double boiler until a thick foam forms. Remove from heat and beat again. Mix together the flour and cornstarch and carefully fold into the beaten mixture. Stir in the melted butter. Line a cake ring with parchment paper and fill with batter. Bake for about 45 minutes. After baking, overturn onto parchment paper sprinkled with granulated sugar. Carefully pull the parchment paper from the cake and remove from the cake ring.

Bake Time: about 45 minutes

Bake Temperature: 350°F (180°C)

Ingredients for 1 Torte
(10in (26 cm) diameter)
8 Eggs
1 cup plus 2 tbsp (250 g)
  Granulated sugar
1 cup (125 g) Flour
1 cup less 2 tbsp (125 g)
  Cornstarch
3½ (50 g) Butter, melted
Granulated sugar for sprinkling

Chocolate Sponge Cake

Preheat oven to 350°F (180°C). Beat the eggs, granulated sugar, salt, and vanilla sugar until creamy. Beat until the batter no longer grows in volume. Carefully fold in flour, cornstarch, and cocoa powder. Finally, fold the oil in gently and bake for 35–40 minutes.

Bake Time: 35–40 minutes

Bake Temperature: 350°F (180°C)

Ingredients for 1 Torte
(10in (26 cm) diameter)
7 Eggs
1 cup less 2 tbsp (200 g)
  Granulated sugar
Dash of salt
Dash of vanilla sugar
¾ cup (100 g) Wheat flour
⅓ cup (50 g) Cornstarch
5 tbsp (35 g) Cocoa powder
¼ cup (50 ml) Oil

The Biscuit Family

In German, sponge cake is called "Biskuit." In the 1893 book The Universal Lexicon of Culinary Arts, *it was written that "Biskuit is one of the most digestible and, if simply prepared, healthiest baked goods. Therefore it is highly recommended for children and the ill and convalescing, as an accompaniment to wine for the latter." Even if modern doctors might not give this advice, sponge cake has not lost its popularity. Maybe it's because sponge cake is only one member of the whole biscuit family, from which there are dozens if not hundreds of different fine baked goods that can be prepared.*

It wasn't always like that. When the ancient Romans invented a twice baked (latin: bis cotus), rock hard provision for their legions, they were not thinking about taste, but about shelf life. From "bis cotus" the French made "bis cuit," and baked it just once, which propelled the biscuit to international success in cake and cookie form.

LIGHT POUND CAKE

Ingredients for 1 Torte or 1 Ring Cake (10in (26 cm) diameter)
5 Eggs
3 Egg yolks
¾ cup (170 g) Granulated sugar
Dash of vanilla sugar
Salt
Lemon zest
¾ cup (100 g) Flour
½ cup plus 1 tbsp (90 g) Corn starch
4½ tbsp (65 g) Butter, melted (or oil)

Preheat oven to 350 °F (180 °C). Beat the eggs with egg yolks, granulated sugar, salt, vanilla sugar, and lemon zest. Sift the cornstarch with the flour and carefully mix in. Stir in the melted butter or oil and bake for about 55 minutes as a torte or ring cake, depending how you want to use it.

Bake Time: about 55 minutes

Bake Temperature: 350 °F (180 °C)

HEAVY POUND CAKE

Preheat oven to 410°F (210°C). Cream the butter with the cornstarch, confectioner's sugar, vanilla sugar, salt, and lemon zest. Mix in egg yolks little by little. Begin to beat the egg whites, add granulated sugar, beat to stiff peaks, and then blend into the butter mixture. Fold in the flour. Fill a buttered torte form and bake for 20 minutes at 410°F (210°C). Open the oven slightly and turn the temperature down little by little to 340°F (170°C). Continue to bake for about 40 minutes.

Bake Time: about 60 minutes

Bake Temperature: 410°F (210°C) lowering to 340°F (170°C)

All about Eggs
Eggs—Vade Mecum of the Sweet Kitchen

Nothing can change our modern eating habits, full of warnings about cholesterol. You can certainly reduce the amount of eggs in a modern cake. But without any eggs, you won't get anywhere.

And you don't have to. Even cholesterol skeptics admit that eggs have their nutritional benefits. In particular, they are relatively low fat and low calorie, especially the egg white, and yet rich in all sorts of vitamins and minerals such as sodium, potassium, calcium, magnesium, and phosphor.

Above all, eggs are ideally suited to baking and binding due to their physiological properties. When the egg whites are beaten, the proteins tear somewhat and are stretched out. The air that they capture in the process makes egg whites an ideal leavening agent.

The protein of the yolk also has its merits. It is somewhat less stable than that of the egg white, but is ideally suited to binding and thickening. But, of course, caution is necessary when heating egg yolk because it congeals easily under too much heat.

Ingredients for 1 Torte (10 in (26 cm) diameter)
2 sticks plus 5 tbsp (300 g) Butter
2⅔ cups (300 g) Wheat flour
or
2 cups (300 g) Cornstarch
1½ cups (190 g) Confectioner's sugar
Dash of vanilla sugar
Dash of salt
Lemon zest
6 Egg yolks
6 Egg whites
½ cup (125 g) Granulated sugar
6 tbsp (50 g) Flour
Butter for the form

SHOPPING FOR EGGS

You can tell a good egg by the shell, which should be clean, undamaged, and even. Otherwise bacteria can get inside easily. That is why damaged eggs spoil more quickly.

Free range eggs exhibit a stronger taste and a more intensively yellow yolk due to the varied feeding situation of the hens. The slightly higher price of free range eggs pays for itself morally and in taste.

STORAGE OF EGGS

- *Store your eggs in a cool, dark, airy place at about 54 °F (12 °C) and about 80 percent humidity.*
- *Keep eggs that you want to store for longer in your refrigerator at a temperature between 34 and 37 °F (1 and 3 °C).*
- *Before using eggs, let them reach room temperature.*
- *Avoid unnecessary temperature swings, because "sweating" can cause eggs to grow mold.*
- *Keep your eggs as protected as possible from other aromas, because they absorb strange smells very easily. For your sweet kitchen, this is especially important, because you don't want your cake to smell of vegetables or fish.*

TESTING FRESHNESS

You can test the freshness of an egg using the water test. Place the egg in a glass of cold water and see what it does. If it sinks to the bottom, it is fresh. If the wide base of the egg floats up, it is about a week old. However, if it floats up off the bottom, it was laid two or three weeks before. You can check the freshness once more after you crack the egg. The egg should have no smell, the white should be compact around the yolk, and the yolk itself should be high and round and brightly colored.

Small, dark flecks are a sign that the egg has been fertilized and should only be used with caution.

At the round end of the egg there is an air pocket which becomes larger as the egg gets older.

HOW DO YOU SEPARATE EGGS?

Gently hit the egg in the middle with the back of a knife over a small bowl. Let the white run into the bowl and dump the yolk into a different bowl. It is particularly important when beating egg whites that there are no bits of yolk mixed into the white. So it makes sense to avoid breaking the eggs over a bowl that is already full of egg whites, because just a little bit of yolk could make them entirely useless.

HOW EGG WHITES ARE SURE TO SUCCEED

- *Use egg whites that are somewhat older. They are better suited to beating.*
- *Keep the bowl as well as the mixing tool—whisk, stand mixer, or hand mixer—as cool as possible.*
- *It is best to use granulated sugar with beaten egg whites.*
- *Beat the egg whites without sugar at first, until it begins to bind together, and only then add the granulated sugar.*
- *Beat the egg whites—unless otherwise directed—until they are firm and so stiff that little "glacier peaks" form.*

ALMOND CAKE

Preheat the oven to 340 °F (170 °C). Knead the marzipan well with water then cream with egg yolks, salt, vanilla sugar, and lemon zest. Beat the egg whites to stiff peaks with the granulated sugar and combine with the marzipan mixture. Sift the flour and cornstarch together and carefully fold in. Last, mix in the clarified butter. Bake for about 50 minutes.

Bake Time: about 50 minutes

Bake Temperature: 340 °F (170 °C)

*Ingredients for 1 Torte
(10 in (26 cm) diameter)*
9 oz (250 g) Marzipan paste
2 tbsp plus 1 tsp (35 ml) Water
7 Egg yolks
Dash of salt
Dash of vanilla sugar
Lemon zest
6 Egg whites
⅔ cup (140 g) Granulated sugar
¾ cup (100 g) Flour
¼ cup (35 g) Cornstarch
2¾ tbsp (40 g) Clarified butter, melted

NUT CAKE

Ingredients for 1 Torte
(10 in (26 cm) diameter)
8 Eggs
1 cup less 2 tbsp (200 g)
  Granulated sugar
Lemon zest
1 oz (25 g) Nougat, melted
7 oz (200 g) Nuts, ground
3 oz (80 g) Breadcrumbs
⅔ cup (80 g) Flour
2 tbsp (3 cl) Rum

Preheat oven to 340 °F (170 °C). Beat the eggs with granulated sugar, vanilla sugar, and lemon zest until creamy. Carefully mix in the nougat. Mix in the nuts, breadcrumbs, and flour and, finally, flavor with rum. Bake for about 55 minutes.

Bake Time: about 55 minutes

Bake Temperature: 340 °F (170 °C)

POPPY SEED CAKE

Ingredients for 1 Torte
(10 in (26 cm) diameter)
2 sticks (220 g) Butter
½ cup (65 g) Confectioner's
  sugar
Dash of salt
Dash of vanilla sugar
9 Egg yolks
9 Egg whites
1 cup (220 g) Granulated
  sugar
10.5 oz (300 g) Poppy seeds,
  ground
4.5 oz (130 g) Hazelnuts,
  ground

Preheat the oven to 340°F (170°C). Mix together the butter, confectioner's sugar, salt, and vanilla sugar until creamy. Add the egg yolks and stir to combine. In a separate bowl, beat the egg whites until stiff. Add granulated sugar gradually and continue to beat until combined. Fold the egg whites and sugar mixture into the batter. Sprinkle the poppy seeds and hazelnuts into the mass.

Bake Time: about 50 minutes

Bake Temperature: 340 °F (170 °C)

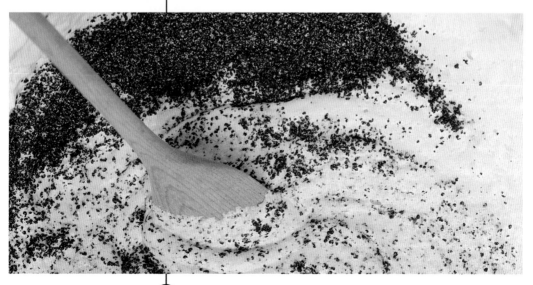

PANAMA CAKE BATTER

Preheat the oven to 340 °F (170 °C). Beat the egg yolks with the granulated sugar, rum, vanilla sugar, salt, and lemon zest until creamy. Heat the chocolate in a double boiler and stir into the batter. Beat the egg whites to stiff peaks with the granulated sugar and fold into the egg yolk mixture. Mix the almonds, hazelnuts, and flour together, then fold into the batter. Fill a buttered form and bake for about 50 minutes, leaving the oven slightly open.

Bake Time: about 50 minutes

Bake Temperature: 340 °F (170 °C) in a slightly open oven

Ingredients for 1 Torte (10in (26 cm) diameter)
7 Egg yolks
2 tbsp (30 g) Granulated sugar
4 tsp (2 cl) Rum
1½ tsp (7 g) Vanilla sugar
Dash of salt
Lemon zest
3 oz (90 g) Couverture chocolate, dark
7 Egg whites
⅔ cup (140 g) Granulated sugar for the egg whites
½ cup (60 g) Flour
3 oz (90 g) Almonds, ground
3 oz (90 g) Hazelnuts, ground
Butter for the form

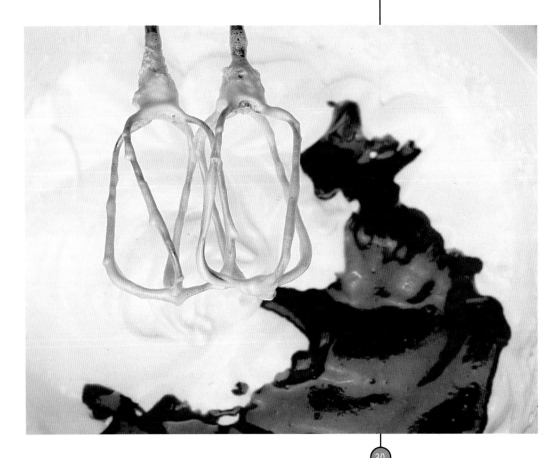

SACHERTORTE BATTER (CHOCOLATE CAKE BATTER)

Ingredients for 1 Torte (10in (26 cm) diameter)
1 stick plus 6 tbsp (200 g) Butter
1⅓ cup (170 g) Confectioner's sugar
9 Egg yolks
7 oz (200 g) Cooking chocolate
9 Egg whites
¾ cup (170 g) Granulated sugar
1⅔ cups (200 g) Flour
Butter for the form

Preheat oven to 340 °F (170 °C). Cream the butter with the confectioner's sugar. Mix in the egg yolks. Heat the cooking chocolate in the oven until it is soft and mix into the butter mixture. Beat the egg whites, add the granulated sugar, and beat to stiff peaks. Carefully fold the beaten egg whites and the flour alternately into the batter. Pour into a buttered springform pan and bake for about 55 minutes.

Bake Time: about 55 minutes

Bake Temperature: 340 °F (170 °C)

Dobos Batter

Preheat oven to 400 °F (200 °C). Cream the egg yolks with the confectioner's sugar. Beat the egg whites, add granulated sugar, and beat to stiff peaks. Fold the beaten egg whites carefully into the yolk mixture along with the flour. On parchment paper, draw six circles of about 9in (23 cm) in diameter, divide up the batter onto the circles, and spread it smooth. Bake all 6 torte bases one after another for about 8 minutes each.

Bake Time: 8 minutes

Bake Temperature: 400 °F (200 °C)

Ingredients
7 Egg yolks
⅔ cup (80 g) Confectioner's
 sugar
7 Egg whites
⅓ cup (70 g) Granulated
 sugar
1 cup plus 1 tbsp (140 g)
 Flour

Esterházy Batter

Preheat oven to 400 °F (200 °C). Begin beating the egg whites, add the granulated sugar, and beat to stiff peaks. Carefully fold in the ground hazelnuts and the vanilla sugar. Line a baking sheet or torte form with parchment paper and spread the batter out 5mm thick. Watch closely while baking until golden brown. Repeat until you have used up all the batter.

Bake Time: 8–10 minutes per sheet

Bake Temperature: 400 °F (200 °C)

*Ingredients for Schnitten
(12× 18in (30× 45 cm)) or for
2 Tortes (10in (26 cm)
diameter)*
About 22 (660 g) Egg whites
3 cups (660 g) Granulated
 sugar
23 oz (660 g) Hazelnuts,
 finely ground
1 tbsp (15 g) Vanilla sugar

Baumkuchen, "Tree Cake"

Ingredients
3 sticks plus 1½ tbsp (360 g)
  Butter
1¼ cup (160 g) Confectioner's sugar
10 Egg yolks
9 oz (260 g) Marzipan, sieved
10 Egg whites
½ cup plus 1 tbsp (130 g)
  Granulated sugar
1 cup plus 1 tbsp (140 g)
  Flour
1 cup less 2 tbsp (130 g)
  Cornstarch

Cream the butter with the confectioner's sugar, mix in the egg yolks little by little, and add the sieved marzipan. Beat the egg whites to stiff peaks with the granulated sugar. Mix together the flour and cornstarch and, alternating with the egg whites, fold into the yolk mixture. Neatly line a baking sheet with aluminum foil (shiny side down), spread out a thin layer of batter and bake for 2–3 minutes with your oven's upper heat at the highest setting and the lower heat at 300 °F (150 °C). Spread another layer, bake briefly once again, and continue until the batter is used up. Let cool, pull off the foil, and use as you please.

Bake Time: 2–3 minutes per layer

Bake Temperature: maximum upper heat, 300 °F (150 °C) lower heat

Use: either as classic baumkuchen or for lining a terrine form for parfaits and mousses

Tips: Classic baumkuchen is brushed with apricot marmalade on top, cut into pieces, and glazed with chocolate. If you happen to have a professional baking spit at your disposal, you can bake the layers on this and achieve the classic ring shape.

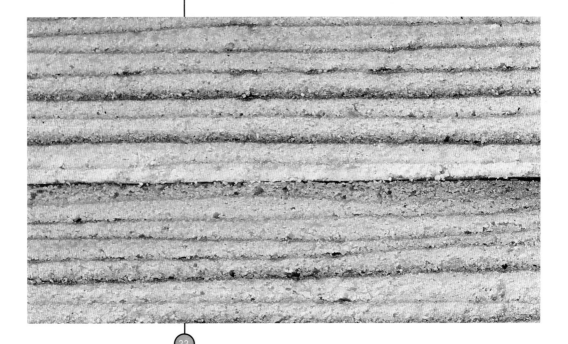

When the Baker is Beaten

Baumkuchen *means "tree cake" and gets its name from the layers of cake that are reminiscent of the age rings on a tree. The technique used to make it goes back to the Greek obelias bread. In the middle ages, it was also known as "Spießkrapfen" or "Prügelkrapfen," meaning skewer or baton cake. In the Austria state of Styria, Prügelkrapfen is still known today as a local specialty that has long been prepared in special ovens. In the kitchens of monasteries and of royalty, a spit with layered batter was turned over an open fire. The preparation lasted at least two days and required two well-rested bakers, who were on the job around the clock. When the cake was done, it had to be pulled from the spit with the help of a cord. If the cord broke, the Prügelkrapfen crashed to the floor. Then the baker would be flogged. (See recipe on p. 34.)*

MACAROON BATTER

Knead together the marzipan paste, confectioner's sugar, nuts, cinnamon, and 1 (!) egg white in a bowl. Little by little, work in the rest of the egg whites until a batter is created that is smooth enough to be squeezed through a pastry bag. Fill a piping bag and use a round nozzle to create small domes on a baking sheet lined with parchment paper. Dust the macaroons with a little bit of confectioner's sugar and let the surface dry out (preferably overnight). Then bake about 12–15 minutes in an oven preheated to 320°F (160°C). While baking, leave the oven open slightly so the steam can escape. Take out the macaroons, let cool, and remove from the parchment paper.

Bake Time: 12–15 minutes

Bake Temperature: 320°F (160°C) in a slightly open oven

Tip: If you lift up the parchment paper—after the macaroons are baked and somewhat cooled—and wipe the underside with a damp cloth, the macaroons will come off the paper with no problem.

Ingredients for about
60 Pieces
16 oz (450 g) Marzipan paste
3¼ cups (400 g) Confectioner's sugar
3 oz (90 g) Hazelnuts or walnuts, ground (can be replaced with almonds)
1 Pinch cinnamon, ground
5 Egg whites
Confectioner's sugar for dusting

MERINGUE BATTER

RECIPE I
Begin to beat the eggs slightly, and then beat to stiff peaks with (50 g) of the granulated sugar. Heat the water to 243 °F (117 °C) with the rest of the sugar to create syrup, let it cool a bit, then slowly fold into the beaten egg whites and mix until cool. Spread the meringue over fruit tortes or fruit schnitten and draw a decorative pattern into it. Brown the surface of the meringue using a "crème brûlée" kitchen torch, which is available in specialty cooking shops, or bake briefly at a high upper heat.

RECIPE II
Beat the egg whites to stiff peaks with the granulated sugar. Then fold in the sifted confectioner's sugar. Spread the meringue over fruit tortes or fruit schnitten and draw a decorative pattern into it. Brown the surface of the meringue using a "crème brûlée" kitchen torch, which is available in specialty cooking shops, or broil briefly in the oven.

GRILLAGE BATTER

First, make basic brittle crumbs (see p. 36). Preheat the oven to 340 °F (170 °C). Mix egg yolks with confectioner's sugar, walnuts, water, vanilla sugar, salt, lemon zest, and cinnamon until creamy. Begin beating the egg whites and then beat to stiff peaks with the granulated sugar. Mix the two mixtures together. Fold in the flour and brittle crumbs. Finally, carefully mix in the oil. Fill a buttered springform pan and bake for about 1 hour.

Bake Time: about 1 hour

Bake Temperature: 340 °F (170 °C)

Ingredients for 2 Tortes (10in (26 cm) diameter) or 1 Cake Base (12×18in (30×45 cm))

Recipe I
10.5 oz (300 g) Egg whites
2¼ cups (500 g) Granulated sugar
½ cup (120 ml) Water

Recipe II
8.5 oz (240 g) Egg whites
1 cup plus 1 tbsp (240 g) Granulated sugar
1⅔ cup (200 g) Confectioner's sugar

Ingredients for 1 Torte (10in (26 cm) diameter)
7 Egg yolks
½ cup (60 g) Confectioner's sugar
2 oz (60 g) Walnuts, ground
2 tbsp (30 ml) Water
2 tbsp (10 g) Vanilla sugar
Dash of salt
Lemon zest
Dash of cinnamon, ground
7 Egg whites
7 tbsp (110 g) Granulated sugar
1 cup less 1 tbsp (110 g) Flour
2 tbsp (30 ml) Oil
Butter for the form

For Brittle Crumbs
2 oz (55 g) Hazelnuts, peeled and roasted
¼ cup (55 g) Granulated sugar
Splash of lemon juice
Oil for the work surface

BRITTLE

Heat half of the sugar with the lemon juice and melt slowly. When the sugar is completely melted, add the rest of the sugar so that it melts quickly, without burning.

Quickly mix in the nuts until they are completely surrounded by sugar. Roll out the mixture with an oiled rolling pin on an oiled work surface (or between two pieces of parchment paper). Let cool and break into pieces or crumbs for further use.

Tip: For a change, you can prepare brittle with chopped almonds or pumpkin seeds.

Ingredients
4½ cups (1 kg) Granulated
   sugar
4 tbsp Lemon juice
18 oz (500 g) Nuts, chopped
Oil for the rolling pin and
   work surface

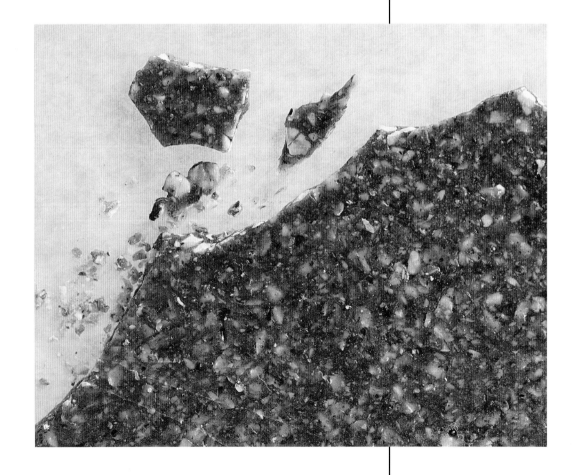

LADYFINGER BATTER

Ingredients for Ladyfingers
for a Charlotte
5 Egg yolks
6 tbsp (50 g) Confectioner's
  sugar
½ tsp Vanilla sugar
5 Egg whites
⅓ cup (70 g) Granulated
  sugar
1 cup (125 g) Flour
Confectioner's sugar for
  dusting

Preheat oven to 400 °F (200 °C). Beat the egg yolks with the confectioner's sugar and vanilla sugar until white and creamy. In a separate bowl, begin to beat the egg whites, add the granulated sugar, and beat to stiff peaks. Fold the two mixtures together, but not completely. Sift the flour and carefully fold it in. Using a piping bag fitted with a round nozzle, pipe ladyfingers onto a baking sheet lined with parchment paper. Dust with powdered sugar and bake for 5–8 minutes. Keep the oven open slightly while baking.

Bake Time: 5–8 minutes, depending on the size of the ladyfingers

Bake Temperature: 400 °F (200 °C) with a slightly open oven

MERINGUE (FOR MAKING MERINGUE MUSHROOMS)

Ingredients
5 oz (150 g) Egg whites
1⅔ cup (200 g) Confectioner's sugar
Cocoa powder for dusting

Preheat oven to 210 °F (100 °C). Beat the egg whites with the confectioner's sugar in a bain-marie until it is not so airy, but is creamy. It should be between 113 and 122 °F (45 and 50 °C). Then beat in an ice bath until it cools. It should thicken without losing volume. Fill a piping bag fitted with a round nozzle and line a baking sheet with parchment paper. To make the mushroom stems, press the piping bag nozzle against the parchment paper and pull it up without squeezing any more. For the mushroom tops, pipe semicircles and dust them with cocoa powder before baking. Dry in the oven for 30 minutes.

Bake Time: 30 Minutes

Bake Temperature: 210 °F (100 °C)

Tip: You can use a hand mixer to beat the eggs, but the last step works best with a whisk.

WAFFLE COOKIES

Mix together the confectioner's sugar, flour, liquid butter, and egg whites. Preheat oven to 350°F (180°C). Spread the batter on a buttered, floured baking sheet in stencils and bake for about 5 minutes.

Bake Time: about 5 minutes

Bake Temperature: 350°F (180°C)

Tip: The thin, cardboard stencils can be arranged in any form on the baking sheet. Then spread the batter thinly, wipe away excess, and bake.

Ingredients
6 tbsp (50 g) Confectioner's sugar
6 tbsp (50 g) Flour
3½ tbsp (50 g) Butter, melted
1 Egg white
Butter and flour for the baking sheet

HONEY WAFFLES

Melt the butter with the honey and stir in the water. Sift the flour and confectioner's sugar, mix in, and place briefly on the range. Remove from heat and let cool. Cut stencils of any shape out of cardboard and place on a baking sheet lined with parchment paper. Spread the batter into the stencils and bake in an oven preheated to 410°F (210°C). Let cool, remove from parchment paper, and store in a dry place for further use.

Bake Time: about 5 minutes

Bake Temperature: 410°F (210°C)

Ingredients
4¼ tbsp (60 g) Butter
4¼ tsp (30 g) Honey
4 tsp (20 ml) Water
⅔ cup (75 g) Confectioner's sugar
¼ cup (35 g) Flour

SESAME WAFFLES

Preheat oven to 400°F (200°C). Mix all the ingredients together. Line a baking sheet with parchment paper and spread out the batter very thinly in any form, such as 4x1in (10x3 cm) strips. Bake for about 5 minutes. Remove from parchment paper and, while still warm, bend into the desired shape by laying the waffles in a small bowl or over a cylinder. Let cool.

Bake Time: 5 minutes

Bake Temperature: 400°F (200°C)

Ingredients
½ cup (100 ml) Orange juice
1⅔ cup (200 g) Confectioner's sugar
½ cup (60 g) Flour
4.5 oz (125 g) Sesame, peeled
1 stick (120 g) Butter, melted

GLAZES

Glazing is considered to require a high level of confectionary skill, and for good reason. A beautiful glaze will tell you how meticulously and professionally even a housewife or amateur chef works. Here, you'll see how it's done.

SIMPLE SYRUP

Slowly bring the water and sugar to a boil. Skim off the foam and continue boiling until the liquid is clear.

Ingredients
4 cups (1 liter) of water
4½ cups (1 kg) Granulated sugar

Tips:

- If you add a few more tablespoons of cold water just before the mixture boils and stir it once more, it will be easier to skim off the foam.
- Cover the pot for a few moments as soon as it begins to boil. The sugar that is stuck to the edge will be dissolved in the steam and will not go to waste.
- Simple syrup is simple to prepare and can be stored in a tightly closed container in a cool place without a problem for 2–3 weeks.

Spinning Tales; or, How to Cook Sugar
Simple syrup is as important to the sweet kitchen as stock is to sauce, from glazing to canning. But simple syrup (see recipe above) is just a basic product. To be able to use it further in any of the many possible ways, it usually must be boiled to a particular consistency, or as they say in the trade, spun. To be as exact as possible, a candy thermometer is absolutely necessary in a professional kitchen. However, there are a few old confectioners'—and housewives'—tricks to knowing the right consistency without a thermometer.

SIMPLE SYRUP
Temperature: (98–100 °C)
How to Tell: The liquid should be clear and transparent.

THREAD
Temperature: just over (100 °C)
How to Tell: The sugar syrup drops from a spoon in wide threads.
Use: for stewed fruit and brushing on baked goods

SOFT THREAD
Temperature: (104–105 °C)
How to Tell: Dampen your thumb and forefinger, put some of the syrup on your finger, and see if a thread forms as you open and close them.
Use: for ice cream, glazes, candied fruit, stewed fruit

HARD THREAD
Temperature: (107–108 °C)
How to Tell: The test is just like the "soft thread," except the sugar threads must be significantly longer.
Use: for compote, jam, and thick glazes

SOFT BALL
Temperature: (112–113 °C)
How to Tell: Quickly dip a wire loop in the syrup and blow on it lightly. The sugar mixture should form small bubbles.
Use: for fondant glazes, shiny glazes, for brushing on Danishes and schnecken pasties

FIRM BALL
Temperature: (114–117 °C)
How to Tell: The test is just like the "soft ball," except the bubbles should be larger and should form a chain.
Use: marmalades, fondant, and meringue

HARD BALL
Temperature: (123–125 °C)
How to Tell: If you dip a silver spoon in ice water, then in the sugar syrup, then in ice water again, the sugar should form a pliable, unbreakable ball.
Use: fondant for bonbons and sugar foam

SOFT CRACK

Temperature: (135–138 °C)

How to Tell: Dampen the end of a wooden chopstick or cooking spoon handle and dip first in the sugar, then in cold water. When the sugar releases from the wood, it should break like glass and, when tasted, should not stick to the teeth.

Use: for candy, sugaring fruit, and for creating sugar thread decorations

HARD CRACK

Temperature: (146–150 °C)

How to Tell: Caramel sugar is light brown/golden, viscous, and uniform.

Use: Grillage and Dobos glaze

CHOCOLATE GLAZE (SACHER GLAZE)

Boil water with granulated sugar for a few minutes at a high heat, then remove from heat and let cool for several minutes. Chop up the cooking chocolate and dissolve little by little in the still-warm sugar solution until a thick, smooth glaze is created. The glaze should remain viscous and be kept lukewarm. If it is too hot, it will not have any gloss and will remain dull after hardening. Pour the glaze over the torte and quickly smooth with two or three strokes of a spatula.

Ingredients for Glaze for One Torte
1 cup plus 3 tbsp (260 g) Granulated sugar
¾ cup (170 ml) Water
7 oz (200 g) Cooking chocolate

Tips:

• Never put a Sachertorte in the refrigerator, otherwise the glaze will start to sweat.
• Since the recipe of the original Sachertorte has been a closely guarded secret since 1832, this Sacher glaze is not the original recipe.

LEMON GLAZE

Mix together sifted confectioner's sugar and lemon juice to a thick consistency.

Ingredients
Confectioner's sugar as needed
Juice of one lemon

The Right Way to Glaze a Torte
Successful glazes don't only delight the eye, but also the palate. Always follow these rules:

- *Always glaze tortes that call for marmalade under the glaze very thinly.*
- *Pour the glaze over the torte while warm and hold a knife ready in the other hand so you can spread the glaze from the middle of the torte out to the edge.*
- *Never push too hard on the glaze with the knife, but rather let the glaze flow slowly and evenly with an angled knife.*
- *To dry out the glaze, set the torte in the half-open, still-warm oven before cooling it.*

EGG WHITE GLAZE

Ingredients
1 Egg white
Juice of 1 lemon
About 2¾ cups (350 g)
   Confectioner's sugar

Mix the egg white with lemon juice, then add sifted confectioner's sugar little by little and stir well.

Tip: The consistency of this glaze can be varied to taste by increasing or lowering the amount of sugar.

GANACHE GLAZE

Ingredients for about 900g
(glaze for 6–7 tortes 10in
(26 cm) in diameter)
1 cup (250 ml) Milk
⅓ cup (85 ml) Whipped
   cream
¼ cup (50 g) Sugar
¼ cup (65 ml) Water
¼ cup (65 ml) Glucose syrup
(viscous starch syrup, see
   tip below)
14 oz (400 g) Dark
   couverture chocolate

Boil all the ingredients except the couverture chocolate in a saucepan. Remove from heat and then stir in the finely chopped chocolate until it is completely melted. Then homogenize the mixture by moving an immersion blender in circles. While blending, do not bring the blender near the surface, or else air will mix in and emulsify the smooth, glossy glaze.

Tip: If you do not have glucose syrup at your disposal, it can be replaced with simple syrup (see p. 40) or you can raise the amount of milk and whipped cream by a total of ¼ cup (65 ml). The finished glaze can be stored for 2–3 weeks and must only be warmed in a warm water bath. You may also want to thin it with some water or make it more viscous by adding chocolate.

FONDANT

A Recipe for Advanced Learners

Stir the granulated sugar into the water, bring to a boil on a high heat, skim, and add glucose. With a wet brush, repeatedly wash the sugar away from the edge. Heat the sugar mixture to 239 °F (115 °F), to the firm ball stage (see simple syrup p. 40). Pour onto a marble board dampened with water, sprinkle the top with water, and pull from the inside to the outside with a wooden spatula until the mixture is body temperature. At first it will be milky white, then become more and more transparent and will finally solidify as you work it. Cover it with a damp towel. Knead until smooth and use as desired.

Use: for punch cakes or punch tortes, for glazing Danish pastries, or for cream schnitten

Tips:

- The glucose syrup in this recipe is a purified, concentrated, liquid solution of edible saccharides from starch. It can be hard to find in a "normal" store, but it makes cooking sugar much easier, unlike the potato syrup that used to be used for this purpose. Put your trust in a confectioner to sell you some of this "wonder ingredient," or ask around in drug-stores.
- Fondant can be stored for longer in a well sealed container covered with aluminum foil.

Ingredients
4½ cups (1 kg) Granulated sugar
5 tbsp (100 g) Glucose syrup
1¾ cups (400 ml) Water

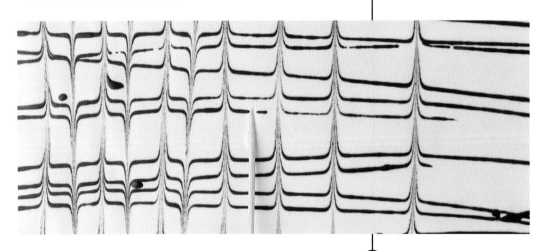

Couverture—The Queen of Chocolate

Chocolate is good, but couverture is better. Based on this motto, patissiers around the world agree that the finest chocolate desserts can only succeed with the most noble chocolate.

Couverture differs from common chocolate in the high quality of all the ingredients, the high proportion of cocoa butter, and a comparatively low sugar content. In addition, it is "conched," or kneaded, until a fine, soft sheen and an irreplaceable aroma appear.

Couverture is never cheap and so it should be used with proper care. So that it shines in the glaze as well as the package, it must be carefully tempered. The cocoa butter has a melting point of 93 °F (34 °C), which is exactly the temperature at which the couverture should be melted in a bain-marie before use. No water should get in the couverture. After being tempered, the couverture can be removed from the heat and stirred cool until just before it hardens.

Now you can really begin to work with couverture. Warm it to 93 °F (34 °C) again and follow the recipe.

And one more thing: If you have soft couverture left over, you can simply let it harden. After being tempered correctly, it will serve you just as well later.

Invitation to a Viennese Coffee Break

SWEET SEDUCTIONS
OF DANISH PASTRY, PUFF PASTRY,
AND PÂTE À CHOUX

CLASSIC COFFEE CAKE

The coffee break is a Viennese institution. Many even believe that it is the most important meal of the day for the Viennese, even if all-day work schedules make it hard to celebrate nowadays. By no means does the coffee itself play the most important role in this meal, but rather the baked goods that are offered alongside it.

GUGELHUPF ["YEAST HOOD"]

Preheat oven to 350 °F (180 °C). Cream the butter with the confectioner's sugar, vanilla sugar, salt, and lemon zest. Mix the egg yolks in little by little. Beat granulated sugar into the egg white, beat egg whites to stiff peaks, and then fold in. Sift flour and cornstarch and carefully fold into the batter along with the raisins. Coat the bundt pan with butter and dust with flour. Pour in the batter and bake for about 1 hour. Let cool, release from pan and dust with confectioner's sugar.

Bake Time: about 1 hour

Bake Temperature: 350 °F (180 °C)

Ingredients for 8in (20 cm) Pan

2 sticks plus 1½ tbsp (250 g) of Butter
3 tbsp (20 g) Confectioner's sugar
2 tsp (10 g) Vanilla sugar
Pinch of salt
Zest of ½ lemon
5 Egg yolks
5 Egg whites
⅔ cup (150 g) granulated sugar
1½ cups (190 g) flour
¼ cup (40 g) Cornstarch
1 oz (30 g) Raisins
Butter and flour for the pan
Confectioner's sugar for dusting

MARBLE GUGELHUPF

Preheat oven to 350 °F (180 °C). Cream the butter with the confectioner's sugar, vanilla sugar, salt, and lemon zest. Mix the egg yolks in little by little. Beat egg whites to soft, beat in granulated sugar, and continue beating until stiff peaks. Then fold into butter mixture. Sift flour and cornstarch together and carefully fold into the batter. Halve the batter and mix cocoa powder and oil into one half. Coat the bundt pan with soft butter and dust with flour. Pour the batters into the pan in turns to achieve a marbling effect. Bake for about 1 hour. Let cool, release from pan and dust with confectioner's sugar.

Bake Time: about 1 hour

Bake Temperature: 350 °F (180 °C)

Ingredients for 8in (20 cm) Pan

2 sticks plus 1½ tbsp (250 g) of Butter
3 tbsp (20 g) Confectioner's sugar
2 tsp (10 g) Vanilla sugar
Pinch of salt
Zest of ½ lemon
5 Egg yolks
5 Egg whites
⅔ cup (150 g) Granulated sugar
1½ cups (190 g) Flour
¼ cup (40 g) Cornstarch
4 tsp (10 g) Cocoa powder
4 tsp (2 cl) Oil
Butter and flour for the pan
Confectioner's sugar for dusting

EMPEROR'S GUGELHUPF

Cream the butter with the confectioner's sugar. Add the eggs little by little, and then add a tablespoon of flour at a time. Dissolve the yeast in lukewarm milk and add along with the rest of the flour. Knead together well. Finally, mix in raisins, salt, and lemon zest. Coat the bundt pan with soft butter and dust with flour. Fill in the dough, cover with a towel, and let rise in a warm place for about 1 hour. Bake for about 1 hour in an oven preheated to 350°F (180°C). Let cool, release from pan, and dust with powdered sugar.

Bake Time: about 1 hour

Bake Temperature: 350°F (180°C)

DANISH GUGELHUPF

Prepare the Danish pastry dough as directed and roll out to a 10x14in (25x35 cm) rectangle on a floured work surface. Blend the butter and confectioner's sugar together until smooth. For the nut filling, boil milk with granulated sugar, vanilla sugar, honey, cinnamon, and lemon zest. Mix in the nuts and let the mixture cool somewhat. Mix in the egg white and rum. Spread the butter-confectioner's sugar mixture on the pastry dough. Then spread first the apricot marmalade and then the cooled nut filling on top. Roll up the dough and cut in half lengthwise. Braid the two pieces into a circle and lay in a buttered, floured bundt pan. Brush with butter and let rise for 20 minutes. Bake for 70 minutes in an oven preheated to 350°F (180°C). After baking, release from pan and top with some apricot marmalade. Sprinkle with roasted almond slices.

Bake Time: about 70 minutes

Bake Temperature: 350°F (180°C)

DANISH GUGELHUPF

Ingredients
3½ cups (430 g) Flour
2 sticks (220 g) Butter
¾ cup (90 g) Confectioner's
  sugar
6 Eggs
¾ cup (170 ml) Milk
5 tbsp (42 g) Yeast
2 oz (60 g) Raisins
Salt
Zest of one lemon
Butter and flour for the pan
Confectioner's sugar for
  dusting

Ingredients
18 oz (500 g) Danish pastry
  dough (see p. 12)
4¼ tbsp (60 g) Butter
½ cup (60 g) Confectioner's
  sugar
1 cup less 2 tbsp (100 g)
  Apricot marmalade
Flour for the work surface
Butter and flour for the pan

For the Nut Filling
½ cup (100 ml) Milk
7 tbsp (100 g) Granulated
  sugar
2 tsp (10 g) Vanilla sugar
2 tbsp (1 kL) Honey
Dash of cinnamon
Zest of one lemon
9 oz (250 g) Walnuts, ground
1 Egg white
4 tsp (2 cl) Rum

For Topping
⅓ cup (40 g) Apricot
  marmalade
Almond slices, roasted

REINDLING

Mix flour, salt, and granulated sugar. Dissolve the yeast in luke-warm milk and mix into the flour along with melted butter and egg yolks. Stir briefly with a cooking spoon and then knead until the dough is elastic and smooth. Cover and let rise in a warm place for 40 minutes. Roll out to a rectangle on a floured work surface. Spread honey on the dough, scatter the raisins and nuts on top, and dust thickly with cinnamon sugar. Roll the dough up like a strudel and lay it in a buttered, floured ring pan. Cover and let rise again for 20 minutes. Bake for 45 minutes in an oven preheated to 375 °F (190 °C). After releasing from the pan, dust with confectioner's sugar.

Bake Time: about 45 minutes

Bake Temperature: 375 °F (190 °C)

Tip: The reindling or reinling is a specialty gugelhupf from the Austrian state of Carinthia, but in its homeland it is not just a dessert. Particularly at Easter, it is served together with Easter eggs, Easter ham, eggs with horseradish, and sausage. At traditional wedding receptions, it is actually served with the meat dish, in which case it is of course prepared without sugar and filled with tarragon leaves instead of raisins and nuts.

The Hooded Monk with the Kugelhopf

Gugelhupf is the icon of Viennese baking. Whether the gugelhupf really originates in Vienna is, like most sweet Viennese legends, not at all clear. After all, the French have their gougelhof, the Germans their Kugelhopf, the Friuli their cuguluf. Linguistically, the roots of these words are very much united and go back to the Middle High German word "gugel," which means "hood" or "headscarf" (creating the old mocking term for a Franciscan monk, "Gugelfranz") and the German word "Hefe," meaning yeast. This would make gugelhupf a "yeast hood."

Ingredients
4 cups (500 g) Flour
¼ cup (50 g) Granulated sugar
5 tbsp (42 g) Yeast
1 cup (250 ml) Milk, luke-warm
3½ tbsp (50 g) Butter, melted
2 Egg yolks
Dash of salt
2 tbsp plus 1 tsp (50 g) Honey
5 oz (150 g) Raisins
5 oz (150 g) Nuts, coarsely ground
1¼ cup (150 g) Confectioner's sugar mixed with cinnamon
Flour for the work surface
Butter and Flour for the pan
Confectioner's sugar for dusting

BÜRGERMEISTER

Ingredients
10.5 oz (300 g) Danish pastry
  dough (see p. 12)
Apricot marmalade for
  spreading
Some fondant (see p. 44)
Almond slices for sprinkling
Flour for the work surface
Butter for brushing

For the Poppy Seed Filling
¼ cup (50 ml) Milk
2 tbsp (1 kL) Honey
1 tbsp (15 g) Granulated
  sugar
2 oz (50 g) Poppy seed,
  ground
1 oz (25 g) Breadcrumbs
½ oz (10 g) Raisins
Zest of one lemon
Dash of cinnamon

For the Nut Filling
¼ cup (50 ml) Milk
2 tbsp (1 kL) Butter
4 tsp (20 g) Granulated sugar
2.5 oz (75 g) Hazelnuts,
  ground
1 oz (20 g) Nougat
Zest of one lemon
Dash of cinnamon
4 tsp (2 cl) Rum

For the Cheese Filling
1½ tbsp (20 g) Butter
3 tbsp (20 g) Confectioner's
  sugar
⅓ oz (10 g) Vanilla pudding
  mix
3.5 oz (100 g) Quark or other
  fresh white cheese
1 Egg yolk
Zest of one lemon
Dash of salt
½ oz (10 g) Raisins

Prepare the Danish pastry dough according to the recipe, roll out into a 10x12in (25x30 cm) rectangle on a floured work surface, and cut three strips 4 in (10 cm) wide.

For the poppy seed filling, boil milk with granulated sugar, honey, cinnamon, and lemon zest. Stir in the poppy seed and breadcrumbs and let the mixture cool a bit. Stir in the raisins. For the nut filling, boil milk, sugar, and butter. Stir in hazelnuts, melted nougat, lemon zest, cinnamon, and rum and let cool a bit. For the quark filling, cream the butter and powdered sugar, stir in quark, vanilla pudding mix, egg yolks, lemon zest, and salt. Finally, mix in the raisins.

Using a piping bag, lay down one filling on each dough strip and roll up the dough lengthwise. Braid the three strips into a round mass and lay in an appropriately sized, buttered pan (about 10x3in (25x8 cm)). Brush with butter and let rise slightly. Bake for about 70 minutes in an oven preheated to 350 °F (180 °C). After removing from the oven, brush with some apricot marmalade. Ice with slightly warmed, thin fondant and sprinkle with roasted almond slices.

Bake Time: about 70 minutes

Bake Temperature: 350 °F (180 °C)

NUT ROLL

Dissolve the yeast in lukewarm milk. Mix in some flour to create a starter dough, cover, and let rise for 20 minutes in a warm place. Add the rest of the ingredients and beat until the dough comes away from the edge of the bowl. Cover again and let rise until the dough has doubled in volume.

For the filling, boil milk with sugar. Stir in honey, nuts, and clove powder and bring to a boil again. Remove from heat, stir in rum and thicken with breadcrumbs.

Knead the dough well one more time and roll out thin on a floured work surface. Spread the cooled filling on top, roll up tightly like a roulade, and lay on a buttered baking sheet. Brush with beaten egg and let rise another 30 minutes. Bake for about 45 minutes in an oven preheated to 375 °F (190 °C). Let cool and dust with vanilla confectioner's sugar.

Bake Time: about 45 minutes

Bake Temperature: 375 °F (190 °C)

Speaking Baking

Anyone who has ever eaten (Bohemian) powidltatschkerln or (Hungarian) Palatschinken knows that Austrian baking comes from a multicultural background. Most dishes make no particular attempt to hide their origins. The German word for a nut roll is "Potitze," which is simply a Germanized version of the Slovenian "potica," which means baked good or cake. Nut rolls came to Austria through Slovenian Styria, where they are still traditionally served as "leavened strudel" with afternoon tea or coffee. And in Czech, kolach very simply means "little pastry" and comes from the Viennese diminutive for a pocket of pastry.

Ingredients
5½ cups (700 g) Flour
1 cup (250 ml) Milk, lukewarm
¼ cup (30 g) Yeast
4 tsp (20 g) Granulated sugar
Dash of salt
2 Egg yolks
7 tbsp (100 g) Butter, melted
1 Egg for brushing
Flour for the work surface
Butter for the baking sheet
Vanilla confectioner's sugar for dusting

For the Filling
7 tbsp (100 g) Granulated sugar
3 tbsp (40 ml) Milk
1 cup plus 3 tbsp (400 g) Honey
18 oz (500 g) Walnuts, ground
Dash of clove powder
2 tbsp (3 cl) Rum
1 oz (30 g) Breadcrumbs

QUARK KOLACH

Ingredients for about
30 pieces
Basic puff pastry dough
 (see p. 11) or about 42 oz
 (1.2 kg) of ready-made
 dough
Flour for the work surface
1 Egg for brushing
Confectioner's sugar for
 dusting

For the Filling
3½ tbsp (50 g) Butter
¾ cup (100 g) Confectioner's
 sugar
¾ oz (20 g) Vanilla pudding
 mix
10.5 oz (300 g) Quark or
 other fresh white cheese,
 strained
2 Eggs
Zest of one lemon
1 tbsp (15 g) Vanilla sugar
Dash of salt
2 oz (60 g) Raisins
4 tsp (2 cl) Rum

Prepare the puff pastry as directed. Preheat oven to 400 °F (200 °C). For the filling, cream the butter with the confectioner's sugar. Stir in all the other ingredients except for the raisins and rum. Finally, mix in the raisins and rum. Roll out the dough on a floured work surface. Keep some of the dough on the side for decoration and cut it into small, 1x1in (2x2 cm) squares. Cut the rest into 4in (11x11 cm) squares. Place some quark filling in the middle, brush the four corners of the square with egg, fold into the center, and brush with egg again. Place the little dough squares in the middle, press down gently, and also brush with egg. Brush with melted butter and place on a buttered baking sheet. Bake at 400 °F (200 °C) at first and then lower to 340 °F (170 °C) and bake for 15 minutes. Dust with confectioner's sugar.

Bake Time: about 15 minutes

Bake Temperature: 400 °F (200 °C) lowering to 340 °F (170 °C)

PLUM KOLACH

Ingredients for about
30 Pieces
Basic Danish pastry dough
 (see p. 12)
1 Egg for brushing
Flour for the work surface
Confectioner's sugar for
 dusting

For the Filling
⅞ cup (200 ml) Red wine
⅓ cup (80 g) Granulated
 sugar
Dash of cinnamon
5 oz (150 g) Dried plums,
 pitted
14 oz (400 g) Plums, pitted
¼ cup (30 g) Cornstarch

Prepare the basic Danish pastry dough. Preheat oven to 400 °F (200 °C). Slice the plums and dried plums. Boil the red wine with granulated sugar and cinnamon. Add the fruit and let boil for a few minutes. Mix the cornstarch into a little bit of water and add to the fruit. Let boil again and then remove from heat. Roll out the Danish pastry dough thin on a floured work surface and cut into 4x4in (11x11 cm) squares. Brush the corners of the squares with egg and fold into the middle without closing them completely. Spoon some of the plum mixture with very little juice into the middle and brush with melted butter. Place the kolaches on a slightly buttered baking sheet and bake at 400 °F (200 °C) at first and then lower to 340 °F (170 °C) and bake for about 15 minutes, depending on size. Dust with confectioner's sugar.

Bake Time: about 15 minutes

Bake Temperature: 400 °F (200 °C) lowering to 340 °F (170 °C)

KARLSBAD KOLACH

Prepare the basic Danish pastry dough. Preheat oven to 400 °F (200 °C). For the filling, boil ¾ of the sour cherry juice with sugar. Mix the rest of the juice with cornstarch and then blend in. Add the sour cherries, stir briefly, then remove from heat. Roll out the Danish pastry dough thin on a floured work surface and cut into 4x4in (11x11 cm) squares. Brush the corners of the squares with egg and fold into the middle without closing them completely. Spoon some of the cherry mixture with very little juice into the middle. Beat the eggs with the granulated sugar until creamy and spoon a teaspoonful of the egg mixture over the cherries. Sprinkle the grated almonds on top. Place the kolaches on a slightly buttered baking sheet and bake at 400 °F (200 °C) at first and then lower to 340 °F (170 °C) and bake for about 15 minutes, depending on size. Dust with confectioner's sugar.

Bake Time: about 15 minutes

Bake Temperature: 400 °F (200 °C) lowering to 340 °F (170 °C)

NUT SCHNECKE

Prepare the basic Danish pastry dough. Preheat oven to 400 °F (200 °C). For the filling, boil milk with granulated sugar, vanilla sugar, honey, cinnamon, and lemon zest. Stir in nuts and let the mixture cool somewhat. Mix in egg whites and rum. On a floured work surface, roll out the dough to an approximately 2.5mm thick, 16x35in (40x90 cm) rectangle. Spread on the nut filling and sprinkle the raisins over it. Roll it up the long way and cut it into about 1in (3 cm) pieces. Place the pieces on a buttered baking sheet and let rise somewhat. Brush with melted butter and bake at 400 °F (200 °C) at first and then lower to 340 °F (170 °C) and bake for about 15 minutes. After baking, brush with apricot marmalade and glaze with warmed fondant. Finally, sprinkle the roasted almond slices on top.

Bake Time: about 15 minutes

Bake Temperature: 400 °F (200 °C) lowering to 340 °F (170 °C)

Ingredients for about
30 Pieces
Basic Danish pastry dough
  (see p. 12)
2 Eggs
¼ cup (50 g) Granulated
  sugar
Flour for the work surface
1 Egg for brushing
5 oz (150 g) Almonds, grated
Butter for the baking sheet
Confectioner's sugar for
  dusting

For the Filling
10.5 oz (300 g) Sour cherries,
  pitted
½ cup (100 ml) Sour cherry
  juice
2 tbsp (30 g) Sugar
2 tbsp (20 g) Cornstarch

Ingredients for about
30 Pieces
Basic Danish pastry dough
  (see p. 12)
2 oz (50 g) Raisins
Flour for the work surface
Butter for brushing
Apricot marmalade
About 3.5 oz (100 g) fondant
  (see p. 44)
Almond slices for sprinkling

For the Filling
⅔ cup (150 ml) Milk
⅔ cup (150 g) Granulated
  sugar
2 tsp (10 g) Vanilla sugar
2 tbsp (1 kL) Honey
Dash of cinnamon
Zest of one lemon
14 oz (400 g) Walnuts,
  ground
1 Egg white
4 tsp (2 cl) Rum

APRICOT DANISH

Ingredients for about
30 Pieces
Basic Danish pastry dough
  (see p. 12)
About 23 apricots, quartered
Butter for brushing
Flour for the work surface
Apricot marmalade for
  brushing
3.5 oz (100 g) fondant
  (see p. 44)
Almond slices

For the Vanilla Cream
1⅔ cup (400 ml) Milk
½ cup (120 g) Granulated
  sugar
1 Egg yolk
2 tsp (10 g) Vanilla sugar
1¾ oz (50 g) Vanilla pudding
  mix
2 Egg whites
2 tbsp (30 g) Granulated
  sugar

Prepare the basic Danish pastry dough. Preheat oven to 400 °F (200 °C). Roll out on a floured work surface and cut into 5x4in (12x10 cm) rectangles. For the vanilla cream, boil ⅓ of the milk with granulated sugar. Mix the rest of the milk together with the egg yolk, vanilla sugar, and vanilla pudding mix and stir into the boiling milk. Let boil briefly, then remove from heat and let cool. Sieve the cooled vanilla cream. Begin beating the egg whites, add the granulated sugar, and beat to stiff peaks. Fold into the vanilla cream.

Pipe a line of vanilla cream with a piping bag on the long side of the rectangle, then fold the other side over and gently press together. Notch the upper edge of the newly formed rectangle about 3in (8 cm) and pull open or push on it a bit. Now place 3 apricot quarters in each pocket and fold the edges over. Place on a buttered baking sheet, brush with melted butter and bake at 400 °F (200 °C) at first and then lower to 340 °F (170 °C) and bake for about 15 minutes. After baking, brush each pastry with apricot marmalade and glaze thinly with slightly warmed fondant. Finally, sprinkle the roasted almond slices on top.

Bake Time: about 15 minutes

Bake Temperature: 400 °F (200 °C) lowering to 340 °F (170 °C)

MANDARIN DANISH

Prepare the basic Danish pastry dough. Preheat oven to 400°F (200°C). Roll out on a floured work surface and cut into 4x4in (11x11 cm) squares. For the vanilla cream, boil ⅓ of the milk with granulated sugar. Mix the rest of the milk together with the egg yolk, vanilla sugar, and vanilla pudding mix and stir into the boiling milk. Let boil briefly, then remove from heat and let cool. Sieve the cooled vanilla cream. Begin beating the egg whites, add the granulated sugar, and beat to stiff peaks. Fold into the vanilla cream.

Spread the vanilla cream in the middle of each square and lay 2 mandarin slices on top. Fold two opposite corners over the filling and press together gently. Place on a buttered baking sheet, brush with melted butter and bake at 400°F (200°C) at first and then lower to 340°F (170°C) and bake for about 15 minutes, according to size. After baking, brush each pastry with apricot marmalade and glaze thinly with slightly warmed fondant. Let dry.

Bake Time: about 15 minutes

Bake Temperature: 400°F (200°C) lowering to 340°F (170°C)

Ingredients for about
30 Pieces
Basic Danish pastry dough (see p. 12)
About 60 mandarin slices
Flour for the work surface
Butter for brushing
Apricot marmalade for brushing
About 3.5 oz (100 g) fondant (see p. 44)

For the Vanilla Cream
1⅔ cups (400 ml) Milk
½ cup (120 g) Granulated sugar
1 Egg yolk
2 tsp (10 g) Vanilla sugar
1¾ oz (50 g) Vanilla pudding mix
2 Egg whites
2 tbsp (30 g) Granulated sugar

POLSTERZIPF ("PILLOW CORNERS")

Prepare the basic Danish pastry dough. Preheat oven to 400°F (200°C). Roll out on a floured work surface and cut into 4x4in (11x11 cm) squares. Spread the red currant marmalade in the middle of each square. Press opposite edges of the squares together well. Brush with beaten egg and bake on a buttered baking sheet at 400°F (200°C) at first. Then lower to 340°F (170°C) and bake for about 15 minutes. Dust with confectioner's sugar.

Bake Time: about 15 minutes

Bake Temperature: 400°F (200°C) lowering to 340°F (170°C)

Tip: Filling polsterzipfe with marmalade is a Viennese tradition. In Upper Austria, they are often served as a sweet main course without filling, but with vanilla sauce.

Ingredients for Polsterzipf
Ingredients yields approx. 30 pieces
Basic Danish pastry dough (see p. 12)
5 cups (600 g) Redcurrant marmalade, unstrained
Flour for the work surface
1 Egg for brushing
Butter for the baking sheet
Confectioner's sugar for dusting

POPPY CRESCENTS

Ingredients for about
30 Pieces
Basic Danish pastry dough
  (see p. 12)
Flour for the work surface
Butter for brushing
Confectioner's sugar for
  dusting

For the Filling
⅔ cup (150 ml) Milk
2 tsp (15 g) Honey
¼ cup (60 g) Granulated
  sugar
2 tsp (10 g) Vanilla sugar
Dash of cinnamon
Zest of 1 lemon
4 tsp (2 cl) Rum
7 oz (200 g) Poppy seed,
  ground
3.5 oz (100 g) Breadcrumbs
  or sponge cake crumbs
4 oz (120 g) Couverture white
  chocolate

Prepare the basic Danish pastry dough. Preheat oven to 400 °F (200 °C). For the filling, mix the poppy seeds with the breadcrumbs. Boil the milk with honey, granulated sugar, vanilla sugar, rum, lemon zest, and cinnamon, then remove from heat and mix in the breadcrumb mixture. Melt the chocolate, mix in, and let the whole thing cool. Roll out the pastry dough on a floured work surface and cut into tall triangles. Spread on the poppy filling, roll up, and form crescents. Brush with melted butter and place on a buttered baking sheet. Bake at 400 °F (200 °C) at first and then lower to 340 °F (170 °C) and bake for about 15 minutes. Dust with confectioner's sugar.

Bake Time: about 15 minutes

Bake Temperature: 400 °F (200 °C) lowering to 340 °F (170 °C)

Tip: Poppy crescents taste even better when they are brushed with apricot marmalade after baking and glazed with some warm fondant.

VANILLA CRESCENT DANISHES

Ingredients for about
30 Pieces
Basic Danish pastry dough
  (see p. 12)
Flour for the work surface
Butter for brushing
1 Egg for brushing
Confectioner's sugar for
  dusting

For the Vanilla Cream
1⅔ cups (400 ml) Milk
½ cup (120 g) Granulated
  sugar
1 Egg yolk
2 tsp (10 g) Vanilla sugar
2 oz (50 g) Vanilla pudding
  mix
2 Egg whites
2 tbsp (30 g) Granulated
  sugar

Prepare the basic Danish pastry dough. Preheat oven to 400 °F (200 °C). For the vanilla cream, boil ⅓ of the milk with the granulated sugar. Mix the rest of the milk with the egg yolk, vanilla sugar, and vanilla pudding mix and stir into the boiling milk. Let boil again briefly, remove from heat and let cool. Sieve the cooled vanilla cream. Begin beating the egg whites, add granulated sugar, and beat to stiff peaks. Fold into the vanilla cream. Roll out the pastry dough on a floured work surface and cut into tall triangles. Spread on the vanilla cream, preferably with a piping bag. Brush the edges of the dough with egg, roll up the triangles, and form crescents. Brush with melted butter and place on a buttered baking sheet. Bake at 400 °F (200 °C) at first and then lower to 340 °F (170 °C) and bake for about 15 minutes. Dust with confectioner's sugar.

Bake Time: about 15 minutes

Bake Temperature: 400 °F (200 °C) lowering to 340 °F (170 °C)

NUT CRESCENTS

Prepare the basic Danish dough. Preheat oven to 400 °F (200 °C). For the filling, mix nuts with the breadcrumbs. Boil the milk with honey, granulated sugar, vanilla sugar, rum, lemon zest, and cinnamon, then remove from heat and mix in the breadcrumbs and nuts. Melt the nougat, mix into the batter, and chill. Roll out the dough on a flour work surface and cut into tall triangles. Spread on the nut filling, roll up the triangle, and form crescents. Brush with melted butter and place on a buttered baking sheet. Bake at 400 °F (200 °C) at first and then lower to 340 °F (170 °C) and bake for about 15 minutes. Halfway through the baking time, brush the crescents with beaten egg and sprinkle with decorating sugar.

Bake Time: about 15 minutes

Bake Temperature: 400 °F (200 °C) lowering to 340 °F (170 °C)

Tip: If you have no decorating sugar, the nut crescents can also be brushed with apricot marmalade and glazed with slightly warmed fondant.

DRIED PEAR FRUIT BREAD

Soak the dried pears, cook until soft, then cut into cubes. Also cut the other fruit into squares and marinate, preferably overnight, in the rum and slivovitz (plum brandy) along with the pears. Mix with the spices and bread dough. Form three loaves and dust well with flour. Place the loaves on a baking sheet lined with parchment paper. Brush with beaten egg, cover, and let rise for about an hour. Bake for about 70 minutes in an oven preheated to 320 °F (160 °C). For a really successful crust, brush the loaves with water after 15 minutes of baking and after baking.

Bake Time: 70 minutes

Bake Temperature: 320 °F (160 °C)

Tip: It is best to get the necessary bread dough for this recipe from a friendly baker.

Ingredients for about 30 Pieces
Basic Danish pastry or brioche dough (see p. 12 and 13)
Flour for the work surface
Butter for brushing
1 Egg for brushing
Decorating sugar for sprinkling

For the Filling
⅔ cup (150 ml) Milk
2 tsp (15 g) Honey
¼ cup (50 g) Granulated sugar
2 tsp (10 g) Vanilla sugar
Dash of cinnamon
Zest of 1 lemon
4 tsp (2 cl) Rum
7 oz (200 g) Walnuts, ground
3.5 oz (100 g) Breadcrumbs or sponge cake crumbs
3.5 oz (100 g) Nougat

Ingredients for 3 Loaves
35 oz (1 kg) Bread dough
Flour for dusting
1 Egg for brushing

For the Fruit Mixture
18 oz (500 g) Dried pears
14 oz (400 g) Dried figs
10.5 oz (300 g) Dried plums
7 oz (200 g) Raisins
5 oz (150 g) Dates, pitted
7 oz (200 g) Dried apricots
5 oz (150 g) Hazelnuts
2 oz (50 g) Candied orange peel
1 oz (20 g) Candied lemon peel
⅓ cup (8 cl) Rum
⅓ cup (8 cl) Slivovitz (plum brandy)
½ oz (10 g) Anise
4 tsp (10 g) Cinnamon
¼ oz (5 g) Clove powder

CHRISTMAS STOLLEN

Ingredients
2¾ cups (350 g) Flour
3 tbsp (25 g) Yeast
½ cup (100 ml) Milk
1 stick plus 2½ tbsp (150 g)
  Clarified butter
1 Egg yolk
6 tbsp (50 g) Confectioner's
  sugar
Dash of salt
2 tsp (10 g) Vanilla sugar
2 tsp (1 cl) Rum
Dash of cardamom
5 oz (140 g) Candied orange
  peel
1½ oz (40 g) Walnuts,
  coarsely chopped
4 oz (120 g) Raisins
7 tbsp (100 g) Butter, melted
¾ cup (100 g) Confectioner's
  sugar for topping

For the Marzipan Filling
2 oz (55 g) Marzipan
1 oz (30 g) Candied orange
  peel, minced
1 Egg yolk

Preheat oven to 300 °F (150 °C). Mix the yeast into the luke-warm milk and add half the flour. Cover the starter dough and let it rise in a warm spot. Mix the clarified butter until creamy. Also mix the egg yolk, salt, sugar, vanilla sugar, cardamom, and rum until creamy. Knead together the starter dough, the clarified butter, and the egg yolk mixture and let rise 15 minutes. Work in the orange peel, raisins, and nuts. Roll the dough out into a rectangle with the long edges thicker.

For the marzipan filling, knead the marzipan with the orange peel and egg yolk and roll into a strand that is as long as the long side of the rectangle. Lay the marzipan in the middle of the dough and fold the sides over each other. Let rise briefly, then bake for 50 minutes. Remove from the oven and, while still hot, brush with liquid butter and roll in confectioner's sugar. Let cool, dust a bit more powdered sugar on top, fold into foil and store in a cool place.

Bake Time: 50 minutes

Bake Temperature: 300 °F (150 °C)

FRUIT BREAD

Prepare the fruit mixture on the previous day. Cube the dried fruit and mix with nuts, almonds, and cinnamon. Marinate with slivovitz and rum to taste. Let soak overnight. On the next day, mix flour, confectioner's sugar, and yeast mixed with lukewarm milk into the fruit. Form two long bricks. Preheat oven to 320 °F (160 °C). For the dough, warm a bit of milk and dissolve the yeast in it. Mix and then warm the egg yolk, milk, confectioner's sugar, vanilla sugar, salt, and lemon zest. Knead the two mixtures together with flour and half melted butter to form dough. Chill. Roll out the dough on a floured work surface, divide in half, and work in the fruit mixture. Brush with beaten egg and yolk, let dry, and brush again. Top with almonds, pistachios, and maraschino cherry halves and bake for about 50 minutes, depending on the size.

Bake Time: about 50 minutes

Bake Temperature: 320 °F (160 °C)

Pretty as a Doughnut

By the time of Maria Theresa, specialty doughnuts and crullers were already the dernier cri of well-to-do bourgeois and aristocrats. In the inn "Zur Goldenen Anten" on Schulerstraße, a Viennese Fasching doughnut sweetened with "real cane sugar" cost five kreutzer. At the time, a Viennese carpenter earned twenty-four kreutzer in a day. The focal points of sweets in Vienna were the "Kunigund" on Bräunerstraße and the "Doughnut Girl" on the Kohlmarkt, who was allegedly "as pretty as a doughnut." The reputation of the doughnut bakers was really not the best in the time of Maria Theresa's Chastity Commission, because many of the "sweet hole-in-the-walls" or "mandoletti," as the bakeries were called, also rented back rooms for gallant adventures. The legend of the invention of the Fasching doughnut in its modern form goes back to the Viennese mandoletti baker named Cäcilie Krapf, called Frau Cilly. However, a similar fried pastry has been known since Carolingian times.

Ingredients
- 4 cups (500 g) Flour
- 3½ tbsp (30 g) Yeast
- 125 ml Milk
- 6 tbsp (50 g) Confectioner's sugar
- 1 stick plus 6 tbsp (200 g) Butter
- 2 Egg yolks
- Vanilla sugar
- Dash of salt
- Zest of 1 lemon
- 1 Egg and 2 egg yolks, beaten
- Halved almonds, pistachios, maraschino cherries as decoration
- Flour for the work surface

For the Fruit Mixture
- 10.5 oz (300 g) Dried plums
- 7 oz (200 g) Dried figs
- 7 oz (200 g) Raisins
- 3½ oz (100 g) Dried apricots
- 3½ oz (100 g) Dated, pitted
- 3½ oz (100 g) Candied lemon peel
- 3½ oz (100 g) Candied orange peel
- 3½ oz (100 g) Nuts, coarsely chopped
- 3½ oz (100 g) Almonds, coarsely chopped slivovitz and rum to taste
- Ground cinnamon
- ¾ cup (100 g) Flour
- 2 tbsp (20 g) Yeast
- 4 tsp (20 ml) Milk

FASCHING DOUGHNUTS

Ingredients for 20 Pieces
6 Egg yolks
7 tbsp (100 g) Butter, melted
5 tbsp (42 g) Yeast
¼ cup (50 g) Sugar
1 cup (250 ml) Milk,
    lukewarm
4 cups (500 g) Flour
Dash of salt
Flour for the work surface
Apricot marmalade for
    brushing
Vegetable oil for frying
Confectioner's sugar for
    dusting

Beat the egg yolks until creamy. Mix in the melted, but not hot, butter bit by bit. Dissolve the yeast with a bit of sugar in 3 tbsp of the lukewarm milk, mix in about ½ of the flour, and mix well into the yolks. Cover with a towel and let rise in a warm place for 30 minutes. Add the rest of the ingredients and beat powerfully until the dough comes away from the edge of the bowl. Cover again and let rise in a warm place until the dough has doubled in size. Knead the dough again, roll out about 5mm thick on a floured work surface, and cut into 2 in (5 cm) strips. Brush each strip with marmalade, cover with another strip, and press lightly on the edges. With a floured, round cookie cutter, cut out doughnuts and overturn them on a floured work surface. Brush with lukewarm oil, cover with a towel, and let rise another 30 minutes. In a deep pan, preheat enough vegetable oil to completely cover a doughnut about 350 °F (180 °C). Place the doughnuts one at a time into the oil and fry. Turn once in the middle. Remove with a straining spoon and let drain well on paper towel. Dust with confectioner's sugar.

SWEET DELICACIES

It's not all about sweet pastries and cake. Classic Viennese confectionary specialties also have a permanent place as an integral part of the "Viennese coffee break."

STRAWBERRY YOGURT TARTLET

Bake the basic sponge cake. Flip onto a sugared sheet pan and pull off the parchment paper. Let the cake cool. Then, with a round cookie cutter, cut out 20 sponge cake bases with a diameter of about 2 inches (5.5 cm). Mix the strawberry marmalade and Cointreau, warm, and saturate the sponge cake bases with the mixture. Set the sponge cake bases into small ring forms. For the yogurt mousse, mix yogurt and confectioner's sugar. Add water to the gelatin, removed excess water, and dissolve it in warmed Cointreau. Stir the Cointreau into the yogurt mixture. Fold in whipped cream, fill each form with yogurt mousse, and chill for about 15 minutes.

For the strawberry mousse, take 2 tablespoons from the strawberry purée and warm over a double boiler. Add water to the gelatin, remove excess water, and dissolve it in the warmed strawberry purée. Mix into the rest of the strawberry purée. Flavor with strawberry liquor and lemon juice. Sweeten whipped cream with confectioner's sugar and fold into the strawberry mixture. Add the strawberry mousse on top of the yogurt mousse and chill for another 20 minutes.

For the strawberry gelatin, take 2 tablespoons from the strawberry purée and warm over a double boiler. Add water to the gelatin, remove excess water, and dissolve it in the warmed strawberry purée. Mix into the rest of the strawberry purée. Cool briefly and then cover the top of each tartlet with gelatin. Chill for 2 hours. Release the sides of each tartlet from each form with a knife dipped in hot water. Garnish with a rosette of whipped cream and half a strawberry each.

Ingredients for 20 Tartlets
(2½ in (6 cm) diameter)
Basic sponge cake for roulades (see p. 22)
2½ tbsp (50 g) Strawberry marmalade
3½ tbsp (5 cl) Cointreau
Granulated sugar

For the Yogurt Mousse
⅔ cups (400 ml) Yogurt
2 tbsp (3 cl) Cointreau
6 tbsp (50 g) Confectioner's sugar
4 Sheets gelatin
1⅕ cups (350 ml) Whipped cream

For the Strawberry Mousse
¾ cup (300 g) Strawberry purée (see p. 200)
5 Sheets Gelatin
2 tsp (1 cl) Lemon juice
2 tbsp (3 cl) Strawberry liquor
⅔ cup (75 g) Confectioner's sugar
1 cup (250 ml) Whipped cream

For the Strawberry Gelatin
½ cup (200 g) Strawberry purée (see p. 200)
2 Sheets gelatin

Garnish
Sweetened whipped cream
10 Strawberries with stems, halved

1
Cut out the sponge cake bases according to the forms.

2
Cover the sponge cakes with a thin layer of strawberry marmalade. Place in the ring forms.

3
Put the yogurt mousse in the ring forms. Let firm and then place the strawberry mousse on top.

4
Dissolve the gelatin in strawberry purée and let cool

5
Spoon the gelatin onto the tartlets. The gelatin should be relatively cool, so that the mousse underneath does not melt!

6
Release the finished tartlets from the ring forms and garnish with whipped cream and a halved strawberry.

Coffee and Chocolate

We know that chocolate was particularly loved by the Habsburgs thanks to a gold chocolate service belonging to Empress Maria Theresa. It can be found today in the Viennese Kunsthistorisches Museum, with its pot, chocolate cups, spoons, and sugar sprinkler. There you can also see an enlightening watercolor of a "chocolate lever," showing the Empress and Emperor with their children, taking their morning chocolate. The artist can certainly not deny having a particularly intimate view of the daily life of the court. After all, she is the Archduchess Maria Christine. In reality, the imperial breakfast was not quite as saccharine as the picture: The gaggle of imperial children was fed barley soup, and only Prince Consort Franz Stephan von Lothringen could never begin the day without his pot of chocolate. The Empress herself drank coffee.

ÉCLAIR WITH MOCHA CREAM

Ingredients for 20 Pieces
Basic choux pastry
  (see p. 20)
1¼ cup (150 g) Apricot
  marmalade
14 oz (400 g) Fondant (see
  p. 44)

For the Mocha Cream
35 oz (1 kg) Pastry cream
  (see p. 247)
2 tbsp (20 g) Instant coffee
  powder
8 Sheets gelatin
1¼ cup (300 ml) Whipped
  cream

Preheat oven to 430 °F (220 °C). Prepare the basic choux pastry. Fill a piping bag fitted with a star-shaped nozzle and pipe approximately (8 cm) strips. Bake briefly at 430 °F (220 °C) then lower heat to 350 °F (180 °C) and bake for about 20 minutes.

For the mocha cream, warm the pastry cream. Add water to the gelatin, remove excess water, and dissolve it in the pastry cream. Sift in the instant coffee powder. Beat in an ice water bath until cool and then fold in the whipped cream.

Let firm for 30 minutes in the refrigerator. Halve the éclairs horizontally. Brush the top half with warmed apricot marmalade. Warm the fondant and pour over the top. Let dry. Pipe the mocha cream onto the lower half with a piping bag fitted with star-shaped nozzle and set the glazed upper half on top.

Bake Time: about 20 minutes

Bake Temperature: 430 °F (220 °C) lowering to 350 °F (180 °C)

PROFITEROLES WITH VANILLA CREAM

Ingredients for 30–35 Pieces
Basic choux pastry
  (see p. 20)
Confectioner's sugar for
  dusting

For the Vanilla Cream
35 oz (1 kg) Pastry cream
  (see p. 247)
4 tsp (2 cl) Cointreau
8 Sheets gelatin
1¼ cup (300 ml) Whipped
  cream

Preheat oven to 430 °F (220 °C). Prepare the basic choux pastry. Fill a piping bag fitted with a star-shaped nozzle and pipe a round puff onto a baking sheet. Bake briefly at 430 °F (220 °C) then lower heat to 350 °F (180 °C) and bake for about 20 minutes.

For the vanilla cream, warm the pastry cream. Add water to the gelatin, remove excess water, and dissolve it in the pastry cream. Flavor with Cointreau. Beat in an ice water bath until cool and then fold in the whipped cream.

Let firm for 30 minutes in the refrigerator. Halve the profiteroles horizontally, so that there are two even halves. Pipe the vanilla cream onto the lower half with a piping bag fitted with a star-shaped nozzle and place the upper half back on top. Dust with powdered sugar before serving.

Bake Time: about 20 minutes

Bake Temperature: 430 °F (220 °C) lowering to 350 °F (180 °C)

Profiteroles with Vanilla Cream Continued

Tip: These profiteroles look particularly enticing when they are made much smaller and served as the main attraction on a petit four plate.

Chestnut Sour Cherry Tartlet

Prepare the basic chocolate sponge cake. Overturn onto a sugared plate and pull off the parchment paper. Cool the cake. Then cut out 20 small sponge cake bases with a round cookie cutter. Place the cake bases in appropriately sized small ring forms and brush with marmalade.

For the sour cherry filling, boil ¾ of the cherry juice with sugar. Mix the rest of the juice with cornstarch and then stir into the boiling mixture. Add cherries, stir briefly, and then remove from heat. For the chocolate mousse, melt chocolate and mix with egg yolks, simple syrup, and heavy cream. Add water to the gelatin and dissolve in slightly warmed rum. Stir into the chocolate mixture. Fold in the whipped cream. Put the chocolate mousse into the forms and add the cherries (without juice) to the middle. Chill for 2 hours.

Release the cooled tartlets from the rings with a knife dipped in hot water. Cover the tartlets all around with sweetened whipped cream. Pipe a ring on top.

Press the chestnut purée through a potato ricer or grater and place on top of each tartlet. Finally, garnish each tartlet with a cherry.

Ingredients for 20 Pieces
(about 2in (6 cm) diameter)
Basic chocolate sponge
  cake (see p. 24), ½ recipe
Sour or sweet cherry
  marmalade

For the Sour Cherry Filling
10.5 oz (300 g) Sour cherries,
  pitted
½ cup (100 ml) Sour cherry
  juice
2 tbsp (30 g) Sugar
2 tbsp (20 g) Cornstarch

For the Chocolate Mousse
15 oz (420 g) Whole milk
  couverture chocolate
6 Egg yolks
½ cup (120 ml) Simple syrup
  (see p. 40)
½ cup (120 ml) Heavy cream
6 Sheets gelatin
2½ cups (600 ml) Whipped
  Cream
¼ cup (6 cl) rum

To Garnish
2 cups (500 ml) Sweetened
  whipped cream
7 oz (200 g) Chestnut purée
20 Sour cherries, pitted

CHOUX SWANS WITH STRAWBERRIES

Preheat oven to 430°F (220°C). Prepare the basic choux pastry. Put in a piping bag fitted with a flat nozzle and pipe 20 "swan necks" into a baking sheet by writing letter S's. With the rest of the dough, pipe round puffs using a star-shaped nozzle. Bake briefly at 430°F (220°C), then lower to 350°F (180°C) and bake for about 20 minutes.

For the strawberry whipped cream, add cold water to the gelatin and warm Cointreau with orange juice. Remove excess water from gelatin and dissolve in the juice mixture. Mix together the strawberry purée, granulated sugar, and gelatin liquid. Carefully fold in the whipped cream and let the mixture firm for 1 hour in the refrigerator. Halve the puffs horizontally. Halve the upper part again to make two "wings." Pipe the cream onto the lower half. Quarter strawberries and place them on the cream. Place the swan necks and wings on top. Dust with confectioner's sugar.

Bake Time: about 20 minutes

Bake Temperature: 430°F (220°C) lowering to 350°F (180°C)

Ingredients for 20 Pieces
Basic choux pastry
  (see p. 20)
20 Strawberries
Confectioner's sugar for
  dusting

For the Strawberry Whipped Cream
7 oz (200 g) Strawberry
  purée (see p. 200)
7 tbsp (100 g) Granulated
  sugar
6 Sheets gelatin
2 tbsp (3 cl) Cointreau
4 tsp (2 cl) Orange juice
1½ cups (375 ml) Whipped
  cream

CREAM CORNETS

Ingredients
18 oz (500 g) Basic puff
   pastry (see p. 11) or
   ready-made dough
4 Egg whites
2¼ cups (280 g)
   Confectioner's sugar
Flour for the work surface
Confectioner's sugar for
   dusting

Preheat oven to 320 °F (160 °C). Prepare the basic puff pastry dough and roll out about 3mm thick on a floured work surface. Cut ½in (1.5 cm) strips using a pastry wheel and roll the strips around cream hold molds. Bake for 10–12 minutes. Let cool.

For the cream, beat the egg whites with the confectioner's sugar in a double boiler for about 5 minutes. The mixture should be very solid and not at all runny. Put the cream in a piping bag and pipe into the cornets. Dust the cream cornets with confectioner's sugar.

Bake Time: 10–12 minutes

Bake Temperature: 320 °F (160 °C)

Tip: Do not shy away from buying cream horn molds, as they cost relatively little. They are available in any good cooking supply store and ensure that your cream cornets will be of professional quality.

DRUNKEN CAPUCHIN

Ingredients for 12 Pieces
4 Eggs
¾ cup (180 g) Granulated
   sugar
2 tsp (10 g) Vanilla sugar
Zest of 1 lemon
Dash of cinnamon
1¼ cups (160 g) Flour
2 oz (60 g) Hazelnuts, ground
1¼ cups (300 ml) Whipping
   cream
2½ cups (300 g) Confectioner's sugar
Butter and flour for the form

To Infuse
7 tbsp (100 g) Granulated
   sugar
4 tsp (2 cl) Orange juice
3 tbsp (4 cl) Water
4 tsp (2 cl) Rum
4 tsp (2 cl) White wine

Preheat oven to 350 °F (180 °C). Beat the eggs with granulated sugar, vanilla sugar, lemon zest, and cinnamon. Mix the hazelnuts with the flour and mix into the eggs carefully. Butter the small pans and dust with flour. Fill with batter and bake about 25 minutes.

For the infusion, boil orange juice with granulated sugar and water. Let cool and mix with rum and white wine. Soak the cooked cakes in the liquid until the entire amount has been absorbed. Whip the cream with the confectioner's sugar and garnish the Capuchins.

Bake Time: about 25 minutes

Bake Temperature: 350 °F (180 °C)

Of Farmers, Liesl, and Capuchins

There are many names in Austria for a cake made of flour, sugar, choco-
late, ground roasted hazelnuts, egg yolks, and beaten egg whites that is
infused with hot spiced wine and served with whipped cream. In Vienna, it
is known mostly as a "drunken Capuchin." The blame probably lies with
the once poor reputation of the Capuchin monks, who allegedly not only
took their vow of celibacy with a grain of salt, but also enjoyed having one
drink too many. In many southern German cookbooks, you will find this
cake called a "drunken Liesl." And when the dish is prepared—somewhat
earthier—with fried crumbs and raisins, then saturated with sugared wine,
then it is tellingly called a "drunken farmer."

FLORA DOUGHNUTS

Mix the nuts with confectioner's sugar, vanilla pulp, cinnamon, and 1(!) egg white. Beat the rest of the egg whites to stiff peaks with granulated sugar. Fold the beaten egg whites bit by bit into the nut mixture. Put the batter in a piping bag fitted with a round nozzle, and pipe 20 equally sized doughnuts onto a baking sheet lined with parchment paper (make half of them slightly flatter to be the bases). Sift confectioner's sugar over them. Place in the oven at about 175–200 °F (80–100 °C), leave the oven door slightly open, and dry more than bake the doughnuts for 2½ to 3 hours. Remove from oven and let cool. Store in a dry place.

For the cream, purée strawberries with confectioner's sugar, sieve, and flavor with Cointreau. Add cold water to the gelatin, remove the excess water, and dissolve the gelatin in some of the strawberry purée, warmed. Add to the rest of the strawberry purée. Whip the cream with confectioner's sugar, fold into the strawberry purée, and chill for 2 hours. Pipe the strawberry mousse onto the bases and set the tops on the mousse.

Bake Time: 1½–3 hours

Bake Temperature: 175–200 °F (80–100 °C)

Tip: With the same recipe, you can make about 20 small petits fours.

Ingredients for 10 Pieces
4 oz (120 g) Nuts, ground
⅓ cup (40 g) Confectioner's sugar
Pulp of 1 vanilla bean
Dash of cinnamon
4 Egg whites
¾ cup (100 g) Granulated sugar
About 4 tbsp Confectioner's sugar for dusting

For the Strawberry Mousse
7 oz (200 g) Strawberries
6 tbsp (50 g) Confectioner's sugar
2 tsp (1 cl) Cointreau
2 Sheets gelatin
½ cup (125 ml) Whipping cream, sweetened with 1 tbsp Confectioner's sugar

INDIAN DOUGHNUTS

Ingredients
8 Egg yolks
10 Egg whites
⅔ cup (140 g) Granulated
  sugar
2 tsp (10 g) Vanilla sugar
¾ cup (100 g) Flour
⅔ cup (100 g) Cornstarch
Apricot marmalade for
  brushing
9 oz (250 g) Sacher or
  ganache glaze (see p. 42
  and 43)
3 cups (750 ml) Whipping
  cream
3 tbsp (25 g) Confectioner's
  sugar

Preheat oven to 375 °F (190 °C). Mix the egg yolks with 1 tbsp (15 g) of granulated sugar and the vanilla sugar until slightly creamy. Beat the egg whites, add the rest of the sugar, and beat to very stiff peaks. Then fold sifted cornstarch, yolk mixture, and last the sifted flour into the egg whites. Fill a piping bag with the batter, and use a round nozzle to pipe 40 domes of 1½in (4 cm) diameter onto a baking sheet lined with parchment paper. Make half of them a little bit flatter, so that as the bases, they are more stable. Bake for about 20 minutes, until light brown. Keep the oven door open a crack while baking, so moisture can escape.

Remove from the oven, brush with apricot marmalade, and let cool. Warm the glaze in a water bath. Dip each half doughnut in the glaze with the help of a fork, set them on parchment paper, and let dry. Whip the cream with the confectioner's sugar and pipe onto the bases with a star-shaped nozzle. Set the tops on the cream.

Bake Time: about 20 minutes

Bake Temperature: 375 °F (190 °C)

Tip: Try making the doughnuts smaller for a change. The result: petits fours that are just as sweet looking as they are sweet tasting.

PUNCH CAKES

Prepare the basic sponge cake batter and bake two cake bases. Remove from the oven, overturn onto a sugared baking sheet, pull off the parchment paper, and let cool. Cut two 8x10in (20x25 cm) rectangles out of the cakes. Cut up the leftover cake for the punch filling and mix in a mixing bowl with the apricot marmalade, rum, and simple syrup. Add the grated chocolate, orange and lemon zest, and cinnamon. Knead the dough until it holds together well. Spread one cake base with apricot marmalade. Place it a baking frame or deep cake pan and spread the punch filling on top. Cover with the second cake layer and weight with a cutting board or similar item for several hours. Remove from the form and cut into 20 squares (2x2in (5x5 cm)). Brush the squares on the tops and sides with slightly warmed apricot marmalade and let cool. Then glaze with warmed fondant. Melt the couverture chocolate in a bain-marie, fill a piping bag, and decorate the tops of the punch cakes.

Confectioners and Pharmacists

Vienna was not always the capital of sugary temptations. The profession of confectioner arose much more in the Netherlands. The first Viennese court confectioner was recruited from there: a certain Matthias de Voss, who was employed at the court as the "sugar baker" for a yearly salary of 93 gulden and 30 kreutzer. Before then, confections and the sale of sugared fruits, spice sticks, nuts, and spun sugar treats was reserved for Viennese pharmacists.

Ingredients for 20 Pieces
Basic sponge cake for schnitten (see p. 23), doubled recipe
Granulated sugar
Apricot marmalade for brushing

For the Punch Filling
½ cup (125 ml) Rum
3 tbsp (40 ml) Simple syrup (see p. 40)
2 oz (50 g) Cooking chocolate
Zest of 1 orange and 1 lemon
Dash of cinnamon
1⅔ cups (200 g) Apricot marmalade

To Glaze
Apricot marmalade
About 9 oz (250 g) fondant, colored with pink food dye (see p. 44)
About 3.5 oz (100 g) dark couverture chocolate

POPPY SQUARES

Preheat oven to 340°F (170°C). Cream the butter with the confectioner's sugar, salt, and vanilla sugar. Add the egg yolks. Beat the egg whites to stiff peaks with the granulated sugar. Carefully fold the egg whites, poppy, and hazelnuts into the egg mixture. Butter and flour a baking frame. Place on a baking sheet lined with parchment paper (or use a deep cake pan) and fill with the poppy batter. Bake for about 45 minutes. Remove from oven, cut around the edges of the frame, overturn onto a sugared baking sheet, and pull off the parchment paper. Cut the poppy cake in half horizontally.

For the cream filling, beat the eggs with vanilla pulp in a bain-marie until creamy. Add honey and continue beating. Add water to the gelatin and dissolve in warmed apple brandy, then mix into the egg. Stir in the melted chocolate and let cool slightly. Carefully fold in the cream that has been not completely whipped.

Brush one poppy cake base with apricot marmalade and spread half of the cream on it. Set the second cake on top, brush with apricot marmalade, and spread the second half of the cream on top. Chill for 2 hours. Cut into 2x2 in (5x5 cm) squares. For the chocolate glaze, bring the cream briefly to a boil and melt the chopped up chocolate in it. Let cool somewhat and then cover the cake squares with it. Let the glaze dry a bit. Melt the white chocolate and place in a cone of parchment paper. Decorate the squares with fine stripes.

Bake Time: about 45 minutes

Bake Temperature: 340°F (170°C)

Tip: If you freeze the poppy squares, they are easier to glaze.

DIPPED FRUIT

Wash the fruit you have chosen and dry with paper towel. Warm the fondant to about 86 °F (30 °C) in a bain-marie. Dip the fruit, set on parchment paper, and let dry. Then melt chocolate in a bain-marie and dip the fruit. Depending on the fruit, you can dip it completely or only partly. Strawberries: it is best to hold the stem and dip ¾ of the way. Ground cherries: hold the leaves (which should stay on for decoration) and dip halfway. Dip bananas entirely. You can dip grapes individually or dip a bunch of 5–6 grapes together. Peel oranges, separate the slices, and dunk each slice completely. Let dry on parchment paper or a drying stand.

Tips:

- Dipped fruit—especially large things like bananas—is particularly attractive when partly decorated with white chocolate and/or sprinkled with brittle.
- It is easiest to dip the fruit if you hold them on a toothpick or a fork.

Ingredients
7–9 oz (200–250 g) Fruit (such as strawberries, bananas, grapes, ground cherries, or oranges)
7 oz (200 g) Fondant (see p. 44)
10.5 oz (300 g) Dark couverture chocolate

Baking Like the Pros
CAKES, TORTES, SCHNITTEN,
AND STRUDEL

CAKE

Cake is the "bread for the sweet tooth." It is nourishing and luxurious at the same time, sweet cheer for every day and a bright light at the weekend. And if they say cake is bad for you, the nutritious ingredients and the huge variety of fruit say that it can only be a rumor.

APRICOT CAKE

Preheat oven to 340°F (170°C). Prepare the basic sponge cake batter, and butter the baking sheet well with melted butter. Place a deep cake pan on it and pour in the batter. Spread the halved apricots on top and bake for about 50 minutes. Warm apricot marmalade with rum and brush thinly on the cake. Roast the grated almonds in a pan until golden brown and then sprinkle on the cake. Let cool before serving.

Bake Time: 50 minutes

Bake Temperature: 340°F (170°C)

Ingredients for 1 Cake Pan
Basic warm sponge cake
  (see p. 24), ½ recipe
Butter for the baking sheet
About 35 oz (1 kg) apricots,
  pitted and halved
1¼ cups (150 g) Apricot
  marmalade
¼ cup (5 cl) Rum
7 oz (200 g) Almonds, peeled
  and grated

APPLE POPPY CAKE

Preheat oven to 340°F (170°C). Cream the butter with the confectioner's sugar. Mix in egg yolks, salt, and lemon zest. Add coarsely chopped apple and rum. Beat the egg whites to stiff peaks. Mix together the nuts, poppy, and flour, and fold nuts and egg whites into the butter and egg yolk mix. Fold the apple slices into the poppy mixture. Like a baking sheet with parchment paper, spread the poppy batter on it, and bake for about 60 minutes. Take the cake out, let cool, and pull off the parchment paper. Cut up and serve dusted with vanilla confectioner's sugar.

Bake Time: about 60 minutes

Bake Temperature: 340°F (170°C)

Ingredients for 1 Cake Pan
2 sticks plus 1½ tbsp (250 g)
  Butter
2 cups (250 g) Confectioner's
  sugar
6 Egg yolks
Salt
Lemon zest
6 Egg whites
7 tbsp (100 g) Granulated
  sugar
8 oz (220 g) Nuts, ground
8 oz (220 g) Poppy seeds,
  ground
½ cup (60 g) Flour
4 Apples, cored, coarsely
  chopped
4 Apples, cored and sliced
3 tbsp (4 cl) Rum
Confectioner's sugar mixed
  with vanilla sugar, for
  dusting

BAKED APPLE CAKE

Ingredients for 1 Cake Pan
Basic pâte brisée (see p. 14),
  ½ recipe
2 sticks plus 1½ tbsp (250 g)
  Butter
⅔ cups (80 g) Confectioner's
  sugar
4 tsp (20 g) Vanilla sugar
Zest of 1 lemon
Dash of salt
2¾ lbs (1.25 kg) Quark or
  other fresh white cheese
6 Egg yolks
8 Egg whites
1 cup less 1 tbsp (210 g)
  Granulated sugar
1 cup (130 g) Flour
3.5 oz (100 g) Preserved
  raisins (see p. 189)
3⅓ lbs (1.5 kg) Apples
  (Golden Delicious)
Juice of 1 lemon
Apple elderflower marma-
  lade to glaze (see p. 197)
Almond slivers, roasted

Preheat oven to 350 °F (180 °C). Prepare the basic pâte brisée dough and chill for about half an hour. Roll out the dough to a thickness of about 2.5mm, lay on a baking sheet, and "stipple" with a fork (poke holes). Bake for about 8 minutes, until light brown. Remove from oven and let cool.

Lower oven heat to 320 °F (160 °C). Peel and core the apples, cut into large cubes, and immediately put them into lemon water to prevent browning. For the quark mixture, cream the butter with confectioner's sugar, vanilla sugar, salt, and lemon zest. Mix in the quark and egg yolk. Begin beating the egg whites, add the granulated sugar, and beat to stiff peaks. Fold the egg whites, flour, and raisins into the quark mixture. Mix in the drained apples. Place a 12x18in (30x45 cm) baking frame around the dough and pour in the apple quark mixture. Bake for about 35 minutes. Remove from the oven, brush with the apple elderflower marmalade, and sprinkle the almond slivers on top. Remove the frame and serve.

Bake Time: about 8 minutes for the dough, then 35 minutes

Bake Temperature: 350 °F (180 °C) for the dough, then 320 °F (160 °C)

Tip: If you do not have access to a baking frame, the cake can of course also be baked in a deeper loaf or cake pan.

Poganze

In Styria, a poganze *is a traditional baked good that is now prepared for Pentecost. Originally, it was either baked noodles or—much more commonly—a flat cake of five leavened layers, filled with apples, raisins, butter, and sugar and baked in a pot. The nineteenth century cookbook of Katharina Prato contained a multitude of poganze recipes with peaches, topfen, raisins, nuts, and semolina, some made with strudel dough. The recipe on the following page is a modern, easy to prepare version.*

APPLE POGANZE

On a work surface, knead the flour with confectioner's sugar, butter, and salt. Quickly knead in the egg yolks, eggs, white wine, and crème fraîche to form a smooth dough. Form a ball and let sit for half an hour in a cool place. Preheat oven to 350 °F (180 °C). Roll the dough out thin. Cut several approximately ½in (1 cm) strips and lay them side by side. Lay the rest of the dough in the buttered cake pan. Peel and core the apples and cut into cubes. Mix with warmed marmalade, lemon juice, breadcrumbs, granulated sugar, and almonds and spread on the dough. Pull up the edges of the dough in the cake pan. Brush the strips of dough with whisked egg and lay decoratively over the poganze. Bake for about 45 minutes. Let cool, dust with powdered sugar, and serve.

Bake Time: about 45 minutes

Bake Temperature: 350 °F (180 °C)

Ingredients for 1 Cake Pan
3⅓ cups (420 g) Flour
½ cup (60 g) Confectioner's sugar
Dash of salt
1 stick plus 2½ tbsp (150 g) Butter
3 Egg yolks
3 Eggs
4 tsp (2 cl) White wine
¼ cup (60g) Crème fraîche
14 Apples
½ cup (50 g) Apricot marmalade
4 tsp (2 cl) Lemon juice
3 oz (80 g) Almonds, peeled and finely chopped
1 oz (30 g) Breadcrumbs
2 tbsp (30 g) Granulated sugar
Butter for the cake pan
Egg white for brushing
Confectioner's sugar for dusting

BERRY MANDL

Preheat oven to 350 °F (180 °C). Cut the brown bread into small cubes, moisten with the milk, and spice with cinnamon and ginger. Place in a buttered casserole dish. Cream butter with honey, then add egg yolks, quark, lemon juice, semolina, and vanilla sugar. Beat the egg whites to stiff peaks with granulated sugar and fold into the egg yolk mixture. Spread the mixture over the bread and place the berries on top. Bake about 40 minutes.

Bake Time: about 40 minutes

Bake Temperature: 350 °F (180 °C)

Garnish Recommendation: Vanilla sauce (see p. 202)

Ingredients for 1 Casserole Dish (9in (20x25 cm))
5 oz (150 g) Brown rye bread, no crusts
5 oz (150 g) Berries (blueberries or blackberries)
7 tbsp (100 ml) Milk
Pinch of cinnamon
Pinch of ground ginger
2¾ tbsp (40 g) Butter
5 tbsp (100 g) Honey
2 Egg yolks
Dash of vanilla sugar
7 oz (200 g) Quark or other fresh white cheese
2 oz (50 g) Wheat semolina
1 tbsp Lemon juice
2 Egg whites
1 tbsp Sugar
Butter for the dish

CHERRY MANDL

Ingredients for 1 Casserole Dish (9in (20x25 cm))
5 oz (150 g) Brown rye bread, no crusts
5 oz (150 g) Sweet cherries, pitted
7 tbsp (100 ml) Milk
¼ cup (6 cl) Lavender Juice (see p. 205)
Mint, cut into strips
Pinch of ground cardamom
2¾ tbsp (40 g) Butter
5 tbsp (100 g) Honey
2 Egg yolks
Dash of vanilla sugar
7 oz (200 g) Quark or other fresh, white cheese
2 oz (50 g) Wheat semolina
1 tbsp Lemon juice
2 Egg whites
1 tbsp Sugar
Butter for the pan

Preheat the oven to 350 °F (180 °C). Cut the brown bread into small cubes, wet with milk and lavender juice, and spice with mint and cardamom. Place in a buttered casserole dish. Cream the butter and honey. Add the egg yolks, quark, lemon juice, semolina, and vanilla sugar. Beat the egg whites to stiff peaks with sugar and fold into the egg yolk mixture. Spread over the bread pieces and lay the pitted cherries on top. Bake for about 40 minutes.

Bake Time: about 40 minutes

Bake Temperature: 350 °F (180 °C)

Garnish Recommendation: Vanilla sauce (see p. 202)

Ingredients for 1 Cake Pan
21 oz (600 g) Basic puff pastry (see p.11) or ready-made pastry
About 3⅓ lbs (1.5 kg) Plums, pitted and quartered
½ cup (200 g) Plum jam
3 tbsp (5 cl) Rum
1¼ cups (150 g) Apricot marmalade and 2 cl rum to glaze
14 oz (400 g) Almond slivers
Dash of cinnamon powder

For the Bavarian Cream
3 Egg yolks
⅓ cup (70 g) Sugar
1 Vanilla bean
4 tsp (2 cl) Slivovitz
2 Sheets gelatin
1¼ cups (300 ml) Heavy cream, half whipped

PLUM CAKE

Preheat oven to 400 °F (200 °C). Prepare the basic puff pastry dough. Roll out, place on a baking sheet, stipple with a fork (gently poke holes), and bake for about 15 minutes, until crispy. Take out and let cool. Mix the plum jam with rum and brush on the pastry.

For the Bavarian cream, halve the vanilla bean and scrape out the pulp with a knife. Beat the egg yolks, sugar, and vanilla pulp in a double boiler until thick and creamy, then beat until cold in an ice water bath. Add water to the gelatin, remove excess water, and dissolve in warmed slivovitz. Mix into the egg yolks. Fold in the not-completely-whipped cream. Let the mixture cool and then spread on the puff pastry base. Lay the plum quarters on top and place the cake in a cool place. Warm apricot marmalade with some rum and brush the plums with it. Sprinkle the almond slivers and cinnamon on top and serve.

Bake Time: about 15 minutes

Bake Temperature: 400 °F (200 °C)

Guillotine and Sunday Cake

It fell as manna from heaven for Moses and was "white as coriander seeds and with the taste of honey cake." In the mythical Land of Plenty, you could pluck cake from the trees. The ancient Egyptians baked honey cake, just like the Greeks and Romans.

But we can speak of cake baking in the current sense as beginning in the eighteenth century, when the art of milling had come far enough that they could grind grain to fine, white flour without large pieces—the birth of sponge cake and pâte brisée was at hand.

But there was one more little kink to work out. The necessary sugar had to be imported at a high cost from countries where it was grown. The luxury to enjoy cake was at first reserved just for the aristocracy, who did not always seem to realize what a privilege it was. During a great famine (the so-called Flour War), when Queen Marie Antoinette was told that her subjects had no more bread, she replied succinctly: "Then let them eat cake." But as a matter of fact, the people had neither bread nor cake, and started a revolution that brought the queen to the guillotine.

Just a few years later, cake was no more expensive than bread. The Berliner chemist, Andreas Sigismund Marggraf (1709–1782), had discovered that a simple beet could be turned into affordable "sweet gold." There were no more limits on the triumph of the "Sunday cake."

MUSCAT GRAPE CAKE

Ingredients for 1 Cake Pan
1 lb (450 g) Basic puff pastry
  (see p.11) or ready-made
  pastry
35 oz (1 kg) Muscat grapes
1¼ cups (300 ml) Heavy
  cream
⅔ cup (150 ml) Muscatel
  wine (or other strong
  white wine)
1 tsp Cinnamon powder
1 cup less 1 tbsp (210 g)
  Granulated sugar
7 Eggs
Dried beans or lentils for
  baking the crust

Preheat oven to 400 °F (200 °C). Prepare the basic puff pastry dough. Roll out thinly and place into an approximately 1in (3 cm) deep cake pan. Stipple with a fork (gently poke holes). Cover the pastry with foil and weight with the dried beans or lentils, so that the dough does not rise while baking. After baking, remove the beans and foil. Wash the grapes and halve or leave whole, as you prefer. Spread the grapes on the puff pastry. Beat the eggs, heavy cream, granulated sugar, cinnamon, and white wine and pour over the grapes. Bake for about 25 minutes, until the batter solidifies. Let cool and serve.

Bake Time: 15–20 minutes for the puff pastry, 25 minutes the second time

Bake Temperature: 400 °F (200 °C)

QUARK STRAWBERRY CAKE

Ingredients for 1 Cake Pan
Basic sponge cake for
  schnitten (see p. 23)
1 cup (120 g) Strawberry
  marmalade
3⅓ lbs (1.5 kg) Strawberries
35 oz (1 kg) Quark or other
  fresh, white cheese
1½ cups (180 g) Confectioner's sugar
3 tbsp (40 g) Vanilla sugar
1⅓ cups (200 g) Cornstarch
Zest of 1 lemon
Zest of 1 orange
Dash of salt
12 Egg yolks
12 Egg whites
1⅓ cups (300 g) Granulated
  sugar

Prepare and bake the basic sponge cake. Place the cake on a baking sheet, brush thinly with strawberry marmalade, and place a baking frame (12x18in (30x45 cm)) around the cake (or place in a deep cake pan).

Preheat oven to 320 °F (160 °C). Wash the strawberries and set aside about 15 pretty ones with their stems. Halve the rest (without stems). Mix the quark with sour cream, confectioner's sugar, vanilla sugar, cornstarch, lemon and orange zest, and a dash of salt until creamy. Mix in the egg yolks. Begin beating the egg whites, add the granulated sugar, and beat to stiff peaks. Fold in carefully. Put the strawberries on the cake and spread the quark mixture on top. Bake for about 35 minutes. Remove from the oven, let cool, and serve. Before serving, garnish each slice with a half strawberry (with the green part).

Bake Time: 10 minutes for the cake, then 35 minutes

Bake Temperature: 400 °F (200 °C) for the cake, then 320 °F (160 °C)

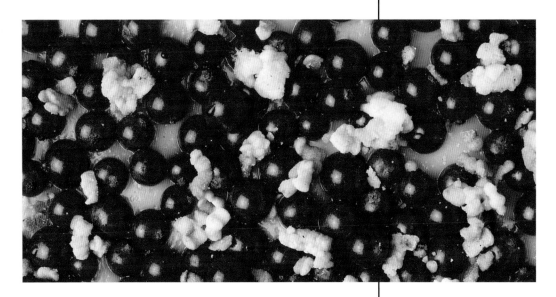

STREUSEL CAKE

Prepare the basic dough for tarts and let sit for 1 hour in a cool place. Preheat oven to 375 °F (190 °C). Roll out the dough thinly, lay on a baking sheet, and place a baking frame around the dough (or use a deep cake pan). Pull up the dough ¾ in (2 cm) around the sides and bake for 10 minutes. Lower the oven heat to 340 °F (170 °C). For the custard royale, beat the egg yolks with milk, heavy cream, vanilla pudding mix, vanilla sugar, salt, and confectioner's sugar. Pour the mixture over the prebaked cake base and bake for another 20 minutes. Let cool. While it is cooling, prepare the basic butter streusel. Spread raspberries on the cooled cake. For the gelatin, warm the raspberry marmalade with water in a double boiler. Add cold water to the gelatin, remove excess water, and dissolve in the marmalade. Pour the gelatin over the raspberries and spread the streusel on top. Let cool and serve.

Bake Time: 10 minutes prebake, then 20 minutes; 5 minutes for the butter streusel

Bake Temperature: 375 °F (190 °C) for prebaking, then 340 °F (170 °C); 340 °F (170 °C) for the butter streusel

Ingredients for 1 Cake Pan
Basic tart dough (see p. 11), ½ recipe
Basic butter streusel (see p. 17), doubled recipe
28 oz (800 g) Raspberries (can be replaced with redcurrants, strawberries, or blueberries)

For the Custard Royale
18 Egg yolks
1 cup (120 g) Confectioner's sugar
3 tbsp (40 g) Vanilla sugar
1.5 oz (40 g) Vanilla pudding mix
Salt
2½ cups (600 ml) Heavy cream
2 cups (500 ml) Milk

For the Gelatin
1½ cups (180 g) Raspberry marmalade
¾ cup (200 ml) Water
3 Sheets gelatin

COCONUT CAKE

Ingredients for 2 Smaller Foil Trays (7×3×2in (18×7×5 cm)) or 1 Larger Loaf Pan
1 stick plus 2½ tbsp (150 g) Butter
1 cup plus 2 tbsp (140 g) Confectioner's sugar
2 tsp (10 g) Vanilla sugar
Dash of salt
Zest of 1 orange
5 Eggs
7 oz (200 g) Coconut flakes
2 oz (60 g) Candied orange peel, finely chopped
6 tbsp (50 g) Flour
1 oz (30 g) Almonds, grated
Some orange marmalade
Grand Marnier
Butter for the pan

For the Orange Glaze
1 Egg white
Juice of 1 orange
3¼ cups (400 g) Confectioner's sugar

Preheat oven to 320 °F (160 °C). Mix the butter with the confectioner's sugar, vanilla sugar, salt, and orange zest until creamy. Add the eggs little by little. So that the batter does not coagulate, add 2 tbsp of coconut flakes. After that, add the rest of the coconut and the candied orange peel. Carefully fold in the flour. Butter the trays. Pour in the batter, sprinkle with almonds, and bake for about 1 hour. Let the cakes cool and remove from the trays. Warm the orange marmalade with a bit of Grand Marnier and brush on the cake.

For the glaze, mix egg whites with orange juice, then little by little stir in sifted confectioner's sugar. Glaze the coconut cake, let harden, and serve.

Bake Time: about 1 hour

Bake Temperature: 320 °F (160 °C)

Tip: The amount of powdered sugar in the orange glaze can be varied to achieve the desired consistency.

A Sweet Ghost

Coconut flakes are to sweet cooking what parmesan is to savory: that is, a truly all-purpose ingredient. Thanks to a high melting point and a flavor that harmonizes ideally with chocolate, fruit, and vanilla, among others, coconut is particularly well-suited to cake baking.

The path from the coconut palm to the bakery is a long one and leads through the mild, nutty flesh of the so-called coconut, which is dried into copra. The coconut palm originated in Southeast Asia, but it was probably given its name by Spanish colonizers. In Spanish, coco means something like "ghost." The pious Spanish got such an idea because of the three openings in the seed, which gave the coconut an eerie, ghostlike appearance to the people of that time. These days, we don't see ghosts in the coconut anymore—at most a good kitchen spirit.

ORANGE CAKE

Preheat oven to 320°F (160°C). Grind the marzipan finely and mix well with water, eggs, and confectioner's sugar. Mix together flour, cornstarch, vanilla sugar, and a dash of salt and carefully mix into the marzipan. Stir in the melted butter along with the candied orange peel and orange zest. Fill a baking frame or a deep, buttered cake pan. Cut the oranges into slices, dust the slices with some flour, and lay on top of the batter. Bake for about 45 minutes. Let cool. Mix Cointreau with orange marmalade and brush on the cake.

For the cream, melt both chocolates to lukewarm and mix with the room temperature butter. Add the Cointreau and cream the whole mixture. Spread the cream on the cake, draw a decorative pattern, and chill. Dust with cocoa powder and serve.

Bake Time: about 45 minutes

Bake Temperature: 320°F (160°C)

Ingredients for 1 Cake Pan
13 oz (360 g) Marzipan paste
4 tbsp Water
10 Eggs
1⅔ cups (200 g)
  Confectioner's sugar
1 cup plus 1 tbsp (140 g)
  Flour
⅓ cup (50 g) Cornstarch
2 tbsp (30 g) Butter
4 tsp (20 g) Vanilla sugar
Salt
Zest of 2 oranges
3.5 oz (100 g) Candied
  orange peel, chopped
8 Oranges
Some flour
⅓ cup (8 cl) Cointreau
Orange marmalade
Butter for the can pan
Cocoa powder for dusting

For the Cream
7 oz (200 g) Milk couverture
  chocolate
3.5 oz (100 g) Dark couverture chocolate
1 stick plus 6 tbsp (200 g)
  Butter
2.5oz (70 g) Cointreau

NUT CAKE

Preheat oven to 375°F (190°C). Prepare the basic pâte brisée dough, chill, and then roll out as thinly as possible. Line a buttered pan with the dough; cut a ¾in (2 cm) strip and place inside for the edge. Stipple the dough with a fork (gently poke holes). For the filling, mix the ground walnuts with confectioner's sugar, vanilla sugar, and the vanilla pulp. Mix eggs, cream, milk, and nut liqueur into the nuts. Pour the mixture onto the cake base, spread evenly, and bake for 25 minutes. Let cool; preferably let sit overnight in a cool place and then serve.

Bake Time: about 25 minutes

Bake Temperature: 375°F (190°C)

Ingredients for 1 Smaller Cake Pan (or 1 Torte, 10in (24 cm) diameter)
9 oz (250 g) Basic pâte bri-
  sée dough (see p. 14)
9 oz (250 g) Walnuts, ground
1 cup (125 g) Confectioner's
  sugar
1 tsp (5 g) Vanilla sugar
Pulp of ½ vanilla bean
3 Eggs
¾ cup (200 ml) Heavy cream
1 cup (250 ml) Milk
1 cup (250 ml) Nut liqueur
Butter for the pan

ROULADES

The roulade is to cake what the galantine is to pie: a distinctive form, not only for showing off the cake, but also to make it taste more succulent.

SPONGE CAKE ROULADE

Preheat oven to 400 °F (200 °C). Prepare the basic sponge cake batter. Line a baking sheet with parchment paper, spread the batter on it, and bake for 15–20 minutes. Remove from the oven, wait until no longer steaming, then overturn onto a lightly sugared cloth or parchment paper. Carefully pull the parchment paper off the cake. Carefully roll up the roulade and let cool. Unroll and spread Apricot marmalade, slightly warmed if desired, on the cake. Roll up the roulade again and dust with confectioner's sugar.

Bake Time: 15–20 minutes

Bake Temperature: 400 °F (200 °C)

Ingredients for about
15 Servings
About 3½ oz (500 g) Basic
  sponge cake for roulades
  (see p. 22)
Apricot marmalade
Granulated sugar
Confectioner's sugar for
  dusting

1
Spread the sponge cake
  batter on a baking sheet
  lined with parchment
  paper.

2
Remove from oven and wait
  until cake is no longer
  steaming, and overturn
  onto a lightly sugared
  cloth or parchment paper.

3
Pull the parchment paper
  off the cake.

4
Press carefully with your
  thumbs on the harder
  edges of the cake, so that
  the roulade is easier
  to roll.

5
Roll up the roulade with the
  cloth or parchment paper
  and let cool

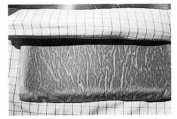
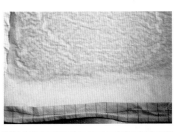
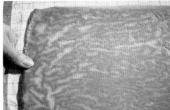

STRAWBERRY NUT ROULADE

Ingredients for
about 15 Servings
Basic nut cake batter
  (see p. 29), ½ recipe
5 oz (150 g) Strawberry
  purée (see p. 200)
⅓ cup (70 g) Granulated
  sugar
4 Sheets gelatin
2 tbsp (3 cl) Cointreau
4 tsp (2 cl) Orange juice
1 cup (250 ml) Whipped
  cream
3.5 oz (100 g) Strawberries,
  washed with stems cut off

For the Garnish
About 1½ cups (350 ml)
  Whipped cream,
  sweetened Chocolate
  shavings
7–8 Strawberries with
  leaves, halved

Preheat oven to 350 °F (180 °C). Prepare the basic nut batter. Line a baking sheet with parchment paper, spread the batter on it, and bake for 12–15 minutes. Take out of the oven and overturn the cake, still hot, onto sugared parchment paper. Carefully pull the parchment paper from the cake.

For the strawberry cream, add cold water to the gelatin, remove excess water, and dissolve in warmed orange juice mixed with Cointreau. Stir in strawberry purée and granulated sugar. Carefully fold in the whipped cream. Spread the cream on the roulade, place the quartered strawberries on top, and let the unrolled roulade sit briefly in a cool place. As soon as the cream begins to harden, roll up the roulade with the help of the parchment paper, wrap the paper tightly around it, and chill for 2–3 hours wrapped in paper. Then remove paper, spread with lightly sweetened whipped cream, and sprinkle with chocolate shavings. Cut the roulade and garnish each piece with a strawberry half.

Bake Time: 12–15 minutes

Bake Temperature: 350 °F (180 °C)

QUARK AND CREAM ROULADE

Preheat oven to 400 °F (200 °C). Prepare the sponge cake batter according to the recipe. Line a baking sheet with parchment paper, spread batter on baking sheet, and bake for 12–15 minutes. Remove from oven and overturn the still hot cake onto parchment paper sprinkled with granulated sugar. Carefully pull the parchment paper from the bottom of the cake. Beat the egg yolks with confectioner's sugar, vanilla sugar, and orange zest until creamy. Add cold water to the gelatin, remove excess water, and dissolve in rum in a double boiler. Beat the egg whites, add granulated sugar, and beat to stiff peaks. Mix the quark with sour cream until smooth and mix in the egg yolk and rum. Alternately fold the whipped cream and egg whites into the quark mixture. Spread the cream on the cake and sprinkle raisins on top. Without rolling it up, chill the roulade briefly. Then roll it up with the help of the paper, wrap tightly in parchment paper, and chill for 2–3 hours. Unwrap from the paper, dust with confectioner's sugar, and slice.

Bake Time: 12–15 minutes

Bake Temperature: 400 °F (200 °C)

Tip: If you do not have preserved raisins, this roulade tastes delicious with other fresh fruits, such as strawberries or grapes.

Ingredients for about
15 Servings
Basic sponge cake batter for roulades (see p. 22), ½ recipe
2 Egg yolks
⅓ cup (40 g) Confectioner's sugar
2 tsp (10 g) Vanilla sugar
Zest of 1 orange
4 tsp (2 cl) Rum
3 Sheets gelatin
7 oz (200 g) Quark or other fresh, white cheese
½ cup (100 ml) Sour cream
2 Egg whites
¼ cup (50 g) Granulated sugar
½ cup (120 ml) Whipped cream
3.5 oz (100g) Preserved raisins (see p. 189)
Granulated sugar
Confectioner's sugar for dusting

CHOCOLATE PEACH ROULADE

Ingredients for about
15 Servings
Basic sponge cake batter
  for roulades (see p. 22),
  ½ recipe
7.5 oz (210 g) White
  couverture chocolate
3 Egg yolks
¼ cup (60 ml) Simple syrup
  (see p. 40)
¼ cup (60 ml) Heavy cream
3 Sheets gelatin
¾ cup (200 ml) Whipped
  cream
2 tbsp (3 cl) Peach liqueur
5 oz (150 g) Preserved
  peaches (see p. 189)
Granulated sugar
Cocoa powder for dusting

For the Chocolate Glaze
5 oz (150 g) Cooking
  chocolate
⅔ cup (150 ml) Heavy cream

Preheat oven to 400 °F (200 °C). Prepare the sponge cake batter according to the recipe. Line a baking sheet with parchment paper, spread the batter on it, and bake for 12–15 minutes. Remove from oven and overturn the still hot cake onto parchment paper sprinkled with granulated sugar. Carefully pull the parchment paper from the bottom of the cake. Melt the chocolate and mix with the yolks, simple syrup, and heavy cream. Add water to the gelatin, remove excess water, dissolve in warmed peach liqueur, and stir into the chocolate. Fold in the whipped cream. Spread the chocolate cream on the cake and then add the preserved peaches on top. Without rolling it up, chill the roulade briefly. Then roll it up with the help of the paper, wrap tightly in parchment paper, and chill for 2–3 hours.

For the glaze, bring the cream to a boil, remove from heat, and melt the chopped chocolate in it. Pour onto a marble pastry board and, using an angled spatula, spread out repeatedly until cool. Put the glaze in a bowl and pour over the roulade. Chill again. Dust the roulade with cocoa powder and slice.

Bake Time: 12–15 minutes

Bake Temperature: 400 °F (200 °C)

Which Flour Goes with Which Dessert?

Add some flour, obviously. It is the essence of almost every baked good. But the type of flour you should use is not always obvious. Not only master bakers, but also experienced housewives know that the very same recipe can have very different results if you use different flour. The most crucial factors are how refined the flour is and the ash content. Ash content means the noncombustible mineral content of the grain, which is mostly found in the husks. After each sieving, the flour is mixed together into specific types of flour according to lightness and ash content.

In Europe, flour is designated by number, and the higher the number— meaning the more completely the grains are ground—the more husks and hulls are contained. The higher the flour type number, the darker the color of the flour and the more minerals it contains. There is also a distinction based on how finely or coarsely the flour is ground.

For sweet baking, aside from whole food baking (see p. 209), the best kind of flour is light colored flour with a low ash content, where only the inside of the grain has been finely ground. Unless otherwise specified, if you use white pastry flour to prepare the recipes in this book (equivalent to Austrian type 450 or 480), nothing can go wrong. This kind of flour absorbs liquid, egg, and fat very well, so it created even dough that is easy to mold. If you cannot find pastry flour, you can mix 1 part cake flour with 2 parts all-purpose flour. You can also use all-purpose or high gluten flour if the recipe you are preparing does not need to be particularly smooth.

No matter what kind of flour you choose, one rule must be followed in the sweet kitchen: always sift the flour before using it. Only then will it be soft and able to easily homogenize with the other ingredients.

Tip: Flour stays fresh longer when it is kept airtight, dry, and especially protected from smells. When the lipids in flour begin to break down after long storage, the flour will become ugly and rancid and can no longer be used. You can easily stop this problem by making sure that your flour is not old—and by baking as often as possible.

SCHNITTEN

The little sister of the torte has many benefits: It is easier to portion out, easier to stack in the fridge, and easier to cut into small pieces when you are counting calories. But schnitten are one thing above all—alluringly sweet.

ESTERHÁZY SCHNITTEN

Ingredients for about 20 Servings (2 cakes of 3×18 in (7×45 cm))
Basic Esterházy tart batter (see p. 32), ½ recipe
1⅔ cups (400 ml) Milk
1 cup less 2 tbsp (200 g) Granulated sugar
4 Sheets gelatin
8 Egg yolks
4 tsp (20 g) Vanilla sugar
Dash of salt
2 sticks (220 g) Butter
3.5 oz (100 g) Nougat
Granulated sugar

For the Glaze
½ cup (70 g) Apricot marmalade
About 5 oz (150 g) fondant (see p. 44)
Dark couverture chocolate

Preheat oven to 400 °F (200 °C). Prepare the Esterházy batter according to the recipe. Line 3 baking sheets with parchment paper, spread the batter out on them, and bake for 8–10 minutes. While still hot, overturn onto a work surface dusted with confectioner's sugar and pull off the parchment paper immediately. Cut into strips 2¾ in (7 cm) wide.

For the cream, mix milk, granulated sugar, vanilla sugar, salt, and egg yolks in a mixing bowl. Continue mixing over steam until the temperature reaches 158 °F (70 °C) and the egg yolks have bound the mixture together somewhat. Dissolve moistened gelatin in the mixture, remove from heat, and mix for 5 minutes with an immersion blender. Chill. Cream the butter, add warmed nougat, and stir in the cooled cream. Spread cream on each strip of cake, set them on top of one another, and spread cream on the side as well (each piece should more or less consist of 7 strips). Coat the top layer with apricot marmalade and chill for 30 minutes.

Melt some dark couverture chocolate. Cover the Esterházy schnitten with a thin layer of fondant. Use parchment paper to create a bag and use it to pipe thin lines of chocolate over the schnitten. Drag a toothpick across the lines of chocolate to create the typical Esterházy pattern. Chill the schnitten until the glaze has dried. To cut the schnitten, it is best to use a serrated knife dipped in hot water.

Bake Time: 8–10 minutes

Bake Temperature: 400 °F (200 °C)

Tip: Esterházy schnitten are not well suited to being stored or frozen. They should be eaten on the day after being prepared, at the latest.

A Man for every Meal

The Esterházys created history not only through valor and cultural vision, but also in the culinary realm. There are countless dishes named after the ancient family of Hungarian magnates, such as Esterházy goulash, Esterházy roast, Esterházy schnitzel, Esterházy torte, and Esterházy schnitten. However, one representative of this family in particular earned the esteem of cooks and bakers: Nikolaus II, Prince Esterházy de Galántha, Count of Forchtenstein (1765–1833), who was an Austrian Field Marshal and politician as well as the founder of a great collection of paintings and engravings. He went down in history for refusing the crown of Hungary offered to him by Napoleon. (See recipe on p. 95.)

CARDINAL SCHNITTEN

Preheat oven to 320 °F (160 °C). For batter I, beat egg whites to stiff peaks with granulated sugar. For batter II (sponge cake), beat eggs, egg yolks, granulated sugar, and vanilla sugar until creamy. Carefully fold in the flour. Set out 3 sheets of parchment paper (about 8in (20 cm) wide). Using a piping bag fitted with a large round nozzle, pipe 3 stripes of egg whites onto each paper, leaving space between the stripes. In between, pipe two strips of cake batter. Do not spread the batter out. Dust with confectioner's sugar and bake for 35 minutes. Let cool and carefully pull off the paper.

For the filling of your choice, whip the cream. For variation I, flavor the cream with vanilla sugar, spread redcurrant marmalade on the first layer and whipped cream on top of that. Place the second cake layer on top, spread with redcurrant marmalade and whipped cream again, and then place the last cake layer on top. For variation II, flavor the whipped cream with confectioner's sugar and instant coffee and then follow the directions as in variation I. Before cutting, dust with confectioner's sugar.

Bake Time: about 35 minutes

Bake Temperature: 320 °F (160 °C)

Ingredients for 15 Servings

For Batter I
12 Egg whites
1¼ cups (270 g) Granulated
  sugar

For Batter II
(Sponge Cake)
3 Eggs
5 Egg yolks
⅓ cup (80 g) Granulated
  sugar
4 tsp (20 g) Vanilla sugar
⅔ cup (80 g) Flour
Confectioner's sugar to dust

For the Filling, Variation I
2 cups (500 ml) Whipping
  cream
4 tsp (20 g) Vanilla sugar
1⅔ cups (200 g) Redcurrant
  marmalade

For the Filling, Variation II
2½ cups (600 ml) Whipping
  cream
3 tbsp (20 g) Confectioner's
  sugar
Instant coffee powder

CREAM SCHNITTEN

Ingredients for 1 Cake Pan
1¾ lbs (800 g) Basic puff
  pastry (see p. 11)
Apricot marmalade and
Rum for brushing
Fondant or egg white glaze
  (see p. 44)

For the Vanilla Cream
4¼ cups (1l) Milk
1⅓ cups (300 g) Granulated
  sugar
3 tbsp (40 g) Vanilla sugar
3 oz (80 g) Vanilla pudding
  mix
7 tbsp (10 cl) Rum
14 Sheets gelatin
6⅓ cups (1.5l) Whipped
  cream

Preheat oven to just under 400 °F (200 °C). Roll out the pre-pared puff pastry dough about 3mm thick and cut into two bases (about 12x18in (30x45 cm) each). Lay the dough on a baking sheet, stipple with a fork (poke gently several times), and bake for 10 minutes. Warm apricot marmalade with some rum and brush on the puff pastry bases.

For the vanilla cream, boil half the milk with granulated sugar and vanilla sugar. Mix the other half of the milk with vanilla pudding mix until smooth and then stir into the boiling milk. Bring to a boil again and then remove from heat. Add cold water to the gelatin, remove excess water, and dissolve in the still-hot vanilla mixture. Stir in rum and chill, but do not let it gel completely. Fold whipped cream into the cooled vanilla cream. Place the puff pastry base in a loaf pan or baking frame, spread the vanilla cream on top, and chill. Separately, glaze the top pastry layer with fondant or egg white glaze, let dry, and place on top just before cutting.

Bake Time: about 10 minutes

Bake Temperature: just under 400 °F (200 °C)

RASPBERRY YOGURT SCHNITTEN

Prepare the sponge cake batter according to the recipe and bake in a cake pan. Warm the raspberry marmalade, mix with the raspberry brandy, and brush the cake base with it. Place a 12x18 in (30x45 cm) baking frame around the cake (or place the cake in a deep cake pan).

For the raspberry mousse, mix the raspberry purée with confectioner's sugar. Add cold water to the gelatin. Dissolve the gelatin in warmed raspberry brandy, then stir into the raspberry purée. Carefully fold in the whipped cream. Spread the raspberry mousse on the cake, smooth, and chill for half an hour.

For the yogurt mousse, mix yogurt, confectioner's sugar, and lemon zest. Add cold water to the gelatin. Warm the orange juice and dissolve the gelatin in it, then stir into the yogurt. Fold in the whipped cream. Spread the yogurt mousse on top of the raspberry mousse, smooth, and chill for another half hour. Wash the raspberries and spread on top of the set mousse.

For the gelatin, boil water with granulated sugar. Remove from heat and stir in lemon juice. Add cold water to the gelatin, remove excess, and dissolve in the still-warm liquid. Let cool, but do not let gel. Pour over the raspberries and chill for about 4 hours. Remove from the mold, portion, and sprinkle with chopped pistachios before serving.

Ingredients for 1 Cake Pan or Baking Frame
Basic chocolate sponge cake batter (see p. 24)
1¼ cup (150 g) Raspberry marmalade
3 tbsp (4 cl) Raspberry brandy (Himbeergeist)
21 oz (600 g) Raspberries
3.5 oz (100 g) Pistachio nuts, chopped

For the Raspberry Mousse
26 oz (750 g) Raspberry purée (see p. 201)
1 cup (120 g) Confectioner's sugar
8 Sheets gelatin
¼ cup (6 cl) Raspberry brandy (Himbeergeist)
1½ cups (375 ml) Whipped cream

For the Yogurt Mousse
4¼ cups (1 l) Yogurt
2 cups (250 g) Confectioner's sugar
12 Sheets gelatin
⅔ cup (150 ml) Orange juice
Zest of 1 lemon
3⅔ cups (875 ml) Whipped cream

For the Gelatin
1 cup (250 ml) Water
7 tbsp (100 g) Granulated sugar
4 tsp (2 cl) Lemon juice
3 Sheets gelatin

REDCURRANT MERINGUE SCHNITTEN

*Ingredients for 1 Cake Pan
or Baking Frame*
Basic sponge cake for
  schnitten (see p. 23)
Redcurrant marmalade for
  brushing
About 35 oz (1 kg)
  Redcurrants, crushed
Basic meringue batter
  (see p. 35)

For the Egg Liqueur Cream
18 oz (500 g) Mascarpone
1 cup (250 ml) Egg liqueur
  (Advocaat or Eierlikör)
¾ cup (100 g) Confectioner's
  sugar
½ cup (100 ml) Orange juice
6 Sheets gelatin
1½ cups (375 ml) Whipped
  cream

Prepare and bake the sponge cake for schnitten according to the recipe. Warm the redcurrant marmalade and brush the cake base with it. Place a 12x18in (30x45 cm) baking frame around the cake (or place the cake in a deep cake pan).

For the cream, mix the mascarpone with confectioner's sugar and egg liqueur until smooth. Add cold water to the gelatin. Warm the orange juice, dissolve the gelatin in it, and mix into the egg liqueur cream. Carefully fold in the whipped cream. Mix in the washed, crushed redcurrants and fill the pan. Smooth and cool for 2 hours.

Prepare the meringue batter according to the basic recipe and spread on top of the redcurrant schnitten. Make a decorative pattern in the top and brown the surface of the meringue using a "crème brûlée" kitchen torch, which is available in specialty cooking shops, or bake briefly at maximum upper heat. Chill. Remove from the pan and serve.

Bake Time: briefly to brown

Bake Temperature: maximum upper heat

APRICOT QUARK SCHNITTEN

Prepare the sponge cake batter for schnitten according to the basic recipe, and bake two cake bases. Brush one cake base with warmed apricot marmalade. Place a baking frame around this cake (or place in a deep cake pan). Mix the quark, mascarpone or sour cream, confectioner's sugar, rum, lemon zest, vanilla sugar, and raisins in a mixing bowl. Warm the orange juice. Add cold water to the gelatin, remove excess water, dissolve in orange juice, and stir into the quark mixture. Now mix in the apricot marmalade. Finally, fold the whipped cream and apricots into the quark cream and fill the pan. Place the second cake on top and chill for 4 hours. Cut with a serrated knife dipped in hot water and dust each piece with confectioner's sugar.

Ingredients for 1 Cake Pan or Baking Frame

Basic sponge cake for schnitten (see p. 23), double recipe
Apricot marmalade for brushing
2 lbs (900 g) Quark or other fresh, white cheese
18 oz (500 g) Mascarpone or sour cream
1 cup (120 g) Confectioner's sugar
3 tbsp (4 cl) Rum
Lemon zest
4 tsp (20 g) Vanilla sugar
Raisins
1¼ cups (300 ml) Orange juice
4 tbsp Apricot marmalade
12 Sheets gelatin
4¼ cups (1 l) Whipped cream
About 4½ lbs (2 kg) preserved apricots (see p. 188 or from a can)
Confectioner's sugar for dusting

Austrian Desserts
Cakes, Tortes, Schnitten, and Strudel

BANANA SCHNITTEN

Ingredients for 1 Loaf Pan or Baking Frame
Basic sponge cake for schnitten (see p. 23)
Apricot marmalade for brushing
12 Bananas, peeled
Juice of 2–3 lemons
½ cup (60 g) Apricot marmalade for the bananas
10.5 oz (300 g) Ganache glaze (see p. 43)

For the Banana Cream
4¼ cups (1 l) Milk
1 cup less 2 tbsp (200 g) Granulated sugar
2 tbsp (30 g) Vanilla sugar
3.5 oz (100 g) Vanilla pudding mix
¼ cup (6 cl) Banana liqueur
18 Sheets gelatin
5 Bananas, peeled
Juice of 1 lemon
4¼ cups (1 l) Whipped cream

Prepare the sponge cake for schnitten according to the basic recipe, let cool, and brush with warmed apricot marmalade. Place the cake base in an appropriately sized baking frame (12x18in (30x45 cm)).

Boil half of the milk with granulated sugar and vanilla sugar. Mix the rest of the milk with vanilla pudding mix, stir into the boiling milk, bring to a boil again and remove from heat. Add cold water to the gelatin, remove excess water, and dissolve in the still-hot vanilla liquid. Cut the bananas into slices and mix into the vanilla cream along with the lemon juice and banana liqueur, using an immersion blender. If the mixture is still hot, chill briefly. Fold whipped cream into the cooled vanilla cream.

Marinate the bananas in a bowl with lemon juice. Remove and roll in the warmed apricot marmalade. Lay the bananas on the cake base and fill the space between the bananas with cream. Chill for 30 minutes. Spread the prepared ganache glaze on top and chill again for 6 hours.

101

CHOCOLATE VANILLA SCHNITTEN

Ingredients for 1 Cake Pan
or Baking Frame
Basic chocolate sponge
　cake batter (see p. 24)
Basic choux pastry batter
　(see p. 20), double recipe
Confectioner's sugar for
　dusting
Cocoa powder for dusting
Chocolate flakes or rolls as
　decoration

For the Vanilla Cream
35 oz (1 kg) Pastry cream
　(see p. 247)
8 Sheets gelatin
Cointreau
1¼ cups (300 ml) Whipped
　cream

For the Chocolate Mousse
21 oz (600 g) Milk couverture
　chocolate
3 Eggs
¾ cups (180 ml) Simple
　syrup (see p. 40)
¾ cups (180 ml) Heavy
　cream
9 Sheets gelatin
4 cups (900 ml) Whipped
　cream
6 tbsp (9 cl) Rum

Preheat oven to 350 °F (180 °C). Prepare the chocolate sponge cake batter according to the recipe. Spread out to 12x18 in (30x45 cm) on a baking sheet lined with parchment paper and bake for 15–20 minutes. Remove from oven, overturn onto a baking tray or cloth dusted with confectioner's sugar, and carefully remove the paper from the bottom of the cake.

Raise the oven temperature to 430 °F (220 °C). Prepare the choux pastry batter according to the recipe. Using a piping bag fitted with a round nozzle, pipe ¾ in (2 cm) strips on a baking sheet lined with parchment paper. Bake briefly at 430 °F (220 °C) then lower to 350 °F (180 °C) and bake for 15–20 minutes. Remove from oven and let cool.

For the vanilla cream, warm the pastry cream. Add cold water to the gelatin, remove excess and dissolve in the pastry cream. Season with a splash of Cointreau, beat until cold, and then fold in the whipped cream. Fill the choux strips with cream by cutting them the long way, pulling them open, and filling with cream. Close them again and chill. For the chocolate mousse, melt the couverture chocolate. Beat the eggs until creamy and mix in the chocolate, simple syrup, and heavy cream. Add cold water to the gelatin, remove excess water, and dissolve in slightly warmed rum. Stir into the chocolate mixture and fold in the whipped cream. Place the cake base in a baking frame or deep cake pan. Spread some chocolate mousse on top. Place the filled choux strips, cover with the rest of the chocolate mousse, smooth, and chill. Before cutting, dust with sifted cocoa powder and garnish with chocolate flakes.

Bake Time: cake: 15–20 minutes; choux pastry: 15–20 minutes

Bake Temperature: cake: 350 °F (180 °C), choux pastry: 430 °F (220 °C) lowering to 350 °F (180 °C)

Tiramisu Schnitten

Place a (8x12 in (22x30 cm)) baking frame on a baking sheet (or use a loaf pan) and line with ladyfingers. Season strong coffee with a large splash of rum and saturate the ladyfingers with it.

For the cream, beat egg yolks, confectioner's sugar, vanilla sugar, and mascarpone until creamy. Add water to the gelatin, remove excess, and dissolve in warmed rum. Mix the rum and lemon juice into the mascarpone. Begin to beat the egg whites, add granulated sugar, and beat to stiff peaks. Fold in the egg whites along with the whipped cream.

Spread a portion of the cream on the ladyfingers. Lay out another layer of ladyfingers on top and saturate with coffee again. The last layer is cream. Chill for several hours. Dust with cocoa powder before serving.

Tip: You can use more or fewer ladyfingers to achieve the desired consistency.

Carpaccio's Sweet Sister

Venice, which was already celebrated in the Middle Ages as a city of sweets, is not only the mother city of marzipan, but also of an old specialty called "tira mi su," which even up until the 80s was hardly known outside of the lagoon city. Today, tiramisu is the sweet sister of carpaccio, which was also invented in Venice, and almost every housewife and hobby chef knows a very special "secret recipe." The tiramisu schnitten described here is a special, enchanting variation.

The meaning of the three strange words that sound like a magic spell remains widely unknown. But they mean plain and simply "pick me up!" which is certainly a reference to the function of this rich dessert: After a long meal, you want to be woken up by the strong coffee that saturates the ladyfingers.

Ingredients for 1 Cake Pan or Baking Frame
About 18 oz (500 g) ladyfingers (see p. 37 or use ready-made)
Rum and strong coffee
Cocoa powder for dusting

For the Cream
5 Egg yolks
6 tbsp (50 g) Confectioner's sugar
9 oz (250 g) Mascarpone
2 Sheets gelatin
2 tsp (10 g) Vanilla sugar
2 tsp (1 cl) Rum
2 tsp (1 cl) Lemon juice
3 Egg whites
¼ cup (50 g) Granulated sugar
½ cup (100 ml) Whipped cream

SHERRY MOCHA SCHNITTEN

Prepare the sponge cake batter for schnitten according to the recipe and bake two cake bases. For the sherry mousse, beat egg yolks with sugar and sherry in a bain-marie until creamy. Add water to the gelatin, remove excess water, and dissolve in the warm sherry mixture. Mix the mascarpone a spoonful at a time into the mixture and fold in the whipped cream. Melt the chocolate in a bain-marie and cover one cake base with it. Let set, then place in a baking frame or deep loaf pan chocolate side down. Mix coffee and sherry and saturate the cake with half of it. Spread half of the sherry mousse on top and cover with the second cake. Saturate with the rest of the sherry coffee mixture and spread the rest of the cream on top. Chill overnight. Dust with cocoa powder before serving.

Ingredients for 1 Cake Pan or Baking Frame
Basic sponge cake for
  schnitten (see p. 23),
  double recipe
3.5 oz (100 g) Dark couverture chocolate
2½ cups (600 ml) Coffee,
  very strong
⅔ cup (160 ml) Sherry
Cocoa powder for dusting

For the Sherry Mousse
12 Egg yolks
¾ cup (170 g) Sugar
¾ cup (200 ml) Oloroso
  sherry (dark, spicy sherry)
28 oz (800 g) Mascarpone
7 Sheets gelatin
4¼ (1 l) Whipped cream

Linzer Schnitten

Preheat oven to 320 °F (160 °C). Cream the butter with confectioner's sugar, salt, vanilla sugar, and lemon zest. Mix in the eggs and egg yolk little by little. Mix hazelnuts, cake crumbs, and flour, and mix into the eggs and butter. Flavor with rum, clove powder, and cinnamon. Place a 12x18in (30x45 cm) baking frame on a baking sheet or use a deep cake pan. Pour in about ⅔ of the batter. Lay down a layer of wafers and brush marmalade on it. Fill a piping bag fitted with a star-shaped nozzle with the rest of the Linzer batter and pipe a lattice on top. Sprinkle with almond slices and bake for about an hour. Let cool and serve.

Bake Time: about 1 hour

Bake Temperature: 320 °F (160 °C)

Tip: Linzer torte can of course be prepared using the same recipe.

For a really successful Linzer dough…
…here are a few old housewives' tips:

- Don't use butter that is cold, but also not room temperature. It is best to take the butter out of the refrigerator about half an hour before using it.
- Mix together the ingredients quickly and evenly, so that the dough stays together properly and does not become crumbly.
- If the dough becomes too crumbly, a few drops of milk will help to make it smooth again.
- Kneading the dough will warm it up, so set it in a cool place so that it becomes firm again.
- Poke holes gently with a fork before baking. The dough will rise better in the oven.
- Make sure that the heat in the oven is not over 320 °F (160 °C).

Ingredients for 1 Cake Pan
2 sticks plus 1½ tbsp (250 g) Butter
2 cups (250 g) Confectioner's sugar
Dash of salt
2 tsp (10 g) Vanilla sugar
Zest of 1 lemon
5 Eggs
1 Egg yolk
9 oz (250 g) Hazelnuts, ground
12.5 oz (360 g) Sponge cake crumbs
1 cup (125 g) Flour
3 tbsp (4 cl) Rum
1 tsp (2 g) Clove powder
2 tsp (5 g) Cinnamon
Wafers
1⅔ cups (200 g) Redcurrant marmalade
Almond slices

STRUDEL

Bubble and boom—that's a strudel, if you go back to the Old High German root "stredan." But it is much more important that this pastry, which came to Vienna through Hungary from Turkey in the sixteenth century, is prepared properly.

APPLE STRUDEL

Ingredients for basic strudel dough (see p. 16) or ready-made dough
3⅓ lbs (1.5 kg) Apples
4¼ tbsp (60 g) Butter
3.5 oz (100 g) Breadcrumbs
½ cup (120 g) Sugar
2 oz (60 g) Raisins
Ground cinnamon
4 tsp (20 g) Vanilla sugar
Zest of 1 lemon
7 tbsp (10 cl) Rum
7 tbsp (100 g) Butter, melted
Flour for the work surface
Confectioner's sugar for
  dusting

Preheat oven to 350 °F (180 °C). Prepare the strudel dough according to the basic recipe. For the filling, heat butter in a pan and lightly brown some of the breadcrumbs in it. Peel, quarter, and core the apple and cut them into thin slices. Mix with raisins, the rest of the breadcrumbs, sugar, vanilla sugar, cinnamon, lemon zest, and rum. Lay a cloth on the work surface and flour evenly. Lightly flour the dough as well and place on the cloth. With a rolling pin, roll the dough out as thinly as possible. Then slide both hands under the dough, palms down, and slowly stretch it in all directions, until it's so thin that you could read a newspaper through it. Be very careful not to tear the dough. Saturate the dough with ¾ of the melted butter. Lay the filling on the dough in a strip. With the help of the cloth, fold the dough over the filling and then fold around once. Cut off extra. Place the strudel with the seam down on a buttered baking sheet and brush with the rest of the butter. Bake for about 40 minutes. Dust with confectioner's sugar and serve while still warm.

Bake Time: 40 minutes

Bake Temperature: 350 °F (180 °C)

Tip: As with all sweet strudels, the best time to eat it is when it is freshly baked and almost still warm. Never serve refrigerated strudel.

PEAR STRUDEL

Preheat oven to 350°F (180°C). Prepare the strudel dough according to the basic recipe. Peel, quarter, and core the pears. Cut the pears into thin slices and mix with raisins, almonds, cake crumbs, sugar, vanilla sugar, lemon juice, and Poire Williams. Lay a cloth on the work surface and flour evenly. Lightly flour the dough as well and place on the cloth. With a rolling pin, roll the dough out as thinly as possible. Then slide both hands under the dough, palms down, and slowly stretch it in all directions, until it's so thin that you could read a newspaper through it. Be very careful not to tear the dough. Saturate the dough with ¾ of the butter. Lay the filling on the dough in a strip. With the help of the cloth, fold the dough over the filling and then fold around once. Cut off extra. Place the strudel with the seam down on a buttered baking sheet and brush with the rest of the butter. Bake for about 40 minutes. Dust with confectioner's sugar and serve while still warm.

Bake Time: 40 minutes

Bake Temperature: 350°F (180°C)

Tip: When served with chocolate sauce and vanilla ice cream, this pear strudel is a delicate, sweet ending to a fine menu.

Ingredients for 10 Servings
Basic strudel dough
  (see p. 16) or ready-made
  dough
3 lbs (1.3 kg) Pears, fully ripe
3.5 oz (100 g) Raisins
3.5 oz (100 g) Almonds,
  grated and roasted
½ cup (120 g) Sugar
5 oz (150 g) Sponge cake
  crumbs
4 tsp (20 g) Vanilla sugar
2 tsp (1 cl) Lemon juice
7 tbsp (10 cl) Poire Williams
7 tbsp (100 g) Butter, melted
Flour for the work surface
Confectioner's sugar for
  dusting

APRICOT STRUDEL

Ingredients for 10 Servings
Basic strudel dough (see p.
  16) or ready-made dough
3⅓ lbs (1.5 kg) Apricots
10.5 oz (300 g) Sponge cake
  crumbs
2 oz (60 g) Pistachio nuts,
  chopped
3.5 oz (100 g) Almond slivers
3.5 oz (100 g) Breadcrumbs
½ cup (120 g) Confectioner's
  sugar
7 tbsp (10 cl) Apricot brandy
7 tbsp (100 g) Butter, melted
Confectioner's sugar for
  dusting
Flour for the work surface

Preheat oven to 350 °F (180 °C). Prepare the strudel dough according to the basic recipe. Blanch the apricots, shock them in ice water, and peel. Pit the apricots and cut them into slices. Mix with almond slivers, pistachios, cake crumbs, confectioner's sugar, and breadcrumbs. Flavor with apricot brandy. Lay a cloth on the work surface and flour evenly. Lightly flour the dough as well and place on the cloth. With a rolling pin, roll the dough out as thinly as possible. Then slide both hands under the dough, palms down, and slowly stretch it in all directions, until it's so thin that you could read a newspaper through it. Be very careful not to tear the dough. Saturate the dough with ¾ of the butter. Lay the filling on the dough in a strip. With the help of the cloth, fold the dough over the filling and then fold around once. Cut off extra. Place the strudel with the seam down on a buttered baking sheet and brush with the rest of the butter. Bake for about 35 minutes. Dust with confectioner's sugar and serve while still warm.

Bake Time: 35 minutes

Bake Temperature: 350 °F (180 °C)

Tip: If you are serving this strudel as dessert, muscatel sabayon (see p. 156) and vanilla ice cream (see p. 350) make an ideal, delicious addition.

QUARK STRUDEL

Preheat oven to 350°F (180°C). Prepare the strudel dough according to the basic recipe. Cream the butter with confectioner's sugar. Mix in the strained quark, sour cream, and egg yolks. Fold in the cornstarch, vanilla sugar, lemon zest, and raisins. Begin to beat the egg whites and then beat them to stiff peaks with the granulated sugar. Carefully fold in the egg whites. Lay a cloth on the work surface and flour evenly. Lightly flour the dough as well and place on the cloth. With a rolling pin, roll the dough out as thinly as possible. Then slide both hands under the dough, palms down, and slowly stretch it in all directions, until it's so thin that you could read a newspaper through it. Be very careful not to tear the dough. Saturate the dough with ¾ of the melted butter. Lay the filling on the dough in a strip. With the help of the cloth, fold the dough over the filling and then fold around once. Cut off extra. Place the strudel with the seam down on a buttered baking sheet and brush with the rest of the butter. Bake for about 40–45 minutes. Dust with confectioner's sugar and serve while still warm.

Bake Time: 40–45 minutes

Bake Temperature: 350°F (180°C)

Ingredients for 10 Servings
Basic strudel dough (see p. 16) or ready-made dough
7 tbsp (100 g) Butter
⅔ cup (150 g) Confectioner's sugar
21 oz (600 g) Quark or other soft, fresh cheese
1¼ cups (300 ml) Sour cream
8 Egg yolks
½ cup (80 g) Cornstarch
2 tbsp (30 g) Vanilla sugar
Zest of 1 lemon
2 oz (50 g) Raisins
8 Egg whites
1 cup less 2 tbsp (200 g) Granulated sugar
7 tbsp (100 g) Butter, melted
Confectioner's sugar for dusting
Flour for the work surface

CREAM STRUDEL

Ingredients for 15 Servings
Basic strudel dough
　(see p. 16) or ready-made
　dough
1 stick plus 6 tbsp (200 g)
　Butter
¾ cup (100 g) Confectioner's
　sugar
9 Dinner rolls
1¼ cups (300 ml) Milk
9 Egg yolks
2 tbsp (30 g) Vanilla sugar
Zest of 1 lemon
⅓ cup (50 g) Cornstarch
1½ cups (375 ml) Sour
　cream
9 Egg whites
7 tbsp (100 g) Granulated
　sugar
7 tbsp (100 g) Butter, melted
Flour for the work surface
Confectioner's sugar for
　dusting

For the Royale
4¼ cups (1 l) Milk
4 tsp (20 g) Granulated sugar
2 Eggs

Preheat oven to 350 °F (180 °C). Prepare the strudel dough according to the basic recipe. Remove the crusts from the rolls, cut into small pieces and saturate with milk. Cream the butter with confectioner's sugar. Fold in the bread, egg yolks, cornstarch, vanilla sugar, sour cream, and lemon zest. Begin to beat the egg whites and then beat them to stiff peaks with the granulated sugar. Carefully fold in the egg whites. Lay a cloth on the work surface and flour evenly. Lightly flour the dough as well and place on the cloth. With a rolling pin, roll the dough out as thinly as possible. Then slide both hands under the dough, palms down, and slowly stretch it in all directions, until it's so thin that you could read a newspaper through it. Be very careful not to tear the dough. Saturate the dough with ¾ of the butter. Lay the filling on the dough in a strip. With the help of the cloth, fold the dough over the filling and then fold around once. Cut off extra. Place the strudel with the seam down on a buttered baking sheet and brush with the rest of the butter. Bake for about 30 minutes. For the Royale, mix all the ingredients together, pour over the strudel, and bake for another 20 minutes, lowering the oven heat to 320 °F (160 °C). Dust with confectioner's sugar and serve while still warm.

Bake Time: about 50 minutes

Bake Temperature: 350 °F (180 °C), then 320 °F (160 °C)

White Strudel from the Red Barn

What would the Viennese bakery be without the accompanying legends? Every legend about the invention of the "Milli cream strudel" leads straight to the inn Zum Roten Stadl—"At the Red Barn"—in Breitenfurt, near Vienna. In the nineteenth century Breitenfurt was famous for its strudel specialties. The absolute bestseller was a strudel made with breadcrumbs, milk, butter, eggs, vanilla, raisins, sugar, and cream, which was apparently named for the cook, Milli. However, a milk cream strudel was listed in a Viennese cookbook from 1696.

DRIED PEAR STRUDEL

Preheat oven to 340°F (170°C). Prepare the strudel dough according to the basic recipe, brush with oil, and let rest. For the filling, cream the butter with confectioner's sugar and egg yolks. Mix in the rest of the ingredients except for the egg whites and granulated sugar. Begin to beat the egg whites and then beat them to stiff peaks with the granulated sugar. Carefully fold in the egg whites. Lay a cloth on the work surface and flour evenly. Lightly flour the dough as well and place on the cloth. With a rolling pin, roll the dough out as thinly as possible. Then slide both hands under the dough, palms down, and slowly stretch it in all directions, until it's so thin that you could read a newspaper through it. Be very careful not to tear the dough. Saturate the dough with ¾ of the butter. Lay the filling on the dough in a strip. With the help of the cloth, fold the dough over the filling and then fold around once. Cut off extra. Place the strudel with the seam down on a buttered baking sheet and brush with the rest of the butter. Bake for about 40 minutes. Dust with confectioner's sugar and serve.

Bake Time: about 40 minutes

Bake Temperature: 340°F (170°C)

Tip: As the crowning moment of a harmonious menu, sabayon (see p. 250) and cranberry compote (see p. 182) make wonderful additions to dried pear strudel.

Drying Pears

In Austria, it is common to dry pears and then bake them into delightful breads, strudel, or cakes. Dried pear bread can be found throughout the Alps around Christmastime. Paolo Santonino, a Bishop's secretary and diarist traveling north out of Italy, first talked about dried pears in 1485, when he went into raptures over a dish "of cooked, sweet pears that, served in a bowl, are covered in butter and semisweet spices."

Ingredients for 10 Servings
Basic strudel dough (see p. 16) or ready-made dough
Oil for brushing
Flour for the work surface
7 tbsp (100 g) Butter, melted
Confectioner's sugar for dusting

For the Filling
2 sticks plus 5 tbsp (300 g) Butter
⅔ cup (80 g) Confectioner's sugar
16 Egg yolks
10.5 oz (300 g) Walnuts, chopped
9 oz (250 g) Dried pears, briefly soaked in water and chopped
3.5 oz (100 g) Raisins, chopped
3.5 oz (100 g) Dried plums
3 oz (80 g) Candied orange peel, chopped
3 oz (80 g) Cooking chocolate, grated
Zest of 1 lemon
Dash of salt
Dash of cinnamon
Dash of cardamom
16 Egg whites
⅓ cup (80 g) Granulated sugar

TORTES

Tortes—the word goes back to the Latin "torquere" and means turned cake—are a pretty challenging task. Baking tortes is considered a high level of Viennese baking for a reason. The rainbow of possibilities goes from simple cake to sweet, edible palaces of confectionary art that can be prepared at home, with some patience.

PANAMA TORTE

Ingredients for 1 Torte
(10in (26 cm) diameter)
Basic Panama cake dough
  (see p. 30)
Almonds, grated and
  roasted

For the Parisian Cream
2 cups (500 ml) Heavy cream
18 oz (500 g) Cooking
  chocolate

Prepare the Panama batter and bake a torte. Let cool and cut horizontally twice. For the Parisian cream, boil the heavy cream, melt the chocolate in it, and then let cool for 2 hours. Before the cream begins to harden, cream with a mixer. Spread cream on each cake piece and set on top of each other. Ice the outside of the torte with cream, but leave some cream for decorating. Chill the torte. Sprinkle with almonds and decorate with the rest of the cream as you wish, such as with rosettes.

Tip: Parisian cream can be prepared in advance and stored in the refrigerator. Before using, it must be warmed and creamed again.

The Canal Torte

The opening of the Panama Canal was as exciting of an event for the people of 1914 as the moon landing was fifty-five years later. Apparently, a cooked chocolate almond torte was served in Vienna for the event, and called a Panama torte. Since there is very little in the world that is really new, recipes for this cake could be found in cookbooks that were published when there was still no pass between the Atlantic and Pacific.

The Ten Commandments of Torte Baking

1. Make sure that the inside of the torte pan is very clean before you fill it with batter and is lightly buttered and floured, unless otherwise specified.
2. For heavy tortes, use only soft, creamed butter so that as much air as possible gets into the batter.
3. Always fold in flour and beaten egg whites last and very carefully. It is the only way to make it come out light and fluffy.
4. Make sure that you only mix the flour and egg whites very briefly with the mixed or beaten batter.
5. Make sure that the butter you use does not become hot, otherwise the torte will be more prone to fall.
6. If the recipe calls for baking powder, always sift it with the flour.
7. Lay the baked torte upside down on a lightly floured board, so that it gets a nice, flat top.
8. Never overfill cream tortes, because they will become not only too rich, but also more difficult to cut.
9. Immediately after filling or icing a cream torte, place it in immediately in the refrigerator or other cool place so that the cream firms quickly.
10. Dip the knife you are using to slice the torte in hot water between each cut. Saw gently when cutting instead of pushing down to prevent cream from spilling out.

SACHERTORTE

Ingredients for 1 Torte
(10in (26 cm) diameter)
Basic Sacher batter
  (see p. 31)
Apricot marmalade
Chocolate or Sacher glaze
  (see p. 42)

Prepare and bake Sachertorte batter according to the basic recipe. Remove from the pan after it has fully cooled. Cut straight on the top, turn over and cut through it horizontally. Brush the lower layer with slightly warmed apricot marmalade, place the top cake layer on top, and brush with marmalade again. Chill. Pour the warm glaze over the torte all at once, smooth quickly with a spatula, and spread around the side of the torte, too. Place on a cake plate and let rest for several hours so the glaze can dry.

Tip: If you want to spare yourself the effort of preparing the Sacher glaze, you can simply use a store-bought chocolate glaze.

The Remains of the Cake Fight

The most famous of all Viennese tortes, and perhaps the most famous torte in the world, was not invented by a great baker. The recipe actually came from a second year apprentice. Franz Sacher, born 1816, baked this chocolate torte for the first time in 1832 as a cooking student in the house of Prince Metternich. Sacher's torte became world famous, but was also to become the topic of many lawsuits between the Hotel Sacher and the Demel Pastry Shop regarding the intellectual property rights of the title "Original Sacher Torte." The most important point of conflict: should the obligatory marmalade layer be in the middle (like Demel's torte) or beneath the glaze (as in the Hotel Sacher and also in the cookbook of Marie von Rokitansky)? Ancestors of the Sachertorte could be found much earlier, like in the 1718 cookbook of Conrad Haggers or in Gartler Hickmann's "Proven Viennese Cookbook" from 1749. Since Katharina Prato presented a "Chocolate torte. À la Sacher" in her "Southern German Cuisine," Chocolate glaze, apricot marmalade, and the name Sacher have been inseparable—no matter where the apricot marmalade is.

CHARLOTTE MALAKOFF

For the cream, mix milk, granulated sugar, vanilla sugar, salt, and egg yolks and heat in a bain-marie until the mixture begins to thicken. Add cold water to the gelatin, remove excess water, and dissolve in the warm mixture. Mix in the rum and chill the cream until it is almost set. Begin to beat the egg yolks, add granulated sugar, and then beat to stiff peaks. Fold the egg whites and whipped cream into the cream. Place the cake base in a torte ring and saturate with some rum. Set aside 7 of the ladyfingers to garnish.

Place the rest of the ladyfingers into 2 or 3 layers alternating with the cream. Before putting the cream on top of the lady-fingers, splash them with rum. Make a final layer of ladyfingers and spread the top and sides with whipped cream. Set a half ladyfinger dipped in chocolate glaze on each slice and sprinkle roasted almonds in the middle.

Mr. Malakoff was Pelissier

The Charlotte Malakoff is a sweet fortress that torte lovers eat their way through like the pudding mountains in the mythical Land of Plenty. This torte gets its name from the storming of a bastion, namely the Russian fortress of Malakov Kurgan at Sevastopol in Crimea, which was conquered by the French General Jean J. Pélissier (1794–1864). However, this torte is neither Russian nor French, but rather came from formerly Austrian northern Italy and quickly became established among the Danube monarchy. Of course, this torte must not be baked, but rather is built on rum-infused ladyfingers and so-called Malakoff cream, similar to tiramisu cream, for which there are many recipes involving whipped cream, butter, milk, mascarpone, and egg yolks. In many old cookbooks you will find that this recipe is not called a torte at all, but rather a "Galician cream."

*Ingredients for 1 Torte
(10in (26 cm) diameter)*
1 Torte base made with ¼
  of the warm sponge cake
  recipe (see p. 24)
9 oz (250 g) Ladyfingers (see
  p. 37 or store-bought)
Rum
Almonds, grated and
  roasted
Chocolate glaze to dip the
  ladyfingers
1⅔ cups (400 ml) Whipped
  cream to garnish

For the Cream
⅔ cup (150 ml) Milk
8 tsp (35 g) Granulated sugar
2 tsp (10 g) Vanilla sugar
3 Sheets gelatin
2 Egg yolks
Dash of salt
4 tsp (2 cl) Rum
1 Egg white
5 tsp (25 g) Granulated sugar
1⅔ cups (400 ml) Whipped
  cream

BLACK FOREST CHERRY TORTE

*Ingredients for 1 Torte
(10in (26 cm) diameter)*
Basic chocolate sponge
  cake batter (see p. 24) or
Basic Sachertorte batter
  (see p. 31)
1 lb (450 g) Sour cherries
  from a jar, with juice
7 tbsp (100 ml) Sour cherry
  juice
¼ cup (50 g) Granulated
  sugar
Dash of cinnamon powder
2 tbsp plus 2 tsp (25 g) Cornstarch
3 tbsp (4 cl) Kirsch (cherry
  liqueur)
3 tbsp (4 cl) Simple syrup
  (see p. 40)
1⅔ cups (400 ml) Whipped
  cream to garnish
Chocolate shavings to
  garnish

For the Parisian Cream
1 cup (250 ml) Heavy cream
9 oz (250 g) Cooking chocolate

*For the Cherry Whipped
Cream*
2 cups (500 ml) Whipped
  cream
4 Sheets gelatin
¼ cup (6 cl) Kirsch (cherry
  liqueur)
4 tsp (2 cl) Water
⅓ cup (40 g) Confectioner's
  sugar

Prepare the chocolate sponge cake or Sachertorte batter and bake a torte. Let cool and slice twice horizontally. Boil the sour cherry juice with cinnamon and sugar. Mix the cornstarch with some water and pour into the juice to thicken it. Set aside 14 cherries to garnish. Bring the rest of the cherries to a boil once in the juice, then remove from heat and let cool. For the Parisian cream, boil the heavy cream, melt the chopped chocolate in it, and let cool for about 2 hours. Before the cream begins to harden, stir it with a mixer. For the cherry whipped cream, add cold water to the gelatin, remove excess water, and dissolve the gelatin in warmed kirsch. Mix in the water and confectioner's sugar and carefully fold it all into the whipped cream.

Place one torte base in a torte ring, mix the kirsch and simple syrup together, and saturate the torte base with half of the mixture. Using a piping bag fitted with a large round nozzle, pipe the Parisian cream onto the torte in 4 rings. Fill the space in between with the cherries. Set the second torte layer on top and saturate with the rest of the kirsch mixture. Spread cherry whipped cream on the second layer and cover with the last torte layer. Chill for about 6 hours. Remove from the torte ring, spread whipped cream on the torte, and garnish with chocolate shavings, whipped cream rosettes, and cherries.

Keller's Cherries

It is celebrated as a traditional jewel of Baden housewifery. But there's one thing: the Black Forest cherry torte has a birthday and an inventor. They say that in 1915 Josef Keller, a confectioner from Radolfzell on Lake Constance, presented a successful new torte creation for his master baker's test in Bad Godesberg by Bonn. On a visit to a student bar in Godesberg called Café Anger, he ate cherries with cream and had the idea to layer chocolate cake saturated with Black Forest kirsch and cherries in whipped cream and garnish the whole thing with chocolate. The only problem with it is the housewives: They still don't believe the story. (See recipe on p. 119.)

PUNSCHTORTE

Prepare the sponge cake according to the recipe, bake a torte, and cut it twice horizontally. For the filling, cut the middle torte layer and the sponge cake chunks into small pieces. Mix with apricot marmalade, rum, simple syrup, orange and lemon zest, and a dash of cinnamon and knead the mixture well until it stays together. Brush the torte base with apricot marmalade and place in a torte ring. Spread the filling on top. Cover with the second torte layer, weight with a board or similar, and chill for several hours. Remove from the torte ring, overturn, brush with marmalade, and glaze the top with fondant. Brush the sides with melted chocolate and press ground hazelnuts against it. Put the rest of the chocolate in a piping bag and decorate the top.

Ingredients for 1 Torte (10in (26 cm) diameter)
Basic sponge cake for tortes (see p. 23)
14 oz (400 g) Sponge cake chunks
⅓ cup (8 cl) Rum
¼ cup (5 cl) Simple syrup (see p. 40)
Zest of 1 orange and 1 lemon
Dash of cinnamon
½ cup (50 g) Apricot marmalade

To Glaze
Apricot marmalade
About 9 oz (250 g) Fondant, colored with pink food dye (see p. 44)
About 7 oz (200 g) Dark couverture chocolate
Hazelnuts, ground

DOBOS TORTE

Ingredients for 1 Torte
(9in (24 cm) diameter)
Dobos batter (see p. 32)
About ⅔ cup (150 g) Granu-
   lated sugar to caramelize
Butter

For the Cream
4 Eggs
⅔ cup (150 g) Granulated
   sugar
½ Vanilla bean
5 oz (150 g) Dark couverture
   chocolate
2 oz (50 g) Nougat
1 stick plus 2½ tbsp (150 g)
   Butter

Prepare the Dobos batter and bake six torte layers. For the cream, beat the eggs with granulated sugar and scraped out vanilla pulp in a double boiler until thick and creamy. Mix in melted chocolate and melted nougat. Let the mixture cool. Cream the butter and mix in the chocolate mixture. Place the first torte layer in a torte ring, spread cream on top, and repeat with the rest of the torte layers. Save the prettiest one for the top and set it aside. Have a buttered spatula and knife ready. Melt the sugar to light caramel and spread it on the top torte layer with a spatula. Cut immediately into equally sized triangle. Set each piece on top of the torte at an angle, then serve.

Two Meter Torte

József C. Dobos, a master confectioner and proprietor of a Budapest deli-catessen, always had an addiction to size. That's why he brought over sixty kinds of cheese and twenty-two kinds of sparkling wine and created a sen-sation when he made a 110lb block of cheese, filled it with burgundy, and set it in his shop window until the cheese had absorbed all the wine as could be sold at a high price. The Dobos torte, first baked in 1885, can thank József C. Dobos's ambition for its existence. He wanted to create a dessert that was suitable for mailing, one that would retain its shape and taste for at least ten days without being cooled properly. It probably surprised even Dobos that the torte not only survived, but still tasted good. Since then, the Hungarians know what they think of József C. Dobos and his torte creation: for its birthday, they carry a two-meter Dobos torte through the streets of Budapest.

ESTERHÁZY TORTE

Prepare the Esterházy batter according to the basic recipe, and bake 6 torte layers. Overturn each torte layer onto a sugared board or cloth and remove the parchment paper immediately.

For the cream, mix milk, granulated sugar, vanilla sugar, salt, and egg yolks in a mixing bowl. Continue mixing in a double boiler until it reaches 158 °F (70 °C) and begins to thicken. Add water to the gelatin, remove excess water, and dissolve in the mixture. Remove from heat and mix with an immersion blender for 5 minutes. Chill. Cream the butter, add warmed nougat, and mix in the cooled cream. Fill a torte ring with the torte layers and the cream alternately. Brush the top layer thinly with apricot marmalade and chill for 30 minutes. Melt some dark chocolate. Glaze the Esterházy torte with fondant. Make a cone with parchment paper and use it to pipe the chocolate onto the torte in thin lines. Immediately pull a toothpick through the lines to create the typical Esterházy pattern. Chill the torte until the glaze dries. Cut the torte with a serrated knife dipped in hot water.

Ingredients for 1 Torte
(10in (26 cm) diameter)
Esterházy batter (see p. 32),
  ½ recipe
Confectioner's sugar for the
  surface

For the Cream
1⅔ cups (400 ml) Milk
1 cup less 2 tbsp (200 g)
  Granulated sugar
4 Sheets gelatin
8 Egg yolks
4 tsp (20 g) Vanilla sugar
Dash of salt
2 sticks plus 4½ tbsp (290 g)
  Butter
3 oz (80 g) Nougat

To Glaze
½ cup (70 g) Apricot mar-
  malade
About 5 oz (150 g) fondant
  (see p. 44)
Some Dark couverture
  chocolate

CAPUCHIN TORTE

This torte recipe for advanced bakers calls for skill and familiarity with baking. Its name comes from the wedge shape of the torte base, which is reminiscent of the garb of the order of Capuchin monks.

Ingredients for 1 Torte
(10in (26 cm) diameter)
Basic nut batter (see p. 29)
1 cup less 3 tbsp (100 g)
  Raspberry marmalade
3 tbsp (4 cl) Raspberry
  liqueur
9 oz (250 g) Raspberries

For the Chocolate Cream
1⅔ cups (400 ml) Heavy
  cream
3 Egg yolks
5 oz (150 g) Milk couverture
  chocolate
2.5 oz (70 g) Dark couverture
  chocolate
1 Sheet gelatin
¼ cup (6 cl) Raspberry
  liqueur

For the Bavarian Cream
3 Egg yolks
⅓ cup (70 g) Granulated
  sugar
1 Vanilla bean
4 tsp (2 cl) Raspberry liqueur
2 Sheets gelatin
1¼ cups (300 ml) Whipped
  cream

For the Chocolate Glaze
3.5 oz (100 g) Dark couverture chocolate
7 tbsp (100 ml) Heavy cream

Prepare the chocolate cream on the day before. Mix the cream and egg yolks. Mix in a double boiler until it reaches 158 °F (70 °C) and the mixture has thickened slightly. Add cold water to the gelatin, remove excess water, and dissolve in the warm cream. Chop up the chocolate and melt in the cream. Mix with an immersion blender for 5 minutes, then chill for 24 hours.

On the next day, prepare the nut batter according to the recipe, bake a torte, and cut it horizontally three times. Brush one torte base with raspberry marmalade. Set another torte layer on top and saturate with raspberry liqueur. Mix the cooled cream with raspberry liqueur and whip like whipped cream. Place a third of the cream in the middle of the torte and spread half the raspberries on top.

With the two remaining torte layers, cut a wedge shape, so that the torte can be rolled into a cylinder without it overlapping. Set the third torte base on top. Spread another third of the cream and the rest of the raspberries on the torte. Roll the fourth layer into a cone as well and set on top.

Make sure that the lower cone is a little flatter than the upper one, so that a pretty dome is created. Smooth the rest of the cream on top and chill for 1 hour.

For the Bavarian cream, beat egg yolks with granulated sugar and the pulp of the vanilla bean in a double boiler until creamy. Add water to the gelatin, remove excess, dissolve in warmed raspberry liqueur, and stir into the cream.

Let cool somewhat and then fold in the whipped cream. Let set for half an hour in the refrigerator. Smooth the Bavarian cream on the Capuchin torte, creating a pretty dome. Chill for another 2 hours.

For the chocolate glaze, boil the heavy cream briefly and melt the chopped chocolate in it. Let cool somewhat and glaze the torte.

Tip: If your freezer is large enough, it is best to freeze the cake for 10 minutes before glazing it. This way glazing will be no problem.

ROULADE TORTE

This master recipe for discerning chefs is relatively involved, but the effort is worth it for a result that not only tastes delicious, but is also a real feast for the eyes.

Ingredients for 1 Torte
(10in (26 cm) diameter)
Basic Sachertorte batter
  (see p. 31)
Hazelnuts, ground

To Soak
5 tsp (25 ml) Simple syrup
  (see p. 40)
3 tbsp plus 1 tsp (5 cl) Apricot brandy

For the Roulade
Basic sponge cake for rou-
  lades (see p. 22), ½ recipe
Apricot marmalade for
  brushing
Sugar for the cloth

For the Whipped Chocolate
Cream
2¼ cups (520 ml) Heavy
  cream
4 Egg yolks
10 oz (290 g) Dark couverture chocolate
¼ cup (6 cl) Apricot brandy
3 Sheets gelatin

For the Glaze
5 oz (150 g) Dark couverture
  chocolate
2 tbsp (30 ml) Oil

Prepare the Sachertorte batter and bake a torte base. Prepare and bake the sponge cake for roulades according to the basic recipe. Let cool off slightly, overturn onto a lightly sugared cloth, and pull off the parchment paper. Roll up the biscuit and let cool. Unroll and brush with apricot marmalade. Roll up tightly and chill.

For the whipped chocolate cream, mix heavy cream and egg yolk. Stir in a double boiler until it reaches 158 °F (70 °C) and the mixture has thickened slightly. Remove from heat and stir in the chopped chocolate. Warm the apricot brandy, dissolve the moistened gelatin in it, and stir into the chocolate mixture. Mix with an immersion blender for about 5 minutes without mixing air in (do not lift the blender to the surface), and chill for 3–4 hours. Then whip like whipped cream.

Place the sachertorte base in a torte ring. Mix simple syrup and apricot brandy and saturate the cake with it.

Smooth some whipped chocolate cream on top. Lay the roulades around on top of the torte. Cover with the rest of the whipped chocolate cream and smooth. Chill for 4 hours.

For the glaze, warm the dark chocolate, stir in the oil, and let cool slightly. Glaze the top of the torte with it and let it become firm. Remove from the ring and sprinkle ground hazelnuts on the sides.

Tip: To cut the torte, use a knife dipped in hot water, otherwise the glaze will break.

CHOCOLATE VANILLA TORTE

A sweet dream for torte freaks who are not afraid of lengthy, precise recipes.

Prepare the chocolate sponge cake batter according to the basic recipe and bake a torte base. Preheat oven to 430 °F (220 °C). Prepare the choux pastry dough and pipe two circular bases (4–5in (10–12 cm) and 8–9in (20–22 cm) diameter) onto a buttered baking sheet using a piping bag fitted with a round nozzle. Bake at 430 °F (220 °C) at first and then lower to 350 °F (180 °C). Bake for 15–20 minutes.

Remove from oven and let cool. In the meantime, warm the pastry cream for the vanilla cream. Add water to the gelatin, remove excess water, and dissolve in the pastry cream. Flavor with some Cointreau. Beat the cream until it cools and then fold in the whipped cream. Slice the cooled choux pastry rings horizontally, fill with cream, and put back together. Chill until needed again.

Melt the milk chocolate. Beat the eggs until creamy. Mix the chocolate, eggs, simple syrup, and heavy cream. Add water to the gelatin, remove excess water, dissolve in warmed rum, and stir into the chocolate mixture. Finally, fold in the whipped cream.

Place the sponge cake base in a torte ring. Put some chocolate mousse on the cake, place the choux rings on top, and spread the rest of the mousse on top. Smooth the top and chill. Remove from the ring before glazing and, if possible, freeze for 1–2 hours (to make the torte easier to glaze).

Prepare the ganache glaze, let cool somewhat, and glaze the frozen torte in one pour. Don't let the mousse soften. Chill the torte again. Garnish with chocolate shavings or rolls and serve.

Bake Time: chocolate sponge cake: 10 minutes; choux pastry: 15–20 minutes

Bake Temperature: chocolate sponge cake: 350 °F (180 °C); choux pastry: 430 °F (220 °C) lowering to 350 °F (180 °C)

Ingredients for 1 Torte
(10in (26 cm) diameter)
Basic chocolate sponge
 cake (see p. 24)
Basic choux pastry
 (see p. 20), ½ recipe
14 oz (400 g) Ganache glaze
 (see p. 43)
Chocolate shavings or rolls
 to garnish
Butter for the baking sheet

For the Vanilla Cream
18 oz (500 g) Pastry cream
 (see p. 247)
4 Sheets gelatin
4 tsp (2 cl) Cointreau
10 oz (150 ml) Whipped
 cream

For the Chocolate Mousse
10.5 oz (300 g) Milk couverture chocolate
2 Eggs
6 tbsp (9 cl) Simple syrup
 (see p. 40)
6 tbsp (9 cl) Heavy cream
5 Sheets gelatin
2 cups (450 ml) Whipped
 cream
2 tbsp (3 cl) Rum

Coconut Nougat Torte

Ingredients for 1 Torte
(10in (26 cm) diameter)
Sachertorte batter
　(see p. 31), ¼ recipe
9 oz (250 g) Ganache glaze
　(see p. 31)
About 3.5 oz (100 g) coconut
　flakes
Coconut liqueur

For the Coconut Mousse
3.5 oz (100 g) White
　couverture chocolate
10 oz (280 g) Coconut purée
4 Sheets gelatin
1¼ cups (300 ml) Whipped
　cream
¼ cups (6 cl) Coconut
　liqueur

For the Chocolate Mousse
2 Egg yolks
4 Eggs
¼ cup (30 g) Confectioner's
　sugar
7 oz (200 g) Dark couverture
　chocolate
7 oz (200 g) Milk couverture
　chocolate
4 Sheets gelatin
⅓ cup (8 cl) Coconut liqueur
3 cups (700 ml) Whipped
　cream

Bake a torte base according to the sachertorte batter recipe and let cool. For the coconut mousse, melt the chocolate. Add cold water to the gelatin. Warm the coconut liqueur and dissolve the gelatin in it. Mix together the coconut purée, chocolate, and coconut liqueur. Carefully fold in the whipped cream. Place a smaller torte ring (7in (18 cm) diameter) on a baking sheet lined with foil, fill with coconut mousse, cover, and freeze.

For the chocolate mousse, melt the chocolate together in a double boiler. Beat the egg yolks and eggs with confectioner's sugar in a double boiler until creamy. Add water to the gelatin, remove excess, and dissolve the gelatin in warmed coconut liqueur. Mix the coconut liqueur and beaten eggs in the chocolate. Carefully fold in the whipped cream.

Place the torte base in a torte ring and saturate with a bit'of coconut liqueur. Set the frozen coconut mousse in the middle. Fill the empty space with chocolate mousse (preferably with a piping bag) and spread the rest of the mousse on top. Freeze the torte again to make glazing easier. Glaze the top with ganache glaze. Remove from the torte ring and press coconut flakes on the sides. Let thaw before serving.

Bailey's Coffee Torte

Prepare the cream the day before. Mix the heavy cream and egg yolks. Continue mixing in a double boiler for about 5 minutes, until it reaches 160 °F (70 °C). Add cold water to the gelatin, remove excess, and dissolve in the warm cream mixture. Chop up the chocolate and melt it in the cream. Mix for 5 minutes with an immersion blender and chill for 24 hours.

Prepare the sponge cake batter and bake a torte. After cooling, slice the torte once horizontally. Brush the first cake base with apricot marmalade and place in a torte ring. Take the prepared cream out of the refrigerator and mix in Bailey's. Whip like whipped cream. Spread half of the cream on the torte and place the second cake layer on top. Mix simply syrup with instant coffee and rum and saturate the cake layer with it. Smooth the rest of the cream on top.

For the coffee whipped cream, whip the cream with confectioner's sugar, adding sifted instant coffee to taste. Smooth the coffee whipped cream on the top of the torte and dust with sifted cocoa powder. Remove from the torte ring, garnish each slice with a preserved apricot quarter and a broken sesame waffle.

Ingredients for 1 Torte
(10in (26 cm) diameter)
Basic warm sponge cake
  batter (see p. 24), ½ recipe
½ cup (50 g) Apricot
  marmalade
14 Preserved apricot
  quarters (see p. 188)
14 Sesame waffles
Cocoa powder for dusting

To Soak
¼ cup (50 ml) Simple syrup
  (see p. 48)
1 tsp Instant coffee powder
4 tsp (2 cl) Rum

For the Cream
3 cups (750 ml) Heavy cream
6 Egg yolks
10.5 oz (300 g) Milk
  couverture chocolate
5 oz (140 g) Dark couverture
  chocolate
4 Sheets gelatin
14 Bailey's

For the Coffee Whipped
Cream
¾ cup (200 ml) Whipping
  cream
4 tsp (10 g) Confectioner's
  sugar
Instant coffee powder

QUARK AND CREAM TORTE

Ingredients for 1 Torte (10in (26 cm) diameter)
Basic warm sponge cake (see p. 24), ½ recipe
½ cup (50 g) Apricot marmalade
About 1⅔ cups (400 ml) Whipped cream
14 Fruit slices (strawberries, apricots, or mandarin oranges, depending on the season)
Hazelnuts, ground

For the Cheese and Cream
4 Egg yolks
⅔ cup (80 g) Confectioner's sugar
4 tsp (20 g) Vanilla sugar
Zest of 1 orange
3 tbsp (4 cl) Rum
6 Sheets gelatin
14 oz (400 g) Quark or other soft, fresh cheese
¾ cups (200 ml) Sour cream
4 Egg whites
7 tbsp (100 g) Sugar
1 cup (250 ml) Whipped cream
3.5 oz (100 g) Preserved raisins (see p. 189)

Prepare the sponge cake batter and bake a torte. Let cook and cut horizontally twice. Place a cake base in a torte ring and brush with warmed apricot marmalade.

For the cream, beat egg yolks with sugar, vanilla sugar, and orange zest until creamy. Beat the egg whites, add sugar, and beat to stiff peaks. Mix the quark with sour cream until smooth. Mix in the egg yolk and rum and fold in the whipped cream and egg whites alternately. Fold in the preserved raisins. Spread somewhat less than half of the cream on the torte base, lay the second layer on top, spread with cream again, and place the third torte layer on top. Spread the rest of the cream about 5mm thick on top, smooth, and chill for several hours. Remove from the torte ring and spread whipped cream on the top and sides. Sprinkle with ground hazelnuts and garnish the top with whipped cream rosettes and fruit slices.

TORTA MERINGA

Bake a torte with the basic sponge cake, let cool and slice into 4 thin torte bases. For the cream, beat egg yolks with sugar and espresso in a bain-marie until creamy. Dissolve the moistened gelatin in the warm egg mixture, let cool, and mix in mascarpone one spoonful at a time. Fold the whipped cream into the cream. For the soaking liquid, mix all the ingredients together. Set one biscuit layer in a torte ring and spread some cream on top (do not saturate the first cake layer). Place the second layer on top, saturate with the liquid and spread cream on top. Repeat until you have used all the cake layers and cream. Chill for 4 hours.

Preheat the oven's upper heat to 480 °F (250 °C). For the meringue, begin beating the egg whites, add the sugar, and beat to stiff peaks. Fold in the sifted confectioner's sugar. Spread the meringue on top of the torte, create a decorative pattern, and bake briefly, until the top is browned. Chill again for several hours, remove from the torte ring, and dust on the top and sides with sifted cocoa powder.

Bake Time: several minutes to brown

Bake Temperature: 480 °F (250 °C)

Tip: Pro bakers brown the meringue with a kitchen torch or place it in a "salamander."

*Ingredients for 1 Torte
(10in (26 cm) diameter)*
Basic sponge cake for tortes
  (see p. 23)
Cocoa powder for dusting

For the Cream
5 Yolks
⅓ cup (65 g) Sugar
⅓ cup (90 ml) Espresso, very
  strong
11 oz (320 g) Mascarpone
4 Sheets gelatin
1¾ cups (420 ml) Whipped
  cream

To Soak
1 oz (30 g) Instant coffee
  powder
3 tbsp (5 cl) Sherry
3 tbsp (5 cl) Rum
¼ cup (120 ml) Water

For the Meringue
2 Egg whites
¼ cup (60 g) Granulated
  sugar
6 tbsp (50 g) Confectioner's
  sugar

Gasparini or Stanislaus?

The question of who first baked beaten egg whites and sugar to make meringue, sometimes called Spanish wind, is the topic of much culinary speculation. Usually, this airy and light dream, which can be filled with ice cream or whipped cream, is attributed to a Swiss pastry chef named Gasparini. He worked as a confectioner in the small east German city of Meiringen, where the dessert is still called "Meringel."

But the Polish also reclaimed the creation of the meringue for themselves and they swear on their marzynka that the personal chef of King Stanislaus I invented it. The King later also became the Duke of Lorraine and allegedly brought meringue to the French. They say that Queen Marie Antoinette was a particularly passionate meringue. (See recipe on p. 130.)

YOGURT POPPY TORTE WITH BLUEBERRIES

Preheat the oven 375 °F (190 °C). Beat the egg whites to stiff peaks with granulated sugar and fold in the poppy and nuts. Place a buttered torte ring on a baking sheet lined with parchment paper (or use a springform). Bake the batter for 15 minutes. Take out of the oven and remove from the pan. Pull off the parchment paper and let cool. Brush the poppy torte base with apricot marmalade and place in a torte ring. For the mousse, mix yogurt, confectioner's sugar, and lemon zest. Add cold water to the gelatin and remove excess. Warm orange juice and dissolve the gelatin in it. Mix into the yogurt. Fold in the whipped cream. Spread washed, well dried blueberries on the torte base, fill with mousse, and chill for 4 hours.

Bake Time: 15 minutes

Bake Temperature: 375 °F (190 °C)

Ingredients for 1 Torte (10in (26 cm) diameter)
5 Egg whites
1 cup plus 3 tbsp (250 g) Granulated sugar
9 oz (250 g) Poppy seeds, ground
2 oz (50 g) Nuts, ground
½ cup (50 g) Apricot marmalade
14 oz (400 g) Blueberries
Butter for the pan

For the Yogurt mousse
2½ cups (600 ml) Yogurt
1¼ cup (150 g) Confectioner's sugar
8 Sheets gelatin
7 tbsp (100 ml) Orange juice
Zest of 1 lemon
2 cups (480 ml) Whipped cream

STRAWBERRY YOGURT TORTE

Ingredients for 1 Torte
(10in (26 cm) diameter)
Basic pâte brisée dough
  (see p. 14), ¼ recipe
Basic sponge cake dough
  for tortes (see p.23),
  ½ recipe
7 tbsp (50 g) Strawberry
  marmalade
¼ cup (50 ml) Cointreau
¾ cup (200 ml) Whipped
  cream, sweetened
Chocolate shavings and
Strawberries with stems to
  decorate

For the Strawberry Yogurt
Mousse
7 oz (200 g) Strawberry
  purée (see p.200)
⅔ cup (150 ml) Yogurt
4 tbsp (2 cl) Cointreau
⅓ cup (40 g) Confectioner's
  sugar
4 Sheets gelatin
1¼ cups (300 ml) Whipped
  cream

For the Strawberry Mousse
7 oz (200 g) Strawberry
  purée (see p. 200)
3 Sheets gelatin
2 tsp (1 cl) Lemon juice
4 tsp (2 cl) Strawberry
  liqueur
6 tbsp (50 g) Confectioner's
  sugar
¾ cup (180 ml) Whipped
  cream

For the Strawberry Gelatin
7 oz (200 g) Strawberry
  purée (see p. 200)
2 Sheets gelatin

Bake 1 torte base out of the pâte brisée and 2 out of the sponge cake batter. Place the pâte brisée in a torte ring and brush thinly with strawberry marmalade. Lay a sponge cake piece on top and saturate with some Cointreau.

For the strawberry yogurt mousse, mix the strawberry purée, yogurt, and confectioner's sugar. Add cold water to the gelatin, remove excess, and dissolve the gelatin in warmed Cointreau. Mix into the strawberry yogurt. Carefully fold in the whipped cream.

Fill the torte ring with the strawberry yogurt mousse and lay the second cake base on top. Saturate with Cointreau again and chill for 20 minutes.

For the strawberry mousse, take 2 tablespoons of the strawberry purée and warm in a double boiler. Add water to the gelatin, remove excess, dissolve in the warmed strawberry purée, then mix into the rest of the purée. Mix in lemon juice, strawberry liqueur, and confectioner's sugar. Fold in the whipped cream. Fill the torte ring with the mousse and chill for another 20 minutes.

For the strawberry gelatin, take 2 tablespoons of the strawberry purée and warm in a double boiler. Add water to the gelatin, remove excess, dissolve in the warmed strawberry purée, then mix into the rest of the purée. Let cool slightly, then pour over the torte. Chill again. Remove from the torte ring. Spread the sides of the torte with sweetened whipped cream and sprinkle with chocolate shavings. Decorate each slice with a halved strawberry with the stem.

RASPBERRY YOGURT TORTE

Bake a torte base using the chocolate sponge cake batter.

Warm the raspberry marmalade, mix with raspberry liqueur, and brush on the chocolate sponge cake base. Place in a torte ring.

For the raspberry mousse, mix raspberry purée with confectioner's sugar. Add cold water to the gelatin and remove excess water. Warm the raspberry liqueur and dissolve the gelatin in it. Stir into the purée. Carefully fold in the whipped cream.

For the yogurt mousse, mix together yogurt, confectioner's sugar, and lemon zest. Add cold water to the gelatin and remove excess water. Warm the orange juice, dissolve the gelatin in it, and mix into the yogurt. Fold in the whipped cream. Fill the torte ring with raspberry and yogurt mousse alternately. Pull a spatula through the mousse in large strokes, so that the mousse is marbled. Smooth the top and chill for 2 hours.

For the gelatin, warm 2 tablespoons of raspberry purée. Add water to the gelatin, remove excess, and dissolve the gelatin in the purée. Stir into the rest of the raspberry purée. Pour the gelatin over the torte. Place washed raspberries around the edge of the torte in the gelatin and chill for another 2 hours. Remove from the ring and sprinkle with chopped pistachios.

Ingredients for 1 Torte (10in (26 cm) diameter)
Basic chocolate sponge cake (see p. 24), ½ recipe
1¼ cup (150 g) Raspberry marmalade
4 tsp (2 cl) Himbeergeist (raspberry liqueur)
5 oz (140 g) Raspberries
Pistachios, chopped, to garnish

For the Raspberry Mousse
26 oz (750 g) Raspberry purée (see p. 201)
1 cup (120 g) Confectioner's sugar
8 Sheets gelatin
¼ cup (6 cl) Raspberry purée
1½ cup (375 ml) Whipped cream

For the Yogurt Mousse
2 cups (500 ml) Yogurt
1 cup (125 g) Confectioner's sugar
6 Sheets gelatin
5 tbsp (75 ml) Orange juice
Zest of 1 lemon
1¾ cups (440 ml) Whipped cream

For the Raspberry Gelatin
7 oz (200 g) Raspberry purée (see p. 201)
2 Sheets gelatin

Welcome to the Age of Yogurt

Every epoch has its own culinary fashions and opinions. That includes ideas about milk. In our time butter, cream, and whipped cream are faced with truly healthy skepticism. On the other hand, yogurt, which was invented by Asian nomads and is particularly loved in Turkey and the Balkans, has become an icon of sensible eating.

For this reason, white, soft, creamy yogurt has quickly established its high value in the bakery.

There is a belief that like Bulgarian shepherds, you can live to be over 100 with the help of yogurt—usually made today from cow milk thickened with special bacteria cultures. The reason for this is its "chemical twist": yogurt contains an abundance of the right twisting lactic acid that detoxifies the body and supports gut flora without putting a strain on the body the way left twisting lactic acid does.

As far as yogurt tortes helping you live to be over 100, that can't be verified here. But it has long been known that they taste delicious, especially in combination with vitamin rich fruits and berries.

POPPY APRICOT TORTE

Ingredients for 1 Torte (10in (26 cm) diameter)

Basic pâte brisée dough (see p. 14), ¼ recipe
Basic poppy batter (see p. 29)
1¼ cup (150 g) Apricot marmalade
4 tsp (2 cl) Apricot Eau de Vie
10.5 oz (300 g) Preserved apricots (see p.188)
Almonds, grated and roasted, to garnish

For the Gelatin

½ cup (70 g) Apricot marmalade
⅓ cup (80 ml) Water
1½ Sheets gelatin

Prepare and bake the pâte brisée dough and poppy batter according to the recipes. Warm apricot marmalade with Eau de Vie and brush the pâte brisée with it. Set the poppy cake base on top and brush it also with apricot marmalade on the top and side. Place in a torte ring. Cut the preserved apricots into slices, lay them on top of the torte, and chill. For the gelatin, warm apricot marmalade with water in a double boiler. Add cold water to the gelatin, remove excess, and dissolve the gelatin in the marmalade. Spread on top of the apricot torte. Chill for 2 hours, remove from the torte ring, and sprinkle roasted almonds on the sides.

WILD BERRY VANILLA TORTE

Prepare the sponge cake batter according to the recipe and bake a torte. After it cools, slice it once horizontally. Place one cake base in a torte ring and brush with marmalade. Boil half the milk with granulated sugar, vanilla sugar, and the halved vanilla bean. Mix the pudding mix with the rest of the milk until smooth, stir into the boiling milk, and bring to a boil again. Remove from heat and take out the vanilla bean. Add cold water to the gelatin, remove excess, and dissolve the gelatin in the mixture. Mix in apricot marmalade and let cool. Stir the mixture until smooth and then carefully fold in the whipped cream.

Spread ¾ of the vanilla cream on the cake base, set the second cake piece on top, and brush with apricot marmalade again. Spread the rest of the cream on top and smooth. Chill for 2 hours. Spread the berries on top of the torte. For the gelatin, boil water with sugar, remove from heat, and stir in the apricot marmalade. Add cold water to the gelatin, remove excess, and dissolve in the sugar water. Carefully pour over the torte and chill.

CARROT TORTE

Preheat oven to 350 °F (180 °C). Mix carrots with ½ cup (60 g) of confectioner's sugar and the lemon zest and let it marinate while you complete the rest of the recipe. Beat the eggs, egg yolks, and the rest of the sugar in a double boiler. Then beat with a mixer until cool and creamy. Carefully fold the carrots into the egg mixture. Mix in flour, baking powder, and hazelnuts. Fold in melted and cooled butter. Butter a torte pan and sprinkle it with chopped almonds. Pour in the carrot batter and bake for 40 minutes. Let cool and overturn onto a cloth or board dusted with confectioner's sugar. Brush with warmed apricot marmalade and glaze with egg white glaze.

Bake Time: 40 minutes

Bake Temperature: 350 °F (180 °C)

Ingredients for 1 Torte (10in (26 cm) diameter)
Basic sponge cake for tortes (see p. 23), ½ recipe
1 cup (120 g) Apricot marmalade
12 oz (350 g) Berries, mixed according to taste

For the Cream
2 cups (500 ml) Milk
¾ cup (180 g) Granulated sugar
4 tsp (20 g) Vanilla sugar
1 Vanilla bean
2 oz (50 g) Vanilla pudding mix
6 Sheets gelatin
¼ cup (30 g) Apricot marmalade
1⅔ cups (400 ml) Whipped cream

For the Gelatin
½ cup (50 g) Apricot marmalade
½ cup (120 ml) Water
⅓ cup (70 g) Granulated sugar
3 Sheets gelatin

Ingredients for 1 Torte (10in (24 cm) diameter)
9 oz (250 g) Carrots, finely grated
1⅔ cup (210 g) Confectioner's sugar
Zest of 1 lemon
5 Eggs
1 Egg yolk
1½ cups (185 g) Flour
2 tsp (10 g) Baking powder
4.5 oz (125 g) Hazelnuts, shelled and grated
1 stick plus 1 tbsp (125 g) Butter, melted and cooled
2 oz (60 g) Almonds, chopped
Apricot marmalade for brushing
Egg white glaze (see p. 43)
Butter for the pan
Confectioner's sugar for the cloth

ORANGE TRUFFLE TORTE

Prepare the Panama cake according to the recipe. Slice the cooled cake twice horizontally. Warm the orange marmalade with Grand Marnier, stir, and brush the first torte layer with it. Place in a torte ring.

For the cream, melt the chocolate in a bain-marie. Beat the egg whites, also in a bain-marie, until creamy, and mix into the chocolate. Add water to the gelatin, remove excess, and dissolve the gelatin in warmed orange juice. Mix orange juice, Grand Marnier, and orange zest into the cream. Whip the cream partway and fold into the cream in two parts. Smooth a third of the cream onto the cake base. Place the second cake piece on top and brush with orange marmalade. Repeat with the third cake. Smooth the rest of the cream onto the top of the torte and chill for 2 hours. Spread whipped cream on top. Remove from the torte ring, dust the sides with cocoa powder, and decorate the top with chocolate shavings and candied orange peel.

Ingredients for 1 Torte
(10in (26 cm) diameter)
Basic Panama batter
1¼ cups (150 g) Orange marmalade
¼ cup (6 cl) Grand Marnier
¾ cup (200 ml) Whipped cream
Chocolate shavings and Candied orange peel to garnish
Cocoa powder for dusting

For the Cream
4 Egg yolks
10.5 oz (300 g) Dark couverture chocolate
¾ cup (150 ml) Orange juice, fresh squeezed
¼ cup (5 cl) Grand Marnier
Zest of 2 oranges
1 Sheet gelatin
1½ cups (350 ml) Whipping cream

LEMON TART WITH MASCARPONE

Preheat oven to 375 °F (190 °C). Line a buttered springform pan with the torte dough and weight with lentils or peas to bake, as described in the basic recipe.

For the filling, beat egg yolks, eggs, and sugar in a double boiler until creamy. Add the butter, lemon juice, and lemon zest and beat well. Beat in the cornstarch, honey, and mascarpone. Slowly heat the mixture, stirring constantly, and simmer until the mixture thickens. Fill the pre-baked crust and bake again for 10 minutes. Chill before serving.

Bake Time: about 12–15 minutes for the dough; 10 minutes to finish

Bake Temperature: 375 °F (190 °C)

Ingredients for 6–8 Portions
Basic dough for tarts (see p. 11), ½ recipe

For the Filling
2 Egg yolks
2 Eggs
½ cup (120 g) Granulated sugar
2¾ tbsp (40 g) Butter
2 tbsp Cornstarch
½ tsp Honey
14 oz (400 g) Mascarpone
¾ cup (180 ml) Lemon juice
Zest of 2 lemons

PASSION FRUIT NOUGAT CHARLOTTE

*Ingredients for 6–8 Portions
(1 Charlotte Pan)*

Basic sponge cake batter
for roulades (see p. 22),
½ recipe
Apricot marmalade for
brushing
7 oz (200 g) Passion fruit
purée (store-bought or
homemade, see Tips)
5 Sheets gelatin
2 Egg yolks
2 tbsp (30 g) Granulated
sugar
4 tsp (2 cl) Cointreau
1 cup (250 ml) Whipped
cream
Sugar for the cloth

For the Nougat Mousse
4 oz (120 g) Nougat
1 Egg
2 Sheets gelatin
⅔ cup (150 ml) Whipped
cream
4 tsp (2 cl) Rum

Bake the sponge cake according to the recipe and overturn onto a sugared cloth. Turn your Charlotte pan upside down and cut out a circular cake base. Set it aside. Slice the rest of the cake lengthwise, brush with marmalade, roll into small roulades, and chill. Cut the roulades into slices 5–8mm thin and line the Charlotte pan with them as thinly as possible. Warm a portion of the passion fruit purée. Add cold water to the gelatin, remove excess, and dissolve the gelatin in the warm purée. Mix with the rest of the purée. Beat the egg yolks with granulated sugar in a double boiler until creamy. Add the passion fruit purée and beat in an ice water bath until cool. As soon as the mixture begins to gel, fold in the whipped cream. Flavor with Cointreau, put in the Charlotte pan, and chill for 20 minutes.

In the meantime, melt the nougat for the nougat mousse. Add water to the gelatin, remove excess, and dissolve in warmed rum. Beat the egg with the rum-gelatin mixture over a double boiler, stir into the nougat, and let cool a bit. Fold in the whipped cream. Fill the Charlotte pan, place the cake base on top, and chill for 2–3 hours. Remove from the pan and brush with warmed apricot marmalade.

Tips:

- It is very easy to make your own passion fruit purée. Just take out the meat of about 10 passion fruits and blend it with more or less simple syrup, according to your personal taste. Sieve—and done.
- If you do not happen to have any passion fruit, you can replace them with strawberries or other fruit. However, the tartness of the passion fruit harmonizes with the sweetness of the nougat wonderfully.

Fruit Pleasures of the World
FINE DESSERTS OF FRUIT
AND BERRIES

COLD TEMPTATIONS

If desserts today are much lighter and easier to digest than in our grandmothers' time, we have to thank the fact that there is less and less sugar and flour but more and more sweet and tart fruits and berries used. Particularly on hot days, such delightfully cool fruit desserts are very popular with health-conscious foodies.

BANANA CHOCOLATE TERRINE WITH KUMQUATS

Prepare the baumkuchen according to the recipe (see p.33), let cool, and cut into thin strips. Lay the strips in a terrine mold the short way.

For the banana mouse, purée the peeled, coarsely chopped bananas with simple syrup and lemon juice. Sieve the purée.

Add water to the gelatin, remove excess, and dissolve in a portion of the banana purée in a double boiler. Mix back into the rest of the purée and beat in an ice bath until it begins to gel slightly.

Beat the egg whites to stiff peaks with sugar and fold into the banana mixture. Fill a terrine mold and chill for 2 hours.

For the chocolate mousse, melt the chocolate in a double boiler and then remove from heat. Mix the simple syrup with peeled, coarsely chopped banana and heavy cream. Pass through a fine sieve and mix into the chocolate along with the egg yolk. Fold in the whipped cream and flavor with banana liqueur. Spread on top of the banana mousse and chill for 4 more hours. Remove from the terrine mold and portion. Place each piece in the middle of a plate, surround with kumquat star anise compote and dust with confectioner's sugar.

Tip: This terrine tastes even more delicate when served with fresh vanilla foam (see p. 203).

Ingredients for 12 Servings
Basic baumkuchen
(see p. 33), ⅓ recipe
About 18 oz (500 g)
  kumquats with star
  anise (see p. 190)
Confectioner's sugar for
  dusting

For the Banana Mousse
2 Bananas
¼ cup (5 cl) Simple syrup
  (see p. 40)
2 tbsp (3 cl) Lemon juice
3 Sheets gelatin
2 Egg whites
4 tsp (20 g) Granulated sugar

For the Chocolate Mousse
4 oz (120 g) Dark couverture
  chocolate
1 Egg yolk
1 Banana
¼ cup (6 cl) Simple syrup
  (see p. 40)
3 tbsp (4 cl) Heavy cream
¾ cup (180 ml) Whipped
  cream
4 tsp (2 cl) Banana liqueur

Berry Lasagna with Strudel Dough Leaves

Ingredients
About 6 oz (180 g) basic
  strudel dough (see p. 16
  or use ready-made dough)
12 oz (350 g) Mascarpone
  cream (see p. 248)
3.5 oz (100 g) Blueberries
3.5 oz (100 g) Raspberries
Strawberry purée
  (see p. 200)
Sour cream and
Mint to garnish
Confectioner's sugar for
  dusting
Butter for the baking sheet

Preheat oven to 430 °F (220 °C). Cut 12 circles out of the pre-pared strudel dough with a round cookie cutter (4 in (10 cm) diameter). Place on a buttered baking sheet, dust with confectioner's sugar, and caramelize in the preheated oven for about 5 minutes. Remove from baking sheet and let cool.

Prepare the mascarpone cream according to the recipe and fill a piping bag fitted with a star-shaped nozzle. Pipe a 1½ in (4 cm) diameter foundation of cream onto each plate. Arrange a variety of berries on and around the cream and cover with a strudel leaf. Repeat with the rest of the berries. Place the prettiest strudel leaves on top of the last cream and berry layer. Surround with strawberry purée and sour cream and dust with confectioner's sugar. Garnish with mint.

Bake Time: about 5 minutes

Bake Temperature: 430 °F (220 °C)

BLUEBERRY BUTTERMILK TARTLETS WITH APRICOTS

Preheat oven to 340°F (170°C). Prepare the basic pâte brisée dough. Roll the dough out 3–4mm thick and poke several times with a fork. Cut out circles of the right size to line the buttered tartlet pans. Place the pans on a baking sheet and bake for about 8–10 minutes. Remove tartlets from the pans and let cool. For the mousse, mix buttermilk with honey, confectioner's sugar, and orange zest. Add water to the gelatin, remove excess water, and dissolve in warmed orange juice. Add to the buttermilk mixture. Stir in an ice water bath until the liquid begins to gel slightly, then fold in the whipped cream. Fill the tartlets with mousse and chill. Place blueberries on top of each tart. Pour blueberry sauce onto each plate and place a tart in the middle. Garnish with preserved apricots and mint and dust with confectioner's sugar.

Bake Time: 8–10 minutes

Bake Temperature: 340°F (170°C)

Ingredients for 8 Servings

Ingredients for 8 Servings
14 oz (400 g) Basic pâte brisée dough (see p. 14)
7 oz (200 g) Blueberries
9 oz (250 g) Preserved apricots (see p. 188)
Blueberry sauce (see p. 201)
Confectioner's sugar for dusting
Mint to garnish
Butter for the pans

For the Buttermilk Mousse
1 cup (250 ml) Buttermilk
2 tbsp (40 g) Honey
6 tbsp (50 g) Confectioner's sugar
Salt
Zest of 1 orange
3 Sheets gelatin
¾ (200 ml) Whipped cream

1
For the dough, knead all the ingredients together and then let rest.

2
Roll out the pâte brisée dough to 3–4mm thick.

3
Cut out dough circles and line the tartlet pans.

4
Stipple the bottoms of the tartlets with a fork. Bake as described.

5
Fill the tartlets with buttermilk mousse and chill.

6
Spread blueberries on top.

PASSION FRUIT TERRINE WITH FRIED STRAWBERRIES

For the passion fruit mousse, add cold water to the gelatin. Warm about 100ml of passion fruit juice. Remove excess water from the gelatin, dissolve in the juice, and then add to the rest of the passion fruit juice. Flavor with Cointreau and mix over an ice bath until the juice begins to gel slightly. Beat the egg white to stiff peaks with the granulated sugar and fold in along with the whipped cream. Fill the terrine mold with the mousse and chill for 1 hour. For the yogurt mousse, mix yogurt with confectioner's sugar. Warm Cointreau and orange juice. Dissolve the moistened gelatin in it. Mix into the yogurt. Fold in the whipped cream. Spread the yogurt mousse on top of the passion fruit mousse and chill for another 3 hours.

For the batter, mix flour, salt, sugar, and oil. Mix in the egg yolks. Add the white wine and strawberry liqueur and mix everything to a smooth batter. Beat egg whites to stiff peaks with sugar and fold into the batter. In a small, deep pan, heat a good amount of oil. Hold the washed strawberries by the stem or on a toothpick, dip into the batter, then fry until golden. Let drain well on paper towels.

Remove the terrine from the mold and portion onto places. Surround each with strawberry purée and place a halved strawberry on top. Garnish with confectioner's sugar and mint.

Garnish Recommendation: add nougat ice cream (see p. 352) or coconut ice cream (see p. 354)

Ingredients for 12 Servings

For the Passion Fruit Mousse
1½ (350 ml) Passion fruit juice
4 Sheets gelatin
3 Egg whites
7 tbsp (100 g) Granulated sugar
4 tsp (2 cl) Cointreau
1 cup (250 ml) Whipped cream

For the Yogurt Mousse
⅔ cup (150 ml) Yogurt
¼ cup (30 g) Confectioner's sugar
4 tsp (2 cl) Cointreau
4 tsp (2 cl) Orange juice
3 Sheets gelatin
⅔ cup (150 ml) Whipped cream

For the Fried Strawberries
12 Strawberries with stems
6 tbsp (50 g) Flour
Dash of salt
½ tbsp Confectioner's sugar
2 tsp (1 cl) Sunflower oil
1 Egg yolk
¼ cup (50 ml) White wine
2 tsp (1 cl) Strawberry liqueur
1 Egg white
4 tsp (20 g) Granulated sugar
Strawberry purée (see p. 200)
Confectioner's sugar and Mint to garnish
Oil for frying

NECTARINE BRITTLE PÂTÉ WITH REDCURRANTS

Ingredients for 8 Servings
8 Wafers (about 2 ½ in (6 cm) diameter)
3 Nectarines
3.5 oz (100 g) Nectarine purée (follow peach purée recipe, p. 200)
3 tbsp (4 cl) Peach liqueur
4 tsp (2 cl) Lemon juice
3 tbsp (4 cl) Simple syrup (see p. 40)
3 Sheets gelatin
14 oz (400 g) Dark couverture chocolate
Brittle crumbs (see p. 36)
7 oz (200 g) Redcurrants
¼ cup (50 ml) Redcurrant juice
4 tsp (30 g) Honey
About 10.5 oz (300 g) Cream ice cream or white chocolate ice cream
Mint to garnish

For the Brittle Cream
1¼ oz (35 g) Dark couverture chocolate
1¾ oz (50 g) Milk couverture chocolate
¼ cup (50 ml) Milk
1½ tbsp (20 g) Butter
.5 oz (15 g) Brittle (see p. 36)

Place each wafer in the same sized mold. For the brittle cream, chop up the chocolates and melt them together in a bain-marie. Mix in milk and butter. Homogenize with an immersion blender, i.e. mix for 5 minutes without letting air in (keep the mixer submerged!). Finally, mix in the brittle, fill the molds, and chill for 2 hours.

In the meantime, cut the nectarines into small cubes. Add cold water to the gelatin. Warm the peach liqueur, lemon juice, and simple syrup. Remove excess water from the gelatin, dissolve in the liqueur mixture, and then stir into the nectarine purée. Add the nectarine cubes. Add this mixture to the molds and chill for about 4–5 hours. Remove the tartlets from the molds.

Melt the dark chocolate in a bain-marie. First dip the lower half of the tartlets in the chocolate, then in the brittle crumbs, and set on parchment paper. Boil the redcurrant juice with honey. Remove from heat, let cool, and mix in crushed redcurrants. In the middle of each dish, place a tartlet, surround with the redcurrants, and place cream ice cream or white chocolate ice cream on top. Garnish with mint

BLACKBERRIES ON A HONEY CREAM ROULADE

For the honey cream, mix yogurt with honey. Add cold water to the gelatin. Warm the lemon and orange juice and dissolve the gelatin in it. Mix with the yogurt. As soon as the mixture begins to gel, fold in the whipped cream. Chill.

For the cake, preheat the oven to 350°F (180°C). Beat egg whites to stiff peaks with granulated sugar. Slowly mix in the yolks, and then fold in the salt, vanilla sugar, and lemon zest. Finally, carefully fold in the sifted flour. Spread on a baking sheet lined with parchment paper. Bake for 10–15 minutes, until golden brown. Let the cake cool, then halve lengthwise. Spread the honey cream on the cake base, roll up, and chill. Then brush the roulades with apricot marmalade and roll in coconut flakes. Slice and arrange the roulades. Melt the white chocolate in a bain-marie and "glue" the blackberries to the roulades with it. Garnish with mint and white chocolate shavings.

Bake Time: 10–15 minutes

Bake Temperature: 350°F (180°C)

Garnish Recommendation: Raspberry purée (see p. 201) and yogurt lemon sauce (see p. 202)

Ingredients for 8 Servings
4 Egg whites
⅓ cup (80 g) Granulated sugar
4 Egg yolks
Vanilla sugar
Lemon zest
Salt
½ cup (80 g) Whole wheat flour
1¼ cups (150 g) Apricot marmalade
Coconut flakes
7 oz (200 g) Blackberries
White couverture chocolate
Mint and white chocolate shavings to garnish

For the Honey Cream
1 cup (250 ml) Yogurt
¼ cup (80 g) Honey
Juice of 1 lemon
Juice of 1 orange
3 Sheets gelatin
¾ cup (200 ml) Whipped cream

A New Peach Melba

Preheat oven to 350 °F (180 °C). Blanch the peaches briefly in salt water, shock in ice water, and peel. Halve and pit. Bring the sauvignon blanc to boil with water, lemon juice, granulated sugar, and honey. Add the peaches and cook until soft. Take the peaches out and set aside. Season the liquid with peach liqueur and boil slowly, until it is thick and syrupy.

Beat the eggs with granulated sugar and salt until thick and creamy. Sieve the flour and cornstarch and fold into the egg. Spread on a baking sheet lined with parchment paper and bake for 6 minutes. Overturn onto a cloth sprinkled with confectioner's sugar and carefully pull away the parchment paper. Cut out circles (about 3 in (7.5 cm) diameter) with a cookie cutter and place in pans of the same size. Brush with warm raspberry marmalade and place the raspberries on top.

Halve the vanilla bean and boil it in milk. Remove from heat and let sit. Beat the egg yolks with granulated sugar in a double boiler until creamy. Remove the vanilla bean and scrape the pulp into the milk. Dissolve the moistened gelatin in the warm milk and then pour into the egg yolk mixture. Continue beating in double boiler until the mixture begins to thicken. You can tell when it is ready because when you blow on the cream while it is coating the cooking spoon, rings will appear that are reminiscent of a rose. Beat in an ice bath until cool. Fold in the whipped cream. Fill the forms and freeze for 2 hours. Remove from the forms.

Cut ten 1½x8 in (4x20 cm) strips of parchment paper. Melt the chocolate in a bain-marie. Brush the paper strips thinly with the chocolate and wrap each tartlet with a strip, chocolate side in. Let harden in the refrigerator and pull off the paper. Cut the peaches into fine slices, but keep them all together in the original shape. Set a peach half on top of each and pour the cooled syrup on top.

Bake Time: about 6 minutes

Bake Temperature: 350 °F (180 °C)

STRAWBERRIES IN CHAMPAGNE GELATIN WITH ELDERFLOWER MOUSSE AND STRAWBERRY FOAM

Wash and quarter the strawberries. Bring the sparkling wine to boil with apple juice, lemon juice, and granulated sugar and then remove from heat. Add cold water to the gelatin, remove excess and dissolve the gelatin in the still warm wine mixture. Cool, letting the liquid almost gel. Put the quartered strawberries in wide glasses (whisky tumblers work best) and cover with the still liquid gelatin. Chill for 1 hour.

For the mousse, add water to the gelatin, remove excess water, and dissolve in a bit of elderflower juice in a double boiler. Stir into the rest of the elderflower juice. Stir in a mixing bowl over ice until the liquid begins to gel. Fold in the whipped cream. Beat the egg whites, add granulated sugar, and beat to stiff peaks. Fold in. Add the mousse on top of the solid gelatin and chill again. Prepare the strawberry foam according to the recipe and foam on top of the mousse with a whipped cream dispenser.

Garnish Recommendation: strawberries with stems and mint

Ingredients for 12 Servings
10.5 oz (300 g) Strawberries
1⅔ cups (400 ml) Sparkling wine (preferably chardonnay)
⅔ cup (150 ml) Apple juice
3 tbsp (4 cl) Lemon juice
⅓ cup (80 g) Granulated sugar
5 Sheets gelatin
Strawberry foam (see p. 274)

For the Elderflower Mousse
1⅔ cups (400 ml) Elderflower juice (see p. 205 or use ready-made juice)
4 Sheets gelatin
½ cup (120 ml) Whipped cream
2 Egg whites
¼ cup (50 g) Granulated sugar

MARINATED PEACHES WITH CAMPARI SABAYON

Ingredients
3–4 Peaches
Confectioner's sugar
4 tsp (2 cl) Grappa
Splash of grenadine
Juice of ¼ lemon
Mint, cut into fine strips
Mint leaves to garnish

For the Campari Sabayon
4 Egg yolks
¼ cup (50 g) Sugar
1 Sheet gelatin
Zest of 1 orange
¼ cup (6 cl) Campari
3 tbsp (4 cl) Orange juice
1 tbsp Whipped cream
Confectioner's sugar

Cut the peaches into thin slices and marinate in grappa, grenadine, lemon juice, mint strips, and confectioner's sugar. Arrange in a rosette on a plate.

For the Campari sabayon, cream the egg yolks with sugar and beat in a double boiler until the mixture binds together and forms a solid, airy foam. Add cold water to the gelatin, remove excess, and dissolve gelatin in the foam. Continue mixing the foam in a cold water bath. Season with orange zest, Campari, and orange juice. Sweeten the whipped cream slightly with confectioner's sugar and fold into the Campari foam before serving. Serve the Campari sabayon over the peaches and garnish with mint leaves.

Garnish Recommendation: Bellini sorbet (see p. 363)

PLUMS IN GELATIN WITH POPPY ICE CREAM AND PLUM FOAM

Ingredients
7 oz (200 g) Plums
7 tbsp (100 ml) Red wine
¼ cup (50 g) Granulated
  sugar
3 Sheets gelatin
2 tsp (1 cl) Armagnac
2 tsp (1 cl) Slivovitz
Plum foam (see p. 274),
  ½ recipe

For the Poppy Ice Cream
Basic vanilla ice cream (see
  p. 350), ½ recipe
¾ oz (20 g) Poppy seeds,
  ground

Half and pit the plums. Boil red wine with granulated sugar. Add the plums and let cook several minutes, until soft. Strain and collect the juice. Add water to gelatin, remove excess, and dissolved gelatin in the juice. Flavor with Armagnac and slivovitz. Now fill cold rinsed single serving molds with the liquid and plums and chill for 3 hours. Prepare the vanilla ice cream according to the recipe. Mix with poppy seed and freeze in the ice cream machine. Prepare the plum foam according to the recipe.

Dip the molds briefly in hot water and overturn one onto each place. Add a scoop of poppy ice cream and the plum foam on top.

GRENADINE PEAR WITH PEAR MOUSSE AND ELDERBERRY PURÉE

Boil the white wine, water, sugar, and grenadine. Cook the peeled pears (with stems) in the liquid until they are soft and let them cool overnight in the mixture. It is best to weight the pears with an overturned plate so that they are completely covered in the liquid.

For the mousse, peel and core the pears and slice into small pieces. Cook until soft in white wine and sugar, blend, and sieve. Dissolve the moistened gelatin in the still-warm pear purée. Beat egg yolks and confectioner's sugar in a double boiler until creamy. Stir in the pear purée, fold in the whipped cream, and flavor with Poire Williams. Chill for 1 hour. Take out the grenadine pears and core them, leaving the pears whole. Fill the pears with the mousse using a piping bag. Portion out the prepared elderberry purée onto plates, set a mousse filled pear on each, and garnish with the rest of the mousse.

Garnish Recommendation: sour ice cream (see p. 355)

Ingredients
4 Pears
1 cup (250 ml) White wine
½ cup (125 ml) Grenadine
¼ cup (60 ml) Water
1 cup plus 2 tbsp (250 g)
 Granulated sugar
Elderberry purée
 (see p. 180)

For the Pear Mousse
1 Pear
¼ cup (65 ml) White wine
¼ cup (50 g) Sugar
2 Egg yolks
¼ cup (30 g) Confectioner's
 sugar
2 Sheets gelatin
3 tbsp (4 cl) Poire Williams
½ cup (125 ml) Whipped
 cream

Beautiful Grenadine

For every bartender, grenadine is like a liquid magic wand. This pomegranate syrup comes from the Caribbean islands of the same name, which lie south of St. Vincent. The main island is the tropical paradise of Granada. Like Campari, invented in 1867 in Milan's Via Rastrelli, grenadine has become part of the world of pastries as well as cocktails, due to its pleasant flavor and luminous color. And here, it proves to be surprisingly child-friendly: in contrast to Campari, grenadine is alcohol free.

MERLOT CHERRIES WITH SOUR CREAM MOUSSE

Halve and pit the cherries. Boil the merlot with the honey and reduce to half. Boil the cherries for 3 minutes. Add the cherry marmalade and orange juice and let come to a boil again. Season with kirsch and chill. For the mousse, mix sour cream with orange zest and confectioner's sugar. Add water to the gelatin, remove excess water, dissolve in warmed kirsch, and mix into the sour cream. Fold in the whipped cream and chill the mousse. Serve the merlot cherries in deep dishes with scoops of mousse on top.

ORANGE SLICES WITH SESAME WAFERS AND MINT SAUCE

Wash the oranges in hot water and dry well. Cut off thin pieces of peel with a knife and cut them into fine strips. Set aside in some cold water. Pull apart the orange slices, collecting the juice. Marinate the orange slices in Grand Marnier and confectioner's sugar.

For the cream, beat egg yolks with granulated sugar in a double boiler until creamy. Add water to the gelatin, remove excess water, and dissolve in slightly warmed orange juice and Grand Marnier. Stir into the egg yolk mixture and beat until cold. Before the mixture begins to gel, fold in the whipped cream. Fill 4 small ring pans (about 2.5 in (6 cm) diameter) with the cream and chill for 3 hours.

For the mint sauce, peel, quarter, and core the pears. Cook in lemon juice and granulated sugar until soft. Blanch the mint in salt water and shock in ice water. Add to the pears and mix everything well. Pass through a fine sieve and season with peppermint liqueur. Remove the cooled cream from the pans onto plates. Lay a sesame waffle leaf on the cream. Arrange orange slices on the leaf and then set another leaf on top. Garnish with mint sauce, mint, orange peels, and confectioner's sugar.

Ingredients for 4–6 Servings
35 oz (1 kg) Sweet cherries
2 cups (500 ml) Merlot (can be replaced with another strong, aromatic red wine)
1¼ cup (150 g) Cherry marmalade
¼ cup (80 g) Honey
Juice of 2 oranges
4 tsp (2 cl) Kirsch

For the Sour Cream Mousse
1¼ cup (300 ml) Sour cream
Zest of 1 orange
4 Sheets gelatin
⅔ cup (80 g) Confectioner's sugar
4 tsp (2 cl) Kirsch
¾ cup (200 ml) Whipped cream

Ingredients
4 Oranges, whole
3 tbsp (4 cl) Grand Marnier
¾ cup (100 g) Confectioner's sugar
8 Sesame waffle leaves (see p. 38)
Mint and confectioner's sugar to garnish

For the Cream
3 Egg yolks
¼ cup (50 g) Granulated sugar
4 tsp (2 cl) Grand Marnier
¼ cup (6 cl) Orange juice
3 Sheets gelatin
1 cup (250 ml) Whipped cream

For the Mint Sauce
4 Pears
⅓ cup (80 g) Granulated sugar
3 tbsp (4 cl) Lemon juice
½ Bundle peppermint
3 tsp (4 cl) Peppermint liqueur
Dash of salt

Mint, Sweet & Sour

The English like to use it in sauces for lamb and beef. The Carinthians, on the other hand, swear that real Carinthian dumplings are not worthy of the name without mint. Most of all, next to lemon balm, mint is one of the most beloved herbs of confectioners. The refreshing scent (in the New Testament, mint is referred to simply as "sweet smelling") covers so many sweets, and the menthol-like "peppery" taste goes perfectly not only with chocolate, but also with sorbets and fruit desserts. By the way, the flavor of fresh mint can also be achieved by using essential peppermint oil.

BURGUNDY PEARS IN BAVARIAN CREAM

Ingredients for 12 Servings, i.e. 2 Triangle Pans of 24oz (700 ml) Volume
⅔ cup (150 ml) Red wine (preferably burgundy)
½ cup (110 ml) Apple juice
¼ cup (50 g) Granulated sugar
4 tsp (2 cl) Poire Williams
4 Sheets gelatin
9 oz (250 g) Pears, peeled and cut into slices

For the Bavarian Cream
5 Egg yolks
½ cup (120 g) Granulated sugar
1 Vanilla bean
2 tbsp (3 cl) Kirsch
5 Sheets gelatin
2 cups (450 ml) Whipped cream

Bring the red wine, apple juice, and granulated sugar to a boil with the pear slices. Remove the pears from the liquid, dissolve the gelatin in it, and season with Poire Williams. Fill the triangular pans about halfway with pears and liquid and chill for 3 hours. Cut the firm pear gelatin out of the molds, place on a sheet lined with parchment paper, and chill again. Wash and dry the pans.

For the Bavarian cream, halve the vanilla bean and scrape out the pulp. Beat the egg yolks with the sugar and vanilla pulp in a double boiler until thick and foamy, then beat until cold in an ice bath. Add water to the gelatin and remove excess water. Dissolve it in slightly warmed kirsch and stir into the egg yolks. Finally, fold in the whipped cream, which should not be too firm. Fill the pans with half of the Bavarian cream. Press the burgundy pears point down into the forms and fill with the rest of the Bavarian cream. Thus it becomes a triangle within a triangle! Chill for 3 more hours.

Garnish Recommendation: preserved dried pears and plums (see p. 187)

Tip: If you do not have triangular pans, it would not change the taste at all to use a terrine.

MUSCAT GRAPES IN GELATIN WITH MUSCATEL SABAYON

Wash and pit the grapes. Bring the sparkling wine, muscatel, grape juice, and sugar to a boil and then remove from heat. Add water to the gelatin, remove excess water, and dissolve in the still-warm wine mixture. Rinse the single serving molds with cold water. First pour in some gelatin, let it set, then place several grapes in the mold. Repeat until you have used up all your ingredients. Always let set in between, so that the grapes do not float to the top. Set in a cool place.

For the sabayon, mix the egg yolks with the sugar and muscatel, then beat until foamy in a bain-marie. Season with grappa and beat well once more. Dip the gelatin molds briefly in hot water, overturn onto plates, and pour sabayon around each one. Garnish with mint, confectioner's sugar, and several grapes.

How Did the Muscat get in the Muscatel?

It is the oldest variety of grape in the world; the Muscat was known to the ancient Greeks and Phoenicians. The knights of the Nibelungen Saga spoke of it with such great joy that it is still known in some places as "Nibelungen wine."

Today, the Muscat grape provides material for noble wines as well as sweet table grapes. Its name comes from its irresistible aroma, which bewitches insects most of all. It was reason enough for the ancient Romans to name the wine after the fly (musca).

The muscatel grape has been found in Austria, specifically Wachau, since 1400. It can be put to use in the sweet kitchen in its fruity, aromatic, tart varieties, depending on the desired taste, or as a high quality Prädikatswein.

Ingredients for 6 Servings
10.5 oz (300 g) Muscat grapes
¾ cup (200 ml) Muscatel
7 tbsp (100 ml) Sparkling wine, preferably chardonnay
7 tbsp (100 ml) White grape juice
¼ cup (60 g) Sugar
4 Sheets gelatin
Confectioner's sugar for dusting
Mint and grapes to garnish

For the Muscatel Sabayon
3 Egg yolks
⅓ cup (80 g) Sugar
½ cup (125 ml) Muscatel
4 tsp (2 cl) Grappa

Jellied Sparkling Chardonnay Soup with Blueberries and Lemon Basil Sorbet

Ingredients for 6 Servings
3 cups (750 ml) Sparkling chardonnay
7 tbsp (100 ml) Savagnin blanc (or another rich white wine)
⅔ cup (150 ml) Elderflower juice (see p. 205 or use ready-made juice)
⅔ cup (150 ml) Apple juice
¼ cup (60 g) Granulated sugar
4 tsp (2 cl) Lemon juice
3 Sheets gelatin
⅓ cup (8 cl) Cointreau
9 oz (250 g) Blueberries
Mint to garnish
About 10.5 oz (300 g) Lemon basil sorbet (see p. 360)

Bring the savagnin blanc to a boil with the elderflower juice, apple juice, lemon juice, and granulated sugar. Remove from heat. Add water to the gelatin, remove excess water and dissolve in the still hot liquid. Add sparkling chardonnay and Cointreau and set in a cool place. Stir until smooth and fill deep dishes. Place a scoop of the prepared sorbet in the middle of each. Garnish with blueberries and mint.

Garnish Recommendation: sesame waffles (see p. 38)

Tip: Although sparkling chardonnay is without a doubt the best option for this fine dish, you can also use other sparkling wines without a problem.

Red Fruit Jelly

Ingredients
1 cup (250 ml) Apple juice
⅓ cup (80 ml) Orange juice
5 oz (150 g) Raspberries for the juice
¼ cup (60 g) Granulated sugar
1 cup (250 ml) Red wine
1 Cinnamon stick
Pulp of 2 vanilla beans
¼ cup (60 g) Vanilla pudding mix
10.5 oz (300 g) Berries, according to taste (such as redcurrants, blackberries, raspberries)

Bring a little less than ½ cup (100 ml) of apple juice to boil with the orange juice, raspberries, granulated sugar, red wine, and cinnamon stick. Let boil for a bit. Pass through a fine sieve. Add the scraped out vanilla bean pulp. Mix the vanilla pudding mix with the rest of the apple juice. Bring the red wine mixture to a boil once more and thicken with the vanilla pudding-apple juice. Remove from heat and add berries. Fill glasses or deep dishes with the fruit jelly and chill overnight.

Garnish Recommendation: Pour cold vanilla sauce (see p. 202) over the jelly or serve it on the side.

BERRY GELATIN WITH AMARETTO

Boil apple juice with Riesling and simple syrup. Remove from heat and let cool for half an hour. Mix in raspberries with an immersion blender and then sieve through cheesecloth without pressing, so that only clear juice comes through. Warm about 200ml of this juice. Add cold water to the gelatin, remove excess water, and dissolve in the warm juice. Add to the rest of the juice with the amaretto. Chill the single serving molds. Stem and wash the berries and mix together. Fill the forms with the cool, but still liquid, gelatin, just to cover the bottom. Put a bit of the berry mixture into each. Let stiffen in the refrigerator, and then fill more with gelatin and berries and let stiffen again. Repeat until you have used all of the berries and gelatin. Let cool for 4 hours. Before serving, set the molds briefly in hot water and release the gelatin.

Garnish Recommendation: yogurt lemon sauce (see p. 202) or various sorbets

Tip: If you do not have access to fresh, seasonal berries, you can use frozen berries. Before using, they must be thawed and patted dry.

Ingredients for 8 Servings
18 oz (500 g) Raspberries
¾ cup (200 ml) Simple syrup (see p. 40)
1¼ cups (300 ml) Apple juice
7 tbsp (100 ml) Riesling (or another rich white wine)
7 tbsp (100 ml) Amaretto
10 Sheets gelatin

For the Berry Mixture
6 oz (180 g) Raspberries
3.5 oz (100 g) Wild strawberries
6 oz (180 g) Blueberries
2 oz (50 g) Redcurrants

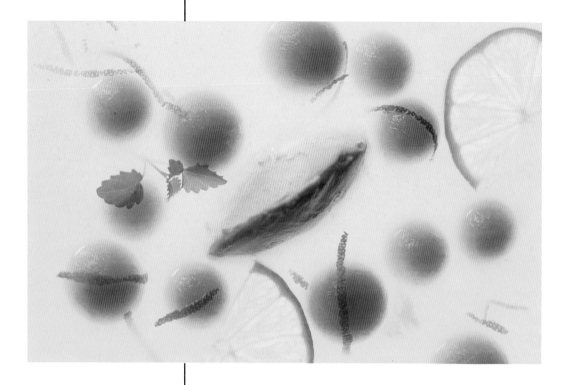

COLD MELON LIME SOUP WITH HONEY WHIPPED CREAM

Ingredients
2 Cantaloupes
  (or honeydews)
¾ cup (180 g) Granulated
  sugar
⅔ cup (150 g) Lime juice
7 tbsp (100 ml) Water
2 Sheets gelatin
5 tbsp Whipping cream
1 tbsp Honey
Lime peel strips and
Mint to garnish

Halve the melons. Remove the pits and scoop out 12 cherry sized melon balls. Cut the rest of the melon meat away from the peel. Boil the lime juice, sugar, and water. Remove from heat. Add cold water to the gelatin, remove excess water, and dissolve in the still-hot lime juice. Mix in the melon meat with a mixer and then sieve. Let chill.

Whip the cream while mixing with honey and chill until needing. Fill deep dishes with the cold melon soup and place three melon balls and a dollop of honey whipped cream into each. Garnish with lime peels and mint.

Tip: This fruit dessert looks particularly decorative when served in the melon rinds. Of course, you must be very careful when scraping out the meat not to damage the rind.

Coconut Soup with Cardamom Oranges and MaiTai Sorbet

Prepare the cardamom oranges the day before. Cut the oranges into 2mm thick slices. Bring water to boil with orange juice, granulated sugar, honey, and cardamom and reduce to half. Flavor with Cointreau. Lay the orange slices flat on a tray or plate and pour the mixture over them. Cover with plastic wrap and let marinate for 24 hours.

For the coconut soup, mix together coconut meat, simple syrup, lime juice, lemon zest, coconut liqueur, peppermint, and ice cubes until all the ice is gone. Before serving, froth with the mixer again. Portion the coconut soup into deep dishes. Drain the orange slices and lay them in the soup. Add a scoop of the prepared Mai Tai sorbet to each and garnish with peppermint.

Ingredients for 8 Servings
2 cups (500 ml) Coconut meat (out of a can or jar)
7 tbsp (100 ml) Simple syrup (see p. 40)
1¼ cups (300 ml) Lime juice
Zest of 1 lemon
1¼ cups (300 ml) Coconut liqueur
4 Peppermint leaves, finely chopped
1 Handful of ice cubes
Mai Tai sorbet (see p. 363)
Peppermint leaves to garnish

For the Cardamom Oranges
2 Oranges, whole
⅔ cup (150 ml) Water
7 tbsp (100 ml) Orange juice
⅔ cup (150 g) Granulated sugar
2 tbsp plus 1 tsp (50 g) Honey
3 tbsp (4 cl) Cointreau
2 tbsp Cardamom, ground

ORANGE SOUP WITH BLUEBERRIES AND COCONUT RAVIOLI

Ingredients for 6 Servings
5 cups (1.2l) Orange juice,
  fresh squeezed
6 tbsp (90g) Sugar
4 tsp (2cl) Grenadine
3 Sheets gelatin
⅓ cup (8cl) Grand Marnier
1 Orange, whole
7 oz (200g) Blueberries
Mint and Confectioner's
  sugar to garnish

For the Ravioli Dough
1⅔ cups (200g) Flour
3 Egg yolks
1 Egg
Dash of salt
2 tsp (10g) Vanilla sugar
1 Egg for brushing
Flour for the work surface

For the Coconut Filling
4 oz (120g) Coconut purée
1 Egg
2 oz (50g) Coconut flakes
4 tsp (20g) Vanilla sugar
4 tsp (2cl) Coconut liqueur

For the Coconut Crumb
3 oz (80g) Coconut flakes
4¼ tbsp (60g) Butter

Sieve the fresh squeezed orange juice and warm with sugar and grenadine. Add cold water to the gelatin, remove excess water, and dissolve in the hot juice. Flavor with Grand Marnier and put in a cool place.

Wash the orange in hot water and rub dry well with a towel. Cut thin pieces of the peel off and then cut them into thin strips. Put aside in some cold water. Peel the oranges completely, take apart the slices, and set aside for garnishing.

For the ravioli dough, knead the flour, egg yolks, egg, salt, and vanilla sugar to a smooth dough. In the meantime, mix together coconut purée, egg, coconut flakes, vanilla sugar, and coconut liqueur for the filling. Roll out the dough thinly on a floured work surface, brush with beaten egg, and cut out 24 circles. Spoon coconut filling into the middle of each one and fold into a pocket. Press the edges together well. Cook the ravioli in boiling salt water for about 3 minutes.

For the coconut crumb, brown the butter in a pan. Add the cooked, drained ravioli and the coconut flakes and stir. Portion the cooled orange soup into deep dishes and add 4 raviolis to each. Add blueberries and the orange pieces in the middle. Garnish with Orange peels and mint and dust with confectioner's sugar.

WARM DELICACIES

What separates Viennese cuisine from most other dessert traditions is its distinctive love for warm desserts. In this tradition, which you will learn much more about in the chapter "Greetings from Flour Heaven," we give you the following warm fruit and berry desserts.

CHOCOLATE RASPBERRY TRIANGLES

For the pâte brisée, beat the egg yolks with sugar and then mix in the room temperature butter. Mix together the flour, baking powder, salt, and lemon zest and knead together with the yolk mixture quickly to form a smooth dough. Chill for about 1 hour. Preheat oven to 400°F (200°C). On a floured work surface, roll out the dough to about 10x4 in (25x10 cm) and about 3mm thick. Lay on a baking sheet lined with parchment paper and bake for 12 minutes. Cut the still warm pâte brisée into 4 right triangles with about 4 in sides.

Spread the prepared pastry cream on the triangles and place the raspberries on top. For the chocolate lemon cream, boil the lemon juice with the heavy cream, then add the water. Remove from heat and melt the chopped chocolate in it. Blend until smooth with an immersion blender. Portion the warm cream onto plates and place a raspberry triangle on each. Garnish with honey waffles and raspberry sorbet and dust with confectioner's sugar.

Bake Time: 12 minutes

Bake Temperature: 400°F (200°C)

Ingredients
2 Egg yolks
⅓ cup (80 g) Granulated sugar
5½ tbsp (80 g) Butter, room temperature
1 cup less 1 tbsp (110 g) Flour
1 tsp (6 g) Baking powder
Dash of salt
Zest of 2 lemons
5 oz (150 g) Pastry cream (see p. 247)
9 oz (250 g) Raspberries
Honey waffles (see p. 38) and raspberry sorbet (see p. 358) to garnish
Flour for the work surface
Confectioner's sugar for dusting

For the Chocolate Lemon Cream
¼ cup (50 ml) Lemon juice
¼ cup (50 ml) Water
⅔ cup (150 ml) Heavy cream
5 oz (150 g) Dark couverture chocolate

STRAWBERRY DATSCHI ON ICED POPPY FOAM

Ingredients for 6 Servings
10.5 oz (300 g) Puff pastry (see p.11)
1¼ cup (150 g) Strawberry marmalade
18 oz (500 g) Strawberries, without stems
Flour for the work surface
Confectioner's sugar for dusting
Strawberries and Strawberry purée (see p. 200) to garnish

For the Poppy Foam
1 cup (250 ml) Milk
3 tbsp (40 g) Granulated sugar
2¾ tbsp (40 g) Butter
2 Egg yolks
⅔ cup (100 g) Cornstarch
Dash of salt
Dash of vanilla sugar
3 oz (80 g) Poppy seeds, ground
½ cup (120 ml) Whipped cream
1.5 oz (40 g) Amaretto

Preheat oven to 350 °F (180 °C). Roll out the puff pastry dough on a floured work surface. Cut out circles (4 in (10 cm) diameter) with a cookie cutter and roll up the edges slightly to create a little ridge. Poke the datschi several times with a fork and brush with strawberry marmalade. Quarter the washed strawberries and place on the datschi. Bake for 15 minutes on a baking sheet lined with parchment paper.

For the poppy foam, mix the egg yolks with cornstarch and a bit of milk. Boil the rest of the milk with sugar, butter, salt, and vanilla sugar. Mix in the egg yolks and remove from heat. Mix with a hand mixer in an ice bath until cool. Fold in the poppy, amaretto, and whipped cream. Portion the iced poppy foam onto plates. Set the warm datschi on top, dust with confectioner's sugar, and garnish with strawberries and strawberry purée.

Bake Time: about 15 minutes

Bake Temperature: 350 °F (180 °C)

APRICOT VANILLA DACQUOISE

Preheat oven to 340 °F (170 °C). Prepare the basic pâte brisée dough. Roll out about 4mm thick and cut out circles (about 3 in (8 cm) diameter) with a cookie cutter. Place in buttered tartlet forms (2½ in (6 cm) diameter). Stipple the bases of the tartlets (poke several times with a fork) and bake for about 10 minutes. Remove tartlets from pans and let cool.

Raise oven temperature to 465 °F (240 °C) or maximum upper heat. For the meringue, beat the egg whites and granulated sugar to stiff peaks. Put one scoop of vanilla ice cream in each tartlet. Halve the apricot halves again and arrange around the ice cream to create a dome. With a piping bag fitted with a small round nozzle, cover the dome in little dots, creating a little "hedgehog." Bake for about 5 minutes. Serve with strawberry purée, mint, frothed sour cream, and confectioner's sugar.

Bake Time: tartlets: about 10 minutes; browning: about 5 minutes

Bake Temperature: tartlets: 340 °F (170 °C); browning: 465 °F (240 °C) upper heat

Unspeakably Sweet

"Dacquoise" may be unpronounceable outside of France, but what is hidden behind this cute little meringue hedgehog is, how you say, delicious. Hiding behind the word "Dacquoise" are the residents of the French town of Dax, north of Bayonne, which has been home to a hot spring since Roman times. And as it always seems to be with spas, Dax is rife with spa romances as well as spa confectioners—and with them, diet cheating in the form of sweet delicacies. What Ischler cakes and Zaunerstollen is to those in Bad Ischl, Dacquoise is to the residents of Dax—and even more, to their spa guests.

Ingredients
7 oz (200 g) Pâte brisée dough (see p. 14)
7 oz (200 g) Vanilla ice cream (see p. 350)
16 Preserved apricot halves
Strawberry purée (see p.200)
Mint and frothed sour cream to garnish
Confectioner's sugar for dusting
Butter for the forms

For the Meringue
2 Egg whites
7 tbsp (100 g) Granulated sugar

FIGS IN COCONUT BATTER WITH CURRANT SAUCE

Ingredients
16 Fresh figs
¾ cup (200 ml) Simple syrup (see p. 40)
⅓ cup (8 cl) Crème de cassis
Clarified butter or oil for frying

For the Coconut Batter
2⅔ cups (300 g) Flour
Dash of salt
2 tbsp (3 cl) Oil
3 Egg yolks
¾ cup (200 ml) White wine
3 Egg whites
2 tbsp (30 g) Granulated sugar
3 oz (80 g) Coconut flakes

For the Currant Sauce
7 tbsp (100 g) Granulated sugar
7 tbsp (10 cl) Crème de cassis
¾ cup (200 ml) Redcurrant juice
7 tbsp (100 ml) Red wine
2 tbsp (20 g) Cornstarch

Blanch the figs and shock in ice water. Peel and poke several times with a fork. Mix together the crème de cassis and simple syrup and pour over the figs. Let marinate for several hours.

For the batter, mix flour, salt, oil, white wine, and egg yolks. Beat the egg whites, add granulated sugar, and beat to stiff peaks. Fold the egg whites and coconut flakes into the egg yolks. Heat a good amount of oil in a deep pan. Let the figs drain well, dip them in the batter (works best on a toothpick) and fry in the hot oil for 6–8 minutes, until golden brown. Let drain on paper towels.

For the currant sauce, caramelize sugar in a pan. Pour in crème de cassis, redcurrant juice, and red wine. Let boil. Mix in cornstarch with a bit of water to thicken the sauce. Pour the sauce onto a dish and place the figs on top.

Garnish Recommendation: fresh strawberries and vanilla ice cream (see p. 350)

CARPACCIO OF BABY PINEAPPLE WITH COCONUT PINEAPPLE GRATIN

Ingredients for 6 Servings

For the Gratin
3 Baby pineapples
1.5 oz (40 g) Coconut meat, unsweetened
2 Sheets gelatin
4 tsp (2 cl) Coconut liqueur
1 Egg white
4 tsp (20 g) Granulated sugar
7 tbsp (100 ml) Whipped cream

For the Carpaccio
2 Baby pineapples
⅔ cup (80 g) Confectioner's sugar
¼ cup (50 ml) Jamaica rum

For the Gratinating Sauce
3 Egg yolks
3 tbsp (50 g) Granulated sugar
4 tsp (2 cl) Coconut liqueur
1 Sheet gelatin
1 oz (30 g) Coconut flakes
Confectioner's sugar for dusting

For the gratin, cut the green off the pineapples. Cut the pineapples in half, scoop out, and purée and sieve the fruit. Add cold water to the gelatin and remove excess water. Warm the coconut liqueur slightly, dissolve the gelatin in it, and stir into the pineapple purée along with the coconut meat. Beat the egg white to stiff peaks with the sugar and fold into the pineapple along with the whipped cream. Fill the empty pineapple halves and chill for 2 hours.

For the Carpaccio, peel the baby pineapples and remove the stem with an apple corer. Cut the fruit into thin slices. Dust with confectioner's sugar, drizzle with rum, and marinate for half an hour.

For the gratinating sauce, beat egg yolks with granulated sugar and coconut liqueur in a double boiler until creamy. Add water to the gelatin, remove excess water, and dissolve in the hot egg mixture. Beat until cold in an ice bath. Fold in the coconut flakes. Spread the gratinating sauce over the pineapple halves and brown for 2–3 minutes in an oven preheated to maximum heat.

Portion the Carpaccio onto plates, place a pineapple half in the middle of each, and dust with confectioner's sugar.

Bake Time: 2–3 minutes

Bake Temperature: Maximum upper heat

Garnish Recommendation: Piña colada sorbet (see p. 363)

A Pinecone Gets Ahead

When Christopher Columbus landed on the island of Guadeloupe in 1493, his men quickly became aware of a particularly refreshing and juicy food that was called "nana meant" by the indigenous people, which means "delicious fruit." The seamen changed the name to "ananas," the genus of the pineapple and its name in many languages. The pineapple is still the culinary emblem of the Caribbean. However, the origin of the pineapple is not the Caribbean, but rather most likely Brazil, where the French and English got a hold of them and brought them to Europe in the sixteenth century. The English called the fruit a pineapple because of its similarity to a pine cone.

STRAWBERRY WITH GREEN PEPPERCORNS AND GRAND MARNIER

Wash the strawberries. Cut large ones in half and marinate the berries in confectioner's sugar and lemon juice. In a pan, froth half of the butter. Add the peppercorns, strawberries, and sugar, and stir. Deglaze with Grand Marnier and flavor with orange and lemon juice. Before serving, stir the rest of the butter into the sauce. Serve the strawberries in deep dishes and garnish with mint.

Garnish Recommendation: Vanilla saffron ice cream (see p. 352) or sour ice cream (see p. 355)

Tip: If you use freeze dried green pepper, you must soak it in water first.

Ingredients
14 oz (400 g) Strawberries
Confectioner's sugar and
  lemon juice to marinate
5½ tbsp (80 g) Butter
2 tbsp (1 kL) Green peppercorns
3 tbsp (4 cl) Grand Marnier
2 tbsp Confectioner's sugar
¼ cup (6 cl) Orange juice
2 tsp (1 cl) Lemon juice
Mint to garnish

BERRIES WITH ALMOND AMARETTO FOAM AU GRATIN

Ingredients
14 oz (400 g) Berries, according to taste
2 tbsp (3 cl) Amaretto
3 tbsp (50 g) Confectioner's sugar
3.5 oz (100 g) Peach purée (see p. 200)

For the Almond Amaretto Foam
2 oz (50 g) Almonds, grated
2 Egg yolks
½ cup (60 g) Confectioner's sugar
3.5 oz (100 g) Pastry cream (see p. 247)
⅓ cup (8 cl) Amaretto
¼ cup (60 ml) Whipped cream

Marinate the washed berries with amaretto and confectioner's sugar. Portion the peach purée into deep dishes and spread the berries on top. For the foam, beat the egg yolks with confectioner's sugar and amaretto until creamy. Fold in the pastry cream, almonds, and whipped cream. Spread the foam on the berries and cook about ½ minute, until golden brown, in an oven preheated to maximum heat (or in the broiler).

Bake Time: about ½ minute

Bake Temperature: Maximum upper heat

Garnish Recommendation: cream ice cream (see p. 353) or honey ice cream (see p. 354)

APPLE RISOTTO WITH CHIPS

Ingredients
9 oz (250 g) Risotto rice
4 Apples (Granny Smith), peeled and cored
7 tbsp (100 g) Sugar
3 tbsp (4 cl) White wine
2 cups (500 ml) Milk
1 Vanilla bean
1 Cinnamon stick
Juice of 1 lemon
1½ tbsp (20 g) Butter
Apple chips (see p. 206)

Let butter begin to melt in a pan and briefly sauté the rice. Add the sugar, and when it begins to caramelized, deglaze with wine and infuse with milk. Slice open the vanilla bean and add to the pan along with the cinnamon stick. Now let the risotto cook, stirring occasionally. Slice the apple thinly. When the risotto is almost done, remove the cinnamon sticks, add the apples, and flavor with lemon juice. Serve with apple chips, prepared according to the recipe.

Cook Time: 18–20 minutes

Garnish Recommendation: Apple ginger sorbet (see p. 361)

STEWED HONEY PEACH WITH LAVENDER ICE CREAM AND ELDERBERRY PURÉE

Preheat oven to 320°F (160°C). Boil the Riesling and sugar. Add the peaches for 2 minutes, then take out and peel. Arrange the peaches in a casserole dish. Add the lavender flowers to the Riesling mixture and reduce to half. Remove the lavender. Stir honey into the mixture and pour over the peaches. Bake for 40 minutes. Remove from oven, let cool just briefly, and place each warm peach on a plate. Scoop lavender ice cream next to each peach. Spoon elderberry purée onto each and dust with confectioner's sugar.

Bake Time: 40 minutes

Bake Temperature: 320°F (160°C)

Garnish Recommendation: vanilla foam (see p. 203)

Ingredients for 5 Servings
2 cups (500 ml) Riesling
⅓ cup (80 g) Granulated sugar
⅔ cup (250 g) Honey
8 Peaches
4 Lavender flowers
14 oz (400 g) Lavender ice cream (see p. 355)
14 oz (400 g) Elderberry purée (see p. 180)
Confectioner's sugar for dusting

From the Honey Cane

It is hard to believe, but until the nineteenth century, the word "sweet" was used almost exclusively in relation to honey, not sugar. Only the truly rich could afford cane sugar, which had to be imported from exotic lands at outrageous prices. Honey, on the other hand, like bees, there was more than enough of. Already by the fourth century, Apicius had collected numerous ancient sweet recipes like boiled ostrich in honey, flamingo with dates and honey, and eggs with honey on top, which display sweetness as the vade mecum of roman gourmet cooking. And as we know from Emperor Nero's house books, 400,000 silver coins were paid for honey alone for a banquet at his court.

In addition to bee's honey, cooks from Assyria to Palestine used date honey, pressed from the fruit, and palm honey or palm juice as sweetener. The word "honey" became synonymous with sweet in early antiquity. So it's no surprise that when people first became aware of sugar cane in the time of Alexander the Great, they called it "honey cane."

The Sweet Pantry

COMPOTE, MARMALADES, SWEET SAUCES, HAND CRAFTED JUICES, AND CARAMELIZED FRUITS

PRESERVES AND COMPOTE

What was once taken for granted by every housewife—marinating, preserving, and canning fruit for winter—is nowadays usually delegated to the delicatessen, where these preserves cost quite a bit. Preserved fruit, marmalade, and gelatin taste best when you prepare them yourself—but, of course, only when you use the best quality fruit.

The Best Apples for the Sweet Kitchen

The apple—Malus domestica—was derived from wild apples and belongs to the rose family. The oldest fossils of apple seeds were discovered in findings from the Tertiary period. Apples have been cultivated since very early on, certainly since the ancient Egyptians, who placed apples in their pharaohs' tombs as provisions for the journey to the afterlife. Of the approximately 50 varieties that are available today, the following are particularly suited to sweet cooking:

COX ORANGE: *Sweet, juicy, and aromatic. Cultivated in 1825 in Buckinghamshire. Season: end of September–mid-November. Ideal for apple strudel, but also for nibbling while you work.*

GLOSTER: *Mildly tart winter apple with juicy and tender flesh. Cultivated in 1969 in Germany. Harvest: October. Ideal for low sugar desserts and stewing.*

GOLDEN DELICIOUS: *Very crisp, sweet flesh. Cultivated in 1890 in West Virginia. Season: October–January. The optimal ingredient for compotes and fruit salads.*

GRAVENSTEINER: *Juicy, very firm, sweet-sour, intensely fragrant. First cultivated in 1669 in Jutland. Season: end of August–end of September. Particularly suited to all kinds of apple cake as well as to baked or dried apples.*

JONAGOLD: *A particularly well-balanced sweet-sour content. Cultivated in 1943 in New York State. Season: beginning of October–mid-December. As good for apple sauce and compote as for apple cake, apple pie, etc.*

APPLE COMPOTE

Ingredients
4 Apples
⅓ cup (80 g) Granulated
   sugar
2 tbsp Lemon juice
Calvados (apple brandy)
¼ cup (50 ml) White wine
7 tbsp (100 ml) Apple juice
½ Cinnamon stick
Dash of vanilla sugar
Raisins
½ tbsp Vanilla pudding mix
Rum to cover
Some water

Preheat oven to 340 °F (170 °C). Peel and core the apples then cut them into slices. Caramelize sugar in a pan. Toss the apples in the sugar and deglaze with lemon juice and Calvados. Pour in the white wine and apple juice, then add the vanilla sugar, cinnamon, and raisins. Cover with parchment paper and let set in the oven until the apples are soft. Stir the vanilla pudding mix with some water and thicken the mixture with it. Fill a hot rinsed canning jar with apple compote. Heat the rum, light it, and pour over the apple compote. Close the jar or jars tightly.

APPLESAUCE

Ingredients
35 oz (1 kg) Apples
Juice of 2 lemons
1 Cinnamon stick
3 Cloves
¼ cup (65 ml) White wine,
   preferably Riesling
¼ cup (65 ml) Water
1 cup less 2 tbsp (200 g)
   Granulated sugar

Peel, quarter, and core the apples. Boil until soft with water, white wine, granulated sugar, lemon juice, cinnamon sick, and cloves. Remove the spices and sieve.

STEWED PLUMS

Ingredients
35 oz (1 kg) Plums
7 tbsp (150 g) Honey
4 tsp (2 cl) Water
4 tsp (2 cl) Slivovitz
5 Cloves
1 Cinnamon stick

Wash, halve, and pit the plums. Break up the cinnamon and place in a burlap spice bag with the cloves. Boil the water with honey and the spice bag. Add the plums and slowly cook until they are soft. Let cool, remove the spice bag, and flavor with slivovitz. Store well sealed.

PEAR COMPOTE

Ingredients
35 oz (1 kg) Pears
Juice of 2 lemons
1¼ cup (300 ml) Water
¾ cup (200 ml) White wine,
  preferably Traminer
1 cup plus 2 tbsp (250 g)
  Granulated sugar
Pulp of 1 vanilla bean
1 Cinnamon stick
3 Cloves
Zest of 1 lemon and
  1 orange
3 tbsp (4 cl) Pear brandy

Peel, core, and quarter the pears. Boil the sugar with the white wine until lightly caramelized. Pour in the water. Add the pear pieces, vanilla pulp, cinnamon, cloves, lemon juice, and orange and lemon zest. Let the whole mixture come to a boil. Remove from heat and let sit. Flavor with pear brandy. Fill hot rinsed canning jars. Heat the rum, light it, and pour into the jars. Shut the jars tightly.

Pears—Not Just for Hélène

It's not only bookkeepers and accountants who heed the popular wisdom that apples and pears should not be mixed. You can also take it literally. Although apples and pears are always named in the same breath (and both belong to the rose family), they really have little in common. Without a doubt, the apple has the worse image of the two. It is not only responsible for Eve's fall, it is also considered earthy, peasant, and sour.

In contrast, the pear is not only less sour and with a much more subtle, seductive aroma than the apple, its form conveys and elegance which has always afforded it a place on the plates of the rich. Even Homer sang about the pear tree in his "Odyssey." Originally, this bottle shaped fruit came from Asia Minor, where the ancient Greeks found it and created almost an edible saint out of it. In the year 1 ACE, when the Greek doctor Dioscorides grappled with the pear from a medical perspective, Greece had already adopted the nickname of "Pearland." The area known as Apia was even officially named after the pear. When Plinius, the great Roman naturalist, counted 21 varieties of pear in his natural history work, the Pyrus communis had already spread through the entire Roman Empire, as well as the Germanic provinces. The Roman colonizers pressed a juice that they called "piracium," which simply means "pear cider."

Since that time, the pear family has grown significantly. At the turn of this century, there were around 1,300 varieties of pear just in Europe. Upscale patisseries treasure the Bartlett pear (mid-August–October) most of all, due to its tender vanilla taste. But the most famous pear in the world is not a variety, but rather a sinfully sweet ice cream dessert of Bartlett pears, vanilla ice cream, and chocolate sauce which was first served on the occasion of the opening night of Offenbach's operetta, "La belle Hélène," and almost surpassed its popularity as the "Hélène pear."

ELDERBERRY PURÉE

Boil red wine with the sugar, honey, and cinnamon stick. Add the elderberries and boil down slowly for about 15 minutes. After 10 minutes, mix in the applesauce or cubed apples. Mix cornstarch with some cold water at your discretion and thicken the purée with it. Finally, season with ginger.

Use: as an addition to quark desserts or kaiserschmarren

Tips:

- Use elderberry season to prepare a larger amount of elderberry purée. It can be frozen without a problem and used in the winter for a fruity change of pace.
- Beware of snacking on elderberries as you pick them in late summer. Raw, they contain a toxic substance that causes nausea and headache, but it is safe after being heated over 212 °F (100 °C)

Ingredients
1 cup (250 ml) Red wine
7 tbsp (100 g) Sugar
2 tbsp Honey
1 Cinnamon stick
1 tbsp (½ kL) Ground ginger
5 oz (150 g) Elderberries
4 tbsp Applesauce or
  2 apples cut into cubes
About 1 tbsp cornstarch

Wild Hunt for Love

The wood of the European Black Elderberry (Sambucus nigra) is entwined in many legends. In pagan times, the elder or "Holder" was the seat of the Goddess Freia, also called Holder, Holla, or Holle. She was honored and feared as the goddess of love as well at the leader of the ghostly Wild Hunt. The berry-like elder fruits, which are rich in vitamins and minerals, are very useful in sweet cooking as well as in the farmer's pantry. The Austrian variety known as Haschberg are particularly aromatic.

Sweet Chaos

Compote probably comes from the Russian "kompot," a thirst-quenching, nonalcoholic drink as well as a "chaos" of different foods. It was Viennese cuisine that first brought a system to the compote chaos. It differentiates between classic compote, which uses just one fruit as its base, which can be whole, halved, or quartered and is stewed in a sugar solution. Closely related to compote is the stewed fruit which originated in Bohemia, most commonly prepared with plums, apricots, and elderberries. It is neither a compote nor a purée. The fruit should be half broken down, but not cooked to a mush. Fruit should only be cooked that much in the case of purée, such as fruit marmalade or classic plum jam. To complete the confusion, Austrian and German dialects have their own words for each of these.

LINGONBERRY COMPOTE

Sort and wash the Lingonberries. Mix with the granulated sugar on low in a mixer with the dough hook attachment until the sugar has completely dissolved. Fill hot rinsed canning jars with the Lingonberries. Heat the rum, light it, and cover the Lingonberries with it. Close the jars tightly.

Lingonberries against Gout

Lingonberries are the fruit of the Vaccinium vitis-idaea *(literally "vine of Mount Ida") of the heather family. Because it is rich in arbutin, tannins, and vitamin C, it is considered to be an effective remedy for diarrhea, flatulence, bladder problems, gout, and rheumatism. Lingonberries are most at home as an addition to game cooking and grilling, but their flesh is also a beloved source of color and flavor in the sweet kitchen.*

Ingredients
18 oz (500 g) Lingonberries
1½ cups (350 g) Granulated
   sugar
Rum to cover

GRAPE COMPOTE

Boil white wine with sugar and honey. Add the washed grapes, remove from heat, and let set. Flavor with grappa.

Wine in Dessert

Everyone who has ever had a glass of sweet Austrian wine such as an Ausbruch or Trockenbeerenauslese knows that wine can be a dessert. (These wines, by the way, make very good gelatin.) The wine grape Vitis vinifera *has a particularly tasty spot not only in Austrian strudel, tortes, schnitten, and crèmes, but also in the form of table grapes, such as the Regina, Italia, Irsai Olivér, Isabella, Muscat, Romulus, or Venus.*

Ingredients
35 oz (1 kg) Grapes
1 cup (250 ml) White wine,
   preferably Traminer
⅔ cup (150 g) Granulated
   sugar
2 tbsp plus 1 tsp (50 g)
   Honey
3 tbsp (4 cl) Grappa

ORANGE RAGOUT

Ingredients for 10 Servings
⅓ cup (80 g) Sugar
Juice of 8 oranges
⅓ cup (8 cl) Grand Marnier
3 tbsp Grenadine
Some cornstarch
10 Oranges, in slices
Some water

Caramelize the sugar to a golden color in a pot and deglaze with orange juice. Pour in Grand Marnier and grenadine and boil halfway. Mix some cornstarch with cold water and thicken the juice with it. Let cool and then add the orange slices.

Use: served cold or slightly warmed with sweet dishes such as chocolate soufflé or semolina dumplings

Fruits of the Cedar
The fruit of the orange tree is the most successful citrus fruit in the world (in the USA alone, 25 billion oranges are harvested yearly), and is available in two main varieties: blond oranges (e.g. Florida, Jaffa, Navel, Sunkist, Valencia) and blood oranges (e.g. Moro, Sanguine, Tarocco). The word "orange" originally comes from Sanskrit and means "cedar apple."

BURGUNDY SOUR CHERRIES

Ingredients
9 oz (250 g) Sour cherries
(can be substituted with sweet cherries), pitted
1 cup (250 ml) Burgundy
(can be substituted with another full red wine)
4 tbsp Honey
1 tbsp Vanilla pudding mix
4 tsp (20 g) Vanilla sugar
⅓ cup (80 g) Granulated sugar
¼ cup (6 cl) Kirsch
Dash of Coriander
3 tbsp Water

Boil the burgundy with honey, vanilla sugar, granulated sugar, and coriander. Reduce to a third. Stir the vanilla pudding mix with the water and sit into the red wine blend. Remove from heat, add cherries, and let set. Season with kirsch.

Use: as garnish for warm baked goods such as cream schmarren or quark soufflé

Tip: Burgundy cherries taste best when served warm.

Berry ragout

Ingredients
10.5 oz (300 g) Berries,
  according to taste (such as
  blackberries, raspberries,
  blueberries)
2 cups (500 ml) Red wine
¼ cup (80 g) Honey
2 tsp (10 g) Vanilla sugar
3 tbsp (4 cl) Grand Marnier

Ingredients
18 oz (500 g) Wild
  strawberries
¼ cup (5 cl) Lemon juice
¼ cup (5 cl) Orange juice
½ cup plus 1 tbsp (130 g)
  Granulated sugar
4 tbsp (20 g) Vanilla sugar
3 tbsp (4 cl) Cognac

BERRY RAGOUT

Let the red wine, vanilla sugar, and honey slowly cook down until the liquid is the consistency syrup. Remove from heat.

Add the washed berries and Grand Marnier, fill canning jars, and close tightly.

WILD STRAWBERRY COULIS

Briefly boil the lemon juice, orange juice, vanilla sugar, and granulated sugar. Mix with half of the wild strawberries. Pass through a fine sieve. Mix in the rest of the strawberries and flavor with cognac.

Sweet and Sour Cherries
Sweet cherries are most suited to cherry cakes. The tart form of this beloved stone fruit is the sour cherry, which has many more uses, from sour cherry marmalade to black forest torte as well as gelatin and fruit sauce.

PRESERVED RHUBARB

Peel the rhubarbs, cut off the ends, and slice into ½-1 in (1–2 cm) wide pieces. Bring the white wine, water, vanilla sugar, granulated sugar, lemon juice, and vanilla bean to a boil. Place the rhubarb pieces in the boiling liquid and then remove from heat. Chop the lemon balm coarsely and place in a spice bag.

Add the spice bag to the rhubarbs, cover with foil, and let sit overnight in a cool place. Remove the spice bag. Fill hot rinsed canning jars, heat the rum, light it, pour over the rhubarbs, and close the jars tightly.

Ingredients
18 oz (500 g) Rhubarbs
½ cup (125 ml) White wine, preferably Riesling
½ cup (125 ml) Water
4 tsp (20 g) Vanilla sugar
⅔ cup (150 g) Granulated sugar
Juice of 2 lemons
1 Vanilla bean
½ Bunch lemon balm
Rum to cover

*The ancient Greeks called this sour stalk—somewhat disrespectfully—
"Rha barbarous" or "root of a foreign tuber," though its delicately bitter
taste is perfect for taking the edge off sweetness. Whether in compote or
cake, old Viennese dessert cuisine loves the rhubarb, particularly in the
time between April and July, as a non-musical counterpoint. After August,
rhubarbs should be avoided for health reasons.*

PRESERVED DRIED PEARS AND PLUMS

Ingredients
18 oz (500 g) Dried pears
10.5 oz (300 g) Dried plums
1¾ cup (400 g) Granulated
  sugar
4¼ (1 l) Red wine
2 cups (500 ml) Water
4 tsp (20 g) Vanilla sugar
2 tbsp (1 kL) Ground ginger
3 Cinnamon sticks
5 Cloves
¼ cup (6 cl) Lavender juice
  (see p. 205)
½ cup (12 cl) Poire Williams

Boil the red wine, water, cinnamon sticks, cloves, sugar, vanilla
sugar, dried pears, and dried plums. Remove from heat and
flavor with ginger, lavender juice, and Poire Williams. Fill hot
rinsed canning jars and close tightly.

Tip: The fruit can be thickened to the desired consistency with
a bit of cornstarch.

Acidic, Bitter, or What?

*The apricot (*Prunus armeniaca, *Latin for Armenian plum) is native to
Europe and is known as an Austrian specialty, but it originally came from
Asia Minor. From there, the proto-apricots were spread through Rome
by merchants. And the ancient Romans brought the "amerellum" (which,
unbelievably, means acidic, sharp, and bitter) north. When Lauriacum was
excavated near Linz, ancient apricot pits were found in amphoras. Wachau
apricots were first mentioned in writing in 1679. Since then, apricots have
become a pillar of Austrian dessert cuisine thanks to apricot dumplings,
strudel, cake, and marmalade. (See recipe on p. 188.)*

PRESERVED APRICOTS

Cut the apricots in half, blanch in boiling water, shock in ice water, and peel off the skin. Quarter and pit the apricots. Boil the white wine with the sugar, vanilla sugar, vanilla bean, and lemon juice. Add the apricots, remove from heat, and let set. Flavor with apricot Eau de Vie. Fill hot rinsed canning jars. Heat the rum, light it, and cover the apricots. Close the jars tightly.

Ingredients
12 Apricots
1 cup (250 ml) White wine
⅝ cup (125 g) Granulated sugar
½ Vanilla bean
1¾ tbsp (20 g) Vanilla sugar
Juice of 1 lemon
3 tbsp (4 cl) Apricot Brandy
Rum to cover

PRESERVED PEACHES

Ingredients
35 oz (1 kg) Peaches
4 cups (900 g) Sugar
¾ cup (200 ml) White wine
¾ cup (200 ml) Water
2 Cinnamon sticks
5 Cloves
10.5 oz (300 g) Glucose syrup
  (can be substituted with
  simply syrup, see p. 40)
2 cups (450 ml) Whisky
  (Bourbon)

Slowly bring the sugar, wine, water, cinnamon, and cloves to a boil. Half and pit the peaches. Blanch the peaches in the slowly boiling mixture and peel off the skin. Let the liquid boil a bit longer, then pass through a sieve and add the sugar syrup and whisky. Put the peaches in hot rinsed canning jars, pour the mixture over them, and place 1 clove and 1 cinnamon stick in each jar. Close the jars tightly.

Not just for Melba

The Romans called the juicy peach a Persian apple. Many natural healers still rely on its diuretic and expectorant effects. Master patissiers also swear and swore on it, above all the great Auguste Escoffier, who invented the presumably most famous peach dish: the "Peach Melba," created for the coloratura soprano Nellie Melba.

PRESERVED RAISINS

Ingredients
35 oz (1 kg) Raisins
2 cups (450 g) Granulated
  sugar
⅓ cup (80 g) Vanilla sugar
4¼ cups (1 l) White wine
2 Cinnamon sticks
Zest of one ½ lemon
Zest of one ½ orange
¼ cup (6 cl) Port wine
¼ cup (6 cl) Rum

Mix together all the ingredients except the rum and let sit for 24 hours in the refrigerator. Then bring to a boil once and fill hot rinsed canning jars. Heat the rum, light it, and pour over the raisins. Close the jars well.

Use: as an addition to various warm sweet dishes like kaiserschmarren, but also an ingredient for apple strudel

Raisins, Zante Currants, Sultanas

When top confectioners can pick out their raisins, they mostly choose dried wine grapes. They are big, reddish raisins with pits and a thick peel, different in appearance and taste from sultanas and Zante currants.

CARDAMOM BERRIES

Boil the red wine with redcurrant juice, honey, granulated sugar, and vanilla sugar, and reduce to half. Stir the vanilla pudding mix with 1tbsp water and thicken the mixture with it. Remove from heat and stir in the berries, cardamom, and ginger. Fill a hot rinsed canning jar, close tightly, and put in a cool place.

Use: as an addition to various desserts, such as cream schmarren or chocolate soufflé

Ingredients
½ cup (125 ml) Red wine
½ cup (250 ml) Redcurrant juice
3 tbsp Honey
1 tbsp Vanilla pudding mix
4 tsp (20 g) Vanilla sugar
⅓ cup (80 g) Granulated sugar
14 oz (400 g) Mixed berries (redcurrants, blackberries, raspberries, wild strawberries, or blueberries)
1 tbsp (½ kL) Cardamom
Pinch of ground ginger
1 tbsp Water

KUMQUATS WITH STAR ANISE

Quickly blanch the kumquats (drop into boiling water) and then shock in ice water. Remove, halve, and pit. Boil the sugar and water for 5 minutes, pour in the orange juice, and boil for a few more minutes. Add lemon juice, grenadine, star anise, and kumquats. Mix the Grand Marnier and Jamaica rum with cornstarch, stir into the ragout, and let boil briefly one more time.

Tip: The kumquat, which originates in East Asia, is mostly used in the modern patisserie as seasoning and decoration due to its distinctive, delicate bitterness. Kumquats taste best warm, perhaps as a delicious addition to an airy chocolate soufflé.

Ingredients
16 oz (450 g) Kumquats
1 cup less 2 tbsp (200 g) Granulated sugar
¾ cup (200 ml) Water
¾ cup (200 ml) Orange juice
2 tsp (1 cl) Grenadine
Juice of one ½ lemon
4 Star anise fruits
¼ cup (6 cl) Grand Marnier
4 tsp (2 cl) Jamaica rum
2 tbsp (20 g) Cornstarch

MARMALADE

Marmalades accompany foodies through the entire year: every day at breakfast or a coffee break, as an essential ingredient of so many sweet pastries, tortes, schnitten, and cakes, or as an important part of many warm desserts, from palatschinken to French toast. Here we present you delicious marmalade recipes that can't go wrong.

BLACKBERRY MARMALADE

Wash the blackberries. Place in a pot with preserving sugar, orange zest, and lemon juice. Cover and let sit overnight in a cool place.

Then bring to a boil, stirring constantly, and let boil briskly for 5–7 minutes. Remove from heat and pass through a fine sieve. Fill hot rinsed canning jars with the hot marmalade, close tightly, and put in a cool place.

Ingredients
35 oz (1 kg) Blackberries
35 oz (1 kg) Preserving sugar
Zest of 1 orange
4 tsp (2 cl) Lemon juice

Blackberries against Sugar

*The fruit of the blackberry bush (*Rubus fruticosus*), which belongs to the rose family, can be found in both wild and cultivated variations. There are styptic, anti-inflammatory, and antidiabetic properties attributed to the blackberry. One of the youngest varieties is the thornlessly cultivated "Thornfree." The Choctaw, Navajo, and Loch Ness varieties are also particularly delicious*

STRAWBERRY MARMALADE

Ingredients
35 oz (1 kg) Strawberries, without stems
35 oz (1 kg) Preserving sugar
Zest of 1 lemon
4 tsp (2 cl) Orange juice

Wash the strawberries and place in a pot with preserving sugar, lemon zest, and orange juice. Cover and let sit overnight in a cool place.

Bring to a boil, stirring constantly, and let boil for 5–7 minutes. Remove from heat and pass through a fine sieve. Fill hot rinsed canning jars with the hot marmalade, close tightly, and put in a cool place.

Tip: If you are fond of the typical seedy texture of berry marmalades, you can skip sieving.

Pretty Girls in the Garden
*The strawberry is, botanically speaking, a "false fruit," but it tastes all the more fruity for it. It has a purifying effect on the blood, is anti-inflammatory, and helps digestion. A total of about four hundred varieties of garden strawberries (*Fragaria ananassa*) of the Rosaceae family are known. Among them is a typical Austrian variation known by the name of "Schöne Wienerin" or "pretty Viennese girl." In upscale patisseries, highly fragrant little wild strawberries enjoy a particular popularity.*

APRICOT MARMALADE

Ingredients
2.5 lbs (1.2 kg) Apricots, fully ripe
35 oz (1 kg) Preserving sugar
4 tsp (2 cl) Lemon juice
4 tsp (2 cl) Apricot Eau de Vie

Pit and quarter the apricots. Boil with the lemon juice and preserving sugar in a shallow pot. While boiling, blend or mash the apricots and then let boil for 5 minutes. Sieve and flavor with the apricot Eau de Vie. Fill hot rinsed canning jars with the hot marmalade, close tightly, and put in a cool place.

REDCURRANT MARMALADE

Remove the currants from the stems and place in a bowl with preserving sugar and orange zest. Cover and let sit overnight in a cool place. Boil in a pot for 5 minutes and mash the currants while boiling. Sieve if you prefer. Fill hot rinsed canning jars with the hot marmalade, close tightly, and put in a cool place.

Tip: You can make gooseberry marmalade with the same recipe. In this case, replace the orange zest with lemon zest or a splash of white wine.

Sweet or Tart?

The refreshingly sour redcurrant is well suited to cakes, marmalade, gelatin, and tortes. Blackcurrants, with their distinctive sharp, sweet taste are more for marmalade and gelatin than baked goods. On the other hand, the less common (and milder) white currant is perfect for eating.

Ingredients
2.5 lbs (1.2 kg) Redcurrants
35 oz (1 kg) Preserving sugar
Zest of 1 orange

WILD BERRY MARMALADE

Place the berries in a bowl with preserving sugar, orange zest, and lemon juice and let sit overnight in a cool place. Bring to boil in a pot and let boil for 5 minutes. Blend the berries and flavor with Grand Marnier. Fill hot rinsed canning jars with the hot marmalade, close tightly, and put in a cool place.

Ingredients
2.5 lbs (1.2 kg) Wild berries, according to taste, without stems
35 oz (1 kg) Preserving sugar
Zest of 1 orange
2 tsp (1 cl) Lemon juice
4 tsp (2 cl) Grand Marnier

Plum Marmalade

Wash, pit, and quarter the plums. Place in a bowl with the preserving sugar and vanilla sugar and chill overnight. Bring to a boil and let boil for 5 minutes in a pot. Blend, sieve, and flavor with slivovitz. Fill hot rinsed canning jars with the hot marmalade, close tightly, and put in a cool place.

Ingredients
3.3 lbs (1.5 kg) Plums
35 oz (1 kg) Preserving sugar
3 tbsp (40 g) Vanilla sugar
4 tsp (2 cl) Slivovitz

Plums Aren't Just Plums

This stone fruit, which originated in Asia Minor and which was brought to Europe by the Romans in 150 BCE, is as appetizing as it is good for digestion. It can be found in about 2,000 varieties, particularly around the Mediterranean and in Central Europe. The most important are the cherry-sized, orange mirabelle plum, the commonly found Prunus domestica, *the yellow-green, firm greengage, and the sweet, juicy damson. All four varieties are suited to sweet cooking, however the damson is the classic plum for sweet Austrian cooking.*

Cherry Peppermint Marmalade

Wash and pit the cherries. Chop the peppermint coarsely and place in a burlap spice bag. Warm the simple syrup and add the peppermint bag, cherries, and preserving sugar. Cover and chill overnight. On the next day, remove the peppermint bag (squeeze it out well), bring the cherries to a boil and let boil for 5 minutes. Blend and sieve. Fill hot rinsed canning jars with the hot marmalade, close tightly, and put in a cool place.

Ingredients
2 cups (500 ml) Simple syrup (see p. 40)
1 Bundle of peppermint
5.5 lbs (2.5 kg) Sweet cherries
70 oz (2 kg) Preserving sugar

APPLE ELDERFLOWER MARMALADE WITH CARDAMOM

Ingredients
4.5 lbs (2 kg) Apples (Golden Delicious)
4.5 lbs (2 kg) Preserving sugar
Ground cardamom

For the Elderflower Syrup
2 cups (500 ml) Water
8 Elderflowers
18 oz (500 g) Preserving sugar
½ Lemon, cut into slices
⅓ oz (10 g) Citric acid

For the elderflower syrup, wash the elderflowers, and then put in a pot with the preserving sugar, lemon slices, and citric acid. Boil water and pour over the elderflower mixture. Cover and keep in a cool place overnight. Strain the syrup. Peel, core, and quarter the apples. Boil in preserving sugar and elderflower syrup, blend, and sieve. Flavor with cardamom to taste. Fill hot rinsed canning jars, close tightly, and put in a cool place.

PEACH VANILLA MARMALADE

Ingredients
2.5 lbs (1.2 kg) Peaches, fully ripe
35 oz (1 kg) Preserving sugar
4 tsp (2 cl) Lemon juice
4 tsp (2 cl) Peach liqueur
1 Vanilla bean

Pit and quarter the peaches. Bring to a boil with lemon juice and preserving sugar and let boil for 5 minutes. Blend and sieve. Bring the marmalade to a boil again and add the vanilla bean, halve lengthwise. Let boil for 2 more minutes. Remove the vanilla bean, scrape out the rest of the pulp, and add it to the marmalade. Remove from heat and stir in the peach liqueur. Fill hot rinsed canning jars with the hot marmalade, close tightly, and put in a cool place.

ORANGE, GRAPEFRUIT, AND LIME MARMALADE

Ingredients
4.5 lbs (2 kg) Oranges
18 oz (500 g) Grapefruits
10.5 oz (300 g) Limes
70 oz (2 kg) Preserving sugar

Peel the oranges and cut into slices. Put half of the peels in warm water and let sit for 24 hours. Change the water 3–4 times during this period. Squeeze the grapefruits and limes. Put the oranges together with the preserving sugar, lime juice, and grapefruit juice in a pot and let boil for 5 minutes. Blend and then sieve the marmalade. Remove the peels from the water, cut away the white parts, and cut into very small cubes. Mix the peel into the marmalade. Fill hot rinsed canning jars, close tightly, and put in a cool place.

Pear Marmalade with Chili

Peel, core, and quarter the pears. Bring to a boil with preserving sugar, citric acid, and lemon juice and let boil briskly for 5–7 minutes. Sieve or purée. Mix in the chili threads or finely chopped chili peppers to taste. Caution: too much chili will make the marmalade too spicy! Fill hot rinsed canning jars with the hot marmalade, close tightly, and put in a cool place.

Ingredients
5.5 lbs (2.5 kg) Pears (Gute
  Luise variety, if available)
70 oz (2 kg) Preserving sugar
1/3 oz (10 g) Citric acid
4 tsp (2 cl) Lemon juice
Chili threads or finely
  chopped chili peppers, to
  taste

1
Prepare the ingredients.

2
Peel and core the pears.
  Chop the chili finely or cut
  into thin threads.

3
Bring the pears to boil with
  the preserving sugar,
  lemon juice, and citric
  acid.

4
Let boil briskly for 5–7
  minutes. Let cool slightly
  and then purée with the
  immersion blender.

5
Sieve the pear marmalade
  and then add the chili.

FRUIT SAUCES AND OTHER SWEET SAUCES

The sweet kitchen is always the healthiest where fruits and berries are involved. Not least—or perhaps above all—are the sweet sauces, which also have their sinful chocolate side.

STRAWBERRY PURÉE

Wash the strawberries and purée with the simple syrup using an immersion blender. Pass through a fine sieve and flavor with Grand Marnier and strawberry liqueur.

Tip: If strawberries are not in season, you can of course use frozen fruit. Just let thaw and then prepare as described above.

Ingredients
35 oz (1 kg) Strawberries
  without stems
9–12 oz (250–350 g) Simple
  syrup (see p. 40), based
  on the sweetness of the
  berries
3 tbsp (4 cl) Grand Marnier
3 tbsp (4 cl) Strawberry
  liqueur

PEACH PURÉE (APRICOT PURÉE)

Wash the peaches or apricots, quarter, and pit. Purée in a blender along with simple syrup, vanilla sugar, and lemon juice then pass through a fine sieve. Flavor with peach liqueur and Cointreau.

Tips:

- If you make the purée out of white peaches, you will have the necessary fruit purée for the "Bellini" cocktail created by Arrigo Cipriani for Harry's Bar in Venice.
- Purists may peel the peaches first, but sieving the fruit ultimately has the same effect.

Ingredients
21 oz (600 g) Peaches (or
  apricots)
5 oz (150 g) Simple syrup
  (see p. 40)
2 tsp (10 g) Vanilla sugar
3 tbsp (4 cl) Lemon juice
3 tbsp (4 cl) Peach liqueur
4 tsp (2 cl) Cointreau

RASPBERRY PURÉE

Ingredients
35 oz (1 kg) Raspberries
About 9 oz (250 g) simple
   syrup (see p. 40), based
   on the sweetness of the
   berries
¼ cup (6 cl) Raspberry
   liqueur
Zest of 1 orange
Dash of ground ginger

Wash the raspberries and purée with the syrup and orange zest. Pass through a fine sieve and flavor with raspberry liqueur and ginger.

The Sweetest Rose
Of all the fruits in the rose family, the raspberry (Rubus idaeus) is without a doubt the sweetest and most enticing. Wild raspberries were already served as food for people by the Neolithic Age, but they have only been cultivated in gardens since the Middle Ages. The particularly flavorful raspberries that are common today first appeared in the Renaissance. But in Europe, they only grew a few kinds of raspberries, whereas in Asia, thought to be the origin of the raspberry, more than two hundred kinds were known.

BLUEBERRY SAUCE

Ingredients
18 oz (500 g) Blueberries
1¼ cups (160 g) Confectioner's sugar
3 tbsp (4 cl) Crème de cassis
   (redcurrant liqueur)
3 tbsp (4 cl) Blueberry
   liqueur

Sort and wash the blueberries, then purée them with the confectioner's sugar. Pass through a fine sieve and flavor with crème de cassis and blueberry liqueur.

A Berry like Red Wine
This fruit of a low bush in the Vaccinium family contains a high amount of tannins and is therefore used as a home remedy against diarrhea and bleeding gums. St. Hildegard von Bingen treasured this very useful berry and created a powder of dried red European blueberries for use against digestive trouble. She wrote that this powder "looks like red wine when mixed with water, and is lovely for quenching your thirst."

YOGURT LEMON SAUCE

Mix all ingredients together. Fold in the whipped cream before serving.

The Sour Charm of the Lemon Trees

The fruit of the lemon tree is most useful in the sweet kitchen exactly because of its natural sourness. Its juice it found in creams, gelatin, sorbets, and ice cream. Its peel flavors many dishes; succade (candied lemon peel) is an irreplaceable baking ingredient. It is the same for its relative, the lime. Unlike the lemon, the lime is seedless and possesses a finer, delicately bitter flavor that ensures it a special place in the modern dessert kitchen.

Ingredients
2 cups (500 ml) Whole milk
  yogurt
1 cup (120 g) Confectioner's
  sugar
⅓ cup (8 cl) Lemon juice
Zest of 2 lemons, fine
4 tbsp Whipped cream

CLASSIC VANILLA SAUCE

VARIATION I

Whisk the egg yolks and sugar until creamy. Add the milk and vanilla bean and slowly heat in a double boiler, until the egg yolks cause the sauce to thicken. Remove the vanilla bean, scrape the pulp into the sauce, and stir the sauce in an ice water bath until cool. Caution: Do not overheat otherwise the egg yolk will coagulate!

VARIATION II

Mix the vanilla pudding mix with 2–3 tbsp of milk and the egg yolks. Boil the rest of the milk with sugar and the vanilla bean. Remove the vanilla bean and scrape the pulp into the sauce. Mix the pudding mixture strongly into the sauce. Let boil up briefly, then stir in an ice bath until cool.

Ingredients
Variation I
6 Egg yolks
7 tbsp (100 g) Granulated
  sugar
2 cups (500 ml) Milk
½ Vanilla bean

Variation II
2 cups (500 ml) Milk
¼ cup (60 g) Sugar
½ Vanilla bean
⅓ oz (10 g) Vanilla pudding
  mix
2 Egg yolks

CANARY MILK

Ingredients
1 cup (220 ml) Milk
¼ cup (50 ml) Heavy cream
⅓ cup (70 g) Granulated
  sugar
Pulp of ½ a vanilla bean
4 Egg yolks
4 tsp (2 cl) Rum

In a double boiler, beat milk, cream, granulated sugar, vanilla pulp, rum, and egg yolks until creamy. Serve right away.

When Canaries Snack on Vanilla

It seems that canaries particularly like the thinner variation of classic vanilla sauce, since in Vienna they are its namesake. It is primarily used on ducat buchteln and milk cream strudel. Perhaps the reason for the relationship between canaries and vanilla is the exotic origins of both the bright songbird and of the aromatic fruit of the orchid, the most precious of which is considered to be Bourbon Vanilla from the island of Réunion (formerly Bourbon). Discriminating canaries—just like pampered foodies—would decline to snack on canary milk that was made with commercially produced vanilla sugar or synthetic vanilla extract instead of a scraped out vanilla bean. Instead of real vanilla, these products contain the synthetic vanilla replacement "vanillin," made of eugenol and guaiacol.

VANILLA FOAM

Ingredients for 4–6 Servings
1 cup (250 ml) Milk
4 tsp (20 g) Sugar
⅓ oz (10 g) Vanilla pudding
  mix

Boil the milk with the sugar. Mix the vanilla pudding mix with a bit of cold water and use it to thicken the milk. Use an immersion blender to foam up the sauce.

Use: as decoration for various desserts

SOUR CREAM FOAM

Put sour cream, milk, and confectioner's sugar in a pot and mix with an immersion blender until creamy.

Use: as a not-too-sweet addition to warm or cold fruity desserts

Ingredients
7 tbsp (100 ml) Sour cream
2 tbsp Milk
¼ cup (30 g) Confectioner's
   sugar

DARK CHOCOLATE SAUCE

Slowly bring milk, heavy cream, and honey to a boil and dissolve the chopped chocolate in it.

Ingredients
6.3 oz (180 g) Dark couverture
   chocolate or cooking
   chocolate, finely chopped
7 tbsp (100 ml) Milk
7 tbsp (100 ml) Heavy cream
1 tbsp (20 g) Honey

WHITE CHOCOLATE SAUCE

Chop the couverture and melt in a double boiler. Be careful not to overheat it! Stir in heavy cream, milk, and Grand Marnier.

Ingredients
7 oz (200 g) White couverture
   chocolate
⅔ cup (150 ml) Heavy cream
¼ cup (60 ml) Milk
4 tsp (2 cl) Grand Marnier

Lavender Pick-Me-Up

An old Viennese saying goes, "You could talk lavender away." It is used to indicate someone who is talking blooming nonsense. The lavender is blooming, too, but its use in the kitchen is anything but nonsense. The blue blossoms of the lavender plant (Lavandula angustifolia) *are not only good for the aromas of perfume makers, but also to give sweet (or sour) dishes a particularly fresh and irreplaceable flavor.*

JUICES

Juicing fruit is not witchcraft. Basically, all you need is a good fruit press or a juicer. The following two recipes are somewhat more refined, but still easy to prepare. And they are not only refreshing; their flavor gives sweet delicacies that special something.

ELDERFLOWER JUICE

Ingredients
8½ cups (2l) Water
2¼ cups (500 g) Granulated
  sugar
1 Lemon
15 Elderflowers
3 tbsp (4 cl) Lemon juice
3 tbsp (40 g) Granulated
  sugar for caramelizing
2 tbsp (6 cl) Vinegar

Boil the water with the sugar and remove from heat. Cut the lemon into slices and add to the liquid along with the elderflowers. Cover and chill for 2 days. Pour through a fine sieve or coffee filter. Melt the over granulated sugar to a light caramel and deglaze with lemon juice and vinegar. As soon as the caramel has dissolved, add to the elderflower juice. Fill canning jars that have been rinsed with hot water and close tightly.

LAVENDER JUICE

Ingredients for about 1 Liter
2½ cups (600 ml) Water
1½ cups (320 g) Granulated
  sugar
2 tbsp (30 g) Vanilla sugar
½ oz (15 g) Citric acid
2 oz (65 g) Lavender flowers
  and leaves

Briefly boil water with granulated sugar, vanilla sugar, and citric acid and remove from heat. Add the washed lavender and let cool. Sieve, fill canning jars that have been rinsed with hot water, and close tightly.

Use: as a refreshing summer drink mixed with mineral water ((4 cl) lavender juice to (0.2l) mineral water) or champagne, or as flavoring

Tips:

- Make sure that you do not boil the lavender mixture, otherwise the juice will become bitter!
- Use—as much as is possible for you—wild lavender, which thrives in higher regions and captivates with its distinct aroma, as opposed to cultured garden lavender.

CARAMELIZED FRUIT

Caramelizing fruit is a delicious way to create sweets that are even sweeter and more enticing. Those who do not wish to leave candying to the confectioners can do it at home without a big investment. The following two basic recipes are easy to modify for many situations.

APPLE CHIPS

Preheat oven to 320°F (160°C). Slice the unpeeled apples very thin, preferably with a bread cutter or mandolin. Lay the apple slices on a baking sheet lined with parchment paper, dust with confectioner's sugar, and caramelize in the oven for a few minutes.

Ingredients
2 Apples, cored
Confectioner's sugar

Bake Time: a few minutes

Bake Temperature: 320°F (160°C)

Use: as decoration for many desserts and sweet dishes, such as apple risotto (see p. 171)

Tips:

- For more delicate, if somewhat more time consuming, apple chips, place the raw apple slices in a vacuum bag with about 21oz (600 g) of simple syrup (see p. 40) and some lemon juice, blanch after 5 minutes, and then chill in ice water. Then take the apple slices out and let dry in the oven for about 8 hours at 120–140°F (50–60°C). Turn the chips over halfway through.
- You can prepare pear chips using the same recipe.

CARAMELIZED APRICOTS

Ingredients
8 Apricots
2 tbsp Sugar or vanilla
   sugar
3 tbsp Butter
1 cup (250 ml) Orange juice
Juice of ½ lemon

Wash and pit the apricots, then slice them thinly. Carefully warm sugar or vanilla sugar in a hot pan until it is liquefied and brown. Add butter and let melt. Add the fruit to the pan, pour in the orange and lemon juices, and cover to steam for a short amount of time. Continuously spoon the juices over the fruit. If the liquid gets too viscous, thin with a little bit of water.

Use: as decoration for countless desserts and sweet dishes

Tip: You can caramelized a multitude of other fruits (peaches, mangos, etc.) using the same recipe.

Snacking Doesn't Have to Be a Sin
THE SWEET HEALTH FOOD KITCHEN

WHOLE FOOD BAKING

Whole foods are not just something for health nuts. It means that healthy minerals, micronutrients, and other nutritious materials remain in the food. But it also signifies the preservation of the individual flavors of the ingredients. Don't be afraid to put it to the test.

The Ten Commandments of Healthy Baking

1. *Replace refined (white) sugar with natural syrups (e.g. pear syrup, molasses, barley malt, etc.) or local honey. However, in many cases (e.g. for confectioner's sugar or when beating egg whites), the "conventional" method is more convenient.*
2. *Try to make your desserts sweet using natural methods, such as using lots of fruit instead of sugar.*
3. *Substitute maple syrup for artificial sweeteners.*
4. *Replace white flour and superfine flour with freshly ground whole meal flour.*
5. *Replace animal fats such as butter or clarified butter with vegetable fats. Instead of gelatin, use agar-agar powder.*
6. *Avoid chemical or manufactured baking additives, food coloring, and artificial flavors. Use natural baking powder!*
7. *Instead of using bread or cake crumbs, use graham cracker or other whole grain crumbs. Many doughs can also be made crunchy by using cereal flakes.*
8. *Use low-fat dairy products!*
9. *For fruit desserts, use garden fruits grown organically and avoid heating them for too long, as it compromises their nutritional value.*
10. *Make sure that you use unsulphured raisins and dried fruits.*

WHOLE GRAIN VANILLA CRESCENTS

Ingredients
1 cup (150 g) Whole wheat
  flour
5 oz (150 g) Almond, ground
1 stick plus 2½ tbsp (150 g)
  Butter or untempered vegetable margarine, cold
⅓ cup (70 g) Raw cane sugar
1 Vanilla bean
2 Egg yolks
Confectioner's sugar mixed
  with vanilla pulp to dust

Preheat oven to 340 °F (170 °C). Mix the flour and almonds. Slice the vanilla bean the long way and scrape out the pulp. Cut the cold butter into small pieces and coat in the flour almond mixture. Add the sugar, vanilla pulp, and egg yolks and quickly knead to a smooth dough. Let rest in the refrigerator for about 10 minutes. Roll the dough into a log, cut off ⅓ oz (10 g) pieces, and shape them into crescents. Place the crescents on a baking sheet lined with parchment paper and bake for 10–15 minutes. Remove from the oven and dust with vanilla sugar while still warm.

Bake Time: 10–15 minutes

Bake Temperature: 340 °F (170 °C)

Tip: Since the warm crescents break very easily, it is a good idea to remove them from the baking sheet with the paper and let them cool.

WHOLE GRAIN CINNAMON STARS

Ingredients
1½ cups (125 g) Whole grain
  oats flakes
⅓ cup (50 g) Whole wheat
  flour
3 tbsp plus 2 tsp (75 g)
  Honey
1 oz (25 g) Almonds, ground
1 stick plus 1 tbsp (125 g)
  Butter or untempered
  vegetable margarine
1 tsp Cinnamon, ground
Zest of 1 lemon
Whole wheat flour for the
  work surface
Butter or untempered veg-
  etable margarine for the
  baking sheet

For the Glaze
4 tbsp Coconut flakes
2 tbsp Arrowroot starch
1 tbsp Milk
1 tbsp Honey

Preheat oven to 350 °F (180 °C). Lightly brown a quarter of the oats in a pan and let cool. Knead all the oats with flour, almonds, honey, butter, cinnamon, and lemon zest. Let rest 20 minutes in the refrigerator. For the glaze, put the coconut flakes in a food processor to make coconut flour. Mix this flour with arrowroot starch, milk, and honey. Roll out the dough 5 mm thick on a floured work surface. Cut out stars and brush them with the glaze. Place them on a buttered baking sheet and bake for about 10 minutes.

Bake Time: about 10 minutes

Bake Temperature: 350 °F (180 °C)

REDCURRANT MUFFINS

Ingredients for 12–15
Muffins

2½ cups (380 g) Whole
  wheat flour
4 tsp (20 g) Baking powder
10.5 oz (300 g) Redcurrants
  (or blackcurrants)
3 Eggs
1 cup (220 g) Brown sugar
2 sticks (220 g) Melted butter
  or untempered vegetable
  margarine
3 tbsp (20 g) Confectioner's
  sugar mixed with vanilla
  pulp
1¾ cups (400 ml) Fat free
  yogurt
Butter or vegetable
  margarine for the pan
Confectioner's sugar for
  dusting

Preheat oven to 350 °F (180 °C). Mix the flour and baking powder. Beat the eggs slightly and add the sugar, melted butter, and vanilla sugar. Stir in the yogurt. Fold in the washed, crushed currants and flour. Spoon the batter into buttered muffin pans and bake for 25 minutes. Let sit for 5 minutes in pans, then dust with confectioner's sugar and serve.

Bake Time: 25 minutes

Bake Temperature: 350 °F (180 °C)

1
Prepare the ingredients.

2
Beat the eggs and add the
  sugar and vanilla sugar.
  Stir in the liquid butter and
  then stir in the yogurt.

3
Fold in the flour mixed with
  the baking powder.

4
Fold in the crushed currants.

5
Spoon the batter into buttered muffin pans and
  bake as described above.

QUARK AND BUTTER CRESCENTS

Knead all the ingredients, except for the egg yolk and milk for egg wash, into a dough and form a log. Wrap in foil and let rest for an hour. Roll out the dough on a floured work surface to an 18x16 in (45x40 cm) rectangle. Cut in half the long way. Cut the two strips into triangles. Brush with melted butter and roll loosely into crescents (from the wide side to the point). Place the crescents on a buttered baking sheet. Mix egg yolks and milk and brush the crescents with the mixture. Let the crescents rise for about half an hour at 86 °F (30 °C). Preheat the oven to 375 °F (190 °C) and bake for about 25 minutes.

Bake Time: about 25 minutes

Bake Temperature: 375 °F (190 °C)

ANISE CURLS

Preheat oven to 350 °F (180 °C). Beat the eggs and sugar until somewhat creamy and fold in the whole wheat flour. Rub a baking sheet with light margarine or line with parchment paper. Spread small circles of batter onto the sheet, sprinkle with anise, and bake for 8–10 minutes, until golden brown. Remove from the baking sheet with a spatula while still warm and form curls over the handle of a cooking spoon. Let cool.

Bake Time: 8–10 minutes

Bake Temperature: 350 °F (180 °C)

Ingredients
2½ cups (250 g) Spelt flour
1 stick plus 1 tbsp (125 g) Butter or untempered vegetable margarine, room temperature
4.5 oz (125 g) Low-fat quark
2 Egg yolks
2 tbsp Milk
Salt
2 tbsp plus 1 tsp (20 g) Dry yeast
Flour for the work surface
About 2 tbsp (30 g) Butter or untempered vegetable margarine for the pan
1 Egg yolk mixed with
1 tbsp Milk for brushing

Ingredients
2 Eggs
¼ cup (50 g) Light brown sugar
¼ cup (40 g) Whole wheat flour
Light margarine
Anise

QUARK KOLACH (WHOLE FOOD)

Ingredients for the Leavened Dough

2⅓ cups (350 g) Whole wheat flour
Zest of 1 lemon
¾ cup (170 ml) Water, luke-warm
2 tbsp Soy flour
2 tbsp plus 1 tsp (20 g) Yeast
3 tbsp plus 1 tsp (70 g) Honey
Dash of salt
2 Egg yolks
2¾ tbsp (40 g) Butter or untempered vegetable margarine
Flour for the work surface
Butter or untempered vegetable margarine for the baking sheet

For the Filling

2 tbsp (30 g) Butter or untempered vegetable margarine
2 tbsp Honey
Pulp of 1 vanilla bean
1 Egg
1 tbsp Brandy
9 oz (250 g) Low-fat quark
1 oz (30 g) Raisins

For the leavened dough mix all the ingredients except for flour and butter with the lukewarm water. Mix in the flour, add the butter, and knead thoroughly. Cover the dough and let it rise in a warm place until it has doubled in size. Knead against and let rise for another 10 minutes.

Preheat oven to 400 °F (200 °C). For the filling, mix the butter well with honey and vanilla pulp. Mix in the quark, egg, and brandy, and then the raisins. Knead the dough again briefly and roll out to about 2 mm on a floured work surface. Cut out 4 in (10 cm) squares. Spoon quark filling into the middle of each square. Brush the corners with water and fold them other each other in the middle. Place the kolaches on a buttered baking sheet, brush them with water, and bake for about 15 minutes.

Bake Time: 15 minutes

Bake Temperature: 400 °F (200 °C)

WHOLE WHEAT BUCHTELN

Warm a little less than 2 cups of milk and mix with yeast and about ⅖ of the whole wheat flour. Cover and let rise for 20 minutes in a warm place. Warm the rest of the milk and mix it with the rest of the flour and honey. Knead with the starter dough, then mix in egg yolks, salt, lemon zest, and room temperature butter. Cover the dough again and let rise for 30 minutes in a warm place. Punch the dough down and then let rise for another 30 minutes. Roll out on a floured work surface and cut out 4in (10 cm) circles with a cookie cutter. Place some plum marmalade on each and fold the edges together. Butter a baking pan and place the buchteln in it close together with the seam down. Brush with melted butter, let rise for another 30 minutes. Preheat oven to 375 °F (190 °C) and bake for about 30 minutes.

Bake Time: 30 minutes

Bake Temperature: 375 °F (190 °C)

Tip: These fine buchteln are not only great served cold with coffee, but also warm as a main course.

Ingredients for 10–12 Servings
3⅓ cups (500 g) Whole wheat flour
1¼ cups (300 ml) Milk
5 tbsp (40 g) Yeast
Dash of salt
7 tbsp (100 g) Butter or untempered vegetable margarine, room temperature
5 tbsp (100 g) Honey
3 Egg yolks
Zest of 1 lemon
Flour for the work surface
Plum marmalade for the filling
Butter or untempered vegetable margarine for the pan

CHERRY TARTLETS

Ingredients for 6 Tartlets
1⅔ cups (250 g) Whole
  wheat flour
1 stick plus 3½ tbsp (170 g)
  Butter or untempered vegetable margarine, room
  temperature
¼ cup (85 g) Honey
2 Egg yolks
Zest of 1 lemon
5 oz (150 g) Hazelnuts,
  ground
18 oz (500 g) Sweet cherries,
  weighed without pits
3 tbsp (60 g) Honey for
  brushing
6 tbsp Cherry or apricot
  marmalade
1 tbsp Kirsch (cherry
  brandy)
Confectioner's sugar for
  dusting
Whole wheat flour for the
  work surface

Put the whole wheat flour on a work surface. Create a depression in the middle and put in the butter, honey, egg yolk, and lemon zest. Knead to a dough. Chill for half an hour. Preheat oven to 375 °F (190 °C). Roll out to 4–5 mm thick on a floured work surface. Cut out six 4½–5 in circles (about 12 cm) and lay them on a baking sheet lined with parchment paper. Warm the honey and brush on the circles. Sprinkle hazelnuts on the honey and spread the cherries on top. Bake for about 15 minutes. Dust lightly with confectioner's sugar and place back in the oven for another 3 minutes. Warm the marmalade with the kirsch. Using a spatula, remove the tartlets from the baking sheet, and glaze with the marmalade.

Bake Time: 15 minutes, then 3 more minutes

Bake Temperature: 375 °F (190 °C)

CHOUX CAKES WITH QUARK CREAM

Ingredients
1⅓ cups (200 g) Whole
  wheat flour
1 cup less 3 tbsp (100 g)
  Buckwheat flour
1 stick (120 g) Butter or
  untempered vegetable
  margarine
About 1⅔ cups (400 ml)
  water
Dash of salt
6 Eggs

For the Quark Cream
14 oz (400 g) Low-fat quark
6 tbsp (120 g) Honey
6 oz (180 g) Whipped cream

Preheat oven to 400 °F (200 °C). Boil the water with butter and salt. Mix the flours together and slowly stir them into the water. Stir the mixture on the stovetop until it is smooth and begins to come away from the pot. Remove from heat and stir in the eggs little by little. Place the dough in a piping bag fitted with a star-shaped nozzle and pipe balls onto a baking sheet lined with parchment paper. Bake for about 35 minutes. Remove from baking sheet and let cool.

For the quark cream, mix the quark with honey until smooth and then fold in the whipped cream. Halve the cakes, pipe quark cream into the middle, and place them back together.

Bake Time: about 35 minutes

Bake Temperature: 400 °F (200 °C)

WHOLE FOOD CAKES, STRUDEL, AND TORTES

Whole food cuisine is not only healthy, but it also brings a bit of change to your everyday baking. Just try one of the following whole food variations on classic recipes and you will be shocked at how well they will turn out.

WHOLE GRAIN SPONGE CAKE ROULADE

Preheat oven to 410 °F (210 °C). Mix the honey, egg yolks, and lemon zest until creamy and then mix in the melted butter. Slowly mix in the whole wheat flour. Beat the egg whites to stiff peaks with a pinch of salt and carefully fold into the mixture. Line a baking sheet with parchment paper and spread the batter on it about ½ in (1 cm) thick. Bake for about 10 minutes. Remove and overturn onto a cloth. Carefully pull off the parchment paper. Roll up the cake while it is still warm and let it cool. Unroll and brush with apricot marmalade. Roll up again and let cool completely.

Bake Time: about 10 minutes

Bake Temperature: 410 °F (210 °C)

Ingredients
1 cup (150 g) Whole wheat flour
6 tbsp (120 g) Honey
6 Egg yolks
6 Egg whites
2¾ tbsp (40 g) Butter or untempered vegetable margarine, melted
Zest of 1 lemon
Dash of salt
1¼ cup (150 g) Apricot marmalade for brushing

APPLE PASTRY

Dissolve the honey in the buttermilk. Mix with the rest of the ingredients and quickly knead to a smooth dough. Let rest for half an hour.

Preheat oven to 480 °F (250 °C). Quarter and core the apples and cut them into slices. Mix together with nuts and raisins. Place an 8in (20 cm) torte ring on a baking sheet lined with parchment paper (or use a springform). Roll two thirds of the dough out to about 5 mm on a floured work surface and place in the buttered torte ring. Pull the dough up a bit on the sides. Bake for about 5 minutes. Lower the oven heat to 320 °F (160 °C). Fill with the apple mixture and smooth. Roll out the rest of the dough, lay on top of the apple, and decorate with dough rosettes. Brush with egg yolk and bake another 25 minutes. Remove from the ring after cooling and slice.

Bake Time: 5 minutes to start, then 25 minutes

Bake Temperature: 480 °F (250 °C) to start, then 320 °F (160 °C)

Ingredients for 1 Torte (8in (20 cm) diameter)
1⅔ lbs (750 g) Apples
3.5 oz (100 g) Hazelnuts, ground
2 oz (50 g) Raisins
Egg yolk for brushing
Flour for the work surface
Light margarine for the pan

For the Dough
3 tbsp Honey
5 tbsp Buttermilk
2⅔ cups (400 g) Whole wheat flour
1½ tbsp (20 g) Butter or untempered vegetable margarine
Pulp of 1 vanilla bean
Dash of cinnamon
Zest of 1 lemon
Dash of salt

PLUM FLECK

For the dough, knead all the ingredients together and let rest for 30 minutes. Preheat oven to 340 °F (170 °C). For the quark filling, cream the butter with honey. Mix in the quark, raisins, and egg yolks. Roll out to a baking sheet sized rectangle on a floured work surface. Lay on a buttered baking sheet and raise up a border around the edge. Cover the dough with a thin layer of quark filling and lay the halved, pitted plums on top (skin side down). Knead the butter with honey and whole wheat flour and roll between your hands to created streusel crumbs. Sprinkle with the streusel and bake for about 30 minutes.

Bake Time: about 30 minutes

Bake Temperature: 340 °F (170 °C)

Ingredients
3⅓ lbs (1.5 kg) Plums
1 stick plus 6 tbsp (200 g) Butter or untempered vegetable margarine
5 tbsp (100 g) Honey
2 cups (300 g) Whole wheat flour
Whole grain flour for the work surface
Butter or untempered vegetable margarine for the baking sheet

For the Dough
3⅓ cups (500 g) Whole wheat flour
4 tsp (2 cl) Oil
Dash of salt
2 tbsp (3 cl) Water, luke-warm
3 Eggs

For the Quark Filling
5 oz (140 g) Low-fat quark
2¾ tbsp (40 g) Butter or untempered vegetable margarine
4 tbsp (2 kL) Honey
¾ oz (20 g) Raisins
2 Egg yolks

Quark Cake with Stewed Apricots

Preheat oven to 375 °F (190 °C). Cream the butter with salt, egg yolk, and honey. Mix in the quark, semolina, raisins, and lemon juice. Beat the egg whites, add sugar, and beat to stiff peaks. Carefully fold into the mixture. Butter an 11in (28 cm) spring-form pan and sprinkle with whole wheat breadcrumbs. Fill with the batter and bake for 35–40 minutes.

For the stewed apricots, quarter and pit the apricots. Heat honey in a pan. Add apricots, water, and vanilla pulp and cook until the apricots are soft. Let the cake cool and serve with the cooled apricots.

Bake Time: 35–40 minutes

Bake Temperature: 375 °F (190 °C)

Ingredients
3½ tbsp (50 g) Butter or untempered vegetable margarine, melted
Dash of salt
4 Egg yolks
6 tbsp (120 g) Honey
14 oz (400 g) Low-fat quark
4 tsp (15 g) Whole wheat semolina
2 oz (60 g) Raisins
Juice of ½ lemon
4 Egg yolks
4 tsp (20 g) Granulated sugar
Butter or untempered vegetable margarine for the pan

For the Stewed Apricots
14 oz (400 g) Apricots, pitted
¼ cup (⅟₁₆ l) Water
Pulp of 1 vanilla bean
3 tbsp Honey

Quark Fruit Cake

Dissolve yeast in some lukewarm water and add to the flour. Mix in the honey, butter, and sea salt and pour in the rest of the water. Knead strongly for 10 minutes. If the dough is too soft, add a bit more flour. Cover and let rise in a warm place for about 45 minutes, until it has doubled in volume.

Preheat oven to 400 °F (200 °C). In the meantime, boil milk for the quark cream. Sprinkle in the rice flour and boil to make a porridge. Mix in honey, quark, egg, and vanilla sugar. Cut the washed fruit into small pieces. Knead the dough well once more, roll out, and place in a buttered cake pan (with a 1in (2 cm) high edge). Spread the quark cream smooth on top and press the fruit into the cream. Bake for about 45 minutes.

Bake Time: about 45 minutes

Bake Temperature: 400 °F (200 °C)

Ingredients
5 tbsp (40 g) Yeast
¾ cup (200 ml) Water, lukewarm
2⅔ cups (400 g) Whole wheat flour
2 tbsp plus 1 tsp (50 g) Honey
3½ tbsp (50 g) Butter or untempered vegetable margarine, room temperature
Dash of sea salt
Light margarine for the pan

For the Cream
¾ cups (200 ml) Milk
½ cup (80 g) Rice flour
¼ cup (80 g) Honey
14 oz (400 g) Low-fat quark
1 Egg
4 tsp (10 g) Confectioner's sugar mixed with vanilla pulp
35 oz (1 kg) Seasonal fruit (e.g. strawberries, grapes, plums, etc.)

WHOLE GRAIN BUTTERMILK APPLE CAKE

Ingredients
6⅔ cups (1 kg) Whole wheat
  flour
4¼ cup (1l) Buttermilk
3 Eggs
Dash of salt
4 tsp (20 g) Organic baking
  powder
7 oz (200 g) Hazelnuts,
  chopped
7 oz (200 g) Raisins
1 cup (200 g) Brown sugar
10 Apples, peeled, cored,
  and cut into slices
6 tbsp Sesame
Butter or light margarine for
  the baking sheet

Preheat oven to 350 °F (180 °C). Mix all the ingredients together, and finally, fold in the apple pieces. Spread the batter on a buttered baking sheet with a high edge (or a large cake pan) and sprinkle with sesame. Bake for 50 minutes.

Bake Time: about 50 minutes

Bake Temperature: 350 °F (180 °C)

BANANA CAKE

Ingredients
5 tbsp (75 g) Butter or
  untempered vegetable
  margarine
⅔ cup (75 g) Confectioner's
  sugar
2 Eggs
1⅓ cups (200 g) Whole wheat
  flour
½ tsp Organic baking
  powder
¼ cup (50 ml) Milk
Salt
3 Bananas
Juice of ½ lemon
3.5 oz (100 g) Almonds,
  grated
Light margarine for the pan
Confectioner's sugar for
  dusting

Preheat oven to 400 °F (200 °C). Cream the butter and confectioner's sugar. Add the eggs. Add the whole wheat flour, baking powder, milk, and salt and knead to a dough.

Peel the bananas, halve the long way, and soak with lemon juice.

Butter a loaf pan. Fill with half of the dough, place the banana halves on the dough, and sprinkle half of the almonds on top. Fill with the other half of the dough, smooth, and sprinkle the rest of the almonds on top. Bake for about 50 minutes. Remove the cake from the pan and dust with confectioner's sugar.

Bake Time: 1 hour

Bake Temperature: 400 °F (200 °C)

REHRÜCKEN FOR DIABETICS

Preheat oven to 300 °F (150 °C). Cream the butter with ⅓ of the sweetener. Mix in the quark and then the egg yolks, little by little. Beat the eggs to stiff peaks with the rest of the sweetener and fold into the quark mixture. Finally, fold in ground almonds, lemon zest, and vanilla sugar. Butter a Rehrücken pan and dust with whole wheat flour, fill with batter, and bake for about 30 minutes. Let cool and remove from pan.

Bake Time: 30 minutes

Bake Temperature: 300 °F (150 °C)

Ingredients
5½ tbsp (80g Butter) or untempered vegetable margarine
⅔ cup (150 g) Artificial sweetener of your choice
2 oz (50 g) Low-fat quark, strained
8 Egg yolks
5 oz (150 g) Almonds, ground
3 Egg whites
Zest of ½ lemon
Dash of confectioner's sugar mixed with vanilla pulp
Light margarine and whole wheat flour for the pan

TEA CAKE

Preheat oven to 350 °F (180 °C). Chop the dates. Boil until soft in half the water, the orange zest, and the rum. Let cool, add the egg yolks, and purée with an immersion blender. Blend ¾ of the flour with baking powder and mix with the rest of the water.

Butter the Rehrücken pan and sprinkle with breadcrumbs. Whip the cream and fold into the batter. Mix the raisins and candied lemon peel with the rest of the flour. Beat the egg whites to stiff peaks with granulated sugar.

Fold the flour with dried fruit into the batter alternating with the egg whites. Fill the Rehrücken pans and bake for about 1 hour.

Ingredients for
2 Rehrücken pans
5 oz (150 g) Dates
1 cup (250 ml) Water
3 tbsp Rum
Zest of 1 orange
4 Egg yolks
1 cup (250 ml) Heavy cream
3.5 oz (100 g) Raisins
2 oz (50 g) Candied lemon peel
2⅔ cup (400 g) Whole wheat flour
4 tsp (20 g) Organic baking powder
4 Egg whites
3 tbsp (40 g) Granulated sugar
Butter or untempered vegetable margarine and Whole wheat breadcrumbs for the pans

MILLET CAKE

Ingredients
7 tbsp (100 g) Butter or
  untempered vegetable
  margarine
⅓ cup (125 g) Honey
3 Egg yolks
¼ cup (60 ml) Milk
2 tbsp Brandy
1 cup less 3 tbsp (100 g) Fine
  millet flour
7 tbsp (50 g) Buckwheat
  flour
3 Egg whites
2.5 oz (70 g) Almonds,
  chopped
Butter or untempered
  vegetable margarine for
  the pan

Preheat oven to 350 °F (180 °C). Cream the butter, honey, and egg yolks. Mix in the milk and brandy. Sift the millet flour and buckwheat flour together and beat the egg whites to stiff peaks. Fold the almonds, flour, and egg whites into the egg yolk mixture. Fill a buttered, floured cake pan or bundt pan and bake for 60 minutes. Let cool and remove from pan.

Bake Time: about 60 minutes

Bake Temperature: 350 °F (180 °C)

ORANGE CAKE (WHOLE FOOD)

Ingredients
1¼ cups (180 g) Whole
  wheat flour
⅔ cup (50 g) Soy flour
1 stick plus 6 tbsp (200 g)
  Butter or untempered
  vegetable margarine
½ cup plus 1 tbsp (200 g)
  Honey
3 Eggs
2 oz (50 g) Coconut flakes
2 tbsp (3 cl) Rum
1 Orange (juice and zest)
Pulp of ½ vanilla bean
Pinch of allspice, ground
2 oz (50 g) Candied orange
  peel
2 tsp (10 g) Organic baking
  powder
1⅔ cup (200 g) Orange
  marmalade to glaze
Butter or untempered
  vegetable margarine for
  the pan

Preheat oven to 340 °F (170 °C). Cream the butter and honey, then slowly mix in the eggs. Add the orange zest, orange juice, rum, vanilla pulp, and allspice. Blend together the whole wheat flour, soy flour, coconut flakes, and baking powder, then mix into the batter. Fold in the candied orange peel. Butter a ring pan or bundt pan and dust with whole wheat flour. Fill with batter and bake for about 60 minutes. After cooling, remove from pan and glaze with warmed orange marmalade.

Bake Time: about 60 minutes

Bake Temperature: 340 °F (170 °C)

WHOLE WHEAT GUGELHUPF

Mix the rum with raisins, almonds, and candied orange peel. Mix the yeast and a little less than half (!) of the flour into the lukewarm milk, cover, and let rise in a warm place for 20 minutes.

Cream the butter, honey, egg yolks, and eggs. Add a dash of salt, heavy cream, and lemon zest. Mix the starter dough with the egg mixture and then knead with the rest of the flour to form a dough. Knead in the fruit, but don't knead the dough for too much longer. Cover and let rise in a warm place for 30 minutes, then punch down. Butter a bundt pan and sprinkle it with grated almonds. Fill with the dough and let rise for another 30 minutes. Preheat oven to 340°F (170°C) and bake for 60–70 minutes.

Bake Time: 60–70 minutes

Bake Temperature: 340°F (170°C)

Ingredients
6⅔ cups (1 kg) Whole wheat flour
2 cups (450 ml) Milk
9 tbsp (80 g) Yeast
Dash of salt
1 cup less 2 tbsp (300 g) Honey
3½ tbsp (400 g) Butter or untempered vegetable margarine
7 oz (200 g) Raisins
3.5 oz (100 g) Almonds, chopped
3.5 oz (100 g) Candied orange peel
6 Eggs
4 Egg yolks
⅓ cups (80 ml) Heavy cream
Zest of 1 lemon
¾ cup (200 ml) Rum
Butter or untempered vegetable margarine and Grated almonds for the pan

WHOLE GRAIN GUGELHUPF WITH DRIED FRUIT

The day before, cover the dried plums, apricots, and apple slices with boiling water and let soak.

Warm the milk. Add the yeast, sugar, and ⅕ of the flour, stir, cover, and let rise in a warm place until it has doubled in size.

Cream the butter, honey, and salt and add the eggs. Mix in the lemon zest, rum, raisins, and the rest of the flour, then knead with the starter dough. Drain the dried fruit, chop into small pieces, and knead into the dough. Butter a bundt pan and sprinkle it with oat flakes. Fill with the dough, cover, and let rise again until it has doubled in size. Preheat oven to 400°F (200°C) and bake for about 1 hour.

Bake Time: about 1 hour

Bake Temperature: 400°F (200°C)

Ingredients
¾ cup (200 ml) Milk
¼ cup (35 g) Yeast
¼ cup (50 g) Brown sugar
2½ cups (250 g) Whole grain spelt flour
1 stick plus 2½ tbsp (150 g) Butter or untempered vegetable margarine
1 tbsp (40 g) Honey
Dash of salt
3 Egg yolks
Zest of ½ lemon
4 tsp (2 cl) Rum
1 oz (25 g) Raisins
2 oz (50 g) Dried plums
2 oz (50 g) Dried apricots
2 oz (50 g) Dried apple slices
Light margarine and Oat flakes for the pan

ALMOND GUGELHUPF

Ingredients
8 oz (220 g) Dates, pitted
1 cup (250 ml) Water
1 tbsp (½ kL) Vanilla
  pudding mix
4 Egg yolks
¼ cup (60 ml) Rum
5 oz (150 g) Almonds, ground
1 cup (250 ml) Heavy cream
1⅓ cups (200 g) Whole
  wheat flour
6 tbsp (3 kL) Organic baking
  powder
4 tbsp Cocoa powder
4 Egg whites
3 tbsp (40 g) Granulated
  sugar
Butter or untempered veg-
  etable margarine and
Breadcrumbs for the pan

Preheat oven to 350 °F (180 °C). Chop the dates and boil with water and pudding mix. Let cool. Add the egg yolks and purée with an immersion blender. Mix the whole wheat flour with baking powder and cocoa powder and mix half of it into the date blend. Also mix in almonds and rum. Whip the cream and fold into the batter. Beat the egg whites to stiff peaks with the granulated sugar. Fold the egg whites and the rest of the flour into the batter.

Butter a bundt pan and sprinkle with breadcrumbs. Fill with the batter and bake for about 90 minutes. Let cool and remove from pan.

Bake Time: 90 minutes

Bake Temperature: 350 °F (180 °C)

BANANA GUGELHUPF WITH COCONUT

Ingredients
12 oz (350 g) Bananas,
  peeled
1⅔ cups (350 g) Brown
  sugar
Dash of salt
Zest of 1 lemon
7 tbsp (100 ml) Half and half
7 tbsp (100 g) Butter or
  untempered vegetable
  margarine
3 Eggs
1 cup plus 2 tbsp (150 g)
  Whole grain rye flour
1⅓ cup (200 g) Whole wheat
  flour
4 tsp (20 g) Organic baking
  powder
Light margarine and
  coconut flakes for the pan
Chocolate glaze (see p. 42)

Preheat oven to 400 °F (200 °C). Blend the bananas with two thirds of the sugar, a dash of salt, the lemon zest, and the half and half. Cream the butter with the rest of the sugar and a dash of salt. Add eggs, then stir in the banana mixture. Sift the flour with the baking powder and fold in. Butter a bundt pan and sprinkle with coconut flakes. Fill with batter and bake for about 1 hour. Let cool slightly, then remove from pan. Glaze with warmed chocolate glaze and sprinkle some coconut flakes on top.

Bake Time: 1 hour

Bake Temperature: 400 °F (200 °C)

POPPY STRUDEL

Dissolve the yeast in about ½ cup of milk and use ⅓ of the flour to create a starter dough. Cover well and let rise about 20 minutes in a warm place. Warm the rest of the milk and knead with the rum, honey, lemon juice, the rest of the flour, and the starter. Mix the egg with salt and slowly add to the dough. Then mix the butter in. Cover and let rise for 30 minutes in a warm place. Knead well one more time and let rise for another 30 minutes.

For the filling, warm milk and mix with the other ingredients.

Divide the dough into 3 pieces and spread them out into circles with the balls of your hands. Let them rise for 10 minutes and then roll them out to 12in (30 cm) squares. Spread the poppy filling on them, roll up, and close the ends well. Place each in a buttered baking tray and let rise for another 60 minutes. Preheat oven to 340 °F (170 °C). Brush with egg and bake for 1 hour.

Bake Time: about 1 hour

Bake Temperature: 340 °F (170 °C)

Ingredients
3⅓ cup (500 g) Whole wheat flour
¾ cup (180 ml) Milk, luke-warm
50g Yeast
2 tsp (10 g) Salt
4 tsp (2 cl) Rum
1 stick plus 2 ½ tbsp (150 g) Butter or untempered vegetable margarine
½ cup less 1 tbsp (150 g) Honey
3 Eggs
4 tsp (2 cl) Lemon juice
Whole grain flour for the work surface
Butter or light margarine for the pan
Egg for brushing

For the Poppy Filling
18 oz (500 g) Poppy, ground
1 cup less 2 tbsp (300 g) Honey
1½ cups (350 ml) Milk
2 oz (50 g) Whole grain breadcrumbs
3.5 oz (100 g) Raisins
1 cup less 2 tbsp (100 g) Plum jam
1 tsp (5 g) Cinnamon, ground

APPLE STRUDEL (WHOLE FOOD)

Ingredients
1⅓ cup (250 g) Whole wheat
  flour
¾ cup (200 ml) Milk,
  lukewarm
1 Egg
Dash of salt
2 tbsp (25 g) Corn oil
Oil and butter or untem-
  pered vegetable margarine
  for brushing
Flour for the cloth

For the Filling
6½ oz (3 kg) Apples, peeled
  and cut into slices
9 oz (250 g) Sweet bread-
  crumbs
¾ cup (250 g) Honey
1 stick plus 6 tbsp (200 g)
  Butter or untempered
  vegetable margarine,
  lukewarm
7 oz (200 g) Raisins
5 oz (150 g) Hazelnuts,
  ground
Lemon zest
2 tbsp (25 g) Cinnamon
  powder

Knead the egg with a dash of salt, lukewarm milk, flour, and oil. Brush the top with oil and let rest for 1 hour. In the meantime, mix the apple slices with sweet crumbs, honey, lukewarm butter, raisins, nuts, lemon zest, and cinnamon to make the filling.

Preheat oven to 400 °F (200 °C). Place the strudel dough on a floured kitchen cloth and roll out to a square. Rub your fingers and the backs of your hands. Slide both hands under the dough and carefully pull it out in all directions until it is so thin that you could read a newspaper through it. Be very careful that the dough doesn't rip. Brush with melted butter and spread the apple filling on it evenly. Roll up with the help of the cloth, fold the ends in, and brush well with butter again. Place on a buttered baking sheet and bake for about 50 minutes, until golden brown. Let cool and then serve.

Bake Time: 50 minutes

Bake Temperature: 400 °F (200 °C)

Quark Strudel (Whole Food)

Warm a bit less than a cup (200 ml) of milk and mix with yeast and ⅖ of the flour. Cover and let rise for 20 minutes in a warm place. Warm the rest of the milk and mix with the rest of the flour and honey. Knead with the starter, then mix in the egg yolk, salt, and room temperature butter. Punch down the dough, cover, and let rise another 30 minutes. Punch down again and let rise for another 30 minutes.

For the filling, cream butter and honey, slowly add the eggs, then mix in the other ingredients. Roll the dough out on a floured work surface to a large rectangle about ⅓ (1 cm) of an inch thick. Brush with the quark filling, leaving a 1½ in (4 cn) border. Roll it up towards yourself the long way. Place on a buttered baking sheet in a U shape. Close the ends well and let rise for another 40 minutes. Preheat oven to 400 °F (200 °C). Brush with egg and bake for about 50 minutes.

Bake Time: 50 minutes

Bake Temperature: 400 °F (200 °C)

Ingredients
3⅓ cups (500 g) Whole wheat flour
⅓ cup (120 g) Honey
1 stick (120 g) Butter or untempered vegetable margarine, room temperature
5 tbsp (40 g) Yeast
1½ cups (350 ml) Milk
3 Egg yolks
2 tsp (10 g) Salt
Whole grain flour for the work surface
Fat for the baking sheet
Egg for brushing

For the Filling
18 oz (500 g) Low-fat quark, strained
7 tbsp (100 g) Butter or untempered vegetable margarine
5 tbsp (100 g) Honey
3.5 oz (100 g) Raisins
5 Egg yolks
Zest of 1 lemon
Dash of salt
Pulp of 1 vanilla bean

Nut Strudel

Dissolve the yeast in a little less than half a cup (100 ml) of milk and make a starter dough by adding about ⅕ of the flour. Cover and let rise in a warm place for about 20 minutes. Warm the rest of the milk and knead with the rum, honey, lemon juice, the rest of the flour, and the starter. Mix the eggs and salt and slowly add to the dough. Knead in the butter. Cover and let rise for 30 minutes in a warm place. Knead well then let rise another 30 minutes. For the filling, warm the milk and mix with the other ingredients.

Ingredients
3⅓ cups (500 g) Whole wheat flour
¾ cup (180 ml) Milk, luke-warm
6 tbsp (50 g) Yeast
2 tsp (10 g) Salt
4 tsp (2 cl) Rum
1 stick plus 2 ½ tbsp (150 g) Butter or untempered vegetable margarine
½ cup less 1 tbsp (150 g) Honey
3 Eggs
4 tsp (2 cl) Lemon juice

Whole grain flour for the
  work surface
Butter or light margarine
  for the pan
Egg for brushing

For the Nut Filling
18 oz (500 g) Walnuts,
  ground
1 cup less 2 tbsp (300 g)
  Honey
¼ cup (5 cl) Rum
1½ cups (350 ml) Milk
2 oz (50 g) Whole grain
  breadcrumbs
1 tsp (5 g) Cinnamon powder

Divide the dough into 3 pieces and spread them out into circles
with the balls of your hands. Let them rise for 10 minutes and
then roll them out to 12 in (30 cm) squares. Spread the nut filling
on the dough, roll up, and close the edges well. Place each in a
buttered baking tray and let rise for another 60 minutes. Preheat
oven to 340 °F (170 °C). Brush with egg and bake for 1 hour.

Bake Time: about 1 hour

Bake Temperature: 340 °F (170 °C)

LINZER TORTE

Ingredients
2 cups (300 g) Whole wheat
  flour
2 sticks plus 1½ tbsp (250 g)
  Butter or untempered
  vegetable margarine
½ cup plus 1 tbsp (200 g)
  Honey
7 oz (200 g) Almonds, ground
5 Egg yolks
5 Egg whites
2 tsp (10 g) Cinnamon,
  ground
2 tsp (10 g) Organic baking
  powder
Zest of 1 lemon
Dash of salt
Redcurrant marmalade
Wafers
Butter or untempered
  vegetable margarine and
Whole wheat flour for the
  torte pan

Preheat oven to 350 °F (180 °C). Cream the butter and honey.
Slowly mix in the egg yolks. Mix the whole wheat flour with
cinnamon and baking powder and gently mix among the
almonds and lemon zest. Beat the egg whites to stiff peaks
with a dash of salt and carefully fold into the mixture. Butter
a torte pan and dust with whole wheat flour. Fill evenly and
smoothly with the dough, leaving enough to cover at the end.
Cover with wafers, brush on the redcurrant marmalade, and
pipe the rest of the dough on top in a lattice and border. Bake
for about 1 hour.

Bake Time: about 1 hour

Bake Temperature: 350 °F (180 °C)

BRAIDED BREAD

Grind the wheat finely and mix with raisins. Dissolve the soy flour, honey, salt, yeast, and rum in lukewarm water. Beat the egg in and mix with the raisin flour. Add melted butter and knead well. Cover and let rise to double the size in a warm place. Punch down and then let rise another 10 minutes. Preheat oven to 340°F (170°C). Roll 9 strips out of the dough and braid four-strand, three-strand, and two-strand braids on a buttered, floured baking sheet.

Brush each braid and each end of a braid with water, so that they stick together better. Let rise again. Brush with cold water and sprinkle with almond slices. Bake for about 50 minutes.

Bake Time: about 50 minutes

Bake Temperature: 340°F (170°C)

Ingredients
23 oz (650 g) Wheat (or 4⅓ cups whole wheat flour)
5 oz (150 g) Raisins
About 2¼ cups (280 ml) water
2 tbsp Soy flour
3 tbsp Rum
1 tbsp (½ kL) Salt
2 tbsp plus 1 tsp (50 g) Honey
¼ cup (30 g) Yeast
1 Egg
3½ tbsp (50 g) Butter or untempered vegetable margarine, melted
Almond slices
Butter or untempered vegetable margarine and
Whole grain flour for the baking sheet

SPONGE CAKE NUT TORTE

Preheat oven to 340°F (170°C). Cream the butter, egg yolks, and lemon zest. Carefully mix in the whole wheat flour and nuts. Beat the egg whites to stiff peaks with a dash of salt and carefully fold into the batter. Fill a buttered and floured torte pan and bake for 50–60 minutes. Cover with parchment paper for half the baking time. Let cool.

For the walnut cream, grind or grate the walnuts very finely. Add water to the gelatin, remove excess water, and dissolve in honey in a double boiler. Let cool. Whip the cream and fold it into the honey along with the nuts. Once the torte is cool, cut it once horizontally and fill with the cream.

Bake Time: 50–60 minutes

Bake Temperature: 340°F (170°C)

Ingredients
1 cup (150 g) Whole wheat flour
6 tbsp (120 g) Honey
3.5 oz (100 g) Walnuts, ground
6 Egg yolks
6 Egg whites
Zest of 1 lemon
Dash of salt
Butter or untempered vegetable margarine for the pan

For the Walnut Cream
3.5 oz (100 g) Walnuts, finely ground
5 Sheets gelatin
5 tbsp 100g Honey
2 cups (500 ml) Heavy cream

WARM WHOLE FOOD DESSERTS

Anyone who has regularly snacked on too much Viennese dessert knows that it contains both delights and sins. But these sins can be forgiven much more quickly and generously (at least by your nice doctor) if you choose the whole food variation.

KAISERSCHMARREN (WHOLE FOOD)

Ingredients for
4–6 Servings
150g Wheat
50g Barley
50g Millet
50g Buckwheat
1¼ cup (300 ml) Water
2 oz (60 g) Dates
2 tbsp Rum
1 cup (250 ml) Milk
Salt
4 Egg yolks
3½ tbsp (50 g) Butter or
  untempered vegetable
  margarine
5 Egg whites

Preheat oven to 350 °F (180 °C). Mix the wheat with the barley, millet, and buckwheat and ground to flour. Mix with the water. Add the finely chopped dates and the rum and let sit for at least 30 minutes. Beat in the milk, egg yolks, salt, and the melted butter with an immersion blender. Beat the egg whites to stiff peaks and fold in. Fill an ungreased nonstick pan and bake for about 12 minutes.

QUARK CASSEROLE WITH RASPBERRY SAUCE

Ingredients
8 oz (225 g) Low-fat quark
3 Egg yolks
Some artificial sweetener
Juice of 1 lemon
3 Egg whites
6 tbsp (85 g) Granulated
  sugar
10g Untempered vegetable
  margarine

For the Raspberry Sauce
1 cup (125 g) Raspberries
Liquid artificial sweetener

Preheat oven to 375 °F (190 °C). Strain the quark. Beat with egg yolks, sweetener, and lemon juice until creamy. Beat the egg whites to stiff peaks with ⅓ cup (65 g) (!) of sugar and fold into the quark. Grease the casserole dish with margarine, sprinkle with the rest of the granulated sugar, and chill. Fill with the quark batter and bake in a water bath for 25 minutes.

For the raspberry sauce, sieve the raspberries and add sweetener. Remove the casserole from the dish and pour the raspberry sauce over it.

Bake Time: about 25 minutes

Bake Temperature: 375 °F (190 °C)

RICE CASSEROLE WITH PEACH SAUCE

Boil the rice in about 1 quart of lightly salted water for 40 minutes, let sit for 15 minutes with the lid on, then let cool. Preheat oven to 400 °F (200 °C). Chop the dates, boil briefly with 4 tablespoons of water and the vanilla pulp, and then remove from heat. Melt the butter in it and then add the egg yolks. Purée with an immersion blender. Mix the date purée into the rice. Beat the egg whites to stiff peaks with the granulated sugar. Fold in. Fill a greased casserole dish and bake for 55 minutes.

For the peach sauce, pit the fruit and purée with the other ingredients, then sieve. Dust the casserole with confectioner's sugar and serve with the peach sauce.

Bake Time: about 55 minutes

Bake Temperature: 400 °F (200 °C)

Ingredients for 10 Servings
10.5 oz (300 g) Organic short
   grain rice
Salt
3 oz (80 g) Dates
Pulp of 1 vanilla bean
2¾ tbsp (40 g) Butter or
   untempered vegetable
   margarine
3 Egg yolks
3 Egg whites
2 tbsp (30 g) Granulated
   sugar
Fat of your choice for the
   pan
Confectioner's sugar for
   dusting

For the Peach Sauce
26 oz (750 g) Peaches
1 cup (250 ml) Sour cream
2 tbsp Low-fat quark
2 tbsp Honey

WHEAT GRITS SCHMARREN

Grind the wheat semi-coarsely and soak it and the minced dates in 1¾ cups (400 ml) of water for 1–2 hours, until soft. Preheat oven to 300 °F (150 °C). Stir the vanilla pulp, cinnamon, confectioner's sugar, eggs, and milk into the grits with a fork. Last, stir in the melted butter. Heat a bit of the fat of your choice in a nonstick pan and pour in the batter. After it has begun to set (about 1 minute), place in the oven and bake for 25–30 minutes. Cut into pieces with two forks and dust with confectioner's sugar.

Bake Time: 25–30 minutes

Bake Temperature: 300 °F (150 °C)

Garnish Recommendation: compote

Ingredients for 6 Servings
10.5 oz (300 g) Wheat
3 oz (80 g) Dates
Pulp of 1 vanilla bean
1 tbsp Confectioner's sugar
Dash of cinnamon
2 Eggs
1 cup (250 ml) Milk
2¾ tbsp (40 g) Butter or
   untempered vegetable
   margarine
Fat of your choice for frying
Confectioner's sugar for
   dusting

1¼ cup (180 g) Whole wheat flour
2 cups plus 2 tbsp (220 g) Spelt flour
2 cups (500 ml) Water
Salt
Zest of ½ lemon
3 Eggs
¾ cup (200 ml) Milk
2¾ tbsp (40 g) Butter or untempered vegetable margarine, melted
Fat of your choice for the pan

For the Filling
3 tbsp Crème fraîche
4 tbsp Honey
3 Egg yolks
Pulp of 1 vanilla bean
18 oz (500 g) Low-fat quark
¾ cups (180 ml) Yogurt
1 oz (30 g) Raisins

For the Royale
1¼ cup (300 ml) Milk
3 Eggs
1 tbsp (10 g) Cornstarch

Ingredients for 4–6 Servings
3 Apples
Some lemon juice
½ cup (125 ml) White wine
¼ cup (80 g) Honey
½ Cinnamon stick
1 tsp Confectioner's sugar mixed with vanilla pulp

For the Palatschinken
1 cup (250 ml) Milk
1 cup (150 g) Whole wheat flour
2 Eggs
1 tsp Brown sugar
Dash of salt
Oil for frying

For the Honey Whipped Cream
3 tbsp Whipped cream
1 tbsp Honey

QUARK PALATSCHINKEN (WHOLE FOOD)

Preheat oven to 350 °F (180 °C). Mix the flours together. Add the water and salt and blend with an immersion blender. Blend in the lemon zest, eggs, and milk. Finally, mix in the melted butter. Fry thin palatschinken in an unbuttered nonstick pan.

For the filling, stir all the ingredients together and spread on the palatschinken. Roll them up and cut into pieces. Place in a greased casserole dish and bake for 15 minutes.

For the royale, beat the eggs, milk, and cornstarch together well. Pour over the palatschinken and bake for another 15 minutes.

Bake Time: 30 minutes
Bake Temperature: 350 °F (180 °C)

APPLE WHOLE GRAIN PALATSCHINKEN

Peel, quarter, and core the apples and cut into slices. Place immediately in water mixed with some lemon juice. Boil the white wine with honey, vanilla sugar, and the cinnamon stick. Remove from heat, add the drained apple slices, briefly bring to a boil again, and then chill. Remove the cinnamon stick.

For the palatschinken batter, mix milk, eggs, sugar, and salt and finally stir in the flour. Heat some oil in a pan, pour some batter in thinly, and make 4–6 golden brown palatschinken. Hold in a warm place. For the honey whipped cream, mix the whipped cream with honey. Fill the palatschinken with the apple mixture, close, and garnish with honey whipped cream.

Tips:

- If you prefer the apples to be thicker, you can add some cornstarch mixed with water to the warm apple mixture.
- The apple palatschinken can be prepared even more quickly if you caramelize the apple slices in honey and stew for just 2 minutes.

MILLET GNOCCHI WITH ELDERBERRY SAUCE

Preheat oven to 400 °F (200 °C). Mix the boiled, cooled millet with low-fat quark, hazelnuts, elderberries, and honey. Mix the chopped apple, lemon juice, lemon zest, coriander, vanilla pulp, cinnamon, and salt into the millet mixture. Finally, add the breadcrumbs. Form 12 gnocchi out of the batter, place on a buttered baking sheet, and bake for 10–12 minutes.

For the elderberry sauce, mix red wine with pudding mix and boil with the clove. Add the elderberries and bring to a boil again. Let cool and stir in the honey. Brush the baked gnocchi with melted butter and sprinkle with almonds. Warm dishes and pour the elderberry sauce onto them. Place 3 gnocchi on each dish in a star formation.

Bake Time: 10–12 minutes

Bake Temperature: 400 °F (200 °C)

Ingredients 150g Millet, boiled (70g raw, boiled with ¾ cup of water)
3.5 oz (100 g) Low-fat quark
1.5 oz (40 g) Hazelnuts, chopped
3 oz (80 g) Elderberries
2 tbsp plus 1 tsp (50 g) Honey
3.5 oz (100 g) Apples, coarsely chopped
Juice of ½ lemon
Zest of ½ lemon
Pinch of coriander, ground
Pulp of ½ vanilla bean
Pinch of cinnamon, ground
Dash of salt
¾ oz (20 g) Brioche crumbs, whole wheat crumbs, or breadcrumbs
3½ tbsp (50 g) Butter or untempered vegetable margarine
2 oz (50 g) Almonds, finely ground
Butter or untempered vegetable margarine for the baking sheet

For the Elderberry Sauce
½ cup (125 ml) Red wine
1 tsp Vanilla pudding mix
1 Clove
5 oz (150 g) Elderberries
2 tbsp plus 1 tsp (50 g) Acacia honey

WHOLE GRAIN QUARK DUMPLINGS IN PUMPKIN

Ingredients for 10–12
Dumplings
9 oz (250 g) Low-fat quark
¼ cup (60 ml) Sour cream
25g Spelt semolina
2 tbsp (10 g) Whole wheat
  flour
1 tsp (5 g) Brown or
  organic sugar
1 Egg
Salt for the water
3 oz (80 g) Pumkin seeds

For the Plum Sauce
10.5 oz (300 g) Plums, pitted
Liquid sweetener
1 tbsp Rum

Knead together the sour cream, semolina, flour, sugar, and egg and chill for about 1 hour. Form dumplings out of the dough and place in boiling salt water for 10 minutes. For the plum sauce, cook the plums until they are soft. Strain, blend with sweetener and rum, and sieve. Chop the pumpkin seeds and roast in a pan without oil. Remove the dumplings, drain, and roll in the seeds. Swerve with the plum sauce.

Cook Time: about 10 minutes

CHOUX APRICOT DUMPLINGS

Ingredients for
20 Dumplings
2½ cups (370 g) Whole
  wheat flour
2 cups (450 ml) Water
2¾ tbsp (40 g) Butter or
  untempered vegetable
  margarine
Salt
2 Eggs
⅓ cup (50 g) Whole wheat
  flour to knead in
20 Apricots, pitted
2¾ tbsp (40 g) Butter or
  untempered margarine to
  pour over
1 oz (30 g) Hazelnuts, ground

Boil water with salt and butter, remove from heat, and stir in the flour. Put back on the stove and stir until the dough comes away from the bottom of the pot. Remove from heat and stir in the eggs little by little. Knead the rest of the flour in by hand and let rest for 30 minutes. Form a long rope of dough and cut off equally sized pieces. Wrap around apricots and form dumplings. Simmer in salt water for 15 minutes. Remove the dumplings and let them drip. Heat butter and pour it over the dumplings. Sprinkle the ground hazelnuts on top.

Cook Time: about 15 minutes

PLUM DUMPLINGS

Cream the butter with salt. Fold in the quark, eggs, and both flours. Knead to a dough and then let rest for 30 minutes. Roll into a rope, cut into equally sized pieces, and wrap around the plums. Form dumplings and simmer in salt water for 10–12 minutes.

Melt the butter with honey and roll the dumplings in it, then in the ground hazelnuts. Dust with confectioner's sugar and serve.

Cook Time: 10–12 minutes

Ingredients for
30 Dumplings
1 cup (150 g) Whole wheat flour
1½ cups (150 g) Spelt flour
4¼ tbsp (60 g) Butter or untempered vegetable margarine
Salt
13 oz (375 g) Low-fat quark
3 Eggs
20 Plums, pitted
2 tbsp (30 g) Butter or untempered vegetable margarine to roll in
1 tbsp Honey
1.5 oz (40 g) Hazelnuts, ground
Confectioner's sugar for dusting

RHUBARB NOODLES

Knead a smooth dough out of flour, water, vinegar, oil, salt, and eggs. Let rest for 1 hour. Preheat oven to 320 °F (160 °C). Roll out to about 1½ mm thick and cut into 1in (2 cm) wide noodles. Peel the rhubarbs, cut into ½in (1.5 cm) pieces and place on a baking sheet. Brush with raspberry purée and sprinkle with some ginger. Cover with aluminum foil and cook for 15 minutes.

Brown the crumbs in butter and sugar. Simmer the noodles in salt water for about 3 minutes. Remove from the water, drain, and mix with the crumbs. Serve with the rhubarbs.

Cook Time: 15 minutes for the rhubarbs, 3 minutes for the noodles

Bake Time: 320 °F (160 °C)

Ingredients for 4–6 Servings
1⅓ cup (250 g) Whole wheat flour
2 tbsp (1 kL) Water, lukewarm
Splash of vinegar
5 tbsp (4 cl) Oil
2 Eggs
Salt
14 oz (400 g) Rhubarbs
¼ cup (50 ml) Raspberry purée (see p. 201)
Dash of ginger, ground
¼ cup (60 g) White or whole wheat breadcrumbs
2¾ tbsp (40 g) Butter or untempered vegetable margarine
1½ tbsp (20 g) Brown or organic sugar

APRICOT PILLOWS

Ingredients for 12 Pieces
1⅓ (200 g) Whole wheat
  flour
Dash of salt
4 tsp (10 g) Yeast
7 tbsp Milk, lukewarm
1¾ oz (50 g) Dates
3 tbsp Rum
2¾ tbsp (40 g) Butter or
  untempered vegetable
  margarine
2 Egg yolks
2 Egg whites
4 tsp (20 g) Granulated sugar
6 Apricots, pitted and halved
Fat of your choice for the
  pan

Dissolve the yeast in lukewarm milk and mix with whole wheat flour and salt. Finely chop the dates and boil in ½ cup (125 ml) water and rum. Add the butter and then let cool. Add the egg yolks and purée with an immersion blender. Beat the egg whites to stiff peaks with the sugar. Mix the date purée into the yeast and flour mixture, knead to a soft dough, and fold in the egg whites. Cover and let rise in a warm place until it has doubled in size. Preheat oven to 375 °F (190 °C). It is best to use an ableskiver pan or an egg frying pan. Grease the depressions in the pan. Place a tablespoon of dough in each, place a half apricot on top, and cover with more dough. Bake for 8–10 minutes.

Bake Time: about 8–10 minutes

Bake Temperature: 375 °F (190 °C)

COUNTESS APPLES

Ingredients for 2 Servings
2 Apples
Sweetener
Some lemon juice
1 Cinnamon stick
1 Clove
1 Egg white
¼ cup (60 g) Sugar-free
  marmalade
Butter or untempered veg-
  etable margarine for the
  dishes

Preheat oven to 400 °F (200 °C). Peel, quarter, and core the apples. Bring 2 cups of water to boil with sweetener, lemon juice, a cinnamon stick, and a clove and stew the apples in it until they are soft. Beat the egg whites to stiff peaks and fold in the sugar-free marmalade. Remove the apples, place each in a greased individual serving size dishes, and cover with egg whites. Bake for 8–10 minutes, until the tip of the egg white is lightly browned.

Bake Time: about 8–10 minutes

Bake Temperature: 400 °F (200 °C)

FILLED BAKED APPLES

Preheat oven to 350 °F (180 °C). For the filling, chop the almonds, raisins, and dried plums and mix with the honey and lemon juice. Core the apples, soak the inside with lemon juice. Fill the apples with the prepared filling, place in a greased casserole dish, and bake for about 20 minutes. Let cool and decorate with whipped cream. Sprinkle almond slivers and confectioner's sugar on top.

Bake Time: about 20 minutes

Bake Temperature: 350 °F (180 °C)

Ingredients for 2 Servings
2 Apples
Lemon juice
Light margarine for the dish

For the Filling
¾ oz (20 g) Almonds
¾ oz (20 g) Raisins
2 oz (50 g) Dried plums
1½ tbsp (30 g) Honey
Juice of ½ lemon

To Garnish
Whipped cream
Almond slivers
Confectioner's sugar

QUINCE GRATIN WITH ROWAN BERRY ICE CREAM

First prepare the ice cream. Wash the rowan berries and boil them for 5 minutes in maple syrup until soft. Purée with an immersion blender and sieve. Boil the milk. Mix together the cream, egg yolk, and honey and stir into the milk. Cook on low heat until the mixture begins to thicken a little. Beat in a cold water bath until cold. Sieve and mix with the rowan berry purée, applesauce, and rowan berry schnapps. Freeze in an ice cream machine. This amount will make about ten scoops.

Peel the quinces, cut into 5 mm slices, pit, and place in lemon water. Heat the red wine with honey and poach the quince slices in it. Pour off the liquid, boil down to about half, and let cool. Cream the egg yolks and honey in a double boiler and bind with cold butter cubes. Fill deep dishes with the egg yolk, place the quince slices on top, and bake for 8–10 on 430 °F (220 °C) upper heat and 300 °F (150 °C) lower heat (or high upper heat). Dust with confectioner's sugar and place the rowan berry ice cream in the middle.

Bake Time: 8–10 minutes

Bake Temperature: 430 °F (220 °C) upper heat and 300 °F (150 °C) lower heat

Ingredients for the Rowan Berry Ice Cream
3.5 oz (100 g) Rowan berries
½ cup (125 ml) Red wine
3 tbsp (4 cl) Maple syrup
1¼ cups (300 ml) Milk
7 tbsp (100 ml) Heavy cream
3 Egg yolks
5 tbsp (100 g) Honey
2 oz (60 g) Applesauce (see p. 177)
4 tsp (2 cl) Rowan berry schnapps

For the Gratin
6 Quinces
Juice of 1 lemon
¾ cup (200 ml) Red wine
1½ tbsp (30 g) Honey to poach
3 Egg yolks
1 tbsp (20 g) Honey to cream
2¾ tbsp (40 g) Butter or untempered vegetable margarine, cold
Confectioner's sugar for dusting

WHOLE FOOD CREAMS

Cakes are not the only thing that you can make healthier. You can easily and playfully use the principles of whole food cooking, as the following recipes deliciously prove, in the preparation of creams. Those who follow a "pure" way of life can replace gelatin in these recipes with agar-agar, an algae extract that gels well. But be careful: it only gels after being boiled for 1–2 minutes in liquid (2 cups (200 ml) to ¼ teaspoon).

ORANGE HONEY CREAM

Add water to the gelatin and remove the excess. Warm some of the orange juice and dissolve the gelatin in it. Mix with the honey and the rest of the gelatin, mix in the egg yolks, and stir over ice bath until cold. Beat the egg whites to still peaks with granulated sugar. Fold into the cream and fill glasses. Garnish with fresh mint.

Ingredients for 6 Servings
1 cup (250 ml) Orange juice, fresh squeezed
2 tbsp plus 1 tsp (50 g) Honey
3 Egg yolks
3 Sheets gelatin
3 Egg whites
4 tsp (20 g) Granulated sugar
Mint to garnish

SOUR MILK GELATIN WITH SPELT LADYFINGERS

Bring the water, white wine, and honey to a boil. Add water to the gelatin, remove excess, and dissolve the gelatin in the warm mixture. Let cool somewhat and mix in the curdled milk. Fill small rings or dishes and chill for 3 hours.

Pit the cherries. Boil for 5 minutes with red wine and a cinnamon stick. Remove from heat, take out the cinnamon stick, and season with honey and cherry brandy. Place the gelatins on dishes. Place the red wine cherries next to them and garnish with spelt ladyfingers and mint.

Ingredients for 6 Servings
2 cups (500 ml) Curdled milk
¼ cup (50 ml) Water
¼ cup (50 ml) White wine
2 tbsp plus 1 tsp (50 g) Honey
5 Sheets gelatin
Ladyfingers according to the basic recipe (see p. 37), made with spelt flour
Mint to garnish

For the Red Wine Cherries
18 oz (500 g) Sweet cherries
1¼ cups (300 ml) Red wine
2 tbsp plus 1 tsp (50 g) Honey
1 Cinnamon stick
4 tsp (2 cl) Cherry brandy

ALMOND CREAM WITH BERRIES

Add water to the gelatin and remove excess. Warm the amaretto and dissolve the gelatin in it. Mix with the sour cream and fold in the almonds. Beat the egg whites to stiff peaks with granulated sugar. Fold into the cream mixture and fill glasses. Chill for 2 hours. Garnish with fresh berries.

Ingredients for 8 Servings
4 Egg whites
3 tbsp (40 g) Granulated sugar
2 oz (50 g) Almonds, ground
2 Sheets gelatin
1½ cups (350 g) Sour cream
6 tbsp Amaretto
9 oz (250 g) Berries of your choice

TOFU CREAM WITH RASPBERRIES

Purée the tofu, honey, and cream in a blender. Lightly crush half of the raspberries with a fork and mix into the tofu cream. Chill briefly. Fill glasses using a piping bag. Garnish with the rest of the raspberries.

Garnish Recommendation: freshly baked sesame waffles (see p. 38)

Ingredients
3.5 oz (100 g) Fresh tofu
½ cup (125 ml) Heavy cream
1 tbsp Honey
9 oz (250 g) Raspberries

MILLET MOUSSE WITH ALMOND CREAM

Boil the millet, vanilla pulp, salt, and milk. Simmer on low for about 25 minutes with the lid slightly opened, then sieve. Slowly bring the agar-agar to a boil in maple syrup, white wine, and water. Remove from heat then bring to a boil again. Mix the liquid agar-agar with the millet mixture. Before it gels, fold in the whipped cream and fill molds with the mousse. Chill for an hour. Remove from the molds and garnish with the almond cream.

For the almond cream, boil the chopped almonds in the cream for 30 minutes. Purée in a food processer. Mix in egg yolks and stir until cool. Sweeten with maple syrup before serving.

Ingredients
2 oz (60 g) Millet, hot rinsed
Pulp of ½ vanilla bean
Dash of salt
2 cups (500 ml) Milk
1 tsp Agar-Agar
2 oz (50 g) Maple syrup
¼ cup (60 ml) White wine
¼ cup (60 ml) Water
½ cup (125 ml) Whipped cream

For the Almond Cream
2.5 oz (70 g) Almonds, peeled and chopped
1 cup (250 ml) Heavy cream
1 Egg yolk
1.5 oz (40 g) Maple syrup

Mill Culture War

White flour versus whole wheat—it's not just a nutritional sciences and medical problem, but also a matter of worldview. Man is a creature of habit, and those who were raised being fed white bread by their mothers often have a bias against whole wheat eaters. And those who swear on whole grains are often fanatics who accuse anyone who doesn't follow their teaching of having an irresponsible relationship to nature in general and their bodies in particular.

A compromise between the two camps (who often come from different generations), is possible. Not every torte made with white flour is "poison" (especially if you don't eat too much), and whole foods can not only be delicious, but they also have scientific pros, such as more dietary fiber, calcium (for the bones), magnesium (for the muscles), or vitamin B (for the nerves).

The bottom line: Those who eat whole foods won't be damaged by a little journey into white flour. And the white flour classicist can make a detour into whole grain—even if it's just for their health.

Dining à la Crème
CREAMS, MOUSSES, AND FOAMS

CREAMS

The "crème de la crème" of the sweet kitchen is the cream itself. It is not only a vital ingredient for holding together fine layers of dough, but can also be the main player in a sweet dish. The requirement is the mastery of a few basic recipes that can be easily followed at home.

BUTTERCREAM (GERMAN BUTTERCREAM)

For the basic cream, cream butter with confectioner's sugar until white. For the German cream, boil ¾ cup (200 ml) of milk (!) with granulated sugar. Mix the rest of the milk with vanilla pudding mix and egg yolks and stir into the boiling milk. Cook briefly, let cool, and sieve. Then mix the vanilla cream into the buttercream one spoonful at a time and use as you wish.

Use: This recipe can be used as a classic torte cream, where the basic buttercream can be mixed with various additions. Aside from the given vanilla cream, you can make hazelnut buttercream (mix in hazelnuts) or chocolate buttercream (mix in chocolate).

Dalai Lama and the Buttercream Torte

The Dalai Lama never thought that his life's work would one day be connected to good old German buttercream. Denis Scheck, the German literature critic and Ingeborg Bachmann Prize judge, was responsible for it. He received a review copy of the collection of Dalai Lama quotes, Daily Advice from the Heart, *about which he said that it contained "wisdom with the intellectual force of a buttercream torte dropped from ten meters." Having said that, buttercream torte doesn't taste so bad at all, and you certainly don't have to drop it from ten meters high.*

Ingredients
For the Basic Cream
2 sticks plus 5 tbsp (300 g) Butter
6 tbsp (50 g) Confectioner's sugar

Variation:
German Buttercream
1 cup (250 ml) Milk
7 tbsp (100 g) Granulated sugar
1 oz (25 g) Vanilla pudding mix
1 Egg yolk

Pastry Cream (Crème Pâtissière)

Ingredients
2 cups (500 ml) Milk
⅓ cup (80 g) Granulated sugar
1 Vanilla bean
3 Egg yolks
1 Egg
4 tbsp (40 g) Cornstarch

Mix the egg yolks, egg, cornstarch, and a third of the milk. Boil the rest of the milk with sugar and the halved vanilla bean. Scrape the vanilla bean pulp into the milk. While stirring constantly, pour the egg and milk mixture into the boiling milk and bring to a boil again. Put the cream in a metal mixing bowl and mix until cold in a cold water bath. Cover with plastic wrap so that it doesn't develop a skin and use as desired.

Use: as a basic cream in pastries

Parisian Cream

Ingredients
1 cup (250 ml) Heavy cream
9 oz (250 g) Dark couverture chocolate or cooking chocolate

Boil the heavy cream, dissolve the chocolate in it, and let cool. Before it hardens completely, beat in a stand mixer until creamy, then use as desired.

Use: as classic torte filling

Tip: Parisian cream can be stored for a while in the refrigerator. Before using, it must be warmed slightly in a water bath and then beaten again.

An Eiffel Tower of Chocolate Cream

Parisian crème doesn't get its name from a confectioner, but rather from a man who is famous for steel instead of snacks. We are talking about Alexandre Gustave Eiffel (1832–1923), whose tower, built for the World's Fair in Paris 1889, gave many confectioners the same idea: to create the shape of the Eiffel Tower on a pâte brisée base and pour chocolate over the whole thing. The chocolate cream used has been called Parisian cream ever sense.

CRÈME À L'ANGLAISE (ENGLISH CREAM)

MASCARPONE CREAM

Slowly mix the egg yolk and sugar until the sugar has dissolved. Boil the milk with the vanilla bean, remove the vanilla bean, and scrape the pulp into the milk. Slowly pour the hot milk into the yolk mixture, stirring constantly. Now pour the cream into a pot and mix constantly while heating it (not boiling!) until the mixture begins to thicken. You can tell when it is ready because when you blow on the cream while it is coating the cooking spoon, rings will appear that are reminiscent of a rose. Then sieve the cream and use as desired.

Use: not as classic vanilla sauce per se, but mostly as a basic pastry cream or as a base for various ice creams

Ingredients
6 Egg yolks
7 tbsp (100 g) Granulated
  sugar
2 cups (500 ml) Milk
½ Vanilla bean

MASCARPONE CREAM

Mix the mascarpone with honey, orange zest, and confectioner's sugar until smooth. Whip the heavy cream. Fold mascarpone mix in the whipped cream and chill.

Use: This quick recipe to prepare cream is perfect as a garnish for marinated fruits and berries, but also as a "quick filling" for a summery fruit torte: spread the cream on a case base, lay fruit on top, and viola!

Ingredients
18 oz (500 g) Mascarpone
2 tbsp Honey
Zest of 1 orange
¾ cup (100 g) Confectioner's
  sugar
7 tbsp (100 ml) Heavy cream

CRÈME SABAYON

Cream egg yolks with sugar in a mixing bowl. Place the bowl in a hot water bath, pour in the wine, and beat until it has doubled in volume. Fill individual serving sized glasses or use as otherwise desired.

Use: works well as a fluffy standalone dessert as well as a garnish for warm and cold desserts

Sabayon is a Zabaglione

Even the French Larousse Gastronomique *admits it: the oft-quoted in cooking jargon "sabayon" is actually the Italian "zabaglione." Sabayon is actually a direct relative of the desserts made famous at the Roman "Café Greco," a warm egg cream beaten with marsala wine and sugar. It is also known as "zabaione" in Italian. The French changed the name a bit and made the famous champagne mousseline that is mostly served with fish and shellfish, but is also still part of dessert. The Austrian zabaglione variant, which is French inspired but not quite a French sabayon, is quite at home with dessert. It is a wine foam, often called "Schado" or "Schato" in old cookbooks, that is mostly served with cakes.*

Ingredients
3 Egg yolks
7 tbsp (100 g) Granulated sugar
½ cup (125 ml) White wine (Riesling, Savagnin, or Muscatel)

BAVARIAN CREAM (BAVAROISE)

Ingredients
3 Egg yolks
⅓ cup (70 g) Sugar
1 Vanilla bean
4 tsp (2 cl) Kirsch (cherry
  brandy)
2 Sheets gelatin
1¼ cups (300 ml) Heavy
  cream

Halve the vanilla bean and scrape out the pulp. Cream the egg yolk with sugar and vanilla pulp in a double boiler, then beat in an ice water bath until cold. Add water to the gelatin, remove excess, and dissolve in warmed kirsch. Stir into the egg mixture. Whip the cream almost completely, then fold in. Fill serving sized dishes and chill for 2 hours.

Garnish Recommendation: fresh berries, fruit purée, or cardamom berries (see p. 190)

Tip: A particular charming addition—especially in the cooler seasons—is preserved dried pears and plums. (See recipe on p. 187.)

The Wittelsbach's Sweet Secret

Even the most cunning culinary historians can't find the answer to the question of just what is so Bavarian about Bavarian cream. There is even a "bavaroise italienne" and a "bavarois mexicaine." Even the "muscovite," created by a French chef for an aristocratic Russian family is a relative of Bavrian cream. The secret of why this basic French pastry cream has its blue and white name must have been taken to the grave by the Wittelsbach royal family. Maybe it was simply the fact that the Bavarian ruling class placed great worth on being served by French chefs.

CRÈME BRÛLÉE

Preheat oven to 185 °F (85 °C). Mix the egg yolk and sugar. Boil the halved vanilla bean in milk and heavy cream. Remove from heat, remove the vanilla bean, and scrape the pulp into the milk. Mix with the egg yolks. Stir in a bain-marie until the mixture thickens. Sieve, portion into dishes, and cook for 40 minutes. Chill for 2 hours. Dust with brown sugar and caramelize in the oven on the highest temperature (or use a kitchen torch).

Cook Time: 40 minutes

Bake Temperature: 185 °F (85 °C)

Ingredients
6 Egg yolks
½ cup (110 g) Granulated
  sugar
1 Vanilla bean
¾ cup (200 ml) Milk
2 cups (500 ml) Heavy cream
¼ (50 g) Brown sugar

Burnt Pleasures

If you study French cookbooks—even modern ones—you will see that crème brûlée rarely appears. And in French restaurants, too, you will not see it on the menu as often you would think based on its worldwide popularity.

Crème brûlée is actually not even as French as mousse au chocolat. Rather, it is an adaptation of the caramel cream called "crema catalona," which existed in Spain by the eighteenth century. The crispy top, however, is claimed by the British, who say that "burnt creams" were enjoyed by Cambridge students in the seventeenth century.

But crème brûlée doesn't owe its status as a fashionable dessert of our time to Spain, England, or France. It conquered the hearts of the globalized dessert world first in 1982, when the fancy New York restaurant Le Cirque called for a "crème brûlée revival."

Panna Cotta

Bring the heavy cream, vanilla bean, vanilla sugar, and granulated sugar to a boil and then simmer on low heat for about
10 minutes. Remove the vanilla bean. Add cold water to the
gelatin, remove excess water, and dissolve in the warm cream.
Flavor with amaretto. Fill individual serving sized molds and
chill overnight.

Garnish Recommendation: fruit purée and sorbets

Ingredients
2 cups (500 ml) Heavy cream
1 Vanilla bean
4 tsp (20 g) Vanilla sugar
3 tbsp (50 g) Granulated
  sugar
3 Sheets gelatin
4 tsp (2 cl) Amaretto

Crème Caramel

Preheat oven to 250 °F (120 °C). Heat the granulated sugar in a
pan, caramelize, and then pour into small molds. Boil the milk,
granulated sugar, and vanilla sugar. Mix together the eggs and
egg yolk, beat into the hot milk, sieve, and then fill the molds.
Fill an appropriately sized pan with 1 in (2 cm) of water, bring to
a boil, then remove from heat. Place the molds in the pan, cover
with aluminum foil, and bake for about 50–60 minutes. Remove
from the water bath, let cool, and then chill for several hours
in the refrigerator. Cut around the crème with a small knife and
overturn onto dishes.

Cook Time: 50–60 minutes

Bake Temperature: 250 °F (120 °C) (lower heat)

Garnish Recommendation: fruit purée and various sorbets

Ingredients for 6 Servings
2 cups (500 ml) Milk
7 tbsp (100 g) Granulated
  sugar to caramelize
⅓ cup (70 g) Granulated
  sugar
3 Eggs
1 Egg yolk
1 tbsp Vanilla sugar

CRÈME CARAMEL

1
Caramelize the granulated sugar in a pan.

2
Cover the bottoms of the molds in caramel.

3
Mix the eggs and egg yolk together and add the boiled milk and sugar mixture.

4
Beat well.

5
Sieve the mixture and fill the molds.

6
Place the molds in a water bath, cover with aluminum foil, and let set in the oven.

WINE CREAM

Beat the egg yolks with sugar in a double boiler until creamy. Add cold water to the gelatin, remove excess, and dissolve the gelatin in warmed lemon juice. Stir into the egg mixture and pour in the wine. Beat everything in the double boiler until it is nice and foamy. Then beat in an ice bath until it begins to gel. Beat the egg whites to stiff peaks with the granulated sugar and fold in. Fill glasses or deep dishes with cream and chill for 3 hours.

Garnish Recommendation: Serve with grape compote (see p. 182) or other fruit compotes.

SEMOLINA FLUMMERY WITH PLUMS

Halve the vanilla bean and scrape out the pulp. Boil in milk with lemon zest and sieve. Boil the vanilla milk again, add the semolina while stirring constantly, and stir in moistened gelatin. Let cool slightly. Cream the egg yolks with sugar and slowly mix into the semolina mixture. Finally, fold in the whipped cream. Fill small molds and chill. Wash, halve, pit, and slice the plums. Place the molds briefly in hot water, then remove the flummery. Garnish with plums.

Garnish Recommendation: stewed plums (see p. 177) or plum marmalade (see p. 196)

Tip: For a change, try a distinctive side dish of cardamom berries (see p. 190) or elderberry sorbet (see p. 359).

SEMOLINA FLUMMERY

Ingredients for 10 Servings
3 Egg yolks
7 tbsp (100 g) Granulated sugar
4 tsp (20 ml) Lemon juice
4 Sheets gelatin
1 cup (250 ml) White wine (Riesling or Savagnin)
4 Egg whites
2 tbsp (30 g) Granulated sugar for the egg whites

Ingredients for 10–12 Servings
2 cups (500 ml) Milk
1 Vanilla bean
Zest of 1 lemon
2 oz (50 g) Wheat semolina
8 Sheets gelatin
5 Egg yolks
1 cup (125 g) Confectioner's sugar
1½ cup (375 ml) Whipped cream
About 10–12 Plums

Sweet as Flummery

The word "flummery" can be puzzling both in English and in German. Flummery is a British word that originally meant "empty blabbering or false compliments," but also "oatmeal." Eventually, it came to mean a kind of semolina pudding, even if it can't be prepared with pudding mix. Traditionally, there is an important distinction between pudding and flummery: pudding can be savory, prepared with fish or shellfish. But a flummery is always sweet. (See recipe on p. 256.)

Chocolate Coffee Cream with Mint

Dissolve the instant coffee, confectioner's sugar, and whiskey in a metal mixing bowl over steam. Add cold water to the gelatin, remove excess water, and dissolve in the warm coffee liquid. Cream the egg yolks and add them to the liquid. Melt and mix in the chocolate. Whip the cream most of the way, then fold in little by little. Fill a large bowl or several individual serving sized molds and chill for 2–3 hours.

For the mint sauce, peel, quarter, and core the pears. Boil with the granulated sugar and lemon juice until soft. Blanch the mint in boiling salt water and shock in ice water. Drain and add the mint to the pears. Blend everything until smooth. Sieve. Flavor with peppermint liqueur. Portion the mint sauce onto plates and place the cream on top. Garnish with finely chopped mint strips and dust with confectioner's sugar.

Ingredients for 8 Servings
8 oz (225 g) White couverture chocolate
3 Egg yolks
¾ oz (20 g) Instant coffee powder
2 tbsp (15 g) Confectioner's sugar
2 Sheets gelatin
1 tbsp Whisky
2 cups (500 ml) Heavy cream
Mint leaves to garnish
Confectioner's sugar for dusting

For the Mint Sauce
4 Pears
⅓ cup (80 g) Granulated sugar
¼ cup (6 cl) Lemon juice
½ Bundle of peppermint
3 tbsp (4 cl) Peppermint liqueur
Dash of salt

EGG LIQUEUR CREAM IN CHOCOLATE WITH COCONUT

Ingredients for 8 Servings
10.5 oz (300 g) Mascarpone
¾ cups (180 ml) Advocaat
  (egg liqueur)
½ cup (60 g) Confectioner's
  sugar
¼ cups (60 ml) Orange juice
Zest of 1 orange
3 Sheets gelatin
1 cup (250 ml) Whipped
  cream
About 7 oz (200 g) dark
  couverture chocolate

For the Coconut Leaves
About 3.5 oz (100 g) strudel
  dough (homemade or
  readymade)
1 Egg for brushing
Coconut flakes

Mix the mascarpone with egg liqueur, confectioner's sugar, and orange zest. Add water to the gelatin, remove excess, and dissolve in warmed orange juice. Mix into the mascarpone. Finally, fold in the whipped cream. Place the mixture in small baking rings (about 2¼ in (6 cm) diameter) and chill for 3 hours. Cut 1½x8 in (4x20 cm) strips of parchment paper.

Melt the dark chocolate in a bain-marie. Fill a parchment paper cone with the melted chocolate and pipe a lattice onto the paper strips. Remove the cooled cream from the rings. Carefully press the paper strips with the chocolate lattice around the cream and freeze for 20 minutes. Carefully pull the paper away, so the chocolate lattice stays on the cream.

Preheat oven to 400 °F (200 °C). For the coconut sheets, cut the strudel dough out into 8 attractive circles or triangles. Brush with egg and sprinkle with coconut flakes. Bake for about 5 minutes, until crispy. Remove from the baking sheet and let cool. Set decoratively on the tartlet before serving.

Bake Time: about 5 minutes

Bake Temperature: 400 °F (200 °C)

Garnish Recommendation: strawberry purée (see p. 200)

Tip: Try pouring some of the egg liqueur over the tartlets—it is not only decorative, but it gives it a little bit of a higher proof taste.

CHOCOLATE LEMON CREAM WITH ORANGE CARDAMOM SYRUP

Place the tartlet rings on a baking sheet lined with parchment paper and chill. For the chocolate mousse, melt the chocolate in a double boiler, remove from heat, and mix in simple syrup and egg yolks. Stir in heavy cream, then fold in whipped cream and season with amaretto. Fill the baking rings halfway and place in the refrigerator to firm for about half an hour.

For the lemon mousse, heat some of the lemon juice with vanilla and granulated sugar. Add cold water to the gelatin, remove excess, and dissolve in the warm lemon juice. Stir in the rest of the lemon juice and chill. As soon as the mixture begins to gel, fold in the whipped cream, flavor with Cointreau, and spread on top of the chocolate mousse. Place in the refrigerator for another ½ hour.

Melt the prepared ganache glaze in a double boiler, remove from heat, and cool to room temperature by placing in the refrigerator for a short time. Pour over the tartlets and chill in the refrigerator for 4–5 hours. For the orange cardamom syrup, reduce the orange juice, cardamom, and honey until it is thick. Cool to room temperature. Remove the chilled tartlets from the rings and pour the syrup around them on plates.

Garnish Recommendation: piña colada sorbet (see p. 363), caramel, and mint

Ingredients for 6 Tartlets
(2½ in (6 cm) diameter)

For the Chocolate Mousse
2.5 oz (70 g) Dark couverture chocolate
1 Egg yolk
¾ oz (20 g) Simple syrup (see p. 40)
¾ cup (200 ml) Heavy cream
7 tbsp (100 ml) Whipped cream
2 tsp (1 cl) Amaretto

For the Lemon Mousse
½ cup (110 ml) Lemon juice
2 Sheets gelatin
1 tbsp (15 g) Vanilla sugar
1 tbsp (15 g) Granulated sugar
⅓ cup (90 ml) Whipped cream
2 tsp (1 c) Cointreau
About 9 oz (250 g) ganache glaze (see p. 43)

For the Orange Cardamom Syrup
2 cups (500 ml) Orange juice
2 tbsp Honey
Cardamom seeds or powder

MOUSSE

The word "mousse" comes from French and means something like foam, airy pastry, or fluffy cream. Gnocchi are often made from mousse and garnished accordingly. If the mousse is placed in a long, rectangular pan, then removed and served, it is called a terrine. Mousses also don't have to be sweet—just think of liver pâté. But the best of these airy, melt-in-your-mouth nothings are from the confectioner, where there is a lot more than "just" the sinfully sweet "Mousse au chocolat."

PRALINE MOUSSE WITH ORANGE RAGOUT

Ingredients for 6 Servings
2.5 oz (65 g) Dark couverture chocolate
2.5 oz (65 g) White couverture chocolate
4.5 oz (125 g) Nougat
1 Egg
1 Egg yolk
Juice and zest of 1 orange
3 Sheets gelatin
2 cups (500 ml) Whipped cream
4 tsp (2 cl) Grand Marnier
Orange ragout according to the basic recipe (see p. 183)

Melt the chocolates and nougat in a bain-marie. Add cold water to the gelatin and whip the cream. Beat the egg and egg yolk in a double boiler and mix into the melted chocolate. Remove excess water from the gelatin and dissolve in warmed Grand Marnier and orange juice. Mix into the nougat. Finally, fold in the whipped cream and the orange zest and chill for 2 hours. In the meantime, prepare the orange ragout and portion onto dishes. Make gnocchi from the mousse and place on the orange ragout.

White Chocolate Mousse with Raspberries

Add water to the gelatin. Beat the egg and egg yolk in a bain-marie until creamy. Remove excess water from the gelatin, dissolve in warmed rum, and mix into the eggs. Melt the chocolate in a bain-marie and stir in. Let cool briefly. Whip the cream, fold in, and chill for at least 2 hours. In the meantime, prepare the raspberry purée and portion onto dishes. Use a spoon to form gnocchi from the mousse and place on the raspberry purée. Garnish with fresh raspberries.

Ingredients for 6–8 Servings
6 oz (175 g) White couverture chocolate
1 Egg
1 Egg yolk
1½ Sheets gelatin
4 tsp (2 cl) White rum
1¼ cups (300 ml) Heavy cream
Raspberry purée (see p. 201)
10.5 oz (300 g) Raspberries

Banana Mousse

Purée the peeled bananas with simple syrup and lemon juice and sieve. Add water to the gelatin, remove excess, and dissolve in some banana purée over steam. Add to the rest of the banana purée and beat over ice until the mixture begins to gel. Beat the egg whites to stiff peaks with sugar and fold into the banana. Fill individual serving size molds and chill for 2 hours.

In the meantime, melt the dark chocolate. Cut out circles about the size of the molds. Fill a parchment paper cone with chocolate and pipe a chocolate lattice onto the circles. Carefully place in the freezer. When they are hard, carefully remove from the paper and lay on top of the finished mousse. Garnish with minced mint.

Tip: You can also make the chocolate lattices in advance and store them in the freezer without a problem. Then you will have a great decoration for many desserts.

Ingredients for 10 Servings
3 Bananas
2 oz (80 g) Simple syrup (see p. 40)
3 tbsp (4 cl) Lemon juice
4 Sheets gelatin
3 Egg whites
2 tbsp (30 g) Granulated sugar
7 oz (200 g) Dark couverture chocolate
Mint to garnish

BUTTERMILK MOUSSE WITH HONEY

Ingredients for 6–8 Servings
2 sticks plus 1½ tbsp
  (250 ml) Buttermilk
3 tbsp (60 g) Honey
3 tbsp (4 cl) Orange juice
Zest of 1 orange
3 Sheets gelatin
¾ cup (200 ml) Heavy cream
10.5 oz (300 g) Burgundy
  cherries (see p. 183)

Mix the buttermilk with warmed honey and orange zest. Whip the cream. Add water to the gelatin, remove excess, and dissolve in warmed orange juice. Stir the orange juice into the buttermilk. Stir over ice until the liquid begins to gel. Fold in the whipped cream and chill for 3 hours. In the meantime, prepare the burgundy cherries and portion into deep dishes. Using a spoon, create gnocchi from the mousse and place on top of the cherries.

MOCHA MOUSSE WITH SESAME WAFFLES AND MANGO PURÉE

Melt both chocolates in a bain-marie. Beat the egg yolks in a bain-marie until creamy and mix into the chocolate. Add cold water to the gelatin, remove excess, warm orange juice, and dissolve the gelatin in it. Stir in orange juice, instant coffee powder, and crème de cacao. Lightly whip the cream and carefully fold in. Chill for at least 2 hours. For the mango purée, peel the mango, pit, and cut into slices. Boil water with sugar and stew the mangos until soft. Blend and sieve. For the coffee sauce, mix the simple syrup with instant coffee powder. Place the finished mocha mousse on dishes and garnish with sesame waffles, mango purée, and coffee sauce.

Ingredients for 6 Servings
2 Egg yolks
3 oz (80 g) Milk couverture chocolate
2 oz (50 g) White couverture chocolate
5 tsp Orange juice, fresh squeezed
½ tbsp Instant coffee powder
4 tsp (2 cl) Crème de cacao (cocoa liqueur)
1 Sheet gelatin
¾ cup (200 ml) Whipped cream
Sesame waffles (see p. 38)

For the Mango Purée
1 Mango (ripe)
3 tbsp (50 g) Sugar
⅓ cup (80 ml) Water

For the Coffee Sauce
3.5 oz (100 g) Simple syrup (see p. 40)
2 tbsp (1 kL) Instant coffee powder

SHERRY MOUSSE WITH STRAWBERRIES

Beat the egg yolks with sugar and sherry in a bain-marie until creamy. Add water to the gelatin, remove excess, and dissolve in the warm egg mixture. Beat the mascarpone into the cooled cream one spoonful at a time. Whip the cream and fold into the sherry cream. Fill small molds or coffee cups and let cool completely. Dip in hot water before removing from the molds and dust with cocoa powder.

Wash and halve the strawberries. Froth half of the butter in a pan. Sprinkle the pepper in the pan, then add the strawberries and sugar and briefly sauté. Deglaze with Grand Marnier. Season with orange juice and lemon juice. Mix in the rest of the butter before serving. Remove the sherry mousse from the molds and garnish with strawberries.

Ingredients for 10 Servings
6 Egg yolks
⅓ cup (75 g) Sugar
7 tbsp (100 ml) Oloroso sherry
13 oz (375 g) Mascarpone
3 Sheets gelatin
2 cups (500 ml) Heavy cream
Cocoa powder for dusting

For the Strawberries
21 oz (600 g) Strawberries
3 tbsp (4 cl) Grand Marnier
3 tbsp Confectioner's sugar
3 tbsp (4 cl) Orange juice
2 tsp (1 cl) Lemon juice
2 tbsp (1 kL) Pepper, black, coarsely ground
4¼ tbsp (60 g) Butter

QUARK MOUSSE WITH STRUDEL LEAVES AND PRESERVED APRICOTS

Beat the egg yolks with sugar, vanilla sugar, and lemon zest until creamy. Add cold water to the gelatin and remove excess. Warm rum, apricot brandy, and marmalade and dissolve the gelatin in it. Beat the egg whites to stiff peaks with granulated sugar. Mix the quark and sour cream. Stir in the egg yolk and apricot gelatin mixture. Alternately fold in the whipped cream and egg whites. Fill small molds—preferably triangular—with mousse and chill.

Preheat oven to 400 °F (200 °C). Prepare the strudel dough according to the recipe, cut into triangles and place on a buttered or parchment paper lined baking sheet. Sprinkle the triangles with confectioner's sugar and bake for about 5 minutes, until the sugar caramelizes. Place the well cooled quark mousse in the middle, place a strudel leaf on top. Place preserved apricots on the strudel and another strudel leaf on top. Garnish with mint and apricot purée.

Bake Time: about 5 minutes

Bake Temperature: 400 °F (200 °C)

Ingredients for 10 Servings
3 Egg yolks
¼ cup (60 g) Sugar
2 tsp (10 g) Vanilla sugar
Lemon zest
1 tbsp Apricot marmalade
3 tbsp (4 cl) Rum
4 tsp (2 cl) Apricot brandy
4 Sheets gelatin
9 oz (250 g) Quark
½ cup (125 ml) Sour cream
2 Egg whites
3 tbsp (50 g) Granulated
  sugar for the egg whites
⅔ cup (150 ml) Whipped
  cream
Strudel dough (see p. 16 or
  readymade)
Preserved apricots
  (see p. 188)
Butter for the baking sheet
Confectioner's sugar for
  dusting
Mint and apricot purée to
  garnish

HONEY POPPY MOUSSE WITH STRAWBERRIES

Ingredients for 6–8 Servings
1 Egg
1 Egg yolk
4 Sheets gelatin
4 tsp (2 cl) Grand Marnier
5 oz (150 g) White couverture chocolate
¼ cup (90 g) Honey
3.5 oz (100 g) White or gray poppy seeds
1½ cups (350 ml) Whipped cream
10.5 oz (300 g) Dark couverture chocolate
14 oz (400 g) Strawberries, fresh
Strawberry purée (see p. 200)
Confectioner's sugar and chopped mint to garnish

Beat the egg and egg yolk in a bain-marie until creamy. Add honey and beat more. Add cold water to the gelatin, remove excess, and dissolve in warmed Grand Marnier. Stir into the egg mixture. Melt the white chocolate in a bain-marie, stir in, and let cool. Carefully fold in the poppy and whipped cream and chill for 2–3 hours.

In the meantime, melt the dark chocolate in a bain-marie. Fill a parchment paper cone, pipe a lattice onto parchment paper, and freeze.

Make gnocchi from the finished honey poppy mousse, place on dishes, and serve with fresh strawberries and some strawberry purée. Break pieces off the chocolate lattice and place decoratively on the mousse. Dust with confectioner's sugar and sprinkle with chopped mint before servings.

Tip: Instead of making a chocolate lattice, it is even easier to spread chocolate thinly on the paper.

LEBKUCHEN MOUSSE WITH ORANGES

Ingredients for 6 Servings
1 Egg
2 Egg yolks
5 tsp (25 g) Granulated sugar
1 Sheet gelatin
4 tsp (2 cl) Rum
4 tsp (2 cl) Kirsch (cherry brandy)
1 tsp (4 g) Lebkuchen or gingerbread spices
2 oz (50 g) Dark couverture chocolate
2 oz (60 g) Lebkuchen
¾ cup (200 ml) Whipped cream
3 Oranges
Confectioner's sugar and Grand Marnier to marinate
Mint, chopped

Beat the egg and egg yolks with granulated sugar in a double boiler and then beat in a cold water bath until cold. Add cold water to the gelatin, remove excess, and dissolve in slightly warmed rum and kirsch. Stir in, add the lebkuchen spices, and carefully mix in the melted chocolate. Cut the lebkuchen into small pieces, mix in, and then fold in the whipped cream. Chill for 3–4 hours.

In the meantime, take the oranges apart and marinate in confectioner's sugar and Grand Marnier. Make gnocchi from the mousse, place on dishes, and garnish with the marinated orange pieces. Sprinkle with chopped mint before serving.

Pear Mousse with Chocolate Sabayon

Peel, halve, and core the pears and cook in a covered pot with white wine and a little less than half (60 g) of the sugar. Purée in a blender and sieve. (You should have about 1 cup (250 ml) of fruit purée.) Beat the egg yolks with the rest of the sugar. Bring the pear purée briefly to a boil, dissolve the moistened gelatin in it, and mix into the egg, stirring constantly. Beat until the mixture is cold and has a creamy consistency. Fold in the whipped cream and flavor with pear brandy. Pour in a bowl and chill for at least 3 hours.

For the sabayon, mix egg yolks with sugar, cocoa powder, and milk and beat in a warm water bath until creamy. Flavor with crème de cacao and beat again. Make gnocchi from the mousse, place on dishes, and serve with chocolate sabayon.

Garnish Recommendation: pear chili sorbet (see p. 362)

Tip: This dish looks particularly decorative when you also garnish with freshly caramelized strudel leaves.

Ingredients for 6 Servings
14 oz (400 g) Pears, ripe
½ cup (125 ml) White wine
½ cup plus 1 tbsp (135 g) Sugar
2 Egg yolks
3 Sheets gelatin
1 cup (250 ml) Whipped cream
⅓ cup (8 cl) Pear brandy

For the Chocolate Sabayon
4 Egg yolks
⅓ (80 g) Sugar
1 tbsp Sugar
½ cup (125 ml) Milk
3 tbsp (4 cl) Crème de cacao (cocoa liqueur)

Yogurt Terrine

Mix the yogurt with the confectioner's sugar. Add water to the gelatin and remove excess. Warm the orange juice and lemon juice together and dissolve the gelatin in it. Mix into the yogurt. Whip the cream and fold it in. Fill a terrine pan and chill for 3 hours. Remove from the form and cut into servings.

Garnish Recommendation: fruit purée and fresh fruit

Ingredients for 6 Servings
1 cup (250 ml) Whole milk yogurt
6 tbsp (50 g) Confectioner's sugar
Juice of ½ lemon
Juice of ½ orange
3 Sheets gelatin
¾ cup (200 ml) Heavy cream

VANILLA CRESCENT TERRINE

Ingredients for 6 Servings
Vanilla crescent batter
  (see p. 378)
Cocoa powder and
Confectioner's sugar for
  dusting

For the Mousse
1 cup (250 ml) Milk
2 Vanilla beans
3 Egg yolks
⅓ cup (70 g) Granulated
  sugar
3 Sheets gelatin
1 cup (250 ml) Whipped
  cream
3 tbsp (4 cl) Whisky
3.5 oz (100 g) Chocolate
  shavings
2 oz (60 g) Almonds, peeled
  and roasted

For the Calvados Sabayon
Sabayon (see p. 250)
3 tbsp (4 cl) Calvados

Preheat oven to 350°F (180°C). Prepare the vanilla crescent dough and let rest for about half an hour. Form rolls that are the length of your terrine. Bake them for about 10 minutes.

For the mousse, boil milk with the halved vanilla beans. Remove the beans and scrape the pulp into the milk. Add water to the gelatin, remove excess, and dissolve in the milk. Beat the egg yolks and sugar in a double boiler then beat in the milk until it begins to thicken slightly. Fold in the whipped cream and flavor with whisky. Fold the chocolate and almonds into the mousse.

Now fill the terrine pan with the vanilla sticks and the mousse alternately and chill for several hours. In the meantime, prepare the sabayon and flavor with calvados. Remove the cooled terrine from the pan and dust with cocoa powder and confectioner's sugar. Cut into servings and serve with the calvados sabayon.

Bake Time: about 10 minutes

Bake Temperature: 350°F (180°C)

Garnish Recommendation: apple compote (see p. 177)

TRIPLE CHOCOLATE TERRINE

For the dark mousse, melt the bittersweet chocolate and mix with egg yolks, simple syrup, and whipping cream. Fold in whipped cream and flavor with Grand Marnier. Fill terrine pans with the mousse and chill for half an hour. In the meantime, melt the milk chocolate and mix with egg yolks, simple syrup, and whipping cream. Add water to the gelatin, remove excess water, dissolve in slightly warmed rum, and stir into the chocolate mixture. Fold in whipped cream. Spread on top of the first layer in the terrine pans and chill another half hour. Now melt the white chocolate and mix with egg yolks, simple syrup, and whipping cream. Add water to the gelatin, remove excess water, dissolve in slightly warmed Bacardi, and stir into the chocolate mixture. Fold in whipped cream. Fill in the third layer in the terrine pan and for best results, let chill overnight.

Garnish Recommendation: fresh fruit and fruit purée

Ingredients for 2 terrine pans

For the Dark Mousse
7.5 oz (210 g) Bittersweet chocolate
3 Egg yolks
2 oz (60 g) Simple syrup (see p.40)
¼ cup (60 ml) Heavy cream
1¼ cup (300 ml) Whipped cream
2 tbsp (3 cl) Grand Marnier

For the Milk Chocolate Mousse
7.5 oz (210 g) Milk chocolate
3 Egg yolks
2 oz (60 g) Simple syrup (see p.40)
¼ cup (60 ml) Heavy cream
3 Sheets gelatin
1¼ cup (300 ml) Whipped cream
2 tbsp (3 cl) Rum

For the White Mousse
7.5 oz (210 g) White chocolate
3 Egg yolks
2 oz (60 g) Simple syrup (see p.40)
¼ cup (60 ml) Heavy cream
3 Sheets gelatin
1¼ cup (300 ml) Whipped cream
2 tbsp (3 cl) Bacardi

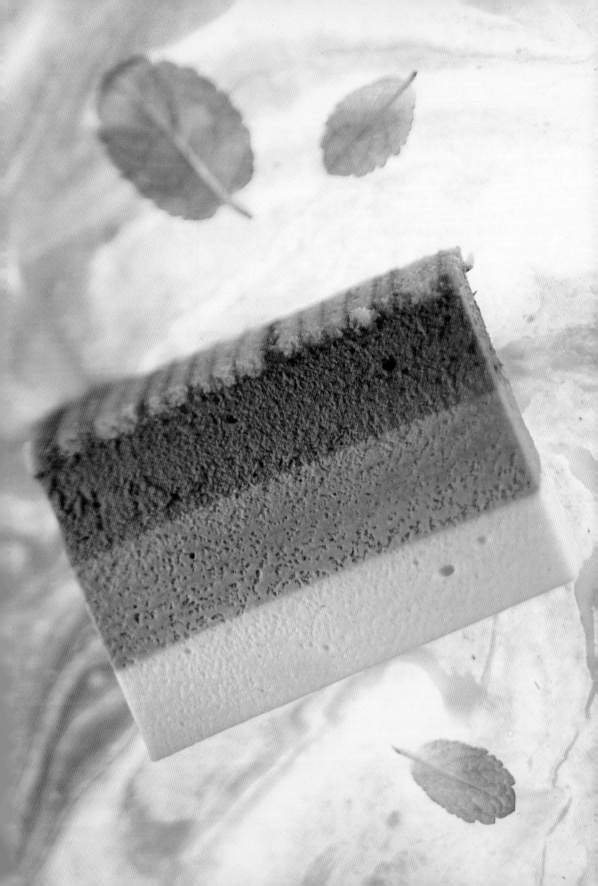

Foams

Foam is a particularly light and modern form of classic mousse. It was invented by the three star Spanish chef Ferran Adriá, who ran one of the most avant garde restaurants in the world, El Bulli, and while there he was concerned with food science and food design.

In the process of his studies, Adriá experimented with whipped cream containers and created a new, airy-light foam dish that can also be made in many fantastical varieties in the home kitchen (and not only for dessert!).

Foams can be a standalone dish or a pretty, delicious garnish. They can be served instead of the classic sorbet in a multi-course meal, but they also make refreshing amuse-bouches and enticing petits-fours. Most of all, foams have the advantage that they can be kept for a long time and prepared in advance of guests.

The perfect flavors for foams are all fruits, herbs, and spices, but also champagne, wine, liqueurs, and brandies—not to mention chocolate.

The requirement for making foam is a cream whipper such as iSi Gourmet Whip, which can be bought anywhere at a well-equipped kitchen store. The following recipes will fill a one (1) quart (1l) cream whipper. If you have a 1 pint cream whipper, you can halve to recipe and use 1 to 2 chargers.

CHOCOLATE MINT FOAM

Ingredients for about
10 Servings
9 oz (250 g) Milk couverture
  chocolate
9 oz (250 g) Dark couverture
  chocolate
⅓ cup (80 g) Granulated
  sugar
2 cup (500 ml) Heavy cream
½ Bundle of mint
3 tbsp (4 cl) Peppermint
  liqueur
Dash of salt

Blanch the mint in salt water and then shock in ice water. Warm cream and sugar in a pot, mix in the mint with an immersion blender, and then sieve. Dissolve the chocolate in the warm cream. Flavor with peppermint liqueur. Stir in an ice water bath until cold and fill a 1 quart cream whipper. Screw in two chargers and shake well. Place in the refrigerator for several hours. Before foaming, shake well with the whipper upside down.

PLUM FOAM

Pit and halve the plums and boil them in red wine and granulated sugar for several minutes. Purée with an immersion blender and then sieve. Add water to the gelatin, remove excess, and stir in. Let firm in the refrigerator. Whisk smooth and fill a 1 quart cream whipper. Screw in two chargers and shake well. Place in the refrigerator for several hours. Before foaming, shake well with the whipper upside down.

Ingredients for 10 Servings
35 oz (1 kg) Plums
¾ cup (160 g) Granulated sugar
7 tbsp (100 ml) Red wine
6 Sheets gelatin

STRAWBERRY FOAM

Add cold water to the gelatin. Warm about ½ cup (100 ml) strawberry purée and dissolve the gelatin in it. Stir in the rest of the purée, flavor with strawberry liqueur and then chill. Let firm in the refrigerator. Whisk smooth and fill a 1 quart cream whipper. Screw in two chargers and shake well. Place in the refrigerator for several hours. Before foaming, shake well with the whipper upside down.

Ingredients for 10 Servings
4¼ cup (1 l) Strawberry purée (see p. 200)
6 Sheets gelatin
3 tbsp (4 cl) Strawberry liqueur

CAMPARI FOAM

Boil the orange juice with sugar and sieve. Add cold water to the gelatin, remove excess, and dissolve in the warm juice. Flavor with Campari and chill. Let firm in the refrigerator. Whisk smooth and fill a 1 quart cream whipper. Screw in two chargers and shake well. Place in the refrigerator for several hours. Before foaming, shake well with the whipper upside down.

Ingredients for about 10 Servings
4 cups (900 ml) Blood orange juice
⅔ cup (150 g) Granulated sugar
⅔ cup (150 ml) Campari
7 Sheets gelatin

Airy, Light, Sweet, & Fluffy

SOUFFLÉS, CASSEROLES, SCHMARREN,
AND PUDDING

SOUFFLÉS

Hot air—it is not only hiding behind so many clever advertising and marketing strategies, it is also the secret to every successful soufflé. In both cases there seems to be more there than there really is. The basic ingredients of a soufflé are mostly quite simple, yet a successful soufflé can be stunning. As long as the outside is crisp and the inside fine and creamy—and it is served quickly enough that it does not fall too soon.

QUARK SOUFFLÉ

Strain the quark, add the egg yolks, cornstarch, a pinch of salt, vanilla sugar, lemon zest, and the sour cream, and mix together. Coat one or several appropriate soufflé ramekins with butter and sprinkle with sugar. Ready a water bath in the oven at 350–425 °F (180–220 °C). Beat the egg whites with sugar until stiff and fold into the quark mixture. Fill the ramekins about ⅔ full, set them in a water bath and bake for about 20 minutes. Remove the soufflés, garnish to your taste, and serve right away.

Bake Time: about 20 minutes

Bake Temperature: 350–425 °F (180–220 °C)

Garnish suggestions: various sorbets, fresh fruit, or pickled apricots (see p.188)

Ingredients for 10 Servings
1 cup (250 g) Quark
3 Egg yolks
4 tsp (20 g) Cornstarch
½ cup (125 ml) Sour cream
1 tbsp Vanilla sugar
Zest of one lemon
Pinch of salt
3 Egg whites
3 tbsp (40 g) Sugar
Butter and sugar for the
  ramekins

CHOCOLATE SOUFFLÉ

Ingredients for 10 Servings
3 oz (90 g) Dark couverture
  chocolate
1 oz (30 g) Milk couverture
  chocolate
3½ tbsp (50 g) Butter
6 Egg yolks
6 Egg whites
3 tbsp (40 g) Granulated
  sugar
Butter and granulated sugar
  for the ramekin

Preheat oven to 400 °F (200 °C). Put both chocolates in a metal mixing bowl and warm over steam. As soon as they are liquid, stir in the butter, remove from heat, and mix in the egg yolks. Beat the egg whites to stiff peaks with the sugar and fold into the chocolate mixture. Butter a ramekin and sprinkle with granulated sugar. Fill the ramekin about ⅔ of the way full and bake in a water bath for about 25 minutes. Remove the soufflé from the ramekin, garnish to taste, and serve right away.

Bake Time: about 25 minutes

Bake Temperature: 400 °F (200 °C)

Garnish Recommendation: fresh fruit or orange ragout (see p. 183)

Tip: Since the chocolate soufflé batter can be prepared days early and frozen, it is perfect for when you are expecting guests. In this case, you simply have to bake for 5 minutes longer.

BANANA SOUFFLÉ

Ingredients for 8 Servings
5½ tbsp (80 g) Butter
⅓ cup (40 g) Confectioner's
  sugar
4 Egg yolks
14 oz (400 g) Bananas
Juice of 2 lemons
2 oz (50 g) Almonds, grated
  and roasted
1.5 oz (40 g) Chocolate
  streusel
4 tsp (20 g) Cornstarch
4 Egg whites
6 tbsp (90 g) Sugar
Butter and granulated sugar
  for the ramekins

Preheat oven to 350 °F (180 °C). Cream the butter with the confectioner's sugar and then add the egg yolks. Purée the bananas, mix with lemon juice, almonds, chocolate streusel, and cornstarch. Mix into the egg yolk mixture. Beat the egg whites to stiff peaks with the sugar and fold in. Butter the ramekins and sprinkle them with sugar. Fill the ramekins about ⅔ of the way full and bake in a water bath for about 20 minutes. Remove the soufflés from the ramekin, garnish to taste, and serve right away.

Bake Time: about 20 minutes

Bake Temperature: 350 °F (180 °C)

Garnish Recommendation: banana slices, chocolate shavings, and mango purée

Bananas, of All Things

Although the banana was only shipped from Asia to Europe in 1885, it is only of the oldest domesticated plants in the world. Alexander the Great met them during his Indian campaign, and in 500BCE, Gautama Buddha used the banana bush as a symbol for the inanity and worthlessness of worldly possession because it cannot fertilize itself and its flowers are sterile.

Bananas owe their worldwide popularity to world famous variety star Josephine Baker, who—clothed only in a banana belt—was a singing propagandist for bananas in the 1920s. She coined that erotic image that the Chiquita company used in 1945 for a famous radio spot which went: "I'm Chiquita Banana and I've come to say / That bananas have to ripen in a certain way. / Any way you want to eat them / It's impossible to beat them." The refrain offered good life advice to unenlightened banana consumers: "But you must never put bananas / In the refrigerator / No-no-no-no." (See recipe on p. 281.)

POPPY SOUFFLÉ

Preheat oven to 400 °F (200 °C). Take the crusts off the bread and saturate them in milk, then sieve. Cream the butter and confectioner's sugar, add the egg yolks little by little, and then mix in the poppy. Mix the sieved rolls, vanilla sugar, salt, and lemon zest into the butter. Beat the egg whites to stiff peaks and fold them and the breadcrumbs into the batter in turns. Butter the ramekins and sprinkle them with sugar. Fill the ramekins about ⅔ of the way full and bake in a water bath for about 20 minutes. Remove the soufflés from the ramekin, garnish to taste, and serve right away.

Bake Time: about 20 minutes

Bake Temperature: 400 °F (200 °C)

Garnish Recommendation: preserved dried pears, preserved apricots (see p. 188), or elderberry purée (see p. 180)

Ingredients for 12 Servings
1 stick plus 2 tbsp (140 g) Butter
⅔ cup (140 g) Confectioner's sugar
5 oz (140 g) Poppy seeds, freshly ground
1½ Dinner rolls
1½ cup (350 ml) Milk
Dash of vanilla sugar
Zest of 1 lemon
Dash of salt
6 Egg yolks
6 Egg whites
1 oz (25 g) Breadcrumbs
Butter and granulated sugar for the ramekins

HAZELNUT SOUFFLÉ

*Ingredients for 8–10
Servings*
3 oz (90 g) Nougat
2¾ tbsp (40 g) Butter
6 Egg yolks
6 Egg whites
3 tbsp (40 g) Granulated
   sugar
3 oz (80 g) Hazelnuts, ground
2 tsp (10 g) Cornstarch
Butter and granulated sugar
   for the ramekins

Preheat oven to 400 °F (200 °C). Put the nougat in a metal mixing bowl and melt over steam. Stir in the butter, remove from heat, and mix in the egg yolks. Beat the egg whites to stiff peaks with the granulated sugar and fold into the nougat along with the ground hazelnuts and cornstarch. Butter the ramekins and sprinkle them with sugar. Fill the ramekins about ⅔ of the way full and bake in a water bath for about 25 minutes. Remove the soufflés from the ramekin, garnish to taste, and serve right away.

Bake Time: about 25 minutes

Bake Temperature: 400 °F (200 °C)

Garnish Recommendation: honey whipped cream and orange ragout (see p. 183)

SEMOLINA SOUFFLÉ

Ingredients
¾ cup (200 ml) Milk
2 tbsp (30 g) Butter
5 tsp (25 g) Granulated sugar
Lemon juice
Dash of salt
Dash of ginger
1 oz (35 g) Semolina
1 tbsp (15 g) Cornstarch
2 Egg yolks
3 Egg whites
Butter and granulated sugar
   for the ramekins
Sour cream and
   confectioner's sugar to
   garnish

Preheat oven to 350 °F (180 °C). Boil the milk with butter, half of the sugar, some lemon juice, ginger, and a dash of salt. Add the semolina and "roast" like choux pastry. That means stir on medium heat until the dough comes away from the edge of the pot. Stir the egg yolk and cornstarch into the batter. Beat the egg whites to stiff peaks with the rest of the sugar and fold in. Butter the ramekins and sprinkle them with sugar. Fill the ramekins about ¾ of the way full and bake in a water bath for about 25 minutes. Remove the soufflés from the ramekins, garnish to taste, and serve right away.

Bake Time: about 25 minutes

Bake Temperature: 350 °F (180 °C)

Garnish Recommendation: berries or orange ragout (see p. 183) and sesame waffles (see p. 38)

CHESTNUT SOUFFLÉ

Ingredients for 6 Servings
3½ tbsp (50 g) Butter
3 Egg yolks
Dash of salt
Dash of vanilla sugar
¾ oz (20 g) Cooking chocolate
2 oz (60 g) Chestnuts, sieved
   (or ready-made chestnut
   purée)
3 Egg whites
3 tbsp (40 g) Sugar
1 oz (30 g) Almonds, ground
⅓ oz (10 g) Breadcrumbs
Butter and granulated sugar
   for the ramekins
Confectioner's sugar for
   dusting

Cream the butter with a dash of salt and the vanilla sugar. Add the egg yolks little by little. Melt the chocolate in a bain-marie and stir into the batter. Beat the eggs to stiff peaks with the sugar. Fold in the egg yolks, chestnuts, ground almonds, and breadcrumbs in turns. Butter the ramekins and sprinkle them with sugar. Fill the ramekins about ⅔ of the way full and bake in a water bath for about 15–20 minutes. Remove the soufflés from the ramekins, garnish to taste, and serve right away.

Bake Time: 15–20 minutes

Bake Temperature: 400 °F (200 °C)

Garnish Recommendation: sauvignon sabayon (see p. 250), grapes, or grape compote (see p. 182)

Chestnuts instead of Grain
The filling "nuc castanea," which became the Spanish chestnut or Italian "marrone," was known to the ancient Romans and traveled north with them from the Mediterranean to Hadrian's Wall in England. As opposed to the equally filling field crops, the chestnut was not a result of agriculture, but rather came from the woods and pastures. The custom of planting edible chestnuts cultured from wild chestnuts instead of old, dead oak trees spread, especially in southern and central Europe. Not, however, to load up the markets of the Middle Ages with roasted chestnuts, but because they hoped to created an emergency replacement for grain with flour made from the chestnuts. In Italy, European chestnuts are still often called "Albero del pane"—tree of bread.

LEBKUCHEN SOUFFLÉ

Preheat oven to 400 °F (200 °C). Melt the chocolate in a bain-marie. Cream the egg yolks and sugar and add the chocolate little by little. Grind the lebkuchen, saturate with milk, and stir into the egg yolk mixture together with the lemon zest, orange zest, vanilla sugar, salt, cardamom, and ground nuts. Begin beating the eggs, then beat to stiff peaks with granulated sugar. Slowly fold into the batter. Butter the ramekins and sprinkle them with granulated sugar. Fill the ramekins about ¾ of the way full and bake in a water bath for about 25–30 minutes. Remove the soufflés from the ramekins and serve right away.

Bake Time: about 25–30 minutes

Bake Temperature: 400 °F (200 °C)

Garnish Recommendation: Cardamom berries (see p. 190) and sabayon (wine foam, see p. 250)

Ingredients for 6 Servings
5½ tbsp (80 g) Butter
3 tbsp (40 g) Confectioner's sugar
3 oz (80 g) Dark couverture chocolate
4 Egg yolks
5 oz (140 g) Lebkuchen
3 tbsp (4 cl) Milk, lukewarm
Zest of 1 lemon
Zest of 1 orange
Dash of vanilla sugar
Dash of salt
Pinch of cardamom
2 oz (60 g) Walnuts, ground
4 Egg whites
3 tbsp (40 g) Granulated sugar
Butter and granulated sugar for the ramekins

MARBLE SOUFFLÉ

Preheat the oven to 400 °F (200 °C). Strain the quark. Add the egg yolks, cornstarch, salt, vanilla sugar, lemon zest. Beat the egg whites to stiff peaks with sugar and fold into the quark mixture. Spilt the batter in half and carefully fold the cocoa powder into one half. Butter the ramekins and sprinkle them with granulated sugar. Fill the ramekins about ¾ of the way full with the two batters and bake in a water bath for about 20 minutes. Remove the soufflés from the ramekins and serve with strawberry purée and fresh fruit.

Bake Time: about 20 minutes

Bake Temperature: 400 °F (200 °C)

Ingredients for 10 Servings
9 oz (250 g) Quark
3 Egg yolks
4 tsp (20 g) Cornstarch
4.5 oz (125 g) Sour cream
Dash of vanilla sugar
Zest of 1 lemon
Dash of salt
3 Egg whites
3 tbsp (40 g) Granulated sugar
1 tbsp Cocoa powder
Butter and granulated sugar for the ramekins
Strawberry purée (see p. 200) and fresh fruit to garnish

LEMON QUARK SOUFFLÉ

Ingredients for 10 Servings
9 oz (250 g) Quark
Zest of 2 lemons
Juice of 1 lemon
3 Egg yolks
4 tsp (20 g) Cornstarch
½ cup (125 ml) Sour cream
Dash of vanilla sugar
Dash of salt
3 Egg whites
3 tbsp (40 g) Granulated
  sugar
Butter and granulated sugar
  for the ramekins

Strain the quark and mix in the egg yolks, cornstarch, salt, vanilla sugar, lemon zest, lemon juice, and sour cream. Butter the ramekin(s) and sprinkle with granulated sugar. Place a water bath in the oven from 350–430 °F (180–220 °C). Beat the egg whites with sugar, fold into the batter, and fill the ramekin ¾ full. Bake in the water bath for about 20 minutes. Remove the soufflé from the ramekin, garnish to taste, and serve right away.

Bake Time: about 20 minutes

Bake Temperature: 350–430 °F (180–220 °C)

Garnish Recommendation: fresh berries and any sorbet

SCHMARREN

In Austrian German, "Schmarren" means complete nonsense. In Viennese baking, Schmarren is actually a quite sensible and particularly delicious dish made with rich ingredients such as semolina, breadcrumbs, potatoes, or flour, made light and fluffy by adding eggs.

KAISERSCHMARREN

Ingredients
4 Eggs
⅓ cup (40 g) Flour
1 tbsp Granulated sugar
Raisins to taste
¼ cup (⅛ l) Milk
Butter for frying
Granulated and
  confectioner's sugar
  for dusting

Preheat oven to 400°F (200°C). Separate the eggs and beat the whites to stiff peaks with the granulated sugar. Fold in the yolks, vanilla sugar, raisins, and flour. Carefully mix in the milk. Heat butter in a pan. Pour in the batter and brown on low heat for about 30 seconds, then bake for about 15 minutes. Take the pan out of the oven and cut the kaiserschmarren into pieces with a fork. Sprinkle with granulated sugar and caramelize in the oven again. Dust with confectioner's sugar before serving.

Bake Time: about 15 minutes

Bake Temperature: 400°F (200°C)

Garnish Recommendation: stewed plums (see p. 177) or compote and/or ice cream

Schmarren alla casa

Next to boiled beef, kaiserschmarren was the favorite dish of Emperor Franz Joseph and also one of the culinary insignia of the Habsburg dynasty—the "House of Austria" or "Casa d'Austria." This relationship indicates to many culinary historians that this most famous of all schmarren can trace its name back to a preparation "alla Casa d'Austria." Another of the many schmarren legends concerns the Emperor's passion for hunting. He allegedly was always looking forward to a "kaserchmarren" in the next alpine hunting lodge. The most popular legend talks about a court chef named Leopold, who wanted to make himself popular with the ruling family with a new recipe of pancake batter and stewed plums. Empress Elisabeth, who was concerned with her figure, allegedly left the dish untouched, at which the Emperor had to step in and order his servant: "Give me that nonsense that our Leopold threw together." And kaiserschmarren was born.

CREAM SCHMARREN

Preheat oven to 350 °F (180 °C). Mix the sour cream with quark, confectioner's sugar, egg yolks, cornstarch, rum, and vanilla sugar. Beat the egg whites, add granulated sugar, and beat to stiff peaks. Fold into the egg yolk mixture. Melt butter in a pan. Put the schmarren batter in the pan and cook until it stiffens. Bake in the oven for about 12 minutes. Tear the schmarren into small pieces and dust with confectioner's sugar.

Bake Time: about 12 minutes

Bake Temperature: 350 °F (180 °C)

Garniture Recommendation: lukewarm burgundy cherries (see p. 183) and vanilla foam (see p. 203)

Ingredients
1 cup (250 ml) Sour cream
2 oz (50 g) Quark
6 tbsp (50 g) Confectioner's
   sugar
3 Egg yolks
⅓ cup (50 g) Cornstarch
1 tbsp Rum
Dash of vanilla sugar
3 Egg whites
¼ cup (60 g) Granulated
   sugar
1½ tbsp (20 g) Butter for
   frying
Confectioner's sugar for
   dusting

SEMOLINA SCHMARREN

Preheat oven to 375 °F (190 °C). Boil the milk, butter, and vanilla pulp. Sprinkle in the semolina and cook through, until it no longer sticks. Pour in a bowl, stir in egg yolks little by little, and add lemon zest and rum. Cream the egg whites with a dash of salt and a third of the sugar, add the rest of the sugar, then beat to very stiff peaks. Fold into the semolina mixture. Melt butter in a pan, put the batter in the pan, then bake for about 15 minutes.

Remove from oven, sprinkle with sugar, and briefly caramelize in the oven again. Cut into small pieces with a fork and serve garnished with strawberry purée and fresh strawberries.

Bake Time: about 15 minutes

Bake Temperature: 375 °F (190 °C)

Garnish Recommendation: peppermint pear sorbet (see p. 362)

Ingredients for 6 Servings
2 cup (500 ml) Milk
4¼ tbsp (60 g) Butter
Pulp of 1 vanilla bean
3 oz (90 g) Semolina
4 Egg yolks
Lemon zest
2 tsp Rum
4 Egg whites
Dash of salt
⅓ cup (80 g) Granulated
   sugar
1½ tbsp (20 g) Butter for
   frying
Confectioner's sugar
Strawberries and
   strawberry purée
   (see p. 200) to garnish

Nut Schmarren with Strawberries

Preheat oven to 400°F (200°C). Melt the nougat in a double boiler. Beat the egg yolks in a double boiler with vanilla sugar, confectioner's sugar, and orange zest until thick and creamy. Stir into the nougat. Begin to beat the egg whites, add granulated sugar, beat to stiff peaks, and fold in along with the hazelnuts. Heat butter in a pan, put the batter in the pan, and fry for about 1 minute on medium heat. Then place in the oven and bake for about 15 minutes. Remove, dust with confectioner's sugar, and cut with two forks. Wash and quarter the strawberries. Marinate in Grand Marnier and some confectioner's sugar, warm in a pan, and serve with the schmarren.

Bake Time: about 15 minutes

Bake Temperature: 400°F (200°C)

Garnish Recommendation: honey ice cream (see p. 354)

Ingredients
6 Egg yolks
2 tsp (10 g) Vanilla sugar
⅓ cup (40 g) Confectioner's sugar
Zest of 1 orange
2 oz (50 g) Nougat
6 Egg whites
1 cup (120 g) Granulated sugar
4 oz (120 g) Hazelnuts, ground
2¾ tbsp (40 g) Butter
Confectioner's sugar for dusting

For the Strawberries
10 oz (280 g) Strawberries
Grand Marnier
Confectioner's sugar

1
Prepare the ingredients.

2
Cream the egg yolk with vanilla sugar, confectioner's sugar, and orange zest in a double boiler and pour in the liquid nougat.

3
Mix the egg and nougat well.

4
Fold the egg whites and ground hazelnuts into the nougat egg mixture.

5
After baking, dust the schmarren with confectioner's sugar and cut into pieces.

6
Serve the nut schmarren with strawberries.

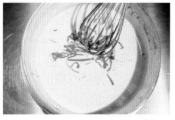

BLUEBERRY SCHMARREN

Ingredients for 6 Servings
4 Egg yolks
6 Egg whites
2 cups 500ml Milk
2 Cups (250 g) Flour
½ cup (125 g) Granulated
  sugar
10.5 oz (300 g) Blueberries
Butter for frying
Confectioner's sugar for
  dusting

Preheat oven to 350 °F (180 °C). Mix the egg yolks with flour and milk to make dough. Begin beating the egg whites, sprinkle in the granulated sugar, beat to stiff peaks, and carefully fold into the dough. Melt butter in a pan and put the dough in the pan. Sprinkle the washed, sorted blueberries into the dough and then bake for about 15 minutes, depending on the height of the dough. Tear up the finished schmarren, dust with confectioner's sugar, and briefly caramelize in the oven again.

Bake Time: about 15 minutes

Bake Temperature: 350 °F (180 °C)

Garnish Recommendation: vanilla ice cream (see p. 350) and honey whipped cream

PUDDINGS

Austrian puddings—called "Koch," also the word for a cook—can be porridges, purées, or sweet casseroles baked in a tall dish. Sometimes they were steamed before being removed from their molds and called steamed puddings.

STRAWBERRY PUDDING SOUFFLÉ

Preheat oven to 350 °F (180 °C). Purée and sieve the strawberries. Mix in a stand mixer for 15 minutes with lemon juice, egg white, and granulated sugar. Begin beating the egg whites, add granulated sugar, and beat to stiff peaks. Carefully fold into the strawberry mixture. Butter and fill individual serving sized molds or deep dishes and bake for 10 minutes. Dust with confectioner's sugar and serve.

Bake Time: about 10 minutes

Bake Temperature: 350 °F (180 °C)

Garnish Recommendation: sour ice cream (see p. 355)

Ingredients for 6 Servings
18 oz (500 g) Strawberries
4 tsp (2 cl) Lemon juice
2 Egg whites
3 tbsp (50 g) Granulated
  sugar
Butter for the molds
Confectioner's sugar for
  dusting

For the Egg Whites
3 Egg whites
½ cup (120 g) Granulated
  sugar

PEACH PUDDING SOUFFLÉ

Preheat oven to 350 °F (180 °C). Mix the peach marmalade, egg white, granulated sugar, and grenadine for 15 minutes in a stand mixer on low, until it becomes viscous. Begin beating the egg whites, add the granulated sugar, and beat to stiff peaks. Carefully fold the egg whites into the peach mixture. Dice the preserved peaches and fold into the mixture. Butter and fill individual serving sized molds or deep dishes and bake for 10 minutes. Dust with confectioner's sugar and serve.

Bake Time: about 10 minutes

Bake Temperature: 350 °F (180 °C)

Garnish Recommendation: vanilla ice cream (see p. 350) and strawberry purée (see p. 200)

Ingredients for 6 Servings
½ cup (50 g) Peach
  marmalade
2 Egg whites
3 tbsp (50 g) Granulated
  sugar
2 tsp (1 cl) Grenadine
3 oz (80 g) Preserved
  peaches (see p. 189)
Butter for the molds
Confectioner's sugar for
  dusting

For the Egg Whites
3 Egg whites
3 tbsp (50 g) Granulated
  sugar

CHOCOLATE ORANGE PUDDING SOUFFLÉ WITH ORANGES

Ingredients for 6 Servings
3.5 oz (100 g) Cooking chocolate, ground
2 Egg whites
2 tbsp (30 g) Granulated sugar
Zest of 2 oranges
Almonds, grated
Confectioner's sugar for dusting
Butter for the molds
Orange slices to garnish
Grand Marnier to marinate

For the Egg Whites
3 Egg whites
5 tbsp (70 g) Granulated sugar

Preheat oven to 350 °F (180 °C). Mix the ground chocolate with orange zest and 1(!) egg white until the mixture becomes viscous. Add the second egg and granulated sugar and mix for another half hour. For the beaten egg whites, begin beating, add the granulated sugar, and beat to stiff peaks. Carefully fold into the chocolate mixture. Butter and fill individual serving sized molds or deep dishes. Dust with confectioner's sugar and sprinkle almonds on top. Bake for 10 minutes. Marinate the orange slices in Grand Marnier and serve with the pudding.

Bake Time: about 10 minutes

Bake Temperature: 350 °F (180 °C)

SPONGE CAKE PUDDING

Ingredients for 6–8 Servings
3.5 oz (100 g) Sponge cake
⅓ cup (150 ml) Heavy cream
3½ tbsp (50 g) Butter
4 Egg yolks
Zest of 1 lemon
2 tsp (10 g) Vanilla sugar
4 Egg whites
3 tbsp (50 g) Granulated sugar
Butter and granulated sugar for the molds
Confectioner's sugar for dusting

Preheat oven to 400 °F (200 °C). Cut the cake into cubes, saturate with heavy cream, and let soak. Cream the butter until it is white. Add the egg yolk, then the cake, vanilla sugar, and lemon zest. Begin beating the egg whites, add granulated sugar, and beat to stiff peaks. Fold into the cake mixture. Butter individual servings sized molds and sprinkle with granulated sugar. Bake in a water bath for 30 minutes. Remove from molds and dust with confectioner's sugar.

Bake Time: about 30 minutes

Bake Temperature: 400 °F (200 °C)

Garnish Recommendation: strawberries, strawberry purée (see p. 200), and vanilla foam (see p. 203)

KIPFERL PUDDING

Preheat oven to 400 °F (200 °C). Cut the rolls into cubes and soak in the milk. Cream the butter with confectioner's sugar until white. Add the egg yolk and lemon zest. Squeeze out some of the excess milk from the rolls and mix into the butter. Beat the egg whites to stiff peaks with granulated sugar and fold into the batter. Butter individual servings sized molds and sprinkle with granulated sugar. Fill and bake in a water bath for 30 minutes. Remove from molds and dust with confectioner's sugar.

Bake Time: about 30 minutes

Bake Temperature: 400 °F (200 °C)

Garnish Recommendation: vanilla sauce (see p. 202) and cinnamon ice cream (see p. 356)

Ingredients for 6–8 servings
5 Crescents, stale
⅓ cup (100 ml) Milk
5 tbsp (70 g) Butter
½ cup (70 g) of Powdered
  sugar
Zest of 1 lemon, grated
5 Egg yolks
3 Egg whites
5 tbsp (60 g) Granulated
  sugar
Butter and granulated sugar
  for the forms

These Crescents are the Top

You can't miss the similarity: the crescent roll, or Kipferl, and the Turkish crescent moon. It would be ridiculous if there were no nice legend to go with it. And history itself assists in that as well. At the time of the Turkish siege of Vienna there was a Viennese baker named Peter Wendler, who had the patriotic idea to bake a crescent shaped egg pastry and call it a "Gipfel," or "tip," after the Turkish crescent moon that adorned the tip of the steeple on St. Stephen's Cathedral along with the cross. Soon the word "Gipfel" became "Kipfel." Etymologists see the story a little differently and believe "Kipferl" comes from the Old High German "kipf" (wagon tongue) and "kife" (chew). For a Christmas celebration in 1227, Leopold VI, the Glorious, received an early form of Kipferl as a gift. But the great Babenbergs couldn't even dream of the glorious Kipferl treat that can be prepared with our recipe.

ALMOND PUDDING

Ingredients for 8 Servings
7 tbsp (100 g) Butter
1 cup (120 g) Confectioner's sugar
2 tsp (10 g) Vanilla sugar
Dash of salt
Zest of 1 lemon
7 Egg yolks
½ cup (120 g) Almonds, ground
1 oz (30 g) Hazelnuts, ground
¾ oz (20 g) Breadcrumbs
4 Egg whites
2 tbsp (30 g) Granulated sugar
Butter and granulated sugar for the molds
Confectioner's sugar for dusting

Preheat oven to 400 °F (200 °C). Cream the butter with confectioner's sugar, vanilla sugar, salt, and lemon zest. Add the egg yolks little by little. Beat the egg whites to stiff peaks with the granulated sugar. Fold into the yolk mixture along with almonds, hazelnuts, and breadcrumbs. Butter individual servings sized molds and sprinkle with granulated sugar. Fill and bake in a water bath for 20 minutes. Remove from molds and dust with confectioner's sugar.

Bake Time: about 20 minutes

Bake Temperature: 400 °F (200 °C)

Garnish Recommendation: preserved apricots (see p. 188) and vanilla sauce (see p. 202)

APRICOTS PUDDING WITH ALMONDS

Ingredients for 6–10 Servings
(according to the size of the molds)
3½ tbsp (50 g) Butter
6 Egg yolks
⅓ cup (80 g) Confectioner's sugar
3.5 oz (100 g) Almonds, peeled and minced
1 Dinner roll
Heavy cream to marinate
5 oz (140 g) Preserved apricots (see p. 188)
3 Egg whites
¼ cup (60 g) Granulated sugar
Butter and granulated sugar for the molds
Confectioner's sugar for dusting

Beat butter with icing sugar until white and foamy, and then stir in egg yolks. Remove the crust from the bread and cut the rest into small cubes and soak in a little cream. Take the soaked bread cubes and mix together with the almonds in the butter mixture. Exercise caution by folding the egg whites into the mixture slowly. Grease matching ramekins with melted butter, then sprinkle with granulated sugar and pour mixture about ⅔ of the way up. Place the ramekins inside a dish filled with a little water and poach in a preheated oven at 400 °F (200 °C) for about 30 minutes. Serve with sprinkled with powdered sugar.

Bake Time: about 30 minutes

Bake Temperature: 400 °F (200 °C)

Garnish Reccomendation: pickled apricots (see page 188) and vanilla sauce (see page 202)

RICE PUDDING

Blanch the short grain rice in boiling salt water, strain, and shock with cold water. Boil the rice with the milk and then simmer on low until the rice is soft and the liquid has almost entirely evaporated. Preheat oven to 400 °F (200 °C). Cream the butter and mix into the cooled rice along with the egg yolks. Begin to beat the egg whites, add the granulated sugar, beat to stiff peaks, and carefully fold into the rice. Butter individual servings sized molds and sprinkle with granulated sugar. Fill and bake in a water bath for 20 minutes. Remove from molds and dust with confectioner's sugar.

Bake Time: about 20 minutes

Bake Temperature: 400 °F (200 °C)

Garnish Recommendation: apple compote (see p.177) and raspberry purée (see p. 201)

Ingredients for 8–10 Servings
4.5 oz (125 g) Short grain rice
2 cups (500 ml) Milk
5½ tbsp (80 g) Butter
5 Egg yolks
5 Egg whites
⅓ cup (80 g) Granulated sugar
Dash of salt
Butter and granulated sugar for the molds
Confectioner's sugar for dusting

CHOCOHUPF

Preheat oven to 400 °F (200 °C). Cream the butter and confectioner's sugar and then add the egg yolks. Remove the excess milk from the soaked rolls and mix into along with the melted chocolate. Beat the egg whites to stiff peaks with granulated sugar and fold into the batter along with the breadcrumbs and nuts. Butter individual servings sized molds and sprinkle with granulated sugar. Fill ⅔ of the way full. Cover and bake in a water bath for about 30 minutes. Remove from molds and place on plates. Serve with warm chocolate sauce and whipped cream.

Bake Time: about 30 minutes

Bake Temperature: 400 °F (200 °C)

Ingredients for 6 Servings
4¼ tbsp (60 g) Butter
½ cup (60 g) Confectioner's sugar
3 Egg yolks
2 oz (60 g) Chocolate, melted
1½ Dinner rolls, stale, soaked in milk
2 oz (60 g) Nuts, ground
2 oz (60 g) Breadcrumbs
3 Egg whites
4 tsp (20 g) Granulated sugar
Butter and granulated sugar for the molds
Chocolate sauce (see p. 204) and whipped cream to garnish

Politically Incorrect, but Delicious

One of the most popular treats of classic Viennese cooking is still the pudding known as a "Mohr im Hemd" or "Moor in a shirt," which has had some political problems in recent years. For example, in New York the Moorish figure in the famous Julius Meinl logo may only be printed in bronze, to avoid accusations of racism. And in Austria, many socially conscious customers wrinkle their noses when they see a pastry stands offering "Moors." What else could we call "a dark pudding with chocolate sauce and whipped cream"? Some new names have been proposed for this good old dish, such as the "Chocohupf."

CHOCOLATE PUDDING WITH CANDIED LEMON AND ORANGE PEEL

Ingredients for 6–8 Servings
2.5 oz (70 g) Cooking chocolate
5 tbsp (70 g) Butter
6 Egg yolks
2.5 oz (70 g) Almonds, chopped
2 oz (50 g) Candied lemon peel
2 oz (50 g) Candied orange peel
4 Egg whites
⅓ cup (70 g) Granulated sugar
Butter and granulated sugar for the molds

Preheat oven to 400 °F (200 °C). Melt the cooking chocolate. Cream the butter with egg yolks and mix in the cooking chocolate, almonds, candied lemon peel, and candied orange peel.

Begin beating the eggs, add granulated sugar, and beat to stiff peaks. Fold into the chocolate mixture. Butter individual servings sized molds and sprinkle with granulated sugar. Fill ⅔ of the way full. Bake in a water bath for about 20 minutes.

Bake Time: about 20 minutes

Bake Temperature: 400 °F (200 °C)

SWEET CASSEROLES

Casseroles enjoy great popularity among economically minded housewives because they can be served in the same dish they are baked in, which saves on dishwashing. Plus, good bakers can be in top form when throwing together a casserole.

SALZBURG GNOCCHI

Ingredients for 4–5 Servings
½ cups (125 ml) Milk or
  heavy cream
2¾ tbsp (40 g) Butter
4 tsp (20 g) Vanilla sugar
10 Egg whites
¼ cup (60 g) Granulated
  sugar
6 Egg yolks
Zest of 1 lemon
¼ cup (30 g) Flour
4 tsp (20 g) Cornstarch
Confectioner's sugar for
  dusting

Preheat oven to 430 °F (220 °C). In a heat safe porcelain dish or a casserole dish, mix the milk or cream, butter, and half of the vanilla sugar. Bake for 5 minutes. Begin beating the egg whites, add the granulated sugar, and beat to stiff peaks. Sift the cornstarch and flour together. Mix the egg yolks with the rest of the vanilla sugar and carefully fold into the egg whites along with the lemon zest and the cornstarch and flour. Form three large gnocchi and place them in the dish. Bake for 8–10 minutes. The gnocchi should still be creamy in the middle. Dust with confectioner's sugar and serve immediately, since they fall quickly as they cool.

Bake Time: 8–10 minutes

Bake Temperature: 430 °F (220 °C)

Garnish Recommendation: lingonberry compote

The Queen of Casseroles
It was described as "wobbly, skin-colored mountains of eggs souffléd with sugar" by James Henderson, the long time travel correspondent of the "Financial Times." And maybe you do have to be a native to really understand and enjoy the virtues of this dessert that is as huge as it is airy and light. But really, Mr. Henderson was not so wrong when he alluded to mountains. The "queen of casseroles" is supposed to look like the mountain ranges around Salzburg just after the first snow.

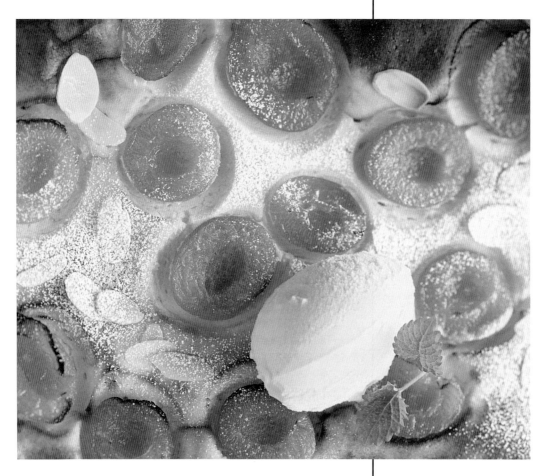

QUARK GRATIN WITH APRICOTS

Mix the quark with cornstarch, confectioner's sugar, egg yolks, rum, vanilla sugar, and lemon zest. Begin beating the egg whites, add granulated sugar, and beat to stiff peaks. Fold into the quark mixture. Pit the apricots and cut into slices. Butter deep oven-safe dishes, portion the quark mixture into each, and lay the apricot slices on top. On maximum upper heat, brown for several minutes in the oven. Dust with confectioner's sugar and serve right away.

Bake Time: several minutes

Bake Temperature: maximum upper heat

Garnish Recommendation: vanilla ice cream (See p. 350) or apricot sorbet (see p. 359)

Ingredients for 6 Servings
18 oz (500 g) Quark
⅓ cup (50 g) Cornstarch
⅓ cup (80 g) Confectioner's sugar
4 Egg yolks
4 tsp (2 cl) Rum
4 tsp (20 g) Vanilla sugar
Zest of 1 lemon
4 Egg whites
7 tbsp (100 g) Granulated sugar
4 Apricots
Butter for brushing
Confectioner's sugar for dusting

Ingredients for 6 Servings
10.5 oz (300 g) Brioche or
  dinner rolls, stale
7 tbsp (100 ml) Milk
1 Egg
1 oz (30 g) Preserved raisins
  (see p. 189)
3 tbsp (4 cl) Rum
1 oz (30 g) Almonds, grated
4 Apples or quinces
Juice of 1 lemon
3½ tbsp (50 g) Butter
2 tbsp (1 kL) Cinnamon
  powder
3 Egg whites
¼ cup (60 g) Granulated
  sugar
2 Egg yolks
2 tsp (10 g) Vanilla sugar
2 tbsp (20 g) Flour
Butter for the dish
Confectioner's sugar for
  dusting

Ingredients for 6 Servings
9 oz (250 g) Dinner rolls or
  brioche
2 Apples
2 oz (50 g) Almonds, grated
  and roasted
Cinnamon
⅓ cup (8 cl) Calvados (apple
  brandy)
2 cups (500 ml) Heavy cream
½ cup (120 g) Granulated
  sugar
7 Eggs
Butter for dish
Confectioner's sugar for
  dusting

For the Elderberry Sauce
4¼ cups (1 l) Red wine
35 oz (1 kg) Elderberries,
  crushed
1 Cinnamon stick
1 cup plus 2 tbsp (250 g)
  Granulated sugar
Cornstarch

CLASSIC SCHEITERHAUFEN ("FUNERAL PYRE")

Preheat oven to 340 °F (170 °C). Mix the milk with the egg. Cut the brioche or rolls into ½ in (1 cm) slices and soak in the egg milk. Cut the apple or quince into slices, sauté briefly in butter, and flavor with lemon juice and cinnamon. Butter a ceramic loaf pan. Arrange the apples and brioche like roof tiles and spread the raisins, rum, and almonds on top. Beat the egg white to stiff peaks with the granulated sugar. Fold in the egg yolk, vanilla sugar, and flour. Spread on top of the Scheiterhaufen. Bake for 25 minutes. Remove from oven and serve dusted with confectioner's sugar.

Bake Time: about 25 minutes

Bake Temperature: 340 °F (170 °C)

APPLE CASSEROLE WITH ELDERBERRY SAUCE

Preheat oven to 400 °F (200 °C). Cut the rolls or brioche into cubes. Peel and core the apples and cut into slices. Mix the bread, apples, and almonds. Beat the cream, eggs, and sugar and fold into the bread mixture. Flavor with cinnamon and Calvados. Fill a buttered dish and bake for about 30 minutes. For the elderberry sauce, boil the red wine, elderberries, sugar, and cinnamon and simmer for 15 minutes. Sieve. Mix a bit of cornstarch with a little bit of water and then stir into the simmering sauce. Remove the apple casserole from the dish and serve with the elderberry sauce and powdered sugar.

Bake Time: 30 minutes

Bake Temperature: 400 °F (200 °C)

Garnish Recommendation: vanilla ice cream (see p. 350)

NOODLE CASSEROLE WITH QUARK

Preheat oven to 350°F (180°C). Boil the pasta in milk, salt lightly, and cook until soft. Remove from heat and mix the strained quark into the warm pasta. Mix in the egg yolk, cornstarch, and vanilla sugar. Fold in the lingonberries. Begin beating the egg whites, add granulated sugar, beat to stiff peaks, and fold in. Butter a casserole dish and fill with the mixture. Bake for about 20 minutes. Dust with confectioner's sugar and serve with compote.

Bake Time: 20 minutes

Bake Temperature: 350°F (180°C)

Ingredients for 12 Servings
7 oz (200 g) Pasta
2 cups (500 ml) Milk
Salt
2 tbsp Lingonberries
9 oz (250 g) Quark
3 Egg yolks
4 tsp (20 g) Cornstarch
Dash of vanilla sugar
3 Egg whites
¼ cup (60 g) Granulated
　sugar
Butter for the dish
Confectioner's sugar for
　dusting
Compote as an addition

NUT CASSEROLE WITH APPLES

Preheat oven to 350°F (180°C). Cream the butter with egg yolks, lemon zest, and cinnamon. Soak the roll in milk, remove excess milk, and sieve. Mix the sieved roll, nuts, and breadcrumbs into the butter. Beat the eggs to stiff peaks with granulated sugar and fold in. Mix in the apple compote. Butter a casserole dish and sprinkle with breadcrumbs. Bake for 45 minutes. Dust with confectioner's sugar.

Bake Time: 45 minutes

Bake Temperature: 350°F (180°C)

Garnish Recommendation: vanilla sauce (see p. 202)

Ingredients for 8 Servings
7 oz (200 g) Apple compote
　(see p. 177)
5½ tbsp (80 g) Butter
4 Egg yolks
Dash of cinnamon powder
Zest of 1 lemon
⅓ cup (80 ml) Milk
1 Dinner roll
3 oz (90 g) Walnuts, ground
1 oz (30 g) Breadcrumbs
4 Egg whites
⅓ cup (80 g) Granulated
　sugar
Butter and breadcrumbs for
　the dish
Confectioner's sugar for
　dusting

RADETZKY RICE

Ingredients for 4–6 Servings
4.5 oz (125 g) Short grain
  rice
Dash of salt
2 cups (500 ml) Milk
1½ tbsp (20 g) Butter
6 tbsp (90 g) Granulated
  sugar
Juice and zest of 1 orange
Juice and zest of 1 lemon
3 tbsp (4 cl) Rum
½ cup (50 g) Apricot mar-
  malade
Butter for the dish
Confectioner's sugar

Blanch the short grain rice in boiling salt water. Sieve and shock in cold water. Slowly boil milk with the rice and add butter, granulated sugar, and the juice and zest of the lemon and orange. Simmer the rice until it is soft. Mix in the rum and apricot marmalade. Butter a casserole dish and fill with the rice. For the egg whites, begin beating them, add the granulated sugar and vanilla sugar, and beat to stiff peaks. Loosely spread the egg whites over the rice and sprinkle almonds on top. Brown for 3–4 minutes in an oven on maximum upper heat. Dust with confectioner's sugar and serve.

Bake Time: 3–4 minutes

Bake Temperature: maximum upper heat

Tip: If you want to serve Radetzy rice in individual servings, use small buttered rings and garnish with homemade fruit purée.

SOUFFLÉD SEMOLINA GNOCCHI

Ingredients
7 tbsp (100 ml) Milk
1 tbsp (15 g) Granulated
  sugar
1 tbsp (15 g) Vanilla sugar
2 oz (50 g) Wheat semolina
Zest of 1 lemon
5 Egg yolks
8 Egg whites
6 tbsp (90 g) Granulated
  sugar for the egg whites
Dash of salt
2 tbsp (20 g) Flour
4 tsp (20 g) Cornstarch
Butter for the dish
Confectioner's sugar for
  dusting

Boil the milk with granulated and vanilla sugar. Mix in semolina and lemon zest and simmer until the semolina is well saturated and the mixture comes away from the pot. Let cool slightly and then mix with the egg yolks. Begin beating the egg whites, add granulated sugar and a dash of salt, and beat to stiff peaks. Fold into the semolina mixture along with flour and cornstarch

Bake Time: 6-8 minutes

Bake Temperature: 392 °F (200 °C)

Garnish Recommendation: Canary Milk (see p. 203) and Wild Strawberry Coulis (see p. 185) or Lingonberry Compote (see p. 182)

SOUFFLÉD STRAWBERRIES

First, let the washed and sorted strawberries soak for a while in some lemon juice and confectioner's sugar. Preheat oven to maximum upper heat. Begin beating the eggs, add the granulated sugar, then beat to stiff peaks. Beat the egg yolks with granulated sugar until they are white. Stir in the strawberry liqueur and beat one more time.

Carefully fold the egg yolk into the beaten egg whites. Place the marinated strawberries in deep, heat resistant dishes, place an equal amount of soufflé batter on top of each, dust with confectioner's sugar, and brown in the oven for 5–8 minutes. Place on saucers, dust with confectioner's sugar, and garnish with mint leaves.

Bake Time: about 5–8 minutes

Bake Temperature: high upper heat

Garnish Recommendation: piña colada sorbet (see p. 363)

Ingredients
300 g (10.5 oz) Strawberries
Confectioner's sugar and
  lemon juice to marinate

For the Soufflé Batter
3 Egg whites
30 g (2 tbsp) Granulated
  sugar for the egg whites
3 Egg yolks
90 g (6 tbsp) Granulated
  sugar for the egg yolks
15 ml (1 tbsp) Strawberry
  liqueur
Confectioner's sugar for
  dusting
Mint to garnish

SOUFFLÉD QUARK PALATSCHINKEN

Ingredients for 8 Servings
Palatschinken dough
  (see p. 18)
Butter for the dish
Confectioner's sugar for
  dusting

For the Filling
4.5 oz (125 g) Quark
⅓ cup (75 ml) Sour cream
2 Eggs
3 tbsp (25 g) Confectioner's
  sugar
1 tbsp (15 g) Vanilla sugar
2 tbsp (20 g) Vanilla pudding
  mix
2 tsp (1 cl) Amaretto
2 tsp (1 cl) Kirsch
Raisins
⅓ cup (70 ml) Whipped
  cream

For the Royale
¾ cup (200 ml) Milk
3 Eggs
2 tbsp (30 g) Granulated
  sugar

Prepare eight palatschinken according to the recipe. Preheat oven to 320 °F (160 °C). For the filling, strain the quark and mix with the other ingredients, folding the whipped cream in last. Fill the palatschinken with the quark mixture, roll up and cut in half. Place the pieces like roof shingles in a well buttered casserole dish. Bake for 5 minutes. In the meantime, beat together the royale ingredients and then pour over the palatschinken. Bake for another 20 minutes. Dust with confectioners sugar before serving on individual plates.

Bake Time: 5 minutes to start, then another 20 minutes

Bake Temperature: 320 °F (160 °C)

Garnish Recommendation: elderberry sorbet (see p. 359)

Tip: These palatschinken taste excellent even without royale. In that case, they should be rolled up with the ends folded under and baked for about 10 minutes in a well buttered casserole dish.

SOUFFLÉD SCHEITERHAUFEN WITH SOUR ICE CREAM AND STRAWBERRIES

Preheat upper and lower oven heat to 400 °F (200 °C). Remove the crusts from the brioche, cut into small pieces, and soak in milk. Separate the eggs. Cream room temperature butter with vanilla sugar, then mix in the egg yolk bit by bit. Squeeze out the excess milk from the brioche well, then mix into the butter along with the raisins. Begin beating the egg whites, add the granulated sugar, and beat to stiff peaks. Fold into the brioche mixture. Brush the ramekins with melted butter, sprinkle with granulated sugar, and fill about ⅔ of the way with batter. Set them in a water bath to bake for about 25 minutes. If they brown too quickly, cover them with aluminum foil. In the meantime, wash and quarter the strawberries and marinate them in Grand Marnier and confectioner's sugar. For the sour cream topping, mix all the ingredients with an immersion blender until foamy. Place the marinated strawberries on plates, place one scheiterhaufen on each place, and garnish with sour ice cream, strawberry purée, and sour cream topping.

Bake Time: about 25 minutes

Bake Temperature: 400 °F (200 °C)

Ingredients for 6–8 Servings
4¼ oz (120 g) Brioche
1 cup (about 250 ml) Milk
3 Eggs
2 tbsp Raisins
4¼ tbsp (60 g) Butter
1 tsp Vanilla sugar
¼ cup (60 g) Granulated sugar
Butter and granulated sugar for the ramekins
Sour ice cream (see p. 355) and strawberry purée (see p. 200) to garnish

For the Marinated Strawberries
9 oz (250 g) Strawberries
4 tsp (2 cl) Grand Marnier
3 tbsp Confectioner's sugar

For the Sour Cream Topping
4 tbsp Sour cream
1 tbsp Lemon juice
4 tsp (10 g) Confectioner's sugar

Souffléd Rice Pudding with Apricot Foam

Ingredients for
8–10 Servings
4½ oz (125 g) Short grain
  rice
Dash of salt
2 Cups (500 ml) Milk
1 Cinnamon stick
1 Vanilla bean
⅔ oz (10 g) Raisins
2 tsp (1 cl) Apricot brandy
4 Egg yolks
5 Egg whites
3 tbsp (50 g) Granulated
  sugar
⅔ cup (150 ml) Heavy cream
2–3 tbsp Peach purée
  (see p. 188)
Butter and granulated sugar
  for the ramekins

Briefly blanch the rice in boiling salt water. Sieve and shock with cold water. Slowly bring the milk and rice to a boil. Preheat oven to 400 °F (200 °C). Add the cinnamon stick, halved vanilla bean, and raisins and simmer the rice over a low heat until it is soft. Remove the cinnamon stick and vanilla bean and stir in the apricot brandy. Let cool slightly and mix in the egg yolks. Begin beating the egg whites, beat to stiff peaks with the granulated sugar, and fold in. Brush the ramekins with melted butter, sprinkle with granulated sugar, and fill about ⅔ of the way with the rice pudding batter. Place in a water bath to bake for about 20 minutes.

Whip the cream in a metal mixing bowl over ice. Carefully fold in the apricot purée. Serve the rice pudding with the apricot foam and preserved apricots.

Bake Time: about 20 minutes

Bake Temperature: 400 °F (200 °C)

Greetings from Flour Heaven

DUMPLINGS, NOODLES, PASTRY POCKETS, GNOCCHI, PANCAKES, BUCHTELN, DALKEN, AND DOUGHNUTS

DUMPLINGS

Sweet dumplings—just the mention of them has always made the mouths of Austrian gourmets water. But at the same time, the calories that come with them awaken some guilt. That doesn't carry so much weight in the following recipes, since the serving sizes have been measured out so that each dumpling is small. And so, there are—almost—no regrets.

FRUIT DUMPLINGS

Strain the quark and mix with soft butter, eggs, and a dash of salt until smooth. Mix in the semolina and chill for 2 hours.

Roll the dough out on a floured work surface and cut out circles with a cookie cutter. Place the washed fruit in the circles, fold up the dough, and form dumplings. Bring a good amount of salt water to boil and boil the dumplings for 10–12 minutes. In the meantime, heat butter in a pan for the cinnamon crumbs. Brown the breadcrumbs with cinnamon in the butter. Remove the dumplings from the water, let drain, and roll in the crumbs. Dust with powdered sugar before serving.

Cook Time: about 10–12 minutes

Tip: This recipe is particularly good for strawberry or plum dumplings. It is entirely up to your personal tastes whether you replace the pit of the small plum with a sugar cube or a piece of marzipan.

Ingredients for
12 Dumplings
1¼ cup (300 g) Quark
2 tbsp (30 g) Butter
2 oz (60 g) Semolina
2 Eggs
Salt
12 Small fruits, according to taste
Flour for the work surface
Confectioner's sugar for dusting

For the Cinnamon Crumbs
7 tbsp (100 g) Butter
6 oz (170 g) Breadcrumbs
Dash of cinnamon, ground

1¾ tbsp (25 g) Butter
2 tbsp Confectioner's sugar
12 oz (350 g) Quark
3.5 oz (100 g) White bread
  crumbs
2 Eggs
Lemon zest
Rum
Dash of salt
12 Apricots
12 Sugar cubes
Confectioner's sugar for
  dusting

For the Sugar Crumbs
7 tbsp (100 g) Butter
3.5 oz (100 g) Breadcrumbs
3 tsp (50 g) Granulated sugar
Dash of cinnamon
Dash of vanilla sugar

Ingredients for
18 Dumplings
Quark dough for filled
  dumplings (see p. 18)

For the Poppy Filling
4.5 oz (125 g) Poppy seeds,
  ground
2.5 oz (70 g) Breadcrumbs
7 tbsp (100 ml) Milk
Lemon zest
Splash of Rum
Dash of cinnamon
Honey
2 tbsp (30 g) Sugar
2 oz (50 g) White chocolate
1 Egg yolk

For the Sugar Crumbs
7 tbsp (100 g) Butter
3.5 oz (100 g) Breadcrumbs
3 tbsp (50 g) Granulated
  sugar
Dash of cinnamon
Dash of vanilla sugar

APRICOT DUMPLINGS

For the quark batter, cream the butter with confectioner's sugar, add the eggs, then mix in the quark, lemon zest, salt, breadcrumbs, and some rum. Let sit for about 2 hours. If the dough is too sticky, mix in 2 more tablespoons of breadcrumbs. Cut open the apricots, remove the pit, replace with a sugar cube, and wrap in dough to create nice round dumplings. Place in boiling salt water and cook for about 15 minutes. For the sugar crumbs, melt the butter and brown the crumbs with the sugar. Flavor with cinnamon and vanilla sugar. Roll the dumplings in the crumbs and serve dusted with confectioner's sugar.

Cook Time: about 15 minutes

Garnish Recommendation: apricot sorbet (see p. 359)

Tip: You can also pit the apricots by pushing them out with the end of a cooking spoon and pushing in the sugar cube.

POPPY QUARK DUMPLINGS

Mix the poppy and breadcrumbs. Boil the milk with sugar, some honey, rum, lemon zest, and cinnamon. Remove from heat and mix in the breadcrumbs. Melt the chocolate and mix in along with the egg yolks. Chill for a while. Prepare the quark dough according to the recipe and wrap the well cooled poppy mixture in it. Let the dumplings sit in hot (not boiling) water for about 12 minutes. For the sugar crumbs, melt the butter and brown the crumbs with the sugar. Flavor with cinnamon and vanilla sugar. Let the dumplings drain, then roll them in the sugar crumbs and serve.

Cook Time: about 12 minutes

Garnish Recommendation: yogurt lemon sauce (see p. 202) and preserved apricots (see p. 188)

SEMOLINA DUMPLINGS WITH HONEY WHIPPED CREAM

Boil the milk, sugar, lemon zest, and vanilla pulp. Sprinkle in the semolina and cook like choux pastry, stirring constantly. Stir butter into the hot mixture. Finally, mix in eggs bit by bit, then place in the refrigerator for 2 hours. Roll the cold dough into dumplings and place in boiling sugar water for about 10 minutes. For the sugar crumbs, melt butter and brown the breadcrumbs. Add lemon zest and orange zest. Season with confectioner's sugar. For the honey whipped cream, mix liquid honey with whipped cream. Let the dumplings drain and then roll them in the sugar crumbs. Garnish with the honey whipped cream and serve.

Cook Time: 10 minutes

Garnish Recommendation: Orange ragout (see p. 183)

PEAR DUMPLINGS

Peel the pears, remove the core, and dice. Boil in sugar water until soft, remove and let drain. Brown granulated sugar and breadcrumbs in the butter. Mix with the pears, eggs, quark, nuts, vanilla sugar, cinnamon, and Poire Williams to make dough. Let rest for 1 hour. Heat a good amount of oil in a deep pan. Form small dumplings from the dough and fry in the hot oil until golden brown. Let drain on paper towels. Dust with confectioner's sugar and serve.

Garnish Recommendation: raspberry purée (see p. 201)

Ingredients for 12–18
Dumplings
2 cups (500 ml) Milk
⅓ cup (75 g) Sugar
Lemon zest
Pulp of ½ vanilla bean
7 oz (210 g) Wheat semolina
1 stick plus 2½ tbsp (150 g)
  Butter, room temperature
2 Eggs
Sugar for the water

For the Sugar Crumbs
7 tbsp (100 g) Butter
2 oz (50 g) Breadcrumbs
Zest of 1 orange
Zest of 1 lemon
Confectioner's sugar

For the Honey Whipped
Cream
1 tbsp Honey
3 tbsp Whipped cream

Ingredients for
18 Dumplings
10.5 oz (300 g) Pears
2 Eggs
7 tbsp (100 g) Granulated
  sugar
2 oz (50 g) Breadcrumbs
1½ tbsp (20 g) Butter
2 oz (50 g) Hazelnuts, ground
2 oz (50 g) Low-fat quark
2 tsp (10 g) Vanilla sugar
Dash of cinnamon, ground
4 tsp (2 cl) Poire Williams
Confectioner's sugar for
  dusting
Granulated sugar for the
  water
Sunflower oil for frying

Pear Dumplings from the Mondsee

Who invented the European dumpling ("Knödel" in German)? Between Prague and Brno, you'll get the answer: the Bohemians, of course, and the Czech word "knedlsk" is proof. But in South Tyrol, people will certainly have a different opinion, and they will not only point to the old minstrel word "knode," but also the Gothic chapel of the Castle d'Appiano, where the frescoes contain the first visual depiction of European dumplings.

"Not so fast," the Upper Austrians and Salzburgers would say. The residents of these states share the Mondsee lake, near which the first Neolithic "dumpling findings" were verified. Culinary archaeology dates the leftover dough, found among grain vessels, millet remains, grindstones, and flat axes, to the time between 2500 and 1800 BCE. It cannot be determined whether they originally contained fruit or meat. Since there were already many pears in the area in that time, it is not unjustified to think that our ancestors might have enjoyed pear dumplings. (See recipe on p. 314.)

CHOCOLATE DUMPLINGS

Ingredients for

24 Dumplings

1¾ tbsp (25 g) Butter
12 oz (350 g) Quark
2 Eggs
½ tbsp Vanilla sugar
3 tbsp (20 g) Confectioner's
  sugar
Zest of ½ lemon
Zest of ½ orange
2 tsp (1 cl) Rum
3.5 oz (100 g) Breadcrumbs
Sugar for the water
Confectioner's sugar for
  dusting

For the Filling
7 tbsp (100 ml) Heavy cream
3.5 oz (100 g) Dark couverture chocolate

For the Cinnamon Crumbs
7 tbsp (100 g) Butter
4 oz (120 g) Breadcrumbs
Dash of cinnamon, ground

For the filling, first melt the dark chocolate in the heavy cream in a double boiler, then chill. In the meantime, make the dough by first creaming the butter and confectioner's sugar. Mix in the quark. Then mix in the eggs, vanilla sugar, rum, orange zest, and lemon zest. Finally, fold in the breadcrumbs. Let the dough rest for 1 hour. Fill a piping bag fitted with a round nozzle with the cooled chocolate and pipe small balls of chocolate. Wrap each ball in dough and form dumplings. Bring sugared water to a boil in a pot and boil the dumplings for 6–8 minutes. While they boil, melt butter in a pan and brown the breadcrumbs with cinnamon. Remove the dumplings, let drip, and roll in the crumbs. Dust with confectioner's sugar and serve.

Cook Time: 6–8 minutes

Garnish Recommendation: strawberry purée (see p. 200)

Tip: If you'd rather skip the step of preparing the chocolate, you can simply use chunks of cooking chocolate as filling.

NUT AND QUARK DUMPLINGS

Prepare the quark dough for dumplings and let rest for 2 hours.

For the filling, mix the nuts and breadcrumbs. Boil the milk with the sugar, honey, rum, lemon zest, and cinnamon. Remove from heat and stir into the nuts. Melt the nougat and stir into the nut mixture with the egg yolks. Chill for a while.

Form small balls from the nut batter and chill them again. Wrap the chilled balls in the prepared dough and form dumplings. Bring a good amount of water to boil and then let the dumplings sit in it for about 12 minutes (do not boil them). For the sugar crumbs, melt butter and brown the crumbs and sugar. Flavor with cinnamon and vanilla sugar. Remove the dumplings from the water, let drip, and roll in the crumbs.

Cook Time: about 12 minutes

Garnish Recommendation: grape compote (see p. 182) and vanilla sauce (see p. 202)

Ingredients for
18 Dumplings
Quark dough for dumplings
(see p. 18)

For the Nut Filling
4.5 oz (125 g) Nuts, ground
2.5 oz (70 g) Breadcrumbs
7 tbsp (100 ml) Milk
Lemon zest
Splash of rum
Dash of cinnamon
Some honey
2 tbsp (30 g) Sugar
2 oz (50 g) Nougat
1 Egg yolk

For the Sugar Crumbs
7 tbsp (100 g) Butter
7 tbsp (100 g) Breadcrumbs
3 tbsp (50 g) Granulated
  sugar
Dash of cinnamon
Vanilla sugar

LEAVENED DUMPLINGS

Ingredients for about
20 Dumplings
4 cups (500 g) Flour
¼ cup (30 g) Yeast
¾ cup (200 ml) Milk,
   lukewarm
5½ tbsp (80 g) Butter,
   melted
¼ cup (60 g) Granulated
   sugar
2 Eggs
2½ cups (300 g) Plum jam
Salt
Zest of ½ lemon
Flour for the work surface

To Sprinkle and Dust
1 stick plus 2½ tbsp (150 g)
   Butter, melted
4 oz (120 g) Poppy seeds,
   ground
3 tbsp (50 g) Confectioner's
   sugar

Dissolve the yeast in half of the lukewarm milk. Add some flour and stir. Sprinkle some flour on top, cover, and let the starter dough rise for 20 minutes. Put the rest of the flour in a bowl. Knead with the starter dough, butter, eggs, the rest of the milk, granulated sugar, a dash of salt, and lemon zest to form smooth dough. Cover and let rise for 30 minutes in a warm place.

Roll the dough out on a floured work surface to about ½ in (1.5 cm) thick and cut into 2¾ in (7x7 cm) squares. Spoon plum jam onto the middle of each square, close the dumplings, and roll into smooth balls in your hands. Place on a floured surface, cover with a towel, and let rise again, until they have nearly doubled in size.

Bring salt water to boil in a large pot. Place the dumplings in the simmering water and let them steep more than boil. Place the lid of the pot on top while they are simmering, slightly ajar. After 10 minutes, remove the lid and turn the dumplings. Cook for another 5 minutes, then remove and immediately poke 2–3 holes with a needle so that they do not collapse.

Place in a casserole dish brushed with melted butter and place in an oven preheated to a low heat until all the dumplings are cooked. Drizzle the dumplings in melted butter and dust with poppy and confectioner's sugar.

Cook Time: about 15 minutes

NOODLES AND PASTRY POCKETS

Pastry pockets, called "Tascherl" in Austrian German, are the link between southern European ravioli, northern European Knödel, and eastern European pierogis. Noodles are often also mentioned in this context, which doesn't necessary mean that the "noodles of the north" always have to be made with classic southern pasta dough. Southern European pasta cooking has long since caught up with old Austrian dumplings, shown in the following recipes.

POPPY NOODLES

Ingredients for 6 Servings
18 oz (500 g) Potatoes, high
   starch
⅔ cup (100 g) Potato flour
1 Egg
Salt
5½ tbsp (80 g) Butter
7 tbsp (100 g) Confectioner's
   sugar
10.5 oz (300 g) Poppy seeds,
   ground

Boil the unpeeled potatoes in salt water until they are soft. Peel and dry in a 200 °F (100 °C) oven. Press through a potato ricer and knead with potato flour, egg, and a dash of salt. Form rolls, cut off small pieces, and roll into noodles approximately 3 in (7 cm) long and finger thick.

Boil salt water and let the noodles simmer for 5 minutes. Melt butter, remove the noodles from the pot, let drip, and roll in the butter. Dust thickly with poppy and confectioner's sugar before serving.

Cook Time: about 5 minutes

"Poppy Pacifier" for Grown Ups

The ancient Egyptians already knew of poppy's medicinal uses, but the Chinese ruined poppy's reputation forever when they discovered that opium could be extracted for narcotic use.

In Austria, however, the narcotic effects of poppy were only used as admittedly controversial way to calm babies. Mostly in rural areas, they made a "poppy pacifier" with the help of poppy and honey, which seemed to have a wonderfully calming effect on the little darlings, letting their parents work the fields in peace. Incidentally, poppy oil was also used to preserve the "Eternal Light" on the church altar during lent. They left production of opium to Asia.

Because of its overall rather harmless use of poppy, Austria is today one of the few countries in which poppy can legally be grown (particularly in the Waldviertel region). It has to be that way, otherwise a whole array of poppy desserts would be threatened with extinction.

Zwettl poppy was even noted in the 1930s in the London stock exchange. There is still hope that the currently notoriously bad economy of Austria could recover thanks to domestic poppy.

PLUM JAM PASTRY POCKETS

Boil the unpeeled potatoes in salt water until they are soft. Peel and dry in a 200 °F (100 °C) oven. Press through a potato ricer and quickly knead with potato flour, egg yolks, semolina, butter, and a dash of salt. Roll the potato dough out to about 4mm thick on a floured work surface. Cut out circles with a 3in (8 cm) round, scalloped cookie cutter. Mix the plum jam with cinnamon and rum and place in the middle of each circle (preferably with a piping bag). Brush the edges with a beaten egg, close the dough, and press the edges together with your thumb and forefinger. Boil salt water and place the pockets in the water for about 5 minutes. For the crumbs, heat butter and brown the crumbs. Remove the pastry pockets from the water, let drip, and roll in the crumbs.

Cook Time: about 5 minutes

Garnish Recommendation: vanilla ice cream (see p. 350)

A Shield for Sweet Tournaments

Anyone who has ever heard the Viennese song of the same name as the pastry—"Powidltatschkerln" written by Hermann Leopoldi and unforgettably interpreted by Peter Alexander—knows that the plum jam pastry is a thoroughly Bohemian incorporation of the multicultural Viennese culinary community. The plum jam, which unlike plum marmalade is thickened without the use of added sugar or gelling agent, is in fact a culinary achievement that goes back to the Czech word "povidli." The accompanying pastries first met the plum jam in Vienna, but they go back to the old French "targe," which means "jousting shield."

Ingredients for 6–8 Servings
21 oz (600 g) Potatoes, high starch
⅔ cup (100 g) Potato flour
¾ oz (20 g) Wheat semolina
2 tbsp (30 g) Butter, melted
2 Egg yolks
Salt
Flour for the work surface
1 Egg yolk for brushing

For the Filling
1⅔ cup (200 g) Plum jam
Dash of cinnamon powder
2 tsp (1 cl) Rum

For the Crumbs
1 stick (120 g) Butter
6 oz (170 g) Breadcrumbs

POPPY APRICOT RAVIOLI WITH VANILLA WHIPPED CREAM

Ingredients for 6–8 Servings
3½ cups (430 g) Flour
3 Eggs
3 Egg yolks
Dash of salt
1 tbsp Vegetable oil
Egg yolk for brushing
Dash of sugar for the water
Mint to garnish

For the Filling
1¾ tbsp (25 g) Butter
2 tbsp Confectioner's sugar
Juice and zest of 1 lemon
3 Egg yolks
2 tsp (1 cl) Rum
9 oz (250 g) Quark
1.5 oz (40 g) White bread
  crumbs
½ cup (50 g) Apricot mar-
  malade
2 Apricots

For the Poppy Crumbs
5½ tbsp (80 g) Butter
2 oz (50 g) Poppy seeds,
  ground
2 oz (50 g) Sponge cake
  crumbs
3 tbsp (20 g) Confectioner's
  sugar

*For the Vanilla Whipped
Cream*
⅔ cup (150 ml) Whipping
  cream
3 tbsp (20 g) Confectioner's
  sugar
Dash of vanilla sugar
Pulp of ½ vanilla bean

Slowly knead the flour, eggs, egg yolks, salt, and oil to a smooth, flexible dough. Form a ball, wrap it in plastic wrap, and chill for 1 hour. In the meantime, cream the butter, sugar, lemon juice and lemon zest for the filling. Stir in the egg yolks, rum, quark, white bread crumbs, and apricot marmalade. Finally, fold in the diced apricot. For the poppy crumbs, foam the butter in a pan. Lightly brown the cake crumbs, poppy, and confectioner's sugar and set aside.

Roll the dough out to thin sheets. On half of the sheets, mark approximately 2in (6 cm) squares, place some filling in the middle of the squares and brush the space in between with egg white. Lay the other sheets on top and press them together well in the spaces between the squares. Poke holes to remove any air bubbles that appear. Cut out the squares with a pastry wheel. For the vanilla whipped cream, whip the cream halfway with confectioner's sugar, vanilla sugar, and vanilla pulp. In a big enough pot, boil water with a bit of sugar. Place the ravioli in the water and let simmer for 3–4 minutes. Remove and let drip. Roll the ravioli in the poppy crumbs and serve garnished with vanilla whipped cream and mint.

Cook Time: 3–4 minutes

Garnish Recommendation: preserved apricots (see p. 188) and apricot sorbet (see p. 359)

CHOCOLATE RAVIOLI WITH MOSCATO SABAYON

First, prepare the filling. Boil the heavy cream, stir in the chopped chocolate, and remove from heat. Mix in the Grand Marnier with an immersion blender and homogenize the mixture (blend for 5 minutes without mixing in any air). Then chill for 1 hour.

For the dough, sift the flour and cocoa powder. Knead to a smooth dough with the eggs and sugar. Wrap in foil and let rest for 30 minutes. Roll out the dough (preferably with a pasta maker). Cut out squares or circles on a floured work surface and place a little bit of filling on each. Brush the edges with beaten egg white, close, and press the edges together well. Bring salt water to boil with a little vanilla sugar. Place the ravioli in the water and let simmer for 5 minutes.

For the moscato sabayon, beat all the ingredients together in a bain-marie until the sabayon is nice and airy. Remove the ravioli and let drain. Serve with orange slices. Garnish with sabayon and confectioner's sugar.

Cook Time: about 5 minutes

Ingredients for about
60 Ravioli
12 oz (350 g) Dark couverture chocolate
1 cup (250 ml) Heavy cream
7 tbsp (10 cl) Grand Marnier
2 cups (250 g) Flour
3.5 oz (100 g) Cocoa powder
4 Eggs
¼ cup (30 g) Confectioner's sugar
Flour for the work surface
Egg white for brushing
Salt and vanilla sugar for the water
Orange slices to garnish
Confectioner's sugar for dusting

For the Moscato Sabayon
4 Egg yolks
3 tbsp Sugar
6 tbsp (9 cl) Muscatel wine
¼ cup (6 cl) Sparkling wine (preferably Chardonnay)

SEMOLINA RAVIOLI WITH STRAWBERRIES

Ingredients for about

40 Ravioli
2 oz (50 g) Durum wheat
  semolina (or wheat
  semolina)
¾ cup (100 g) Flour
2 Egg yolks
2 Eggs
Dash of cinnamon
Dash of salt
Dash of vanilla sugar for the
  water
Flour for the work surface
Egg white for brushing
18 oz (500 g) Strawberries
Strawberry purée
  (see p. 200)

For the Filling
1 cup (250 ml) Milk
4¼ tbsp (60 g) Butter
2 tsp (10 g) Granulated sugar
2 tsp (10 g) Vanilla sugar
Pulp of ½ vanilla bean
Dash of salt
2 oz (60 g) Wheat semolina
1 Egg
Zest of 1 lemon

For the Butter Crumbs
1 stick (120 g) Butter
6 oz (170 g) Breadcrumbs
Dash of cinnamon

For the dough, mix the flour and semolina. Knead with the eggs, egg yolks, cinnamon, and salt to a smooth dough. Wrap in foil and let rest for 50 minutes. For the filling, boil the milk, butter, granulated sugar, vanilla sugar, vanilla pulp, and salt. Stir in the semolina and simmer for 3–5 minutes, until it is soaked. Remove from heat. Let cool, then stir in the egg and lemon zest.

Roll out the dough (preferably with a pasta maker). Cut out squares or circles on a floured work surface and place a little bit of filling on each. Brush the edges with beaten egg white, close, and press the edges together well. Bring salt water to boil with a little vanilla sugar. Place the ravioli in the water and let simmer for 4–5 minutes. For the butter crumbs, heat butter and brown the breadcrumbs with cinnamon. Remove the ravioli, let drip, and roll in the crumbs. Pour strawberry purée onto dishes, place the ravioli on it, and garnish with the washed, quartered strawberries.

Cook Time: 4–5 minutes

Garnish Recommendation: vanilla ice cream (see p. 350)

NUT FLECKS

Knead the flour with eggs and salt. Add lukewarm water little by little and knead until the dough is nice and smooth. Add flour as needed. Wrap in foil and let rest for 30 minutes. Roll out to about 2 mm on a floured work surface. Cut into 2in (5 cm) wide strips, lay on top of each other, and cut again into approximately ½ to ¾in strips. Then cut small squares out of the strips. Boil salt water and cook the flecks for 1–2 minutes. Pour out the water, shock in cold water, and let drip. Roll them briefly in hot lard, so that they don't stick together.

Preheat oven to 350°F (180°C). For the cream batter, mix the egg yolks with confectioner's sugar and vanilla sugar. Beat the egg whites to stiff peaks with the granulated sugar and fold into the egg yolk mixture. Add raisins and lemon zest. Mix the flecks with the cream batter. For the nut batter, boil milk with sugar and cinnamon. Sprinkle in the nuts. Place half of the flecks in a buttered casserole dish. Spread the nut batter on top and cover with the rest of the flecks. Bake for about 20 minutes. Cut into equally sized pieces and serve.

Cook Time: 1–2 minutes for the flecks

Bake Time: about 20 minutes

Bake Temperature: 350°F (180°C)

Ingredients for 6–8 Servings
4 cups (500 g) Flour
4 Eggs
Dash of salt
2 tbsp Water, lukewarm
Flour for the work surface
Some lard

For the Cream Batter
3 Egg yolks
6 tbsp (50 g) Confectioner's sugar
2 tsp (10 g) Vanilla sugar
2 oz (50 g) Raisins
Zest of 1 lemon
3 Egg whites
3 tbsp (50 g) Granulated sugar

For the Nut Batter
1 cup (250 ml) Milk
7 tbsp (100 g) Granulated sugar
5 oz (150 g) Walnuts, ground
Dash of cinnamon

GNOCCHI

Gnocchi, or Nocken in German, are really one of the sweetest temptations of traditional Austrian dessert cuisine. And yet the rainbow of gnocchi stretches from fluffy, soft quark gnocchi to airy, weightless egg white gnocchi.

QUARK GNOCCHI

Ingredients
21 oz (600 g) Quark
3½ tbsp (50 g) Butter
3 Eggs
Zest and juice of 1 lemon
2 tsp (1 cl) Rum
⅓ cup (40 g) Confectioner's sugar
4.5 oz (130 g) White bread crumbs
Dash of salt

For the Butter Crumbs
7 tbsp (100 g) Butter
3.5 oz (100 g) Breadcrumbs
⅓ cup (70 g) Granulated sugar
1 tsp Cinnamon

Using a clean cloth, squeeze out the quark well and then sieve. Cream the butter and confectioner's sugar, then mix in the quark and egg. Flavor with lemon juice and rum. Finally, fold in the white bread crumbs and let the dough rest for 2 hours. Bring lightly salted water to a boil, use a tablespoon to form gnocchi out of the dough, and simmer them for about 8 minutes.

For the butter crumbs, melt butter. Brown the crumbs and sugar in it and flavor with cinnamon. Remove the gnocchi from the water, let drain, and roll in the crumbs.

Cook Time: about 8 minutes

Garnish Recommendation: stewed plums (see p. 177) or elderberry purée (see p. 180)

POPPY QUARK GNOCCHI IN ICED APPLE SOUP

Mix the quark well with butter and eggs in a bowl. Add granulated sugar, breadcrumbs, and lemon zest and let rest for 30 minutes. For the apple soup, first cut the peeled, cored apples into cubes. Boil them with water and wine, blend, and sieve (you will need about 4 cups (just under 1l) of apple juice). Heat the preserving sugar, stirring constantly, until it begins to caramelize. Deglaze with the prepared apple juice and dissolve the caramel completely. Add the lemon juice, boil the apple soup, and then mix in a bowl over ice until it is cold. Flavor with Calvados. Use a spoon to form gnocchi from the dough, and simmer in salt water for 8 minutes. For the poppy crumbs, melt butter and quickly brown breadcrumbs, poppy, sugar, and a pinch of cinnamon. Remove the gnocchi, let drain, and roll in the poppy crumbs. Pour the apple soup into dishes and place the gnocchi in them.

Cook Time: about 8 minutes

Garnish Recommendation: apple slices or apple balls with apple ginger sorbet (see p. 361)

Ingredients for 4–6 Servings
10.5 oz (300 g) Quark
1¾ tbsp (25 g) Butter
2 Eggs
Zest of 1 lemon
2 tsp (10 g) Granulated sugar
2 oz (60 g) Breadcrumbs
Salt for the water

For the Apple Soup
3⅓ lbs (1.5 kg) Apples (Boskoop, Golden Delicious, or Elstar)
1 cup (250 ml) White wine (preferably Riesling)
1 cup (250 ml) Water
9 oz (250 g) Preserving sugar
Juice of 2 lemons
5 tbsp (75 ml) Calvados

For the Poppy Crumbs
5½ tbsp (80 g) Butter
1 oz (30 g) Breadcrumbs
1 oz (30 g) Poppy seeds, ground
4 tsp (20 g) Granulated sugar
Cinnamon

SEMOLINA GNOCCHI WITH RHUBARB STRAWBERRY RAGOUT

Ingredients
2 Dinner rolls, stale
½ cup (125 ml) Milk
2¾ tbsp (40 g) Butter
1 Egg
1 Egg yolk
Zest of ½ lemon
Dash of salt
Dash of cinnamon
3 oz (80 g) Durum wheat semolina (or wheat semolina)
Confectioner's sugar for dusting

For the Rhubarb Strawberry Ragout
10.5 oz (300 g) Rhubarb
2 cups (500 ml) Riesling (or other white wine)
½ cup (120 g) Granulated sugar
Pulp of ½ vanilla bean
2 tbsp Cornstarch
7 oz (200 g) Strawberries
Mint, cut into fine strips

For the Cinnamon Crumbs
About 5 tbsp (70 g) Butter
3.5 oz (100 g) Breadcrumbs
Dash of cinnamon

Take the crusts off the rolls, cut them into small cubes, and saturate with milk. Cream the butter. Squeeze the excess milk from the bread and sieve. Add to the butter along with the egg and egg yolk and mix everything well. Mix in the lemon zest, salt, cinnamon, and semolina well and let rest for 30 minutes.

Wash and peel the rhubarbs and cut them into bite-sized pieces. Boil the peels with wine and granulated sugar and sieve. Boil the liquid again with the vanilla pulp. Mix the cornstarch with a little bit of water and then use it to thicken the mixture. Add the rhubarb and simmer for 1 minute. Remove from heat and let cool. Wash and quarter the strawberries and mix into the cooled rhubarbs along with the mint.

Boil lightly salted water. Form gnocchi from the semolina dough using a spoon and simmer on low heat for 12–15 minutes. For the cinnamon crumbs, heat butter and brown the breadcrumbs and cinnamon. Remove the gnocchi, let drain, then roll in the crumbs. Portion the rhubarb strawberry ragout into dishes and place gnocchi in each. Dust with confectioner's sugar.

Cook Time: 12–15 minutes

Egg White Gnocchi

Ingredients for 8 Servings
8 Egg whites
¾ cup (160 g) Granulated
  sugar
3 cups (750 ml) Milk
Pulp of ½ vanilla bean
2 tsp (10 g) Vanilla sugar

Begin to beat the egg whites, add the granulated sugar, and then beat them to stiff peaks. Bring the milk to a boil with vanilla pulp and vanilla sugar. Spoon gnocchi from the egg whites and simmer for 2 minutes in the milk. Turn them over and let sit them sit in the milk for another 2 minutes at reduced heat. Remove from the milk and let drain.

Cook Time: about 4 minutes

Garnish Recommendation: vanilla sauce (see p. 202)

Tip: These gnocchi look particularly good when drizzled with melted caramel.

Swimming Islands in Bird Milk
Egg white gnocchi is a dish that appears in many countries under many different names. Preparation varies slightly from place to place, of course. But they are always fluffy balls of beaten egg whites served floating, more or less, in sweet vanilla sauce. In France, they have "îles flottantes"—floating islands, while in Transylvania there is a very similar dish which enjoys great popularity, known as "bird milk." And since in Vienna, egg white gnocchi are often served with "canary milk" (see p. 203), a thin vanilla sauce, it comes full circle.

PALATSCHINKEN AND PANCAKES

Palatschinken, or Austrian style crepes, are a product that can be described with the fashionable work "fusion cuisine." The word "Palatschinke" came to Vienna from the Romanian "placinta" and the Hungarian "pálácsintá." Both refer to the old Transylvanian custom of cooking pancakes on hot stones, which can still be seen at some local fairs. The Viennese "Palatschinken" appeared in the nineteenth century, before which they mostly spoke of "Pfannkuchen" or "Eierkuchen." These were different from other, much more viscous pancakes. Palatschinken are mostly cooked on smaller pans, while these Austrian style pancakes get their crispy brown surface, as in the following recipes, from a large pan or the oven.

VANILLA PALATSCHINKEN

Make 8 palatschinken according to the basic recipe. Preheat oven to 350°F (180°C). Boil heavy cream, granulated sugar, vanilla sugar, and the halved vanilla bean. Beat the egg yolks, remove the hot cream from the stove, and stir into the yolks. While stirring constantly, bring to a boil again. Sieve, stir, and let cool. For the egg whites, beat the whites to stiff peaks with sugar and fold into the vanilla mixture. Fill the palatschinken with the vanilla, roll up, fold in the ends, dust with confectioner's sugar, and place in a buttered casserole dish. Brown in the oven for a few minutes.

Bake Time: several minutes

Bake Temperature: 350°F (180°C)

Garnish Recommendation: elderberry purée (see p. 180) or vanilla sauce (see p. 202)

Ingredients for 8 Pieces
Palatschinken Dough
  (see p. 18)
Confectioner's sugar for
  dusting
Butter for the pan

For the Filling
¼ cup (50 ml) Heavy cream
4 Egg yolks
¾ cup (60 g) Granulated
  sugar
1 Vanilla bean
2 tsp (10 g) Vanilla sugar

For the Egg Whites
4 Egg whites
2 tbsp (30 g) Granulated
  sugar

Ingredients for 8 Pieces
Palatschinken dough
  (see p. 18)
Apricot marmalade
Rum
Confectioner's sugar for
  dusting

Ingredients for 8 Pieces
Palatschinken dough
  (see p. 18)
Oil for the parchment paper
Confectioner's sugar for
  dusting

For the filling
4 tsp (20 g) Sugar
2 tsp (1 cl) Water
2 oz (60 g) Pumpkin seeds
½ tsp Vanilla sugar
2 tsp (10 g) Butter
7 tbsp (100 ml) Whipped
  cream
4 tsp (2 cl) Rum
3 tbsp (20 g) Confectioner's
  sugar
3 Oranges, peeled and in
  slices

APRICOT PALATSCHINKEN

Make 8 palatschinken according to the basic recipe. Warm the apricot marmalade with some rum and brush the palatschinken with it. Roll up and dust with confectioner's sugar before serving.

ORANGE PALATSCHINKEN

Make 8 palatschinken according to the basic recipe. For the filling, cook sugar and water in a pan to make a light caramel. Remove from heat, mix in the pumpkin seeds, and mix well with vanilla sugar and butter. Spread out the batter on oiled parchment paper, let cool, then break with a rolling pin. Mix the whipped cream with rum and confectioner's sugar and spread on the prepared palatschinken. Place the pumpkin seed brittle and orange slices on top and roll up the palatschinken. Dust with confectioner's sugar before serving.

Garnish Recommendation: orange ragout (see p. 183)

CAKE PANCAKES

Preheat oven to 400 °F (200 °C). Beat the egg yolks with lemon zest and vanilla sugar. Beat the egg whites to stiff peaks with granulated sugar. Carefully fold the egg whites into the egg yolks. Sift the flour in and slowly fold it in. Finally, fold in the hot, browned butter.

In a pan, melt some butter and place batter in the pan according to your desired size of pancake. Smooth the top with a spatula. Let cool on the stovetop for about 1 minute and then finish baking in the oven for about 10 minutes. While still in the pan, brush with apricot marmalade and fold closed. Place on plates and garnish with fruit.

Bake Time: about 10 minutes

Bake Temperature: 400 °F (200 °C)

Variation I: Schönbrunner pancakes are prepared the same way, but filled with fruit compote.

Variation II: The classic filling for Stephanie pancakes (Omelette Stéphanie) is made of wild strawberries, pineapple, and pears.

Variation III: Apricot pancakes are not only filled with apricot marmalade, but also preserved apricots (see p. 188) and raisins. Vanilla sauce (see p. 202) fits them very well.

Ingredients
3 Egg yolks
Zest of ½ lemon
2 tsp (10 g) Vanilla sugar
6 Egg whites
7 tbsp (100 g) Granulated sugar
⅓ cup (40 g) Flour
2¾ tbsp (40 g) Butter, melted
Butter for cooking
2 tbsp Apricot marmalade
Fruit according to taste to garnish (such as strawberries, orange slices, or kiwi slices)

PANCAKE SOUFFLÉ

Ingredients for 2 Servings
3 Egg yolks
Zest of ½ lemon
Pulp of ½ vanilla bean
7 tbsp (110 g) Granulated
   sugar
5 Egg whites
1 tsp Potato flour
Butter for brushing
Confectioner's sugar for
   dusting

Preheat oven to 400 °F (200 °C). Cream the egg yolk, lemon zest, vanilla pulp, and about 1½ tablespoons of granulated sugar. Beat the egg whites with the rest of the granulated sugar to stiff peaks. Using the whisk, carefully fold the potato flour into the egg whites. Carefully mix the egg whites into the egg yolks with a spatula. Butter a metal sheet or appropriate casserole dish and dust with some sugar. With a dough scraper, place ¾ of the batter on the sheet in an oval shape like a boat. Make a 3in (8 cm) slit in the surface. Put the rest of the batter in a piping bag fitted with a star-shaped nozzle and decorate the upper and lower edges with rosettes. Bake for 10–12 minutes. Dust with confectioner's sugar before serving.

Bake Time: 10–12 minutes

Bake Temperature: 400 °F (200 °C)

Garnish Recommendation: burgundy cherries (see p. 183)

BUCHTELN AND DALKEN

Buchteln are one of the classic contributions of legendary Bohemian cuisine to the Viennese kitchen. There were thousands of recipes for "buchticky." The majority of these leavened specialties were originally filled with plum jam and served with vanilla sauce. In the nineteenth century, a particularly popular variety was Ternobuchteln, named after the lottery, called the "Terno" at the time. They had notes with lucky numbers baked into them by an industrious innkeeper on the Hermannskogel hill in the Vienna Woods.

But on the other hand, dalken were not very lucky to begin with. Quite the opposite: They were called ash cakes and included any unlucky baked good that a clumsy ("dalkert") chef had botched. This is a bitter injustice to the fine Bohemian dalken, also called livance. In reality, they taste delicious, but require a special dalken pan with several round depressions. Similar pans can be found in America under the name of pancake puff pan or aebleskiver pan, or you can use an egg pan.

BUCHTELN WITH VANILLA SAUCE

Ingredients for 6 Servings
1 cup (125 g) Flour, fine
1 cup (125 g) Flour, coarse
1 Egg
3 tbsp (4 cl) Oil
½ cup (125 ml) Milk,
  lukewarm
2 tbsp (15 g) Yeast
3 tbsp (25 g) Confectioner's
  sugar
Dash of salt
1¼ cup (150 g) Apricot
  marmalade
2 tsp (1 cl) Rum
About 7 tbsp (100 g) butter,
  melted, for brushing
2 cups (500 ml) Vanilla sauce
  (see p. 202)
Confectioner's sugar for
  dusting

For the dough, mix the flour together. Mix the yeast with the lukewarm milk in a bowl. Mix in half of the flour, sprinkle more flour on top, cover, and let rise in a warm spot for about 30 minutes. Beat the rest of the flour, the salt, egg, sugar, and oil into the starter dough with a cooking spoon until the dough comes away from the side of the bowl. Cover and let rise another 20 minutes.

Roll out to ½ in (1 cm) and cut out circles with a 2½ in (6 cm) cookie cutter. Mix the apricot marmalade with rum and spoon onto each circle. Bring the edges together, and dip them in butter. Place the buchteln with the edges down in a buttered pan. Preheat oven to 350 °F (180 °C). Let the buchteln rise for another 20 minutes. Brush with melted butter and bake for about 30 minutes. In the meantime, prepare the vanilla sauce. Dust the buchteln with confectioner's sugar before serving with the warm vanilla sauce.

Bake Time: about 30 minutes

Bake Temperature: 350 °F (180 °C)

LINGONBERRY DUCAT BUCHTELN IN PEAR SOUP WITH SOUR CREAM WHITE PEPPER ICE CREAM

First prepare the ice cream by mixing the sour cream with confectioner's sugar, lemon juice, heavy cream, and pepper and freezing in the ice cream machine. For the pear soup, peel, halve, and core the pears. Stew in a small covered pot with wine, water, and sugar. Purée in a blender and sieve.

For the buchteln, mix the flours. Stir the yeast into the lukewarm milk and mix in half of the flour. Sprinkle more flour on top, cover, and let rise in a warm spot for about 30 minutes. Beat the rest of the flour, the salt, egg, sugar, and oil into the starter dough with a cooking spoon until the dough comes away from the side of the bowl. Cover and let rise another 20 minutes. Roll out to ½in (1.5 cm) and cut out circles with a 2 ½in (6 cm) cookie cutter. Spoon lingonberry compote onto each. Bring the edges together, and dip them in butter. Place the buchteln with the edges down in a buttered pan. Preheat oven to 320°F (160°C). Let the buchteln rise for another 20 minutes. Brush with melted butter and bake for 25 minutes, brushing with butter again halfway through. Pour the pear soup into dishes, dust the buchteln with confectioner's sugar and place in the soup. Scoop the ice cream on top and garnish with mint.

Bake Time: 25 minutes

Bake Temperature: 320°F (160°C)

Tip: If the lingonberry compote is too liquid, freeze it briefly before filling.

BOHEMIAN DALKEN

Put the flour in a bowl. Dissolve the yeast in some lukewarm milk, stir into the flour, and let rest for 10 minutes. Mix salt, melted butter, the rest of the milk, the egg, egg yolk, and 1 tablespoon (!) of the sugar with the starter dough and let rest for 1 hour. Beat the egg white to stiff peaks with the rest of the sugar and fold into the batter.

Ingredients for
10–12 Servings
For the Sour Ice Cream
2 cups (500 ml) Sour cream
1¼ cups (150 g)
  Confectioner's sugar
Juice of 1 lemon
¼ cup (5 cl) Heavy cream
1 tsp (5 g) Pepper, white,
  ground

For the Pear Soup
18 oz (500 g) Pears, fully ripe
1 cup (250 ml) White wine
1 cup (250 ml) Water
7 tbsp (100 g) Sugar
3 tbsp (4 cl) Pear Brandy

For the Ducat Buchteln
1 cup (125 g) Flour
1 cup (125 g) Flour, coarse
1 Egg
3 tbsp (4 cl) Oil
Dash of salt
½ cup (125 ml) Milk, lukewarm
2 tbsp (15 g) Yeast
3 tbsp (25 g) Confectioner's
  sugar
3½ tbsp (50 g) Butter,
  melted
Lingonberry compote for
  filling (see p. 182)
Flour for the work surface
Butter for the pan
Confectioner's sugar for
  dusting
Mint to garnish

Ingredients for 4–6 Servings
1 cup (125 g) Flour
4 tsp (10 g) Yeast
3 tbsp (40 g) Granulated
  sugar
Dash of salt
1 tbsp (15 g) Butter

1 cup (250 ml) Milk, lukewarm
1 Egg
1 Egg yolk
2 Egg whites
Butter for the pan
9 oz (250 g) Lingonberry
  compote (see p. 182)
Confectioner's sugar for
  dusting

For the Quark Cream
10.5 oz (300 g) Quark
1 Egg
⅓ cup (80 g) Granulated
  sugar
Zest of 1 orange
1 tbsp Raisins
1 Egg white
1 tbsp Granulated sugar for
  the egg white

Ingredients for 6–8 Servings
18 oz (500 g) Berries
4 tsp (2 cl) Grand Marnier and
Some confectioner's sugar
  to marinate
1 cup (250 ml) Sour cream
1⅔ cup (200 g) Flour
7 Egg yolks
Dash of salt
Dash of vanilla sugar
Lemon zest
7 Egg whites
7 tbsp (100 g) Granulated
  sugar
Butter for frying
Confectioner's sugar for
  dusting

For the Quark Sauce
5 oz (150 g) Quark
2 Egg yolks
6 tbsp (50 g) Confectioner's
  sugar
1½ tbsp Sour cream
2 tsp (1 cl) Rum
Zest of ½ lemon
½ cup (125 ml) Heavy cream

For the quark cream, mix the quark, egg, granulated sugar, orange zest, and raisins. Beat the egg white to stiff peaks with sugar and fold in. Butter the dalken pan (or aebleskiver pan). Heat the pan on medium and fill the depressions with dalken batter. Fry each side for about 3 minutes, until light brown. Place two dalken on each plate with a spoonful of lingonberry compote and quark cream on top and cover with dalken. Dust with confectioner's sugar and serve.

Cook Time: about 6 minutes

Tip: If you don't have the right pan, you can make dalken in a regular frying pan, as long as you have egg rings.

SOUR CREAM DALKEN WITH BERRIES

Wash the berries and marinate in Grand Marnier and powdered sugar. Mix the sour cream, salt, egg yolk, vanilla sugar, and lemon zest. Begin to beat the eggs, add granulated sugar, and beat to stiff peaks. Carefully fold the egg whites and the flour into the yolk mixture. Butter the dalken pan (or ableskiver pan), heat on medium, pour in the batter, and fry, turning the dalken once.

For the quark sauce, strain the quark and mix with egg yolks, confectioner's sugar, sour cream, rum, and lemon zest. Whip the cream slightly and hold in. Place one dalken on each plate, place the marinated berries and quark sauce on top, then top with another dalken. Dust with confectioner's sugar.

FRIED FOODS

If we were talking about classic Austrian cuisine, this chapter would have to be called "Lard Fried Foods," since a real Viennese, Hungarian, or Bohemian house-wife would have been able to choose between only butter or lard for frying the following dishes. Since then, our ideas about animal fat have changed, and modern sweet cuisine prefers lighter, more nutritious, and lower cholesterol vegetable oil for frying. But it doesn't make the recipes any less delicious.

FRIED APPLE SLICES

Peel the apples, remove the core with an apple corer; and cut into ½ in (1 cm) slices. Cover with lemon juice and rum and dust with confectioner's sugar. For the batter, knead together the flour, wine, oil, egg yolks, and salt. Beat the egg whites to stiff peaks with the granulated sugar and fold into the batter. Heat a good amount of oil in a pan. Dip the apple slices in the batter and fry on both sides until golden brown. Remove, let drain well on paper towels, and dust with a cinnamon powdered sugar mixture.

Garnish Recommendation: vanilla sauce (see p. 202) or vanilla ice cream (see p. 350)

Ingredients for 8 Servings
8 Apples, as tender as
  possible
Juice of 2 lemons
2 tbsp Rum
¾ cup (100 g) Confectioner's
  sguar
Sunflower oil for frying
Confectioner's sugar and
  cinnamon for dusting

For the Frying Batter
2¾ cups (350 g) Flour
1½ cups (375 ml) White wine
¼ cup (50 ml) Oil
3 Egg yolks
Dash of salt
3 Egg whites
2 tbsp (30 g) Granulated
  sugar

FRIED ELDERFLOWERS

Wash the flowers in cold, flowing water and let drain on paper towels. For the batter, mix flour, white wine, oil, egg yolks, and salt until smooth. Beat the egg white to stiff peaks with granulated sugar and fold into the batter. Heat a good amount of oil in a pan. Dip the elderflowers in the batter, let excess drip off, and fry the flowers until golden brown. Remove and let drain on paper towels. Dust with a mixture of cinnamon and confectioner's sugar.

Garnish Recommendation: vanilla sauce (see p. 202)

(see p. 202)

Ingredients for 10 Servings
20 Elderflowers
2¾ cups (350 g) Flour
1½ cups (375 ml) White wine
¼ cup (50 ml) Vegetable Oil
3 Egg yolks
Dash of salt
3 Egg whites
2 tbsp (30 g) Granulated
   sugar
Sunflower oil for frying
Confectioner's sugar and
   cinnamon for dusting

1
Prepare the ingredients.

2
Mix the flour, white wine, oil, egg yolks, and salt. Last, fold the egg whites into the batter.

3
Wash and dry the elderflowers.

4
Dip the elderflowers in the batter and let the excess drip off.

5
Fry in hot oil until golden brown.

6
Remove and drain on paper towels. Dust with a mixture of confectioner's sugar and cinnamon before serving.

SCHLOSSERBUBEN

Soak the dried plums in cold water for half an hour. Remove, let drip dry, and push a peeled almond in place of each pit. For the frying batter, mix the flour, wine, oil, egg yolk, and salt until smooth. Beat the egg whites to stiff peaks with the granulated sugar and fold into the batter. Heat a good amount of oil in a pan. Dip the plums in the batter and fry until golden brown on all sides. Remove and let drip on paper towels. Dust with confectioner's sugar and cocoa powder.

Garnish Recommendation: vanilla sauce (see p. 202) and plum sorbet (see p. 358)

Ingredients for
12–15 Servings
60 Dried plums, as big
  as possible
60 Almonds, peeled
2¾ cups (350 g) Flour
1½ cups (375 ml) Wine
¼ cup (50 ml) Oil
3 Egg yolks
Dash of salt
3 Egg whites
2 tbsp (30 g) Granulated
  sugar
Sunflower oil for frying
Confectioner's sugar and
  cocoa powder for dusting

WÄSCHERMÄDELN

Halve and pit the apricots. Cover with apricot liqueur, dust with confectioner's sugar, and let sit for a short time. Make small balls out of the marzipan and put them in the place of the pits. Put the apricots back together. For the frying batter, mix the flour, wine, oil, egg yolk, and salt until smooth. Beat the egg whites to stiff peaks with the granulated sugar and fold into the batter. Heat a good amount of oil in a pan. Dip the apricots in the batter and fry until golden brown on all sides. Remove and let drip on paper towels. Dust with confectioner's sugar.

Garnish Recommendation: vanilla sauce (see p. 202) and apricot sorbet (see p. 359)

Tip: To be sure that the apricot halves will stay together while frying, you can attach them with toothpicks. You can also cut the apricots open carefully on one side and remove the pits that way.

Ingredients for 10 Servings
20 Apricots
7 oz (200 g) Marzipan paste
7 tbsp (100 ml) Apricot
  liqueur
2¾ cups (350 g) Flour
1½ cups (375 ml) Wine
¼ cup (50 ml) Oil
3 Egg yolks
2 tbsp (30 g) Granulated
  sugar
Sunflower oil for frying
Confectioner's sugar

TYROLEAN POPPY BALLS WITH WHITE CHOCOLATE SAUCE

Mix all the ingredients for the poppy balls together and let sit for 5 minutes. Form 12 equally sized balls and chill them. For the frying batter, mix the white wine, flour, egg yolk, and salt until smooth. Beat the egg whites to stiff peaks with the granulated sugar and fold into the batter. Heat a good amount of oil in a pan. Dip the poppy balls in the batter and fry until golden brown on all sides. Remove and let drip on paper towels. Pour the prepared white chocolate sauce into dishes and place 3 poppy balls in the middle of each. Garnish with fresh raspberries and dust with confectioner's sugar.

Ingredients
½ cup (125 ml) White wine
1 cup (120 g) Flour
3 Egg yolks
Dash of salt
3 Egg whites
4 tsp (20 g) Granulated sugar
White chocolate sauce (see p. 204)
Raspberries to garnish
Confectioner's sugar for dusting
Sunflower oil for frying

For the Poppy Balls
2 oz (60 g) Poppy seeds, ground
1 cup less 2 tbsp (100 g) Plum jam
Dash of vanilla sugar
4 tsp (10 g) Confectioner's sugar
1 tbsp Rum

ARME RITTER (FRENCH TOAST)

Take the crusts off the brioche rolls by grating them, setting the crumbs aside. Mix the milk with egg yolk, vanilla sugar, granulated sugar, and rum. Pour over the brioche rolls and let them become saturated. After 15 minutes, squeeze out the excess liquid, cut open to the middle, and fill with chopped dried plums and lingonberry compote. Form the brioche rolls into balls. Beat the egg white a bit, dip the brioche dumplings in it, and roll in the crumbs. Heat oil in a pan and fry until golden on all sides. Remove from the oil and let drip on paper towels. Mix cinnamon and confectioner's sugar. Place the French toast on plates and dust with cinnamon sugar.

Garnish Recommendation: Preserved dried pears and plums (see p. 187) or Cardamom berries (see p. 190)

Ingredients for 6 Servings
6 Brioche rolls, stale
3 Eggs
½ cup (125 ml) Milk
4 tsp (20 g) Vanilla sugar
3 tbsp (50 g) Granulated sugar
4 tsp (2 cl) Rum
3 Egg whites
3.5 oz (100 g) Dried plums, chopped
3.5 oz (100 g) Lingonberry compote
½ tsp Cinnamon and confectioner's sugar for dusting
Oil for frying

APRICOT FRENCH TOAST WITH HONEY WHIPPED CREAM

For the honey whipped cream, mix the whipped cream with liquid honey and then chill. Take the crusts off the brioche rolls by grating them, setting the crumbs aside. Halve the rolls, brush with apricot marmalade, and fill with apricot pieces. Put the rolls back together. For the vanilla milk, beat all the ingredients together. Dip the brioche on both sides, roll in the crumbs, and fry in hot oil until golden brown on all sides. Remove from the oil and let drain on paper towels. Place on dishes and garnish with honey whipped cream. Dust with confectioner's sugar before serving.

Garnish Recommendation: lukewarm or cold cardamom berries (see p. 190)

Tip: This French toast can also be prepared with fresh French toast. In that case, you don't need as much milk, since fresh bread can't absorb as much.

Ingredients
4 Brioche rolls, stale
2 Apricots, pitted and diced
Apricot marmalade
Oil for frying
Confectioner's sugar for
  dusting

For the Vanilla Milk
½ cup (125 ml) Milk
1 Egg
Dash of vanilla sugar

For the Honey Whipped Cream
3 tbsp Whipped cream
½ tbsp Honey

FRIED POTATO NOODLES WITH VANILLA FOAM

Ingredients
2 tbsp (15 g) Yeast
2 tbsp (25 ml) Heavy cream, lukewarm
1 cup (125 g) Flour
3 oz (75 g) Potatoes, high starch, boiled and sieved
1 tbsp (15 g) Butter, melted
1 Egg
2 Egg yolks
Salt
Flour for the work surface
Sunflower oil for frying
Confectioner's sugar for dusting
5 oz (150 g) Blueberries to garnish

For the Vanilla Foam
½ cup (125 ml) Heavy cream
⅓ cup (80 ml) Milk
Pulp of 1 vanilla bean
2 tbsp (30 g) Granulated sugar
3 Egg yolks

Dissolve the yeast in lukewarm cream. Knead to a dough with the flour, potatoes, butter, egg, egg yolks, and a dash of salt. Cover and let rise in a warm place. Roll out on a floured surface and form noodles that are about a finger's thickness and 3in (7 cm) long. Heat a good amount of oil in a pan. Fry the potato noodles in the hot oil until they are golden brown all over. Remove from oil and let drain on paper towels.

For the vanilla foam, boil the cream, milk, vanilla pulp, and granulated sugar. Pour into the egg yolks while stirring constantly, then beat in a double boiler until it is nice and creamy. Place the noodles in dishes, pour the vanilla foam over them, and garnish with fresh blueberries. Dust with confectioner's sugar.

Viennese Baked Goods and the "Small Joy"

Psychologists and social researchers have long known that in times that are scary and shaken by crises, the demand for sweets goes up—along with that, more energy in the form of sugar. After the discovery of cheap beet sugar, sugar went from being a luxury of the aristocrats and the rich to a cheap folk food, which brought so much joy to the table during lean times. Most of the famous baked goods of Austrian-Bohemian cuisine—such as plum jam dumplings, cream strudel, buchteln, or leavened dumplings—have the advantage of being not only delicious, but also affordable to prepare. Even the warm Viennese baked goods of the nineteenth century were not at all a "small joy in cheerful poverty," as it may seem today, but rather the often desperate attempt to put cheap, filling, and good tasting food on the table in times of bitter distress.

The Home Ice Cream Parlor
ICE CREAM, SORBET, GRANITA, AND PARFAIT

ICE CREAMS

To make ice cream, it helps to have an ice cream machine. It is not only practical, but it is also fast. If you want to make several different kinds of ice cream, it makes sense to use this trick from the pros in the ice cream parlors: always begin with a light ice cream (milk or cream) and gradually work toward the darkest (chocolate). If you do not have access to an ice cream machine—which is not such an expensive purchase—it is best to put the ice cream mixtures in a metal form and deep freeze for 2–3 hours, stirring occasionally.

Vanilla Ice Cream

Boil the milk, heavy cream, halved vanilla beans, and half of the granulated sugar. Cream the eggs with the rest of the granulated sugar in a metal mixing bowl. Remove the vanilla bean from the milk and scrape any remaining pulp into it. Boil the vanilla milk once more and then stir in to the eggs, stirring constantly. Stir in a double boiler, until the mixture begins to thicken. Sieve and then beat until cool. Place the cooled cream in the ice cream machine or freeze in a shallow pan, stirring occasionally.

Ingredients for
12–14 Servings
2 cups (500 ml) Milk
2 cups (500 ml) Heavy cream
¾ cup (160 g) Granulated
   sugar
3 Vanilla beans
6 Egg yolks
4 Eggs

NOUGAT ICE CREAM

Boil the milk and heavy cream. Cream the egg yolks, eggs, and granulated sugar. Add the milk/cream mixture and mix the whole thing in a double boiler for a few minutes, until it begins to thicken. Melt the chocolate and nougat. Add the egg mixture and mix in cocoa powder. Finally, stir in the Cointreau. Place in the ice cream machine or freeze in a shallow pan, stirring occasionally.

WHITE CHOCOLATE ICE CREAM

Boil the milk and heavy cream. Cream the egg yolks, eggs, and granulated sugar. Add the milk/cream mixture and mix the whole thing in a double boiler for a few minutes, until it begins to thicken. Melt the chocolate. Add the egg mixture and then stir in Bacardi. Place in the ice cream machine or freeze in a shallow pan, stirring occasionally.

VANILLA SAFFRON ICE CREAM

Boil the milk, heavy cream, halved vanilla bean, saffron, and half of the granulated sugar. Cream the eggs with the rest of the granulated sugar in a metal mixing bowl. Remove the vanilla bean from the milk and scrape any remaining pulp into it. Boil the vanilla milk once more and then add to the egg, stirring constantly. Stir in a double boiler, until the mixture begins to thicken. Sieve and then beat until cool. Place the cooled cream in the ice cream machine or freeze in a shallow pan, stirring occasionally. Before serving, place a saffron thread on each scoop.

Ingredients for
8–10 Servings
1¼ cups (300 ml) Milk
1¼ cups (300 ml) Heavy cream
3 Egg yolks
2 Eggs
3 tbsp (50 g) Granulated sugar
1.5 oz (40 g) Dark couverture chocolate
2 oz (60 g) Nougat
4 tsp (10 g) Cocoa powder
3 tbsp (4 cl) Cointreau

Ingredients for 7–9 Servings
1⅔ cups (400 ml) Heavy cream
7 tbsp (100 ml) Milk
⅓ cup (80 g) Granulated sugar
4 Egg yolks
2 Eggs
4.5 oz (125 g) White couverture chocolate
3 tbsp (4 cl) Bacardi

Ingredients for 12–14 Servings
2 cups (500 ml) Milk
2 cups (500ml) Heavy cream
¾ cup (160 g) Granulated sugar
3 Vanilla beans
Dash of saffron
6 Egg yolks
4 Eggs
Saffron threads to garnish

CREAM ICE CREAM

Ingredients for 7–9 Servings
¾ cup (170 g) Granulated
  sugar
1.5 oz (40 g) Dried milk
  powder
2 cups (500 ml) Milk
¾ cups (200 ml) Heavy
  cream

Mix the granulated sugar with the dried milk powder. Add the milk and cream and bring to a boil once. Mix for 5 minutes and then sieve. Place in the ice cream machine or freeze in a shallow pan, stirring occasionally.

Who Invented Ice Cream?

What do noodles have in common with ice cream? They say that both were discovered by Marco Polo in China and brought back to Europe. But neither is really true. In 1200 ACE, the Chinese poet Yang Wan Li did describe the "frozen milk" in the cellar and the technology to make ice cream from water and saltpeter, but it (like pasta) came from the Arabs, who called their ice cream "sharbat" or "sherbet," via Sicily. The ancient Romans already had "nature ice," which was made simply using snow from Mount Vesuvius or Mount Aetna. The critical philosopher Seneca tried to rouse the Roman senate against the bad habit of selling the snow, preserved from the winter at a high price, for eating instead of storage.

It is also said of Alexander the Great that he had his messengers bring him snow during his travels to India, which he then mixed with honey, fruit, and spices. Alexander also discovered a useful "side effect" to the ice: he had the ice-filled barrels covered with oak planks, where he stored the wine for his troops, who he knew loved to have a cool drink. Maybe that is an explanation for why Alexander so often left the battlefield as the victor, despite his youth.

The first ice cream cookbook in history, The De Sorbetti *by Filippo Baldinini, appeared in 1784 in Italy, which is also where J. W. von Goethe, who had quite a sweet tooth, discovered his professed love for raspberry ice cream.*

Thanks to the invention of Linde's refrigerating machine in 1876, ice cream could become available for public consumption instead of simply being a luxury for aristocrats and bourgeois.

BEER ICE CREAM

Cream the egg yolks with honey and sugar in a mixing bowl over steam. Boil the beer and quickly mix about a ladleful of beer with the egg. Add this mixture to the rest of the beer and heat over steam again, to about 175 °F (80 °C), whisking the entire time. Place the mixing bowl in ice water and beat until cold. Mix in the heavy cream, sieve, and place in the ice cream machine or freeze in a shallow pan, stirring occasionally.

Ingredients for 7–9 Servings
6 Egg yolks
1 tbsp Honey
7 tbsp (100 g) Granulated
  sugar
2 cups (500 ml) Dark beer
½ cup (125 ml) Heavy cream

HONEY ICE CREAM

Boil the heavy cream and milk. Mix the egg yolks with honey and beat into the cream/milk mixture in a double boiler, until the mixture begins to thicken. Sieve and place the cooled cream in the ice cream machine or freeze in a shallow pan, stirring occasionally.

Ingredients for 4–6 Serving
1 cup (250 ml) Heavy cream
½ cup (125 ml) Milk
6 tbsp (125 g) Honey
4 Egg yolks

COCONUT ICE CREAM

Boil heavy cream, granulated sugar, and coconut purée. Beat the egg whites to soft peaks. Remove the coconut mixture from heat and fold the egg whites in. Add water to the gelatin, remove excess, and dissolve in warmed coconut liqueur. Mix into the ice cream mixture. Blend everything well with an immersion blender. Let cool and place the cooled cream in the ice cream machine or freeze in a shallow pan, stirring occasionally.

Ingredients for 6–8 Servings
1 cup (250 ml) Heavy cream
1 cup (250 ml) Coconut
  purée
½ cup (120 g) Granulated
  sugar
4 Egg whites
1 Sheet gelatin
4 tsp (2 cl) Coconut liqueur

LAVENDER ICE CREAM

Ingredients for 7–8 Servings
1 cup (250 ml) Milk
1 cup (250 ml) Heavy cream
6 tbsp (90 g) Granulated
  sugar
1 tbsp (20 g) Honey
7 tbsp (100 ml) Lavender
  Juice (see p. 205)
1 Egg
4 Egg yolks

Boil the heavy cream and milk and add the lavender juice. Cream the egg, egg yolks, honey, and sugar and add to the hot lavender milk, stirring constantly. Whisk in a double boiler, until it begins to thicken. Remove from heat and stir until cool. Sieve and place in the ice cream machine or freeze in a shallow pan, stirring occasionally.

RUM ICE CREAM WITH RAISINS

Ingredients for 6–7 Servings
½ cup (120 g) Brown sugar
¼ cup (6 cl) Rum
1¼ cup (300 ml) Heavy
  cream
1 cup (250 ml) Milk
½ Vanilla bean
2 tbsp (30 g) Sugar
2 Eggs
2 Egg yolks
3 oz (80 g) Preserved raisins
  (see p. 189)

Cook the sugar to a light caramel and deglaze with rum. Mix in the cream, milk, and vanilla bean and let boil until the caramel dissolves. Cream the eggs, egg yolks, and sugar. Add the hot caramel milk and stir for 5 minutes in a double boiler. Sieve and let cool. Place in the ice cream machine or freeze in a shallow pan, stirring occasionally. Mix the raisins into the finished ice cream.

SOUR ICE CREAM WITH LIME

Ingredients for 6–7 Servings
2 cups (500 ml) Sour cream
⅔ cup (150 g) Granulated
  sugar
¼ cup (50 ml) Water
Juice and peel of 2 limes

First, wash the limes in hot water, rub dry with a towel, and wash again. Cut the peel off in thin strips, or use a zester. Squeeze out the juice. Heat the water with the sugar, until the sugar dissolves. Stir into the cream. Finally, stir in the lime zest and lime juice. Place in the ice cream machine or freeze in a shallow pan, stirring occasionally.

Ice Cream from the Paradeisgartl

In 1797—while the Napoleonic troops were pressing forward over Villach and Klagenfurt into Styria—sugar-saturated Vienna had two things on its mind aside from the French occupiers: "G'frorne" or "frozen" and "lemonade tents." The former is simply ice cream, and it was sold next to other iced and sweet delicacies in tent-like establishments called lemonade tents, which were set up on the side of the road or in the marketplace.

The success of this totally new form of sweet cuisine was so big that the Viennese theater newspaper reported on 6,000 cups of ice cream that were eaten nightly just in the Milano coffee house in the Paradeisgartl in Vienna. The widow Kleopha Lechner opened more tents in the marketplace to serve the promenading Viennese ladies and gentlemen "all types of frozen treats, in various forms." The Demel Konditorei in Vienna began its career then too, as an ice cream parlor across from the old Burgtheater in Michaelerplatz.

CINNAMON ICE CREAM

Boil the milk with heavy cream, cinnamon sticks, honey, and sugar. Remove the cinnamon, beat the egg yolks, mix them in, and remove from heat. Sieve and place in the ice cream machine or freeze in a shallow pan, stirring occasionally.

Ingredients for
8–10 Servings
2 cups (500 ml) Milk
¾ cup (200 ml) Heavy cream
2 Cinnamon sticks
6 tbsp Honey
3 tbsp (40 g) Sugar
5 Egg yolks

SORBET

The fruit ice that we call sorbet started out as nothing but naturally occurring ice or snow mixed with fruit juice. Even though using an ice cream machine to make sorbet is convenient, they can also be made by hand. The only important thing is using high-quality fruit, sugar syrup, and, if need be, a splash of liqueur. Then you only need to follow the methods of the famous French ice cream makers, Berthillon:

- Pour the sorbet mixture into a stainless steel bowl with a flat bottom.
- Place the bowl in the freezer.
- Every hour, stir or blend well, so that the mixture freezes evenly and no large ice crystals occur.
- Let freeze again.
- Repeat until the sorbet is nice and creamy.

Attention: The serving sizes given in this chapter are the right size for an intermediate course in a full course meal!

CHOCOLATE SORBET

Ingredients for 10 Servings
6 tbsp (85 g) Granulated sugar
⅓ cup (85 ml) Water
3 tbsp (4 cl) Grand Marnier
Zest of 2 oranges
7 oz (200 g) Dark couverture chocolate
7 tbsp (100 ml) Heavy cream
1 tbsp Confectioner's sugar
Orange peels
Chocolate shavings

To make simple syrup, boil water with granulated sugar, remove from heat and add Grand Marnier and orange zest. Melt the chocolate in a bain-marie and stir into the syrup. Place in the ice cream machine or freeze in a stainless steel bowl, stirring occasionally. Remove from the freezer approximately 15 minutes before serving, so that the sorbet is not too hard. Mix the heavy cream with the confectioner's sugar and whip halfway, spoon on top of each scoop, and garnish with chocolate shavings and orange peels.

Tip: This sorbet is particularly decorative if you fill small espresso cups with it before freezing.

STRAWBERRY SORBET

Purée all the ingredients with a blender and sieve. Place in the ice cream machine (or freezer, stirring repeatedly).

Ingredients for
12–14 Servings
18 oz (500 g) Strawberries
2 tbsp (30 ml) Lemon juice
4 tsp (20 ml) Strawberry
  liqueur
⅓ cup (150 g) Granulated
  sugar

RASPBERRY SORBET

Boil the water with sugar and add the washed raspberries. Purée with a blender and sieve. Flavor with raspberry liqueur and place in the ice cream machine (or freezer, stirring repeatedly).

Ingredients for
18–20 Servings
28 oz (800 g) Raspberries
¾ cup (180 g) Granulated
  sugar
¼ cup (50 ml) Water
3 tbsp (4 cl) Raspberry
  liqueur

PLUM SORBET

Cut the washed, pitted plums into slices. Boil the red wine with granulated sugar, add the plums, and let marinate. Purée with a blender and sieve. Flavor with cinnamon and slivovitz. Place in the ice cream machine (or freezer, stirring repeatedly).

Ingredients for
12–14 Ingredients
18 oz (500 g) Plums, pitted
¼ cup (50 ml) Red wine
⅔ cup (150 g) Granulated
  sugar
Dash of cinnamon
3 tbsp (4 cl) Slivovitz

MANDARIN SORBET

Melt sugar in a pan. Add mandarin juice, orange juice, and mandarin zest. Remove from heat and let cool. Place in the ice cream machine (or freezer, stirring repeatedly).

Ingredients for
10–12 Portions
2 cups (500 ml) Mandarin
  juice
⅔ cup (150 g) Granulated
  sugar
Zest of 3 untreated man-
  darins
Juice of 1 orange

APRICOT SORBET

*Ingredients for 8–10
Servings*
9 oz (250 g) Apricot purée
  (sieved apricots)
7 tbsp (100 ml) Sparkling
  wine (preferably Chardonnay)
½ cup (50 g) Apricot
  marmalade
Juice of ½ lemon
4 tsp (2 cl) Apricot brandy
2 oz (60 g) Simple syrup (see
  p. 40)

Mix the apricot purée, apricot marmalade, lemon juice, and simple syrup. Add the apricot brandy and sparkling wine and place
in the ice cream machine (or freezer, stirring repeatedly).

MUSCAT GRAPE SORBET

*Ingredients for 18–20
Servings*
7 tbsp (100 ml) Water
1 ⅓ cup (300 g) Sugar
3 ⅓ lbs (1.5 kg) Muscat
  grapes, halved
1⅔ cups (400 ml) White wine
  (preferably muscatel)
2 tsp (10 g) Vanilla sugar
2 tsp (1 cl) Lemon juice
2 tsp (1 cl) Brandy

Boil water with sugar until the liquid is clear. Briefly boil the
halved grapes with white wine in the syrup and then let marinate
overnight. Sieve without crushing the fruit. Stir the grape juice
with vanilla sugar, lemon juice, and brandy and place in the ice
cream machine (or freezer, stirring repeatedly).

ELDERBERRY SORBET

*Ingredients for 14–16
Servings*
18 oz (500 g) Elderberries,
  crushed
⅔ cup (150 ml) Water
¾ cup (180 g) Granulated
  sugar
¼ cup (5 cl) Elderberry
  brandy

Bring the elderberries to a boil with water and sugar. Purée with
a blender and sieve. Flavor with elderberry brandy. Place in the
ice cream machine (or freezer, stirring repeatedly).

ELDERFLOWER SORBET

*Ingredients for
12–14 Servings*
2.5 cups (600 ml) Elder-
  flower Juice (see p. 205)
7 tbsp (100 ml) Sparkling
  wine or champagne
4 tsp (2 cl) Lemon juice

Stir the elderflower juice together with the sparkling wine and
lemon juice. Place in the ice cream machine (or freezer, stirring
repeatedly).

PUMPKIN SORBET

Bring all the ingredients to a boil and let them simmer until the pumpkin is very soft. Blend smooth and sieve. Let cool and place in the ice cream machine (or freezer, stirring repeatedly).

Ingredients for
12–15 Servings
7 oz (200 g) Pumpkin flesh
⅔ cup (150 ml) Apple juice
⅔ cup (150 ml) Water
7 tbsp (100 g) Sugar
Peel of 1 untreated orange,
  cut into strips
3 tbsp (4 cl) Lavender juice
  (see p. 205, or substitute
  elderflower syrup)

LEMON BASIL SORBET

Blanch the basil in some boiling salt water. Shock in ice water. Boil the lemon juice with granulated sugar and water. Remove from heat and add the lemon zest. Squeeze out the basil and mix in with an immersion blender. Sieve and place in the ice cream machine (or freezer, stirring repeatedly).

Tip: Because of its tart, sour notes, this sorbet is not only great as a refreshing dessert, but particularly as an invigorating intermediate course in a full course meal.

Ingredients for
10–12 Servings
1¼ cups (300 ml) Lemon
  juice
¾ cup (180 g) Granulated
  sugar
⅔ cup (150 ml) Water
Zest of 1 lemon
½ Bundle of basil
Salt

APPLE GINGER SORBET

Ingredients for
8–10 Servings
9 oz (250 g) Apples (Granny Smith)
2 tbsp (30 ml) Lemon juice
1 tbsp (15 ml) Calvados (French apple brandy)
7 oz (200 g) Simple syrup (see p. 40)
Ginger, ground (or fresh ginger slices)

Peel, core, and dice the apples. Purée with lemon juice, Calvados, and simple syrup. Flavor with the ground ginger or purée the fresh ginger with the other ingredients. Sieve and immediately place in the ice cream machine (or freezer, stirring repeatedly).

PEPPERMINT PEAR SORBET

Peel, quarter, and core the pears. Boil the pears in white wine, sugar, and vanilla pulp until they are soft. Purée the mixture. Blanch washed mint in boiling water and then shock it in ice water. Cut the leaves small, add to the pear mixture, and blend again. Add the peppermint liqueur, sieve the mixture, and place in the ice cream machine (or freezer, stirring repeatedly).

Ingredients for
16–18 Servings
10 Pears, ripe
¾ cups (200 ml) White wine
1 cup plus 2 tbsp (250 g) Sugar
Pulp of 1 vanilla bean
1 Bundle of peppermint
2 tbsp (30 ml) Peppermint liqueur

PEAR CHILI SORBET

Peel, quarter, and core the pears. Bring the pears, water, lemon juice, and sugar briefly to a boil. Purée with a blender and sieve. Let cool somewhat. Flavor with pear brandy and chili. Place in the ice cream machine (or freezer, stirring repeatedly).

Tip: If you want this sorbet to be less fiery, simply reduce or leave out the chili.

Ingredients for
10–12 Servings
14 oz (400 g) Pears, fully ripe
¼ cup (50 ml) Water
½ cup plus 1 tbsp (130 g) Granulated sugar
¼ cup (50 ml) Lemon juice
4 tsp (2 cl) Pear brandy
Chili threads or ¼ of a chili pepper (without seeds), finely chopped

BELLINI SORBET

Ingredients for 6–8 Servings
9 oz (250 g) Peach purée
  (sieved peaches)
3.5 oz (100 g) Simple syrup
  (see p. 40)
Juice of ½ lemon
4 tsp (2 cl) Grappa
⅓ cup (8 cl) Champagne
Champagne to serve

Mix all the ingredients together well, sieve, and place in the ice cream machine (or freezer, stirring repeatedly). To serve the sorbet, pour champagne over each scoop in a chilled glass.

PIÑA COLADA SORBET

Ingredients for
13–15 Servings
2 cups (500 ml) Pineapple
  juice
5 oz (150 g) Coconut purée
3.5 oz (100 g) Simple syrup
  (see p. 40)
4 tbsp Rum

Blend the pineapple juice with coconut purée and simple syrup, sieve, and flavor with rum. Place in the ice cream machine (or freezer, stirring repeatedly).

MAI TAI SORBET

Ingredients for
10–12 Servings
1 cup (250 ml) Orange juice,
  fresh squeezed
⅓ cup (80 ml) Lemon juice,
  fresh squeezed
⅔ cup (150 g) Granulated
  sugar
¼ cup (50 ml) Water
3 tbsp (4 cl) Cointreau
3 tbsp (4 cl) Brown rum
Lime peel, cut into fine
  strips

Boil the water with the granulated sugar to make a thick syrup (see p. 40). Mix with the other ingredients and place in the ice cream machine (or freezer, stirring repeatedly).

MELON SORBET WITH GRAPPA

Ingredients for
8–10 Servings
10.5 oz (300 g) Melon flesh
  with juice (honey or cha-
  rentais melon)
¼ cup (60 ml) Late harvest
  wine (Beerenauslese)
1 tbsp Honey
3 tbsp (40 g) Granulated
  sugar
7 tbsp (100 ml) Grappa

Scoop out the seeds of the melon and press them through a sieve, collecting the juice. Peel the melons and dice the flesh. Heat the wine with honey and granulated sugar. Blend with the melon and melon juice. Sieve and flavor with Grappa. Place in the ice cream machine (or freezer, stirring repeatedly).

MOCHA CARDAMOM SORBET

Simmer the water and sugar for 3 minutes. Remove from heat, stir in the instant coffee powder, and flavor with cardamom. Let cool. Place in the ice cream machine (or freezer, stirring repeatedly).

Ingredients for
18–20 Servings
3 cups (700 ml) Water
1 cup less 2 tbsp (200 g)
   Granulated sugar
2 oz (50 g) Instant coffee
   powder
Pinch of cardamom

GRANITA

When you put a mixture of fruit juice or fruit purée and sugar syrup in a bowl in the freezer and stir it occasionally, the mixture crystallizes and becomes granita. Granita is ideal as an intermediate course in a long meal or as an ultra cool dessert on hot days.

BEERENAUSLESE GRANITA

Ingredients for 6–8 Servings
7 tbsp (100 g) Granulated sugar
1 cup (250 ml) Water
1½ cup (375 ml) Late harvest Riesling (Beerenauslese)
Mint to garnish

Boil the water and granulated sugar. Let cool and add the wine. Pour onto a stainless steel sheet pan and freeze. As soon as a layer of ice forms, stir it with a spoon. Freeze again and stir after half an hour. Repeat this process until the entire thing is frozen into ice crystals. Fill chilled glasses, garnish with mint, and serve.

RASPBERRY GRANITA

Ingredients for 2–4 Servings
7 oz (200 g) Raspberries
⅓ cup (75 g) Sugar
Juice of 2 lemons
Sparkling wine (preferably Chardonnay) to taste

Stir all the ingredients together until the sugar has dissolved. Press through a sieve and freeze on a stainless steel sheet pan, stirring multiple times during the freezing process. Shave pieces off the finished granita with a spoon and fill chilled glasses. Fill the glasses with a bit of champagne, to taste.

Tip: Granitas can easily be prepared with other sour fruit juices, dry wines, or champagnes, but the liquid must be appropriately sweetened.

Don Carlos and the Snow Water

In 1568, when Don Carlos, that Infante of Spain immortalized by Friedrich von Schiller and Guiseppe Verdi, died suspiciously in a Madrid jail, the official cause of death was pronounced to be drinking too much snow water. That made complete sense to the contemporaries of the unlucky Infante, since all doctors of the time were in agreement that it was very unhealthy to drink cold liquids. This idea came from Hippocrates, who had proclaimed that "it is dangerous to overheat or overcool the body. Anything excessive is an enemy of nature." In the meantime, we have become a little wiser: in modern nutritional medicine, sorbets and low sugar fruit ices are recommended in many diets, because they are among the lowest calorie desserts. Just so long as there is more ice in it than chocolate. (See recipe on p. 365.)

PARFAITS

The semifreddo, or "half cold," counts among the highest level for master confectioners. But you can make parfaits easily at home, just as long as you use high-quality ingredients and temper them correctly. Because a parfait that is too cold to be scooped up in creamy spoonfuls has missed its mark.

HAZELNUT PARFAIT

Ingredients for 6–7 Servings
10.5 oz (300 g) Brittle (see p. 36)
3 Egg yolks
3 tbsp (40 g) Granulated sugar
2 Egg whites
2 oz (50 g) Nougat
¾ cup (200 ml) Heavy cream
3 tbsp (4 cl) Nut liqueur

Prepare the brittle according to the recipe and grind coarsely. Cream the egg yolks with half of the granulated sugar. Beat the egg whites to stiff peaks with the rest of the sugar. Melt the nougat in a double boiler and stir into the egg yolk. Carefully fold in the egg whites. Whip the cream halfway and fold it in along with the brittle. Flavor with nut liqueur. Fill a terrine pan and freeze for at least 3 hours, but preferably overnight. Let the parfait thaw slightly before serving, so that it is not too hard.

BAILEY'S PARFAIT

Ingredients for 10–12 Servings
4 Eggs
2 Egg yolks
7 tbsp (100 g) Sugar
3 oz (80 g) Milk couverture chocolate
2 oz (60 g) White couverture chocolate
2 cups (500 ml) Whipped cream
¾ cup (200 ml) Bailey's
Cocoa powder for dusting

Beat the eggs, egg yolks, and sugar in a mixing bowl over steam until cream. Place the bowl in ice water and beat until cool. Melt the milk chocolate and white chocolate in a bain-marie and mix with the egg. Fold in the whipped cream and then the Bailey's. Fill mold and freeze overnight. Before serving, dip each mold in hot water, remove the parfaits, and lightly dust with cocoa powder.

Garnish Recommendation: preserved apricots (see p. 188) or strawberries and some vanilla foam (see p. 203)

CAPPUCCINO PARFAIT

Beat the egg yolk and sugar in a double boiler. Beat in a stand mixer until cool. Meanwhile, boil the coffee in a pot and double the concentration. Whip the cream halfway and fold the coffee and whipped cream into the egg mixture. Flavor with the coffee liqueur. Fill coffee cups and freeze for at least 3 hours, but preferably overnight. Let the parfait thaw somewhat before serving, so that it is not too hard.

Tip: The cappuccino parfait tastes particularly good when garnished with fresh seasonal berries.

Ingredients for 4–6 Servings
2 Eggs
1 Egg yolk
⅓ cup (75 g) Granulated
   sugar
7 tbsp (100 ml) Coffee,
   strong
3 tbsp (4 cl) Coffee liqueur
1¼ cup (300 ml) Whipped
   cream

Ingredients for 18 Servings
For the Coconut Parfait
4 Eggs
2 Egg yolks
7 tbsp (100 g) Sugar
Dash of salt
12.5 (350 g) White chocolate
12.5 (350 g) Coconut purée
½ cup (12 cl) Coconut
  liqueur
2 cups (500 ml) Whipped
  cream

For the Nougat Parfait
1 Egg
1 Egg yolk
4 tbsp (2 cl) Grand Marnier
3.5 oz (100 g) Nougat
1 cup (250 ml) Whipped
  cream
Coconut flakes and
Cocoa powder to garnish

COCONUT NOUGAT PARFAIT

For the coconut parfait, beat the eggs, egg yolks, granulated sugar, and salt in a double boiler until creamy, then place the bowl in ice water and beat until cold. Melt the chocolate in a double boiler (watch out, don't let it get too hot!). Mix with the eggs, stir in coconut purée and coconut liqueur and fold in the whipped cream. Fill a terrine pan or individual molds ¾ of the way and freeze for at least 3 hours. For the nougat parfait, cream the egg and egg yolk. Soften the nougat in a double boiler and stir into the egg. Fold in the whipped cream and flavor with Grand Marnier. Spread the nougat parfait on top of the frozen coconut and freeze overnight. Place the molds briefly in hot water to remove the parfaits. Coat them in coconut flakes and dust with cocoa powder.

Garnish Recommendation: mango purée or fresh strawberries

PRALINE PARFAIT

Beat the eggs, egg yolks, granulated sugar, and a dash of salt in a double boiler until creamy, then place bowl in ice water and beat until cold. Melt the chocolate in a double boiler (watch out; don't let it get too hot!), and stir into the egg. Stir in Bacardi and cognac and fold in the whipped cream. Fill a terrine pan or individual containers and freeze overnight. Let thaw slightly before serving, so that it isn't too hard.

Garnish Recommendation: cardamom berries (see p. 190) or burgundy cherries (see p. 183) and vanilla foam (see p. 203)

Tip: The praline parfait tastes even more delicate if you first line the terrine with baumkuchen slices.

Ingredients for
10–12 Servings
4 Eggs
2 Egg yolks
⅓ cup (80 g) Granulated sugar
Dash of salt
4.5 oz (125 g) Dark couverture chocolate
2 cups (500 ml) Whipped cream
4 tsp (2 cl) Bacardi
4 tsp (2 cl) Cognac

The Ice of Poets, Knights, and Kings

Great artists have always liked the topic of ice cream. "Where is the snow of the bygone year?" asked François Villon, who wasn't thinking of winter sports, but rather iced desserts. The crusaders brought the technology for creating ice cream from the Arabic lands back to France. Soon the French landed aristocracy could show their wealth not only through their well-stocked wine cellars, but also ice cellars where they stored iced fruit in all colors of the rainbow. Ice cream traveled from France to England, where King Charles I so jealously guarded the recipe for his favorite ice cream that he made it an official state secret. It remains such until the execution of the kind under the puritan Oliver Cromwell.

POPPY CINNAMON PARFAIT

Ingredients for 10 Servings
1.5 oz (40 g) Poppy seeds, ground
¾ cups (200 ml) Milk
1 tbsp Cinnamon
4 Eggs
2 Egg yolks
⅔ cup (150 g) Granulated sugar
1⅔ cups (400 ml) Whipped cream
Dash of salt

Simmer the poppy for about 2 minutes in ¾ of the milk, then set aside. Boil the rest of the milk, add the cinnamon, and let steep for 5 minutes. Set aside. Beat the eggs, egg yolks, granulated sugar, and salt in a double boiler until creamy, then place the bowl in ice water and beat until cold. Fold in the whipped cream. Halve the mixture. Mix one half with the poppy and the other with the cinnamon. Alternate layers of the mixtures in the container of your choosing and freeze for at least 3 hours (preferably overnight). Let thaw slightly before serving, so that it's not too hard.

Garnish Recommendation: Burgundy cherries (see p. 183) or berry ragout (see p. 185)

NOUGAT ORANGE PARFAIT

Beat the eggs, egg yolks, granulated sugar, and salt in a double boiler until creamy, then place bowl in ice water and beat until cold. Warm nougat in a bain-marie and stir until smooth. Mix the egg with the nougat, stir in Cointreau, and fold in whipped cream. Fill a terrine pan or individual containers and freeze overnight. Let thaw slightly before serving, so that the parfait is not too hard.

Garnish Recommendation: orange ragout or burgundy cherries (see p. 183)

Tip: Very clever amateur chefs can try this refined presentation for this parfait: roll a 4–5 in (10–12 cm) cone out of parchment paper and secure with a rubber band. Cut the wide end so that it can stand securely. Fill halfway with melted dark couverture chocolate and roll it around to coat the entire inside of the cone. Place on a lightly oiled glazing rack and freeze for 30 minutes. Fill with the cooled parfait mixture and freeze the cones with the points downward (you can place them in glasses). Before serving, remove the paper and simply place the cone on a dish.

Ingredients for
10–12 Servings
5 Eggs
3 Egg yolks
⅓ cup (80 g) Granulated
 sugar
14 oz (400 g) Nougat
⅓ cup (80 ml) Cointreau
4 cups (900 ml) Whipped
 cream
Dash of salt

QUARK RUM PARFAIT

Bring the water and granulated sugar to a boil and then simmer for about 1 minute. Remove from heat. Mix the quark with rum, lemon juice, and vanilla sugar until smooth, then mix in the sugar syrup you made. Whip the cream halfway and fold it in along with the preserved raisins. Fill a terrine pan and freeze overnight. Let thaw slightly before serving, so that the parfait is not too hard.

Garnish Recommendation: fresh strawberries and sesame waffles (see p. 38)

Ingredients for
10–12 Servings
1 cup (220 g) Granulated
 sugar
¾ cup (180 ml) Water
17.5 (500 g) Quark
Juice of 1 lemon
4 tsp (20 g) Vanilla sugar
1¼ cups (300 ml) Heavy
 cream
2 oz (60 g) Preserved raisins
 (see p. 189)
¼ cup (6 cl) Rum

ELDERFLOWER PARFAIT

Beat the eggs, egg yolks, and granulated sugar in a double boiler until creamy. Boil the elderflower juice. In the meantime, add cold water to the gelatin. Remove excess water, remove the elderflower juice from heat, and dissolve the gelatin in it. Beat the egg with the elderflower juice over ice until cold. Whip the cream halfway and fold it in along with the elderberry brandy. Fill a terrine pan and freeze overnight. Let thaw slightly before serving, so that the parfait is not too hard.

Garnish Recommendation: berry ragout (see p. 185) or preserved peaches (see p. 189)

Ingredients for 12 Servings
4 Eggs
2 Egg yolks
6 tbsp (90 g) Granulated sugar
1½ cups (350 ml) Elderflower juice (see p. 205)
2 Sheets gelatin
4 tsp (2 cl) Elderberry brandy
2 cups (500 ml) Heavy cream

GRAPPA PARFAIT

Beat the eggs, egg yolks, granulated sugar, and salt in a double boiler until creamy, then place bowl in ice water and beat until cold. Warm the apricot marmalade and honey in a double boiler, stir until smooth, and mix with the egg. Stir in the grappa. Whip the cream halfway and fold in. Fill a terrine pan and freeze overnight. Let thaw slightly before serving, so that the parfait is not too hard.

Garnish Recommendation: marinated warm blackberries

Tip: This classic ice cream dish, also called a soufflé glace, looks particularly attractive if you line the terrine with baumkuchen slices before filling it with the parfait.

Ingredients for
8–10 Servings
2 Eggs
2 Egg yolks
⅓ cup (80 g) Granulated sugar
Dash of salt
1 cup (100 g) Apricot marmalade
5 tbs (100 g) Honey
1⅔ cups (400 ml) Heavy cream
½ cup (120 ml) Grappa

GRAND MARNIER ICE CREAM SOUFFLÉ

Ingredients for 6 Servings
2 Eggs
4 Egg yolks
7 tbsp (100 g) Granulated
 sugar
¼ cup (60 ml) Grand Marnier
1⅔ cups (400 ml) Whipped
 cream
1 tbsp Cocoa powder

First, wrap the ramekins in parchment paper so that the paper is ½in (1.5 cm) higher than the top. Cream the eggs, egg yolks, and granulated sugar in a double boiler. Add the Grand Marnier and beat over ice until cold. Whip the cream halfway and fold in. Fill the ramekins. Freeze overnight. Dust the tops with cocoa powder and then remove the paper.

Garnish Recommendation: marinated oranges or orange ragout (see p. 183) and kumquats with star anise (see p. 190)

Beethoven and Ice Cream Season
In the nineteenth century, the increasing love of the Viennese for ice cream corresponded to the fear that it would soon run out, since they were limited to the store of naturally occurring ice. In the mild winter of 1793–94, ice cream freak Ludwig van Beethoven asked whether there would be enough ice cream in Vienna the next summer. Because if there wouldn't, he would rather pass the summer in the mountains.

The Microcosm of Sweets

COOKIES AND CANDIES

COOKIES

"Show me your cookie jar, and I'll tell you who you are." It could almost be an Austrian saying. Nowhere else will you find such a variety of sweet little baked goods as you will in the coffee- and Christmas-cookie scented Alps.

VANILLA CRESCENTS

Preheat oven to 350 °F (180 °F). Coat the butter in the flour on a pastry board. Knead with confectioner's sugar and ground nuts to a smooth dough. Chill for about half an hour. Form a log from the dough. Cut off small pieces and shape them into crescents. Set them on a baking sheet lined with parchment paper and bake for about 10 minutes. Carefully (they break easily!) roll the still-hot crescents in a mixture of confectioner's sugar and vanilla sugar.

Bake Time: 10 minutes

Bake Temperature: 350 °F (180 °F)

Ingredients
1 stick plus 6 tbsp (200 g) Butter
2¼ cups (280 g) Flour
⅓ cup (80 g) Confectioner's sugar
3.5 oz (100 g) Nuts, ground
Confectioner's sugar and vanilla sugar to coat

VANILLA OR VANILLIN

For centuries, vanilla, along with saffron, was one of the most expensive and noble spices in the world. People tried over and over to find substitutes, but never got past garlic, which used to be called "the vanilla of the poor man" and is the reason there is a German dish called vanilla roast beef that contains no vanilla. But in 1874, the German scientist Wilhelm Haarman managed to create a synthetic substitute for vanilla. He called in "vanillin" and manufactured it in factories. Since then, the aroma of vanilla, previously only available to the rich, could be smelled in the kitchens of farmers, petty bourgeoisie, and workers. Vanilla crescents quickly became the most popular cookie for Christmas and tea time, despite the fact that they should be called vanillin crescents. Now that most people use synthetic vanilla in their baking.

Nut Kisses

Ingredients
Macaroon batter made with
    hazelnuts (see p. 34)
Confectioner's sugar to dust
2⅓ cups (300 g) Raspberry
    marmalade

Prepare the macaroon batter according to the recipe. Line a baking sheet with parchment paper and pipe domes onto the baking sheet using a piping bag fitted with a round nozzle. Dust with some confectioner's sugar and let dry (preferably overnight). Preheat oven to 320 °F (160 °C) and bake for 12–15 minutes. Keep the oven open a crack so that the steam can escape. Remove the kisses from the oven, let cool, and remove from the paper. Brush half of them with raspberry marmalade and place the others on top.

Bake Time: 12–15 minutes

Bake Temperature: 320 °F (160 °C)

COCONUT KISSES

Preheat oven to 320 °F (160 °C). Beat the egg whites to stiff peaks with the confectioner's sugar. Fold in the coconut flakes and honey. Place little domes of batter on a baking sheet lined with parchment paper and bake for about 10 minutes. Let cool.

For the cream, cream butter and sugar and mix in the grated chocolate bit by bit. Cut 1in (3cm) circles out of the wafers. Spread cream on them and set a coconut kiss on top of each one. Chill until the cream is firm. Melt the chocolate glaze and dip the bottom of each cookie.

Bake Time: about 10 minutes

Bake Temperature: 320 °F (160 °C)

Ingredients
1 cup less 2 tbsp (200 g) Confectioner's sugar
3 Egg whites
7 oz (200 g) Coconut flakes
2 tbsp (1 kL) Honey
Wafers
About ⅔ cup (150 g) Chocolate glaze to dip (see p. 42)

For the Crème"
2 sticks plus 1½ tbsp (250 g) Butter
1¼ cup (150 g) confectioner's sugar
3 oz (80 g) Cooking chocolate, ground

LINZER EYES

Preheat oven to 350 °F (180 °C). Knead the flour, room temperature butter, confectioner's sugar, ground hazelnuts, cinnamon, and milk to dough and let rest for half an hour. Roll out the dough and split into two halves. Cut circles out of one half, and rings of the same size out of the other half. Place on a baking sheet lined with parchment paper and bake for about 10 minutes. Let cool, brush the circles with apricot marmalade, and place the rings on top. Dust with confectioner's sugar.

Bake Time: about 10 minutes

Bake Temperature: 350 °F (180 °C)

Ingredients
2 cups (240 g) Flour
2 sticks plus 1 tbsp (240 g) Butter
⅔ cup (140 g) Confectioner's sugar
6 oz (170 g) Hazelnuts, ground
2 tbsp (1 kL) Cinnamon, ground
2 tbsp Milk
About 1¼ cup (150 g) apricot marmalade for brushing
Confectioner's sugar for dusting

LINZER STICKS

Preheat oven to 320°F (160°C). Cream the butter with sugar, salt, vanilla sugar, and lemon zest. Mix in the egg and then fold in the flour. Using a piping bag fitted with a star-shaped nozzle, pipe strips onto a baking sheet lined with parchment paper. Bake for about 10 minutes. Let cool and brush half of the sticks with marmalade. Place another one on each. Dip to the middle in melted chocolate glaze and sprinkle with decorative sugar.

Bake Time: about 10 minutes

Bake Temperature: 320°F (160°C)

Ingredients
2 sticks plus 1½ tbsp (250 g) Butter
6 tbsp (90 g) Confectioner's sugar
2⅓ cups (330 g) Flour
1 Egg
Dash of salt
Dash of vanilla sugar
Lemon zest
About 1¼ cup (150 g) apricot marmalade for brushing
About 5.5 oz (150 g) chocolate glaze for dipping (see p. 42)
Colorful decorating sugar

LIEUTENANT'S KISSES

Preheat oven to 340°F (170°C). Knead dough out of butter, sugar, almonds, and chocolate. Make small balls and place an almond slice on top of each. Place on a baking sheet lined with parchment paper and bake for about 10 minutes.

Bake Time: about 10 minutes

Bake Temperature: 340°F (170°C)

Ingredients
1 stick (120 g) Butter
1 cup plus 2 tbsp (250 g) Confectioner's sugar
4 oz (120 g) Almonds, ground
4 oz (120 g) Cooking chocolate, ground
Almond slices

FLORENTINES

Preheat oven to 320°F (160°C). Chop up the candied orange peel and raisins. Mix well with the grated almonds, flour, confectioner's sugar, and whipped cream. Make little heaps on a baking sheet lined with parchment paper and press them into flat circles with fork. Bake for 12–15 minutes and then let cool. Melt the chocolate and spread thinly on parchment paper. Place the Florentines in the chocolate. Before the chocolate hardens, cut them out. Remove the paper and press a wave pattern into the chocolate with a fork. Let harden.

Bake Time: about 12–15 minutes

Bake Temperature: 320°F (160°C)

Ingredients
3.5 oz (100 g) Ground orange peel
5.5 oz (150 g) Almonds, grated
3.5 oz (100 g) Raisins
6 tbsp (50 g) Flour
¾ cup (100 g) Confectioner's sugar
½ cup (125 ml) Coffee or plain whipped cream
About 5.5 oz (150 g) dark couverture chocolate

Sweet Greetings from the Medicis
The Medici family gave its home city of Florence more than just impressive tombs and the invention of "Grand Cuisine," exported to Paris by Catherine de' Medici. They also gave it this treat, made—according to the original recipe—of almonds, candied citrus, honey, and spices. But how does it concern the Medicis? Simple—the noble Florentine women reportedly passed time by pressing wave patterns into the chocolate dipped underside of these cookies with their beautiful combs.

ISCHLER TALER

Preheat oven to 300 °F (150 °C). Knead together flour, butter, sugar, hazelnuts, and cinnamon to form pâte brisée dough. Let rest for 30 minutes. Roll out to about 3mm thick and cut out circles with a cookie cutter. Place on a baking sheet lined with parchment paper and bake for about 10 minutes. Brush half of the cookies with apricot marmalade and place a plain one on top of each. Place on a cooling rack and glaze with liquid chocolate glaze.

Bake Time: 10 minutes

Bake Temperature: 300 °F (150 °C)

Ingredients
2 cups (240 g) Flour
2 sticks plus 1 tbsp (240 g) Butter
1 cup plus 2 tbsp (140 g) Confectioner's sugar
6 oz (170 g) Hazelnuts, ground
Pinch of cinnamon
1 cup (100 g) Apricot marmalade
About 5.5 oz (150 g) Chocolate glaze

Cakes or Taler?
The above recipe is a particularly delicious variation of a well-known sweet that was one of the favorites of Emperor Franz Joseph and Empress Sissi. We are talking about the famous Ischler Cakes which are popular in Bad Ischl to this day. They are made with pâte brisée, but instead of apricot marmalade, they are filled with buttercream and dipped in chocolate. Before the chocolate hardens, "Original Ischler Cakes" are decorated with a blanched, dipped almond.

GINGER COOKIES

Knead together confectioner's sugar, flour, ginger, baker's ammonia, and eggs. Let rest briefly. Roll out to 3–4mm thick and cut out with a scalloped cookie cutter. Let dry for 12 hours on a floured pastry board. Preheat oven to 300 °F (150 °C). Place cookies on a baking sheet lined with parchment paper and bake for about 8 minutes.

Bake Time: 8 minutes

Bake Temperature: 300 °F (150 °C)

Tip: This classic cookie is made the traditional way with a special, jagged edged, cookie cutter. If this is not available a scalloped cookie cutter will work just as well.

Ingredients
2 cups (250 g) Confectioner's sugar
2 cups (250 g) Flour
¼ cup (15 g) Ginger, ground
2 tbsp (1 kL) Baker's ammonia (can be replaced with baking powder)
2 Eggs
Flour for the work surface

LEBKUCHEN STARS

Preheat oven to 350 °F (180 °C). For the dough, warm the honey. Boil the sugar and water, mix in the honey, and let cool to about 86 °F (30 °C). Make dough by kneading with the rye flour and wheat flour. Let rest.

Beat the egg yolks with the lebkuchen spices and work into the dough along with milk and flour. Roll out the dough to about 4mm thick. Cut out stars with a cookie cutter and place them on a baking sheet lined with parchment paper. Brush with milk, place almonds or other nuts on top, and bake for 15–20 minutes. Cover with egg white glaze while still hot.

Bake Time: 15–20 minutes

Bake Temperature: 350 °F (180 °C)

Tip: You can store the cookies for several days or even weeks wrapped in plastic (before glazing, of course!).

Ingredients to Start the Dough
2 cups (660 g) Honey
2¾ cup (220 g) Confectioner's sugar
⅓ cup (75 ml) Water
5 cups (500 g) Rye flour
1⅔ cup (200 g) Wheat flour

To Complete the Dough
2 Egg yolks
1 oz (30 g) Lebkuchen spice mix (or gingerbread spice mix, preferably a 9 spice mix)
¼ cup (6 cl) Milk
2⅔ cups (300 g) Wheat flour
Milk for brushing
Almonds, hazelnuts, or walnuts to decorate
Egg white glaze (see p. 43), to taste

Why Are There Cookies for Christmas?

The twelve days of Christmas are a dangerous time in Germanic folklore. The origin of Christmas cookies is an old superstitious belief that the evil spirits of the Wild Hunt, a ghostly hunting party that foretold disaster, could be placated with sweet goodies. Of course, the cookies that were placed in windows were not really eaten by demons, but by children, beggars, and peddlers.

The snacks for demons were not complicated Christmas goodies, but rather, for the most part, simple gingerbread. The delicious and decorative cookies that are baked today appeared in the nineteenth century.

WACHAU HEARTS

Ingredients
2 cups (250 g) Flour
1¼ cups (150 g)
 Confectioner's sugar
1 stick plus 2½ tbsp (150 g)
 Butter
4 tsp (20 g) Vanilla sugar
1 Egg
About 1¼ cup (150g)apricot
 marmalade for brushing
About 150g milk couverture
 chocolate for dipping

Preheat oven to 340 °F (170 °C). Coat the butter in the flour. Knead to a smooth dough with the confectioner's sugar, vanilla sugar, and egg. Chill briefly. Roll out to about 3mm thick and cut out heart with a cookie cutter. Place the hearts on a baking sheet lined with parchment paper and bake for about 10 minutes. After cooking, brush half of the hearts with marmalade and place a plain heart on top of each one. Melt the chocolate and dip each heart halfway.

Bake Time: 10 Minutes

Bake Temperature: 340 °F (170 °C)

POLOS

Preheat oven to 340 °F (170 °C). Cream the butter with sugar, salt, and vanilla sugar. Mix in the eggs and egg yolks little by little and then carefully fold in the flour. Using a piping bag fitted with a round nozzle, pipe round cookies onto a baking sheet lined with parchment paper. Bake for about 12 minutes, leaving the oven cracked open. Remove from oven and let cool. Turn over half the cookies and brush with marmalade. Place the other halves on top. Melt chocolate and pipe thin lines on the cookies with a piece of parchment paper rolled into a cone.

Bake Time: about 12 minutes

Bake Temperature: 340 °F (170 °C)

Ingredients
2 sticks plus 1½ tbsp (250 g) Butter
1 cup plus 2 tbsp (140 g) Confectioner's sugar
Dash of salt
2 tsp (10 g) Vanilla sugar
2 Eggs
1 Egg yolk
1¾ cup (230 g) Flour
About 2½ cups (300 g) apricot marmalade
Some dark couverture chocolate for decorating

NEROS

Preheat oven to 340 °F (170 °C). Cream the butter with sugar, salt, and vanilla sugar. Mix in the eggs and egg whites little by little and carefully fold in the flour and cocoa powder. Using a piping bag fitted with a round nozzle, pipe round cookies onto a baking sheet lined with parchment paper. Bake for about 12 minutes, leaving the oven cracked open.

Melt the chocolate with nougat, mix in the heavy cream, and let cool briefly. The mixture should not harden completely, but should be flexible and soft enough to decorate with. Turn over half of the cookies and pipe nougat cream onto them with a piping bag. Cover with the other half of the cookies.

Bake Time: about 12 minutes

Bake Temperature: 340 °F (170 °C)

Ingredients
2 sticks plus 1½ tbsp (250 g) Butter
1 cup plus 2 tbsp (140 g) Confectioner's sugar
Dash of salt
2 tsp (10 g) Vanilla sugar
2 Eggs
1 Egg yolk
1½ cup (180 g) Flour
50 g Cocoa powder

For the Filling
200 g Couverture chocolate
200 g Nougat
1¼ cups (300 ml) Heavy cream

HAMBURG SCHNITTEN

1⅔ cup (200 g) Flour
1 stick plus 2 tbsp (140 g)
  Butter
⅔ cup (70 g) Confectioner's
  sugar
2.5 oz (70 g) Almonds,
  ground
Dash of cinnamon, ground
Dash of clove, ground
3 Egg yolks
3 Egg whites
1 cup less 1 tbsp (210 g)
  Granulated sugar
Dash of vanilla sugar
2.5 oz (70 g) Almonds,
  ground
2 tbsp (1 kL) Coffee, ground
About 1¼ cup (150 g) apricot
  marmalade

Preheat oven to 350 °F (180 °C). Quickly knead together the flour, butter, confectioner's sugar, almonds, cinnamon, cloves, and egg yolks to make a pâte brisée dough. Let the dough rest for 20 minutes. Line a baking sheet with parchment paper. Roll the dough out to the size of the baking sheet and bake for about 12 minutes. Remove and lower the oven heat to 320 °F (160 °C). Brush with marmalade. Beat the egg whites to stiff peaks with the granulated sugar. Fold in the vanilla sugar, almonds, and coffee. Spread the mixture on the baked dough and bake again for 25 minutes. Cut into rectangles or squares.

Bake Time: 12 minutes to start, then 25 minutes to finish

Bake Temperature: 350 °F (180 °C) to start, then 320 °F (160 °C)

ALMOND SCHNITTEN

Ingredients
1 stick plus 2½ tbsp (150 g)
  Butter
7 Egg yolks
1¼ cup (150 g)
  Confectioner's sugar for
  the yolk mixture
Salt
1 cup plus 3 tbsp (150 g)
  Flour
Pinch of Baking powder
7 Egg whites
1¼ cup (150 g)
  Confectioner's sugar for
  the egg whites
3.5 oz (100 g) Almonds,
  ground
3.5 oz (100 g) Chocolate,
  ground
1 tbsp Rum
Butter for the baking sheet
About 1¼ cup (150 g) apricot
  marmalade
Some couverture to
  decorate

Preheat oven to 340 °F (170 °C). Cream the butter with egg yolks, a dash of salt, and sugar. Fold in flour and baking powder. Spread on a buttered baking sheet and brush with marmalade. Beat the egg whites to stiff peaks with confectioner's sugar and fold in the ground almonds and chocolate. Flavor with rum. Spread the egg whites evenly on top of the dough. Bake for about 35 minutes. Cut into little squares. Melt chocolate, fill a parchment paper cone, and pipe thin lines across the schnitten.

Bake Time: about 35 minutes

Bake Temperature: 340 °F (170 °C)

Filled Lebkuchen

Preheat oven to 300°F (150°C). Knead together all the ingredients for the dough and then let rest for half an hour. Split the dough in half. Roll out one half and lay on a buttered baking sheet. For the filling, mix all the ingredients together and spread on the dough. Roll out the second half of the dough and place on top. Bake for about 25 minutes. Cut into small rectangles or squares.

Bake Time: about 25 minutes

Bake Temperature: 300°F (150°C)

A Chicken for Lebkuchen

Linguists have been known to fight bitterly over whether the word "Lebkuchen" comes from a "Laib Kuchen" ("loaf cake"), "Fladenkuchen" ("flat cake"), or "Lebenskuchen" ("life cake"). It is certain, however, that the oldest lebkuchen were called honey cakes and were buried with the ancient Egyptian pharaohs. In 1296 near Ulm, the patrician name Lebzelter was documented for the first time. In 1395, an entry appears in the ledger of the Nuremburg Teutonic Order stating that the fee of one chicken was levied as rent for a Lebzelter house. Real foodies won't have to think long about whether that was a good exchange.

Ingredients
3 cups (300 g) Rye flour
¾ cup (180 g) Sugar
1 tsp (20 g) Lebkuchen spice mix (or gingerbread spice mix, preferably a 9 spice mix)
2 tsp (10 g) Baking powder
Zest of ½ lemon
2 tbsp Honey
2 Eggs
Butter for the baking sheet

For the Filling
2 cups (250 g) Redcurrant marmalade
2 oz (50 g) Candied orange peel
2 oz (50 g) Candied lemon peel
2 oz (50 g) Nuts
2 oz (50 g) Raisins

Ingredients

Ingredients
2 cups plus 2 tbsp (270 g)
  Flour
1 stick plus 6 tbsp (200 g)
  Butter
¾ cup (110 g) Confectioner's
  sugar
2 Egg yolks
2 oz (50 g) Cooking chocolate, ground
About 5.5 oz (150 g) Chocolate glaze for dipping (see
  p. 42)

For the Cream
1 cup (250 ml) Milk
1 oz (20 g) Vanilla pudding
  mix
3 tbsp (40 g) Vanilla sugar
2 sticks plus 1½ tbsp (250 g)
  Butter
1⅔ cup (200 g) Confectioner's sugar

Ingredients
2 cups (250 g) Flour
1 stick plus 1½ tbsp (130 g)
  Butter
¾ cup (100 g) Confectioner's
  sugar
3.5 oz (100 g) Walnuts,
  ground
1 tbsp Sour cream
1 tbsp Coffee, ground
2 Egg yolks
Coffee beans to garnish

For the Cream
2 sticks plus 1½ tbsp (250 g)
  Butter
1¼ (150 g) Confectioner's
  sugar
1 tsp Instant coffee powder
4 tsp (2 cl) Rum

For the Glaze
2 cups (250 g) Confectioner's
  sugar
3–4 tbsp Coffee

WACHAU CAKES

Preheat oven to 340 °F (170 °C). Coat the butter in flour. Knead to a smooth dough with sugar, egg yolks, and cooking chocolate. Roll the dough out to 3mm thick and cut out circles with a cookie cutter. Place on a baking sheet lined with parchment paper and bake for about 10 minutes.

For the cream, boil half of the milk with vanilla sugar. Mix the rest of the milk with the vanilla pudding mix and then stir into the boiling milk. Remove from heat and let cool.

Cream the butter with confectioner's sugar. Mix the pudding smooth with an immersion blender and then mix into the butter a spoonful at a time. Fill a piping bag fitted with a round nozzle. Pipe cream onto half of the cooled cookies and place the other half on top. Melt the chocolate glaze and dip the cakes only to cover the cookies—the cream should still be visible. Let dry.

Bake Time: about 10 minutes

Bake Temperature: 340 °F (170 °C)

MOCHA BOATS

Preheat oven to 320 °F (160 °C). Coat the butter in the flour. Knead to a smooth dough with the sugar, nuts, cream, coffee, and egg yolks. Chill. Roll out the dough to about 2–3mm thick. Cut out boat shapes with a cookie cutter Place on a baking sheet lined with parchment paper and bake for 10–12 minutes.

For the cream, cream butter with sugar. Dissolve the instant coffee in some rum and mix into the butter. Spread half of the cooled cookies with cream and place the other half on top. For the glaze, mix the sugar with the coffee until cool. Pour over the mocha boats and set a coffee bean in the middle of each.

Bake Time: 10–12 minutes

Bake Temperature: 320 °F (160 °C)

Cookies, Cakes, or Biscuits?

The ancient Egyptians had little honey cakes. By 3,000 BCE the Indians were also making bite-sized treats of nougat and marzipan. But what we would call a cookie today had its origin, in unsweetened form, in ancient Rome, where the so-called wafer biscuit appeared in the third century BCE. Cookies get their sweetness from the Dutch, who appreciated the little dry cakes as long-lasting provisions for seamen—not least for those sailors who brought sugarcane home on their schooners from slave islands. Additionally, cookies played a nearly ritualistic role in Dutch peasant weddings. Each guest had to place the "kockje" he had brought with him in a big pile which became like a many layered wedding cake. Eventually, tradition has it that the "kockje" and this custom reached over the English Channel and were immediately renamed "cookies" or "cakes."

At that time the German word for cookie, "Keks," had not yet been born. It appeared at the beginning of the century as a popular word, and was nothing more than a Germanized version of the word "cakes." Subsequently, a bitter feud around the word sparked between Hermann Bahlsen, the owner of one of the first "cakes & biscuits factories" in Europe, and German cultural fanatics.

When Bahlsen insisted that the word "Keks," which was increasingly used in the German language, be included in the dictionary, the German nationalist "language police" got bent out of shape and hosted a contest to find the best replacement for the unloved English loan word. The somewhat awkward "Knusperchen," from the word for "crispy," was chosen from countless entries—and it cost Mr. Bahlsen a years-long fight against the German purist lobby, until the word "Keks" was finally put in the dictionary in 1915.

CANDIES

No one can argue with the fact that pralines, bonbons, truffles, and other sweet snacks are sinful as well as sinfully delicious. Reaching into the candy bowl too often can lead to a growing waistline, but—how can we say this nicely?—lots of little sins are always better than one big one.

COCONUT TRUFFLES

Ingredients
3 cups (380 g) Confectioner's sugar
2 sticks plus 1½ tbsp (250 g) Butter
4.5 oz (130 g) Coconut flakes
2 tbsp (1 kL) Cocoa powder
2 tbsp (3 cl) Rum
4 tsp (20 g) Vanilla sugar
Coconut flakes to coat

Cream the butter and sugar. Mix in the coconut flakes, cocoa powder, rum, and vanilla sugar. Chill the mixture until it can be molded. Make little balls, roll them in coconut flakes, and place in paper candy cups.

MARZIPAN POTATOES

Ingredients
14 oz (400 g) Marzipan paste
¾ cup (100 g) Confectioner's sugar
Cocoa powder to coat

Knead the marzipan with confectioner's sugar. Form a log, cut off ½ in (1 cm) pieces, and shape them into balls. Roll in cocoa powder immediately and cut three slits in the top (so that they look like baked potatoes that burst open).

CORNFLAKE CANDY

Ingredients
4 oz (120 g) Dark couverture chocolate
10.5 oz (300 g) Nougat
2¾ tbsp (40 g) Butter
4 oz (120 g) Cornflakes, crushed

Melt the chocolate and nougat in a bain-marie. Mix in the butter and let cool somewhat. Quickly fold in the crushed cornflakes. Spoon small lumps of the mixture onto parchment paper or right into paper candy cups.

GRENADINE MARZIPAN CANDY

Knead the marzipan with the confectioner's sugar and grenadine. Make a ½ in (1cm) high rectangle on a baking sheet lined with parchment paper. Cut into small squares and dip them in the melted, slightly cooled chocolate with the help of a fork. Place on parchment paper and press a decoration into them with the fork.

Ingredients
17.5 oz (500 g) Marzipan paste
¾ cup (100 g) Confectioner's sugar
3 tbsp (4 cl) Grenadine
About 5.5 oz (150 g) dark couverture chocolate for dipping

APRICOT TRUFFLES

Dice the dried apricots finely, put in a bowl, and mix well with apricot brandy, nuts, sugar, and chocolate. If the mixture becomes too firm, add a tablespoon more of brandy. Cut approximately ¾ oz (20 g) pieces off and form balls.

Melt the dark chocolate until it is lukewarm. Put a little chocolate in the palm of your hand and roll the balls between your palms to coat with chocolate. Immediately roll them in the chopped hazelnuts and let dry. Place in paper candy cups.

Ingredients
3.5 oz (100 g) Dried apricots, without pits
6 tbsp Apricot brandy
7 oz (200 g) Walnuts, ground
1⅔ cup (200 g) Confectioner's sugar
7 oz (200 g) Dark chocolate, ground

To Coat
7 oz (200 g) Hazelnuts, coarsely chopped
3.5 oz (100 g) Dark chocolate

MARZIPAN BRAIDS

Knead the marzipan with confectioner's sugar. Boil the heavy cream with honey and melt the chopped chocolate in it. Knead into the marzipan and chill for 2 hours. Form a log, cut into about 20 pieces, and make each piece into a small braid. Let dry overnight. For the glaze, melt chocolate, mix with oil, and pour over the braids.

Ingredients
14 oz (400 g) Marzipan paste
¾ cup (100 g) Confectioner's sugar
2 tbsp (3 cl) Heavy cream
2 tbsp (40 g) Honey
3.5 oz (100 g) Dark couverture chocolate

For the Glaze
10.5 oz (300 g) Dark couverture chocolate
¼ cup (50 ml) Oil

COCONUT PINEAPPLE CANDIES

Chop up the chocolate and melt in a bain-marie with butter, coconut oil, and heavy cream. Stir until smooth and chill for 2 hours. Mix with an immersion blender for about 5 minutes, adding the liqueur little by little. Fold in the chopped pineapple and spread the batter out to about 3x12 in (9x27cm) on a baking sheet lined with parchment paper. Chill overnight. Melt the white chocolate in a bain-marie and let cool. Cut the batter into approximately 1in squares. Dip the candies in the chocolate with the help of a fork and set them on parchment paper. Sprinkle with coconut flakes.

Ingredients
10.5 oz (300 g) Milk couverture chocolate
80g Candied pineapple, finely chopped
2 tbsp (30 g) Butter
1 oz (30 g) Coconut oil
½ cup (125 ml) Heavy cream
3 tbsp (4 cl) Coconut liqueur
Coconut flakes
About 5.5 oz (150 g) white couverture chocolate to dip

MASCARPONE TRUFFLES

Mix the mascarpone, butter, ladyfingers, and vanilla sugar in a mixing bowl. Dissolve the instant coffee in amaretto and add to the mascarpone mixture. Mix everything carefully to a solid mass and chill for a few hours. Form small balls and roll in ground white chocolate. Place in paper candy cups.

Ingredients
9 oz (250 g) Mascarpone
7 tbsp (100 g) Butter, room temperature
9 oz (250 g) Ladyfingers, crushed
4 tsp (20 g) Vanilla sugar
4 tbsp (2 kL) Instant coffee powder
¼ cup (6 cl) Amaretto
100g White couverture chocolate

ALMOND RAISIN SLIVERS

Preheat oven to 350 °F (180 °C). Mix the almond slices with the simple syrup. Spread on a baking sheet lined with parchment paper and dust with confectioner's sugar. Roast until browned, mixing several times. Let cool somewhat and mix with the drained raisins Melt the chocolates and add to the mixture. Place small heaps on parchment paper or in paper candy cups.

Ingredients
5.5 oz (150 g) Almond slices
1 oz (30 g) Simple syrup (see p. 40)
3 tbsp (20 g) Confectioner's sugar
2 oz (50 g) Preserved raisins (see p.189)
3 oz (80 g) Milk couverture chocolate
1.5 oz (40 g) Dark couverture chocolate

Marzipan Amaretto Truffles

Ingredients
10.5 oz (300 g) Marzipan paste
¼ cup (6 cl) Amaretto
7 oz (200 g) Hazelnut spread
  (Nutella)
Cocoa powder to coat

Knead the marzipan with the amaretto and soft hazelnut cream, preferably with a mixer. With damp hands, form balls (or sticks) and roll in cocoa powder. Place the finished truffles in paper candy cups.

Nougat Grappa Truffles

Ingredients for 50 Pieces
3.5 oz (100 g) White
  couverture chocolate
3.5 oz (100 g) Nougat
50 Chocolate truffle shells
  (small, hollow chocolate
  balls)
2 oz (50 g) Almonds,
  chopped and roasted
Confectioner's sugar for
  dusting

For the Grappa Cream
3 tbsp (40 ml) Heavy cream
2 oz (60 g) Milk couverture
  chocolate
1 oz (20 g) Dark couverture
  chocolate
1½ tbsp (20 g) Butter
2 tbsp (3 cl) Grappa

Melt the white chocolate and nougat in a bain-marie and let cool (it should not be warmer than 82–86 °F (28–30 °C), otherwise the truffle shells will melt!). Fill a piping bag fitted with a small round nozzle and use it to fill the truffle shells partway. Chill for 2 hours.

For the Grappa cream, briefly boil the cream and butter. Mix in the chopped chocolate and flavor with Grappa. Let the cream cool, then fill the truffle shells with it. Chill for 1 hour. Sprinkle with chopped almonds and dust with confectioner's sugar. Chill completely.

Ingredients for 45 Pieces
3.5 (100 g) Dark couverture
  chocolate
14 oz (400 g) Milk couverture
  chocolate
⅔ cup (150 ml) Heavy cream
1½ tbsp (30 g) Glucose syrup
  (or simple syrup)
7 tbsp (10 cl) Kirsch (cherry
  brandy)
45 Chocolate truffle shells
  (small, hollow chocolate
  balls)
45 Preserved sour cherries
White couverture chocolate
  to decorate
Confectioner's sugar for
  dusting

Black Forest Cherry Truffles

Chop up the chocolate and melt in a bain-marie. Boil the cream with sugar syrup and let cool. Flavor with kirsch and cream with a hand mixer. Using a piping bag fitted with a star-shaped nozzle, fill the truffle shells partway with cream. Place a cherry inside each one and cover with cream. Shave white chocolate over the truffles and dust with confectioner's sugar.

Tip: If you don't have truffle shells available, you can pipe the cream right into paper candy cups.

GRAND MARNIER MARZIPAN

Chop the candied orange peel finely and knead with the marzipan, hazelnuts, and Grand Marnier. Roll out to ½ in (1 cm) thick on parchment paper. Cut into 1in (2.5 cm) squares. Melt the dark chocolate, let cool briefly, dip the candies, and place them on parchment paper. Dust with cocoa powder.

Ingredients
4 oz (120 g) Candied orange peel
14 oz (400 g) Marzipan paste
1 oz (30 g) Hazelnuts, finely chopped
3 tbsp (4 cl) Grand Marnier
About 5.5 oz (150 g) Dark couverture chocolate to dip
Cocoa powder for dusting

NOUGAT ORANGE CANDIES

Melt the dark chocolate and nougat in milk. Stir in the Grand Marnier and orange zest and let cool. Line a baking sheet with parchment paper and spread the mixture out to about 6x9 in (15x24 cm). Chill overnight.

Melt the dark chocolate in a bain-marie and let cool. Cut the candy into squares slightly larger than 1in (3cm) and cover in chocolate. Place on parchment paper and sprinkle with candied orange peel and brittle.

Ingredients
14 oz (400 g) Nougat
7 oz (200 g) Dark couverture chocolate
¼ cup (50 ml) Grand Marnier
¼ cup (50 ml) Milk
Zest of 2 oranges
About 5.5 (150 g) dark couverture chocolate for dipping
Candied orange peel and some brittle (see p. 36) to decorate

AMARETTO TRIANGLES

Melt both chocolates in a bain-marie. Boil the cream and mix into the chocolate along with the butter. Flavor with amaretto. Homogenize with an immersion blender, i.e. mix for 5 minutes without letting air in. (Don't lift the mixer out of the liquid!) Let the mixture cool.

Spread the mixture out on a baking sheet lined with parchment paper to 3½x8 in (9x20 cm) and chill overnight. Cut into about 50 same sized triangles and dip them in the melted milk chocolate with the help of a fork, wiping off excess. Place on parchment paper. Melt the dark chocolate, let cool slightly, and use a parchment paper cone to pipe thin lines across the triangles.

Ingredients
5.5 oz (150 g) Milk couverture chocolate
5.5 oz (150 g) Dark couverture chocolate
⅓ cup (80 ml) Heavy cream
2 tsp (10 g) Butter
⅓ cup (8 cl) Amaretto
About 5.5 oz (150 g) milk couverture chocolate for dipping
Some dark couverture chocolate to decorate

Pralines for the Sun King

Even the most flattering portraits of the Sun King, Louis XIV, can't hide the fact that the ruler was a great gourmand. It was not only quail, partridge, rabbit, and other delicacies of the forest and field that contributed to his size, but also, and most of all, sweets. Louis XIV could thank a certain Maréchal du Plessis-Praslin for one of his favorite desserts. The sergeant stumbled over a delicacy by accident: an inexperienced kitchen boy had spilled icing over a bowl of roasted almonds. Although the sergeant wanted to punish him for it, he changed his mind when he tasted it. The name of the kitchen boy remained unknown, but Sergeant Praslin boasted in the court of the Sun King that he had invented a new sweet, which he gave his own name, "Praslin," which became "praline" as the original "recipe" was refined.

WHITE TRUFFLES WITH GRAND MARNIER

Ingredients for about 120 Pieces
¾ cup (200 ml) Heavy cream
5 tbsp (70 g) Butter
50 g Glucose syrup (or simple syrup, see p. 40)
17.5 oz (500 g) White couverture chocolate
⅔ cup (160 ml) Grand Marnier
120 White chocolate truffle shells (small, hollow chocolate balls)
About 17.5 oz (500 g) White couverture chocolate for dipping

Boil the heavy cream, butter, and glucose syrup briefly and then remove from heat. Chop up the white chocolate and melt in the cream. Flavor with Grand Marnier. Let cool. (It should not be warmer than 82–86 °F (28–30 °C), otherwise the truffle shells will melt!) Using a piping bag fitted with a round nozzle, fill the truffle shells and let them cool overnight.

Melt the white chocolate and let cool. Using a parchment paper cone, fill the shells to the top, creating a cover over the hole. Chill for 1 hour. Using a fork, dip the truffles in the rest of the chocolate. Place on a glazing rack and roll them around to create a pattern. Place on parchment paper and let harden.

BUTTER TRUFFLES

Boil the heavy cream with sugar, salt, and vanilla sugar and stir in the chopped up chocolate. Remove from heat and let cool. Cream the butter and slowly stir into the chocolate. Line a baking sheet with parchment paper. Using a piping bag fitted with a round nozzle, make balls on the paper. Chill and let harden. Before glazing, let them sit at room temperature for a short time. Melt the dark chocolate, let cool, dip the truffles using a fork, and let excess drip off. Roll in cocoa powder and shake off excess.

Ingredients
⅔ cup (150 ml) Heavy cream
¼ cup (60 g) Granulated
  sugar
Dash of salt
2 tsp (10 g) Vanilla sugar
9 oz (200 g) Dark couverture
  chocolate, chopped
9 oz (250 g) Milk couverture
  chocolate, chopped
2 sticks plus 1½ tbsp (250 g)
  Butter
About 5 oz (150 g) Dark
  couverture chocolate for
  dipping
Cocoa powder to coat

Tea Truffles

Chop up the chocolate and melt in a bain-marie. Boil the milk with the cream and glucose syrup. Add the tea and let steep for 4 minutes. Sieve through cheese cloth and press all the liquid out of the cloth.

Mix the liquid and the butter into the melted chocolate. Homogenize the mixture with an immersion blender, i.e. mix for 5 minutes without letting air in. (Don't lift the blender out of the liquid!) Let cool, then cream with a hand mixer. Fill a piping bag fitted with a round nozzle and pipe many lines onto parchment paper. Chill until firm in the refrigerator. Cut into 1¼ in (3.5 cm) pieces. Melt the milk chocolate, let cool, and cover the truffles with it. Dust with cocoa powder.

Ingredients
2.5 (70 g) Dark couverture chocolate
3.5 (100 g) Milk couverture chocolate
5 tbsp (70 ml) Milk
2 tbsp (30 ml) Heavy cream
1½ tsp (10 g) Glucose syrup (or simple syrup, see p. 40)
1 oz (20 g) Black tea leaves (such as Earl Grey)
2 tsp (10 g) Butter
About 150 g milk couverture chocolate for dipping
Cocoa powder for dusting

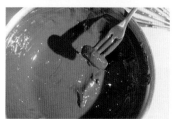

1
Prepare the ingredients

2
Boil the milk, cream, and glucose syrup. Add the tea and steep for 4 minutes.

3
Strain and mix into the melted chocolate along with the butter.

4
Pipe the cream onto a baking sheet lined with parchment paper in many lines. Let harden in the refrigerator.

5
Melt the milk chocolate and let cool. Dip the fully cooled pieces.

6
Let drip on a glazing rack. Dust with cocoa powder.

MOCHA TRUFFLES

Briefly boil the heavy cream, butter, honey, and instant coffee powder and then remove from the heat. Melt both chocolates and dissolve them in the cream. Flavor with coffee liqueur. Let cool. (It should not be warmer than 82–86 °F (28–30 °C), otherwise the truffle shells will melt!) Fill a piping bag fitted with a round nozzle and fill the truffle shells. Chill the truffles overnight.

Melt the dark chocolate and let cool. Cover the hole in the truffle shell using a parchment paper cone to pipe the dark chocolate. Chill for another hour. Dip the truffles in the rest of the chocolate with the help of a fork. Place on a glazing rack and roll around to create a pattern. Place truffles on parchment paper and let harden.

Ingredients for about
120 Pieces
¾ cup (200 ml) Heavy cream
3½ tbsp (50 g) Butter
1½ tbsp (30 g) Honey
3 tbsp Instant coffee powder
14 oz (400 g) Milk couverture chocolate
3.5 oz (100 g) Dark couverture chocolate
⅓ cup (8 cl) Coffee liqueur
120 White chocolate truffle shells (small, hollow chocolate balls)
About 17.5 oz (500 g) Dark couverture chocolate to coat

APRICOT PRALINES

(or simple syrup, see p. 40)

(see p. 36)

Ingredients for about

120 Pieces

¾ cup (200 ml) Heavy cream
5 tbsp (70 g) Butter
1 tbsp (20 g) Glucose syrup
  (or simple syrup, see p. 40)
500g White couverture
  chocolate
½ cup (120 ml) Apricot
  brandy
3 tbsp (40 ml) Apricot liqueur
120 Milk chocolate truffle
  shells (small, hollow
  chocolate balls)
About 10.5 oz (300 g) Milk
  couverture chocolate for
  dipping
3 oz (80 g) White couverture
  chocolate for decorating
Brittle, finely ground
  (see p. 36)

Briefly boil the heavy cream, butter, and glucose syrup and then remove from the heat. Chop up the white chocolate and melt in the cream. Flavor with apricot brandy and liqueur. Let cool. (It should not be warmer than 82–86 °F (28–30 °C), otherwise the truffle shells will melt!) Put the mixture in a piping bag fittd with a round nozzle and use it to fill the truffle shells. Chill, preferably overnight.

Melt the milk chocolate and let cool. Fill a cone made with parchment paper and pipe the chocolate in to cover the hole in the truffle shell. Chill for another hour. Dip the pralines in the rest of the chocolate with the help of a fork and let them drip completely. Place on a baking sheet lined with parchment paper. Temper the white chocolate, fill a parchment paper cone, and use it to pipe thin lines over the pralines. Sprinkle with finely ground brittle and let dry.

BARTLETT PEAR PRALINES

Ingredients for about

120 Pieces

¾ cup (200 ml) Heavy cream
4¼ tbsp (60 g) Butter
2½ tbsp (50 g) Glucose syrup
  (or simple syrup, see p. 40)
16 oz (450 g) Milk couverture
  chocolate
½ cup (120 ml) Poire
  Williams
120 Milk chocolate truffle
  shells (small, hollow
  chocolate balls)
About 10.5 oz (300 g) milk
  couverture chocolate for
  dipping
Confectioner's sugar

Briefly boil the heavy cream, butter, and glucose syrup and then remove from the heat. Chop up the milk chocolate and melt in the cream. Flavor with Poire Williams. Let cool. (It should not be warmer than 82–86 °F (28–30 °C), otherwise the truffle shells will melt!) Put the mixture in a piping bag fitted with a round nozzle and use it to fill the truffle shells. Chill, preferably overnight. Melt the milk chocolate and let cool. Fill a cone made with parchment paper and pipe the chocolate in to cover the hole in the truffle shell. Chill for another hour. Dip the pralines in the rest of the milk chocolate with the help of a fork and let them drip completely. Roll in confectioner's sugar and shake off the excess.

RIESLING BRANDY PRALINES

Briefly boil the heavy cream, butter, and glucose syrup and then remove from the heat. Chop up the milk and dark chocolate and melt in the cream. Flavor with Riesling brandy. Let cool. (It should not be warmer than 82–86 °F (28–30 °C), otherwise the truffle shells will melt!) Put the mixture in a piping bag fitted with a round nozzle and use it to fill the truffle shells. Chill, preferably overnight.

Melt the dark chocolate and let cool. Fill a cone made with parchment paper and pipe the chocolate in to cover the hole in the truffle shell. Chill for another hour. Dip the pralines in the rest of the dark chocolate and let them drip completely. Roll in cocoa powder and shake off the excess.

Ingredients for about
120 Pieces
¾ cup (200 ml) Heavy cream
4¼ tbsp (60 g) Butter
2½ tbsp (50 g) Glucose syrup
 (or simple syrup, see p. 40)
14 oz (400 g) Milk couverture
 chocolate
3.5 oz (300 g) Dark couverture chocolate
½ cup (120 ml) Riesling
 brandy
120 Dark chocolate truffle
 shells (small, hollow
 chocolate balls)
About 10.5 oz (300 g) Dark
 couverture chocolate for
 dipping
Cocoa powder to coat

A Short History of Chocolate

Chocolate—the word comes from the Aztec "chocolatl"—originally meant "bitter water." When the first Spanish conquistadors stepped onto American ground, they found the native people enthusiastically slurping on a drink that was anything but sweet. On the contrary, for European palates, this treat must have tasted like hell. From the cocoa beans picked from the caucauatl tree, the natives prepared a drink that was cooling, yet flavored with chili pepper. In Europe, this met with as much approval as the tomato and potato, which were thought to be poisonous.

When the chilies were replaced with sugar and the cold water with hot water, chocolate became a favorite drink of feudal society, creating as much of a sensation in Versailles as in the chambers of the Spanish-Austrian Habsburg houses. This expensive luxury product that was used to make the sought-after "Indian brew" was celebrated as a "delicious bad luck" and an "Indian knockout that delights the palate in summer and winter."

Chocolate became a status symbol. They infused it with schnapps, created strange dishes like "polenta balls with chocolate," and flavored snuff with it, which led to hideously smeared nostrils. In her famous letters, even the widely traveled Marquise de Sevigné knew that chocolate was not only positive: "it flatters the palate for a while, and warms for a moment, then flares up a deadly fever."

Whether deadly or immortal, this elite delicacy lost its exclusivity when chocolate production was industrialized. Just in "Sweet Vienna," there were eleven chocolate factories with 402 workers at the beginning of the eighteenth century. But was that just rampant lust for sweets in the Danube metropolis? It's not surprising that 55,000 lbs of chocolate were imported per year. Since then, chocolate imports have just increased. But the lust for sweets has always been the same.

Mörwald's Sweet Greetings
THE BEST OF TONI
M.'s PÂTISSERIE

Toni Mörwald is not only an avid gastronome, but also a passionate host. In this chapter he reveals for the first time the delicious sweets with which he and his wife Evi pamper their private guests.

WILD STRAWBERRIES WITH MINT GELATIN

Wash the mint, let drip, and pull off the leaves. Boil with champagne, lemon juice, and sugar, let cool, and let steep for a day in the refrigerator, covered.

Warm slightly, sieve, and stir in moistened gelatin. Stir over ice until cold. Sort the wild strawberries and place on chilled plates. Cover with mint gelatin, dust with confectioner's sugar, and garnish with mint leaves.

Ingredients
1⅔ cup (400 ml) Champagne (or dry sparkling wine)
1 Small bundle of mint
Juice of 3 lemons
5 tbsp Granulated sugar
3 Sheets gelatin
10.5 oz (300 g) Wild strawberries
Confectioner's sugar for dusting
Mint leaves to garnish

BERRIES WITH HONEY ICE CREAM SAUCE

For the honey ice cream sauce, boil milk, cream, and half of the honey. Beat the egg yolks, eggs, and the rest of the honey. Mix in the hot milk mixture, stirring constantly. Whisk the liquid in a bain-marie until the consistency becomes thicker. Let cool and freeze in an ice cream machine. Add the whipped cream while it is freezing. Let the ice cream sit at room temperature for a short time. Mix with champagne just before serving.

Sieve about 5 tbsp of the berries and mix this purée with the rest of the berries and the confectioner's sugar. Warm the chocolate, fill a small paper cone or piping bag, and pipe onto plates decoratively, such as in a leaf shape. Place the honey ice cream sauce and marinated berries on the plates and garnish with mint leaves.

Ingredients for 4–6 Serving
1 cup (250 ml) Milk
1 cup (250 ml) Heavy cream
¾ cup (250 g) Honey
4 Egg yolks
2 Eggs
1 cup (250 ml) Whipped cream
7 tbsp (100 ml) Champagne (or dry sparkling wine)
About 1.25 lbs (600 g) berries according to taste (such as wild strawberries, raspberries, blackberries, etc.)
1 tsp Confectioner's sugar
3.5 oz (100 g) Couverture chocolate
Mint leaves to garnish

PRICKLY PEAR WITH RASPBERRIES AND ALMOND FOAM

Ingredients

7 tsp (100 ml) Almond
milk (reduced milk with
almonds soaked in it for
½ a day, can be replaced
with heavy cream flavored
with almond oil)
½ cup Double cream (can be
replaced with equal parts
mascarpone and heavy
cream)
4½ cups (550 g)
Confectioner's sugar
4 Prickly pears
7 oz (200 g) Raspberries

Mix together the almond milk, double cream, and confectioner's sugar. Fold in the whipped cream. Halve the prickly pears and spoon out the meat. Place some almond foam on plates and some in the prickly pears halves. Place raspberries on top and the meat of the prickly pear next to it.

Ingredients for 6–8 Servings

¼ cup (60 g) Granulated
sugar to caramelize
¼ cup (6 cl) Lime juice
2 Sheets gelatin
7 tbsp (100 ml) Yogurt for
the cream
2–3 Egg whites
About 1 tbsp granulated
sugar for the egg whites
2–3 tbsp whipped cream
8–10 Medium sized kiwis
2 tbsp Simple syrup
(see p. 40)
1 tbsp Bacardi rum
½ cup (125 ml) Yogurt to
garnish
1–2 Sprigs of mint to
garnish
Butter for the molds
Confectioner's sugar for
dusting

LIME CREAM WITH KIWI

Cook the sugar with ⅓ of the lime juice to a light brown caramel. Deglaze with the rest of the lime juice. Add cold water to the gelatin, remove excess, and dissolve in the caramel. Stir in the yogurt and sieve the mixture. Stir over ice until cold. Beat the egg whites to firm peaks with sugar and fold into the cooled mixture. Finally, fold in the softly whipped cream. Fill lightly buttered molds with the lime cream and chill for 1–2 hours.

Cut the peeled kiwis into thin slices—set one aside to garnish—and marinate for about 1 hour in simple syrup and Bacardi. Sieve the set aside kiwi with the seeds and mix with yogurt. Set the cream forms briefly in hot water and place the creams in the middle of plates. Place the drained kiwi slices around them and spoon some kiwi yogurt over the lime cream. Garnish with mint and dust lightly with confectioner's sugar.

Tip: Don't use kiwis that are too ripe, otherwise the typical sour taste of kiwi will be lost.

Sweet Woodruff Cream with Lime Sauce

Remove the sweet woodruff from the stems and boil for 1–3 minutes in milk. Pour through a sieve and dissolve moistened, wrung out gelatin in the milk. Cream the egg yolks, eggs, and sugar and pour the milk in slowly while stirring constantly. Stir until cool. Mince the woodruff and fold in with whipped cream. Fill molds and chill for 3 hours.

For the lime sauce, cook butter and sugar to medium brown caramel while stirring. Stir in half of the lime juice a spoonful at a time. Mix the hot liquid with the egg yolks in a blender and then mix in the rests of the lime juice. Place the molds briefly in hot water. Place lime sauce on each plate and a sweet woodruff cream on top. Garnish with woodruff and mint.

Bartlett Pear Charlotte

Peel, halve, and core the pear. Boil the simple syrup with ⅔ of the white wine, ⅔ of the champagne and a bit of the lemon juice. Poach 5 pear halves in the liquid. Boil the rest of the pears with the rest of the white wine, champagne, and lemon juice to make a purée and then sieve.

Cut the poached pear halves the long way into thin slices and line 5 small charlotte molds in a fan pattern. Warm the pear brandy, dissolve the moistened gelatin in it, and mix into the pear purée. Beat the egg whites to stiff peaks with sugar and fold into the pear purée. Fill the molds and chill for about 2 hours.

For the blackcurrant sauce, mix all the ingredients together, sieve, and thin with blackcurrant juice if the sauce is too thick. Pour the sauce onto dishes, place pear charlottes on top, and garnish with mint.

Ingredients for 8 Servings
2.5 oz (70 g) Fresh sweet woodruff
7 tbsp (100 ml) Milk
3 Sheets gelatin
2 Egg yolks
2 Eggs
⅓ cup (80 g) Granulated sugar
1¼ cups (300 ml) Whipped cream
Mint and woodruff leaves to garnish

For the Lime Sauce
⅓ cup (80 g) Granulated sugar
4¼ tbsp (60 g) Butter
4 tbsp Lime juice
1 Egg yolk

Ingredients for 5 Servings
2 lbs (1 kg) Bartlett pears, fully ripe
4¼ cup (1 l) Simple syrup (see p. 40)
½ cup (125 ml) White wine
¾ cup (200 ml) Champagne (or dry sparkling wine)
Juice of 1 lemon
1 Sheet gelatin
2 tbsp Pear brandy
2 Egg whites
1 tbsp Granulated sugar
Mint leaves to garnish

For the Blackcurrant Sauce
4.5 lbs (2000 g) Blackcurrants, crushed
4 tbsp Sugar
3 tbsp Blackcurrant liqueur
Blackcurrant juice as needed

Ingredients
2 Bartlett pears, ripe
7 tbsp (100 ml) White wine
7 tbsp (100 g) Granulated
  sugar
1 Vanilla bean
Juice of 1 lemon
20 Violet flowers to garnish
2 oz (50 g) Almond slices,
  roasted

For the Almond Foam
7 tbsp (100 ml) Almond
  milk (reduced milk with
  almonds soaked in it for ½
  a day, can be replaced with
  heavy cream flavored with
  almond oil)
3.5 oz (100 g) Double cream
  (can be replaced with
  equal parts mascarpone
  and heavy cream)
¾ cup (200 ml) Whipped
  cream
6 tbsp (50 g) Confectioner's
  sugar

Ingredients for 4–6 Servings
7 tbsp (100 ml) Water
1 tsp (5 g) Black tea leaves
2 oz (50 g) Pineapple slices
Zest of 1 orange
3 tbsp (4 cl) Orange juice
¼ cup (5 cl) Rum
4 tsp (2 cl) Sherry
4 tsp (2 cl) Kirsch (cherry
  brandy)
1 Cinnamon stick
1 Vanilla bean
3 tbsp (4 cl) Red wine
4 tbsp Red wine reduction
1 Clove
3 tbsp (50 g) Sugar
4 tsp (20 g) Cornstarch

For the Lebkuchen Mousse
2 Eggs
1 Egg yolk
2 tbsp (30 g) Sugar

POACHED PEARS WITH ALMOND FOAM AND VIOLETS

Peel, halve, and core the pears and poach them in a pot with white wine, sugar, lemon juice, and a vanilla bean. Let cool. Take out the pear halves and cut into thin slices.

For the almond foam, mix the almond milk with double cream and confectioner's sugar and fold in the whipped cream. Place the pear slices on dishes, cover with almond foam, and garnish with almond slices and violets.

LEBKUCHEN MOUSSE WITH PUNCH SAUCE

Boil water for the punch sauce, pour over the tea leaves, steep for 5 minutes, then sieve. Boil the tea with all the ingredients but the cornstarch. Then thicken with the cornstarch and let sit in the refrigerator for 2–3 days, covered.

For the lebkuchen mousse, beat the eggs, egg yolk, and sugar in a double boiler until it thickens. You can tell when it is ready because when you blow on the cream while it is coating the cooking spoon, rings will appear that are reminiscent of a rose. Add water to the gelatin, remove excess, and dissolve in warmed kirsch. Add to the mousse. Chop up the chocolate and grate the lebkuchen. Stir both into the egg mixture and add the lebkuchen spices. Finally, fold in the whipped cream and chill for 2 hours.

Make a circle of sauce on each dish. Form gnocchi from the mousse and place three on each dish.

COFFEE PARFAIT WITH MASCARPONE SAUCE

Beat egg whites with ¼ cup (60 g) of sugar. Boil the rest of the sugar with water to soft thread (see p. 40). Pour into the egg mixture and beat until cold in an ice water bath. Carefully fold in the cold mocha, rum, and whipped cream. Fill small molds and freeze for at least 1 hour.

For the mascarpone sauce, beat the egg yolks with sugar until creamy. Mix in the mascarpone, flavor with rum and lemon juice and fold in the whipped cream. Portion the sauce onto chilled plates. Place the molds briefly in hot water, remove the parfaits, and place them on the plates. Garnish with whipped cream and wild strawberries.

PANNA COTTA IN MY STYLE

Preheat oven to 270 °F (130 °C). Heat the milk and cream until they are lukewarm. Cut the vanilla beans the long way, add to the milk, and simmer briefly. Whisk the sugar, eggs, and egg yolks. Mix in the milk cream mixture and let sit for a good half an hour. Pour it all through a sieve. Take out the vanilla beans and scrape the pulp in. Fill shallow molds about an inch high and bake for about 30 minutes in a water bath. Remove and place in the refrigerator for about 2 hours. Before serving, sprinkle with brown sugar and briefly caramelize under highest upper heat (or under a salamander).

Bake Time: about 30 minutes

Bake Temperature: 270 °F (130 °C), then maximum heat

1 Sheet gelatin
4 tsp (2 cl) Kirsch (cherry brandy)
2.5 oz (75 g) Dark couverture chocolate
2.5 oz (75 g) Lebkuchen
1 tsp (5 g) Lebkuchen spice (or gingerbread spice)
1 cup (250 ml) Whipped cream

Ingredients for 10 Servings
10 Egg yolks
1 cup (220 g) Granulated sugar
5 tbsp Water
4 tbsp Strong mocha, cold
10 tbsp Rum
2 cups (500 ml) Whipped cream
Wild strawberries and Whipped cream to garnish

For the Mascarpone Sauce
4 Egg yolks
6 tbsp (50 g) Confectioner's sugar
5 oz (150 g) Mascarpone
1 tbsp Rum
1 tbsp Lemon juice
⅔ cup (150 ml) Whipped cream

Ingredients for 4–6 Servings
2 cups (500 ml) Heavy cream
2 cups (500 ml) Milk
⅔ cup (140 g) Granulated sugar
4 Vanilla beans
2 Eggs
3 Egg yolks
Brown sugar for sprinkling

ALMOND BLOSSOM SORBET

Ingredients
¾ cup (200 ml) Champagne
  (or dry sparkling wine)
¾ cup (200 ml) White wine
1½ lemons
3.5 oz (100 g) Almond
  blossoms (can be replaced
  with almond oil)
¾ cup (200 ml) Almond
  milk (reduced milk with
  almonds soaked in it for ½
  a day, can be replaced with
  heavy cream flavored with
  almond oil)

Boil the white wine, champagne, chopped lemon and almond blossoms and let cool. (Set several almond blossoms aside to garnish.) Cover and let sit in the refrigerator for 2–3 days. Add the almond milk, pour through a sieve, and freeze in an ice cream machine. Serve garnished with an almond blossom.

COFFEE SABAYON WITH VANILLA ICE CREAM

Ingredients for 8 Servings
For the Vanilla Ice Cream
1⅔ cups (400 ml) Heavy
  cream
1¼ cups (300 ml) Milk
2 Vanilla beans
½ cup (120 g) Granulated
  sugar
2 Eggs
4 Egg yolks

For the Coffee Sabayon
5 Egg yolks
½ cup (120 g) Granulated
  sugar
⅔ cup (150 ml) Strong coffee
2 tbsp Instant coffee powder
3 tbsp Rum
2 Sheets gelatin
1 cup (250 ml) Whipped
  cream
Mocha beans to garnish

Boil the cream, milk, and the scraped out vanilla pulp with ⅓ cup (70 g) of sugar. Beat the eggs, egg yolks, and the rest of the sugar until creamy. Slowly pour in the hot milk mixture while stirring, place in a bain-marie, and beat until creamy. The mixture should have a thick consistency. Sieve and let cool. Freeze in an ice cream machine.

For the sabayon, beat the egg yolks in a metal mixing bowl. Boil coffee, half of the rum, sugar, and instant coffee powder and add the egg yolks while stirring constantly. Add the gelatin dissolved in the rest of the rum, beat in an ice bath until cold, and fold in the whipped cream. Form gnocchi from the ice cream with tablespoons and place 2 each in chilled glass bowls. Pour the coffee sabayon over them. Garnish with mocha beans before serving.

Tip: You can decorate this sabayon with piped chocolate decorations however you like.

TRIPLE CHOCOLATE PARFAIT

For the first chocolate, boil ¼ cup (60 g) (!) of sugar. Beat the egg yolks and 4 teaspoons (20 g) of sugar. Slowly pour in the hot sugar water and beat until the mixture has cooled. Chop up the chocolate, melt in a bain-marie, and add to the mixture along with the alcohol. Finally, fold in the whipped cream. Fill a terrine pan and freeze for 2 hours. (The terrine pan should be ⅓ full.)

For the second chocolate, follow the same directions as the first. Fill the terrine pan to the ⅔ mark and freeze for another 2 hours. Prepare the third chocolate the same way, fill the terrine pan, and freeze for another 2 hours.

For the almond sauce, whip the cream halfway, and flavor with almond milk syrup and some almond extract. Dip the parfait briefly in hot water and remove from the pan. Pour a circle of sauce onto a plate. Cut the parfait into slices and serve on the sauce.

Ingredients for 16 Servings

For Chocolate I
¼ cup (60 g) Granulated sugar for boiling
4 tsp (2 cl) Water
3 Egg yolks
4 tsp (20 g) Granulated sugar for the egg
2 tbsp Rum
4 oz (120 g) Dark couverture chocolate
1 cup (250 ml) Heavy cream

For Chocolate II
¼ cup (60 g) Granulated sugar for boiling
4 tsp (2 cl) Water
3 Egg yolks
4 tsp (20 g) Granulated sugar for the egg
3 tbsp Kirsch (cherry brandy)
4 oz (120 g) White couverture chocolate
1 cup (250 ml) Heavy cream

For Chocolate II
¼ cup (60 g) Granulated sugar for boiling
4 tsp (2 cl) Water
3 Egg yolks
4 tsp (20 g) Granulated sugar for the egg
3 tbsp Nougat liqueur
4 oz (120 g) Milk couverture chocolate
1 cup (250 ml) Heavy cream

For the Almond Sauce
1¼ cup (300 ml) Heavy cream
Almond milk syrup (milk reduced to syrup consistency with almonds soaked in it for ½ a day, can be replaced with heavy cream flavored with almond oil)
Bitter almond extract

FIG TERRINE

Ingredients for 1 Terrine
(About 8×3×2 in (10×8×6 cm))
3½ tbsp (50 g) Butter
2 tsp (10 g) Granulated sugar
2 Egg yolks
3.5 (100 g) White couverture
  chocolate
2 tbsp Kirsch (cherry
  brandy)
3 Sheets gelatin
2 oz (50 g) Pistachios, finely
  ground
¾ cup (200 ml) Whipped
  cream
6 Figs, small but ripe
5.5 oz (150 g) Raspberries
2 tbsp Blackcurrant
  marmalade to garnish

For the Marzipan Cover
5.5 oz (150 g) Marzipan paste
¾ cup (100 g) Confectioner's
  sugar

For the Almond Foam
1¼ cup (300 ml) Whipped
  cream
Almond milk syrup (milk
  reduced to syrup consistency with almonds soaked
  in it for ½ a day, can be
  replaced with heavy cream
  flavored with almond oil)
Bitter almond extract

Cream the butter and confectioner's sugar, mix in the egg yolks, and beat for a few more minutes. Chop up the chocolate and melt in a bain-marie. Warm the kirsch and dissolve the moistened gelatin in it. Fold the chocolate and kirsch into the egg yolk mixture, add the pistachios, and fold in the whipped cream.

Knead the marzipan and confectioner's sugar together well. Roll out to a 14×8 in (35×20 cm) rectangle. Line the terrine pan with plastic wrap and the marzipan. Peel the figs and sort the raspberries. Fill the terrine pan about 1 in (2 cm) high with the mousse. Place the figs along the middle, fill with the rest of the mousse, and place raspberries the long way. Fold the marzipan over and close and chill for about 3 hours.

For the almond foam, whip the cream halfway and flavor with almond milk syrup and almond extract. Remove the terrine from the pan. Portion the almond foam onto chilled plates and serve the terrine cut into slices. Create decorative patterns in the sauce with blackcurrant marmalade.

ARMAGNAC PLUM MOUSSE WITH TEA SAUCE

Warm Armagnac to about 140 °F (60 °C) (but don't boil!) and pour over the plums. Cover well and let steep for 3 hours. Pour through a sieve, warm the liquid, pour over the plums again, and let steep again. Repeat this process two more times over the course of two weeks. Always close the container well, so that the alcohol doesn't evaporate. Sieve the plum juice and have 5 tbsp (70 ml) ready.

For the mousse, beat eggs, egg yolks, sugar, Armagnac, and plum juice in a bain-marie. Fold in the whipped cream. Chop the plums up finely and mix in. Fill molds and chill.

Prepare a strong tea with Ceylon tea and water. Bring to a boil, add sugar, and bind with cornstarch. Let cool and fold in the whipped cream and rum. Dip the molds briefly in hot water. Put some tea sauce on plates and place a plum mousse on each.

12 Dried plums, pitted
1 cup (250 ml) Armagnac (or cognac or other brandy) to marinate
2 Eggs
2 Egg yolks
⅔ cup (70 g) Confectioner's sugar
5 tbsp (70 ml) Armagnac for the mousse
5 tbsp (70 ml) Armagnac plum juice (from the Armagnac and plums)
3 Sheets gelatin
1¼ cup (300 ml) Whipped cream

For the Tea Sauce
1 oz (20 g) Ceylon tea leaves
1¼ cup (300 ml) Water
2 tbsp (30 g) Granulated sugar
½ tsp Cornstarch
⅔ cup (150 ml) Whipped cream
3 tbsp Rum

BANANA TERRINE WITH PINEAPPLE PUNCH

For the punch, mix all the ingredients well and let sit, covered, in the refrigerator.

For the terrine, beat egg yolk, egg white, and sugar in a warm water bath. Add the moistened and wrung out gelatin and beat in a cold water bath until cold. Stir in the liqueur, puréed banana, and lemon juice, then fold in the whipped cream. Fill a terrine pan and place in the refrigerator for about 3 hours.

Preheat oven to 350 °F (180 °C). For the cake base, beat the egg and sugar in a warm water bath, set aside, and continue beating until it has a thick consistency and is cold. Carefully fold in the remaining ingredients. Brush the baking sheet with oil and line with parchment paper (so that the paper stays in place). Spread the batter on it and bake for 8–10 minutes, until golden. Overturn onto a kitchen towel, pull off the paper, and let cool. Cut out 2in (5cm) round cake bases.

For the chocolate cover, chop up chocolate and melt in a warm water bath. Let cool slightly and quickly spread out about 1mm thick on a 20in (50cm) parchment paper square. Let set, but before it gets too hard, cut 2in (5cm) circles out with a cookie cutter. Place briefly in the refrigerator, then remove the chocolate from the paper.

Dip the terrine briefly in hot water, remove from the pan, and cut into 1in (3cm) slices. With the cookie cutter, cut out 2in (5cm) circles. Cut these circles again with a 1½in (4cm) cookie cutter to create rings. Chill.

Place a cake base on each plate. Place a banana terrine ring on each, fill with the punch, and cover each with a chocolate top. Pour some punch over and garnish with strawberries.

Bake Time: about 8–10 minutes

Bake Temperature: 350 °F (180 °C)

Ingredients for the Terrine
2 Egg yolks
1 Egg white
3 tbsp (50 g) Granulated sugar
2 Sheets gelatin
1 Banana, puréed
5 tbsp Banana liqueur
Juice of 2 lemons
½ cup (120 ml) Whipped cream
3.5 oz (100 g) Dark couverture chocolate for the chocolate tops
8 Strawberries to garnish

For the Cake Base
1 Egg
5 tsp (25 g) Granulated sugar
3 tbsp (25 g) Flour
2 tsp (10 g) Cornstarch
2 tsp (1 cl) Heavy cream
Oil for the baking sheet

For the Pineapple Punch
⅔ cup (150 ml) Champagne (or dry sparkling wine)
⅔ cup (150 ml) Dry white wine
3.5 oz (100 g) Fresh pineapple, cut into small cubes
Juice of 2 lemons
3 tbsp (50 g) Granulated sugar
A few leaves of sweet woodruff

CHOCOLATE LEAVES WITH MANDARIN FLOWERS

Ingredients
10.5 (300 g) Dark couverture
  chocolate
Mandarin flowers and man-
  darin leaves to garnish
  (or fresh mint leaves)

For the Filling
5.5 (150 g) Dark couverture
  chocolate
1 oz (30 g) Milk couverture
  chocolate
3 Egg whites
2 tbsp (30 g) Granulated
  sugar
9 oz (250 g) Double cream

For the Mandarin Sauce
2 cups (500 ml) Mandarin
  juice
2 tsp (10 g) Cornstarch
Some Armagnac (or cognac
  or other brandy)

Chop up the chocolate and melt in a bain-marie. Let cool while stirring, warm again, and spread about 1mm thick on parchment paper. After it hardens, cut into 2x2½ in (5x6 cm) diamonds (or squares) and place briefly in the refrigerator.

For the filling, melt the milk and dark chocolate in a bain-marie. Beat the egg white and sugar. Lightly beat the double cream and mix with the egg whites and warm chocolate.

For the sauce, put the mandarin juice in a pot, reduce to half, and bind with cornstarch. Flavor with Armagnac and let cool.

Fill a piping bag with cream. Remove the chocolate leaves from the parchment paper and layer 4 leaves per person with the cream. Pour circles of sauce onto chilled placed, place the filled chocolate leaves on the sauce, and garnish with mandarin flowers and leaves.

POPPY MOUSSE WITH BRAIDED BREAD

For the dough, mix the yeast with some sugar and a little bit of lukewarm milk, cover, and let rise from about 20 minutes. Put the flour in a bowl and knead together with liquid butter, the rest of the sugar, eggs, the rest of the lukewarm milk, raisins, and the starter dough. Beat the dough until it is soft and smooth. Cover and let rise in a warm place. Punch down and let rise again. Now divide the dough into three ropes and make a braid. Place on a buttered baking sheet and let rise again. Preheat oven to 350°F (180°C). Brush the braid with beaten egg and bake for 60 minutes. Remove and let cool.

For the mousse, boil poppy with milk and then let cool. Cream the butter and confectioner's sugar, add the egg yolks, and beat more. Chop up the chocolate, melt in a bain-marie, and fold into the butter with kirsch. Finally, fold in the cooled poppy and whipped cream. Fill a bowl with with mousse and chill for about 2 hours. Cut the braided loaf into slices and serve with the poppy mousse.

Bake Time: about 60 minutes

Bake Temperature: 350°F (180°C)

Ingredients for 8 Servings
8 cups (1kg) Wheat flour
5 tbsp (40g) Yeast
3 tbsp (40g) Granulated sugar
1 stick (120g) Butter
4 Eggs
About 1 cup (250ml) Milk
3.5 oz (100g) Raisins
1 Egg for brushing
Butter for the baking sheet

For the Poppy Mousse
2 oz (50g) Poppy, ground
½ cup (125ml) Milk
2¾ tbsp (40g) Butter
4 tsp (10g) Confectioner's sugar
2 Egg yolks
3 oz (90g) White couverture chocolate
2 tbsp Kirsch (cherry brandy)
¾ cups (200ml) Whipped cream

TARTLETS WITH CARAMELIZED HAZELNUTS

Ingredients for 50 Pieces
¾ cup (100 g) Confectioner's
  sugar for the dough
1 stick plus 6 tbsp (200 g)
  Butter
2⅔ cups (300 g) Flour
1 Egg
Some vanilla pulp
10.5 oz (300 g) Hazelnuts,
  whole
⅔ cup (150 g) Granulated
  sugar to caramelize
¼ cup (50 ml) Water
5 oz (150 g) Hazelnut nougat
2 oz (50 g) Pistachios,
  ground
5 oz (150 g) Semisweet
  couverture chocolate
Flour for the work surface
Butter for the molds

Quickly knead confectioner's sugar, butter, flour, egg, and vanilla pulp to asmooth dough and let rest for half an hour, covered, in the refrigerator. Preheat the oven to 400 °F (200 °C). Roast the hazelnuts briefly in a preheated oven, so that the skins will come off more easily when you grate them. Grate off the skins. Mix the hazelnuts, granulated sugar, and water, and caramelize over medium heat. Remove from heat and stir until the nut cool.

Roll the pâte brisée out thin and line small tartlet pans with the dough. Press the edges down well and bake until light brown, about 25 minutes. Remove from the pans. Warm the chocolate and brush the tartlets with it. Press nougat into the tartlets and place three caramelized hazelnuts. Sprinkle the ground pistachios over and pour more chocolate on top.

Bake Time: about 25 minutes

Bake Temperature: 400 °F (200 °C)

PÂTE BRISÉE BOATS WITH STRAWBERRIES AND WHITE MOUSSE

Quickly knead the confectioner's sugar, butter, flour, egg, and vanilla pulp, cover, and let rest in the refrigerator for half an hour. For the mousse, cream the butter and confectioner's sugar. Add the egg yolks and beat for 5 more minutes. Chop up the chocolate and melt in a bain-marie. Mix the kirsch and melted chocolate into the egg yolk mixture and fold in the whipped cream. Chill the mousse.

Preheat oven to 400 °F (200 °C). Roll the pâte brisée out thinly on a floured work surface, fill small buttered pans with the dough, press the edges down well, and bake for about 25 minutes, until light brown. Remove from the pans and brush with warmed chocolate. Place 3–4 raspberries in each boat, fill with mousse, and smooth. Pour some chocolate over the top.

Bake Time: about 25 minutes

Bake Temperature: 400 °F (200 °C)

Ingredients for 50 Pieces
¾ cup (100 g) Confectioner's sugar
1 stick plus 6 tbsp (200 g) Butter
2⅔ cups (300 g) Flour
1 Egg
Some vanilla pulp
5 oz (150 g) Semisweet couverture chocolate for brushing
About 7 oz (200 g) raspberries
Flour for the work surface
Butter for the pans

For the Mousse
3 tbsp (45 g) Butter
4 tsp (10 g) Confectioner's sugar
2 Egg yolks
3.5 oz (100 g) White couverture chocolate
2 tbsp Kirsch (cherry brandy)
¾ cup (200 ml) Whipped cream

SAVARIN WITH GRAPES AND WINE FOAM

Ingredients for 15 Pieces
1½ cup (180 g) Flour
4 tsp (10 g) Yeast
5 tbsp Milk, lukewarm
5½ (80 g) Butter
4 tsp (20 g) Granulated sugar
Salt
½ tsp Lemon zest
2 Eggs
Butter and flour for the pans

For the Syrup
1 cup (250 ml) Water
⅓ cup (80 g) Sugar
2 tbsp plus 1 tsp (50 g) honey
Zest of 1 orange
1 tsp Lemon juice
2 tbsp Cognac

For the Grapes
7 oz (200 g) Grapes, as small
  as possible
½ cup (125 ml) Water
¼ cup (60 g) Granulated
  sugar
½ Vanilla bean
2 tbsp Cognac

For the Wine Foam
7 tbsp (100 ml) White wine
7 tbsp (100 ml) Marsala (or
  another strong, aromatic
  dessert wine)
7 tbsp (100 g) Granulated
  sugar
2 Eggs
2 Egg yolks

Sift the flour into a bowl, press a depression into the middle. Place the yeast in the depression and mix with lukewarm milk. Cover and let rise in a warm place. Melt the butter and knead into the dough along with eggs, sugar, salt, and lemon zest. Punch it down strongly. (But the dough should not become too hard.) Let rise in a warm place again. Butter small savarin pans or ring pans, dust with flour, and fill halfway with the dough. Cover and let rise again. Preheat oven to 350 °F (180 °C) and bake for 12–15 minutes. Remove and let cool.

For the syrup, boil with sugar, honey, and orange zest, let cool, and sieve. Flavor with lemon juice and cognac and soak the savarins with it.

Peel the grapes. Bring water with sugar and the vanilla bean to a boil and set aside. Remove the vanilla bean and add the grapes and cognac. Let everything cool. For the wine foam, mix all the ingredients together well and beat in a warm water bath until creamy. Place the savarins on plates, put the grapes in the middle, and serve with wine foam.

Bake Time: 12–15 minutes

Bake Temperature: 350 °F (180 °C)

Toni's Cherry Torte

Ingredients
6 Eggs
⅔ cup (150 g) Granulated sugar
1 cup plus 3 tbsp (150 g) Flour
⅓ cup (50 g) Cornstarch
5½ tbsp (80 g) Butter, melted
Butter and flour for the pan
⅔ cup (15 cl) Kirsch (cherry brandy) for soaking
Almonds, grated and roasted
Confectioner's sugar for dusting

For the Meringue Base
6 oz (180 g) Egg whites
⅓ cup (80 g) Granulated sugar
6 oz (180 g) Hazelnuts, finely ground
⅓ cup (40 g) Flour
Butter and flour for the baking sheet

For the Vanilla Cream
⅓ cup (80 g) Granulated sugar
3 Egg yolks
¾ cup (200 ml) Milk
Pulp of 1 vanilla bean
3 Sheets gelatin
¾ cup (200 ml) Heavy cream
4 tsp (10 g) Confectioner's sugar for the cream

Preheat oven to 350 °F (180 °C). Beat the eggs and sugar in a bain-marie until creamy, remove from heat, and beat until the mixture has a thick consistency and is cold. Carefully fold in the flour, cornstarch, and melted butter. Butter a 10in (26 cm) diameter round pan, dust it with flour, and fill with batter. Bake for about 60 minutes.

For the meringue base, beat egg whites until they are almost stiff, slowly sprinkle in the sugar, and continue beating until they are stiff. Fold in the rest of the ingredients and spread in two 10in (26 cm) diameter circles (preferably with a spatula) on a buttered and floured baking sheet. Bake for about 15 minutes. Remove from the sheet while still hot.

For the vanilla cream, whip the cream with the confectioner's sugar. Mix together the granulated sugar, egg yolk, milk, and vanilla pulp and slowly heat while stirring, but do not boil. Dissolve moistened gelatin in the milk mixture. Stir until cold in an ice bath. Before it sets, fold in the whipped cream.

Spread vanilla cream about 5mm thick on the first meringue base, place the cake base on it, soak with kirsch, spread another 5mm of vanilla cream on the cake, and cover with the second meringue base. Spread the rest of the vanilla cream over the torte and sprinkle the sides with almonds. Dust the top with confectioner's sugar and make a lattice design with a spatula or knife.

Bake Time: about 60 minutes for the torte base, about 15 minutes for the meringue bases

Bake Temperature: 350 °F (180 °C)

LEMON CREAM ROULADE

Preheat oven to 400°F (200°C). Beat the eggs and sugar in a bain-marie, set aside, and continue beating until it has a thick consistency. Fold in the flour, cornstarch, and melted butter. Butter a baking sheet and line it with parchment paper. Spread the batter on it and bake for about 15 minutes.

For the lemon cream, bring sugar, white wine, egg yolk, lemon juice, and lemon zest to a boil while stirring. Remove from heat and stir until it thickens. Add the moistened and wrung out gelatin. Sieve, stir until cool, and fold in the whipped cream. Overturn the baked cake onto parchment paper sprinkled with granulated sugar. Spread lemon cream on top, roll up, and chill. Dust with confectioner's sugar.

Bake Time: about 15 minutes

Bake Temperature: 400°F (200°C)

RUM GUGELHUPF WITH RED WINE PEARS

For the red wine pears, bring all the ingredients to a boil in a pot and boil the peeled, cored, pear halves briefly. Let it all marinate at room temperature for about 6 hours.

Preheat oven to 350°F (180°C). Cream the butter with half of the sugar. Add the egg yolks, hazelnuts, chocolate, cinnamon, rum, and flour little by little and mix everything together well. Beat the egg whites to stiff peaks with the rest of the sugar and fold into the mixture. Butter individual serving sized bundt pans and sprinkle with breadcrumbs. Fill with the batter. Bake for about 18 minutes. Cut the pears into slices. Place in deep dishes, place the gugelhupfs on each, and serve warm.

Bake Time: about 18 minutes

Bake Temperature: 350°F (180°C)

Ingredients
6 Eggs
⅔ cup (140 g) Granulated sugar
1 cup plus 3 tbsp (150 g) Flour
⅓ cup (50 g) Cornstarch
5 tbsp (70 g) Butter, melted
Butter for the baking sheet
Granulated sugar to overturn
Confectioner's sugar for dusting

For the Lemon Cream
⅓ cup (80 g) Granulated sugar
60 ml White wine
3 Egg yolks
Juice and zest of 2 lemons
4 Sheets gelatin
1⅔ cups (400 ml) Whipped cream

Ingredients for 4 Servings
For the Red Wine Pears
18 oz (500 g) Pears, fully ripe
1 Small vanilla bean
1 Small cinnamon stick
1 Clove
¾ cup (200 ml) Red wine
⅓ cup (70 g) Granulated sugar
Juice of ½ lemon
Juice of ½ orange

For the Rum Gugelhupf
½ cup (120 g) Granulated sugar
5½ (80 g) Butter
2 Egg yolks
2 oz (50 g) Hazelnuts, roasted and ground
1.5 oz (40 g) Chocolate, ground
Pinch of cinnamon powder
½ cup (70 g) Flour
1 tbsp Rum
3 Egg whites
Butter and breadcrumbs for the pans

Toni's Cake Fight

Not every master fell from heaven. Even Toni M. "served" in many great houses during his apprentice and journeyman years. At one of the greatest, he assisted in cooking courses, and learned there that even the greats are not infallible. After the master chef had explained a complicated torte recipe to the students, he went about baking the torte for the coffee get together after the course. When the torte was finished, it turned out to be an unattractive piece of dough that could under no circumstances be served. Then the master had an idea: He instructed Toni to trip and drop the torte as he brought the torte to the waiting women. Toni M. agreed hesitantly, received a big laugh, and spared the great master a serious disgrace.

"In my own cooking courses, nothing like this has happened yet," Toni asserts.

MARBLE SOUFFLÉ WITH NOUGAT SAUCE

Ingredients
For the Nougat Sauce
3.5 oz (100 g) Nougat
7 tbsp (100 ml) Heavy cream
½ tsp (3 g) Cornstarch
3 tbsp Simple syrup
  (see p. 40)
3 tbsp Rum
7 tbsp (100 ml) Whipped
  cream

For the Marble Soufflé
7 oz (200 g) Quark
3 Egg yolks
3 Egg whites
¼ cup (60 g) Sugar
1 tsp Sugar
Butter and sugar for the
  ramekins

For the nougat sauce, warm the heavy cream and dissolve the nougat in it. Mix the cornstarch and simple syrup in some water and then add to the cream. Mix together well and let cool. Finally, fold in rum and whipped cream.

Preheat oven to 480 °F (250 °C) lower heat and 320 °F (160 °C) or 375 °F (190 °C) upper heat. Heat a pan of water in the oven. For the soufflé, sieve the quark and carefully mix with the egg yolks. Beat the egg whites to soft peaks with the sugar and fold into the quark. Fold cocoa powder into a quarter of the mixture. Butter small (about 3 in (8 cm)) ramekins, sprinkle with sugar, fill with both mixtures alternately, and smooth. Bake in a boiling water bath for about 20–25 minutes. Immediately place the soufflés on plates and pour the nougat sauce over them.

Bake Time: about 20–25 minutes

Bake Temperature: 480 °F (250 °C) lower heat, 320 °F (160 °C) or 375 °F (190 °C) upper heat

GRATIN OF RASPBERRY AND MANGO WITH ALMOND CREAM

Peel the mango, pit, and cut the meat into cubes. Press $\frac{1}{8}$ of the raspberries through a sieve. Carefully mix the rest of the raspberries with the mango pieces, confectioner's sugar, the raspberry purée, and lemon juice, and let marinate.

For the cream, beat egg yolks with sugar until creamy, and mix well with strained quark. Add the almond milk and bitter almond oil. Beat the egg whites and granulated sugar to soft peaks and carefully mix with the quark. Finally, fold in the whipped cream. Warm the marinated fruit in the oven, place on deep dishes, and cover with almond cream. Gratinate in the oven at 575°F (300°C) or maximum upper heat.

Bake Time: several minutes

Bake Temperature: 575°F (300°C) or maximum upper heat

Ingredients
1 Mango, fully ripe
About 14 oz (400 g)
  Raspberries
1 tsp Confectioner's sugar
Some lemon juice

For the Almond Cream
4 Egg yolks
$\frac{1}{3}$ cup (80 g) Sugar
3 oz (80 g) Quark
3 tbsp Almond milk
  (reduced milk with
  almonds soaked in it for
  $\frac{1}{2}$ a day, can be replaced
  with heavy cream flavored
  with almond oil)
Several drops of bitter
  almond oil
4 Egg whites
$\frac{1}{3}$ cup (80 g) Granulated
  sugar for the egg whites
1¼ cups (300 ml) Whipped
  cream

PEAR TARTLET WITH BUTTER CRUMBS

Roll the puff pastry out on a floured work surface to about 1.5mm thick, cut out 4 round, 6in (15 cm) diameter sheets and let them rest in the refrigerator for several hours.

Preheat oven to 430 °F (220 °C). For the topping, mix the marzipan with hazelnuts and 1 tablespoon of water. Spread the marzipan thinly on the dough circles. Peel, halve, and core the pears. Cut into thin slices and lay on the bases in a fan pattern. Bake for about 20 minutes. Warm the apricot marmalade with 1 tablespoon of water, stir smooth, and pour over the tartlets. Whip the cream halfway and season with sugar and rum. For the crumbs, melt butter and brown the breadcrumbs. Stir in sugar and cinnamon. Place the pear tartlets on large plates, sprinkle with butter crumbs, and serve with rum whipped cream.

Bake Time: about 20 minutes

Bake Temperature: 430 °F (220 °C)

Ingredients
12 oz (350 g) Puff pastry (see p. 11 or use ready-made dough)
1 oz (30 g) Marzipan paste
1 tbsp Hazelnuts, ground
4 Pears, very ripe
2 tbsp Apricot marmalade
1 cup (250 ml) Heavy cream
1 tbsp Confectioner's sugar
3 tbsp Rum
Flour for the work surface

For the Butter Crumbs
4¼ tbsp (60 g) Butter
2 oz (50 g) Breadcrumbs
3 tbsp (40 g) Sugar
½ tsp Cinnamon

MOCHA SPRITZ COOKIES

Preheat oven to 400 °F (200 °C). Cream the butter, sugar, and egg. Dissolve the coffee powder in the rum and add along with the almond, cocoa powder, and flour. Mix together well. Fill a piping bag fitted with a medium sized round nozzle. Pipe small crescents onto a buttered and floured baking sheet, bake for about 5 minutes, and remove from the sheet.

Warm the nougat, stir smooth and brush on the flat sides half of the crescents. Place the other half on top. Melt the chocolate in a bain-marie and dip each filled cookie in it. Place on a cooling rack while the chocolate cools.

Bake Time: about 5 minutes

Bake Temperature: 400 °F (200 °C)

Ingredients for 35 Pieces
1 stick plus 3½ tbsp (160 g) Butter
⅔ cup (80 g) Confectioner's sugar
1 Egg
2 tbsp Rum
2 tbsp Instant coffee powder
2 oz (60 g) Almonds, finely ground
1 tbsp Cocoa powder
1 cup plus 3 tbsp (150 g) Flour
4 oz (120 g) Nougat
4 oz (120 g) Dark couverture chocolate
Butter and flour for the baking sheet

LEMON HEARTS

Ingredients for 50 Pieces
3 Egg yolks
⅓ cup (120 g) Granulated
  sugar
1 tsp Vanilla sugar
Juice and zest of 1 lemon
9 oz (250 g) Hazelnuts,
  ground
Confectioner's sugar for
  rolling out the dough
Butter for the baking sheet

To Glaze
¾ cup (100 g) Confectioner's
  sugar
1 2 tbsp Lemon juice

Preheat oven to 400 °F (200 °C). Beat the egg yolks with sugar and vanilla sugar until creamy. Add the lemon juice, lemon zest, and hazelnuts and knead together well. Roll the dough out on a work surface dusted with confectioner's sugar, cut out small hearts, and lay them on a buttered baking sheet. Bake for 8–10 minutes, until golden.

For the glaze, sift the confectioner's sugar and mix with the lemon juice. Sprinkle the baked lemon hearts with the lemon glaze and let dry.

Bake Time: about 8–10 minutes

Bake Temperature: 400 °F (200 °C)

WALNUT MARZIPAN PRALINES

Ingredients for 20 Pieces
7 oz (200 g) Marzipan paste
3.5 oz (100 g) Walnuts,
  ground
3 tbsp Bénédictine (or other
  herbal liqueur)
Confectioner's sugar for
  rolling out the dough
7 oz (200 g) Milk couverture
  chocolate
About 20 pretty walnuts to
  decorate

Knead the marzipan with walnuts and Bénédictine to make dough. Roll out to about ½in (1 cm) thick on a work surface dusted with confectioner's sugar. Cut out small circles. Warm the chocolate in a bain-marie, pour over the marzipan circles, and set a walnut on each. Let drip on a rack and then place in paper candy cup.

Tip: These pralines can be stored for longer in an airtight container.

Sweet Greetings from Austria
A Brief Foray through the History of Austrian Desserts

When the Ostarrîchi Document marked the birth of Austria in 996, cooking with sugar had been around for more than 15,000 years, but was unknown in Austria. The ancient Melanesians had already discovered that an enticing sweetness could be extracted from sugarcane. Alexander the Great also knew the joy of cane sugar, and when the Caliph of Baghdad celebrated his wedding in 807, he is said to have consumed, along with his court, a formidable 40 tons of confections.

In the area that is today Austria, the only known sweetener was honey, and it would remain so for a while, at least for a certain social class. In the year 1096—Ostarrîchi could have celebrated its hundredth birthday—the first crusade began, and its participants returned three years later with their packs heavy with jewels, spices, perfumes, and Middle Eastern sugarloaves.

From that point on, what would later be called the "Austrian dessert heavens" began to gradually open. Since sugar was so scarce, it was as costly as gold or jewels, and so it took a while for baking and cooking with sugar was common knowledge.

Nevertheless, in the twelfth century, they were already talking about confectioners in Venice and it can be assumed that they were exporting their confections to the Viennese court. Confectioners only became common in Austria on a grand scale when Emperor Ferdinand I, who was raised in Spain and the Netherlands, set up his residence on the Danube in 1522. He hired a host of confectioners from the Netherlands and Spain at the Viennese court.

The year 1555 was the birthday of Austrian confection, which found a benevolent supporter in Emperor Ferdinand.

In the history of Austrian desserts, another date is at least as important as the sudden appearance of the Viennese bakers, when sweets turned from an expensive luxury to something for the common people.

In the Rococo era, a kilogram of sugar cost the equivalent of 27 Euros. That changed in 1747 when the Berlin chemist Andreas Sigismund Marggraf published the essay "Chemical experiments in manufacturing true sugar from indigenous plants." Instead of expensively imported sugar cane, it was now possible to get the same sugar from beets. The following century created the necessary infrastructure thanks to a process developed by Franz Carol Achard in 1798: In 1801 the first beet sugar factory in the world was opened in Cunern/Schlesien. And just two years later, Austria had come so far that it could open the first sugar factory in St. Pölten.

This basic ingredient that helps to create all the dreams of the Viennese dessert heavens was now accessible to all classes—and the sweet horn of plenty could be emptied over the city of Vienna.

The Sweet ABC
PRINCIPLES OF THE SWEET KITCHEN
FROM A TO Z

AGAR- AGAR   The word comes from Malayan and means "gelling food made from algae." It is mostly used in dessert making as a substitute for gelatin.

ANGELICA   An herb

BAIN-MARIE   For warming and melting chocolate, milk, gelatin, etc., to prevent burning or overheating. Water is heated in a large pot. A smaller pot or mixing bowl is placed in it with the ingredients to be warmed.

BAKING PAN   Steel molds of various sizes and shapes for baking batters

BALL SUGAR   See p. 40

BAVARIAN CREAM   Also called crème bavaroise, a basic pastry cream made with egg yolk, vanilla, sugar, gelatin, and heavy cream (see also p. 251)

BLANCH   To briefly boil fruit to prepare it for further use

BRIOCHE   A type of leavened wheat bread

BRITTLE   Brown caramel mixed with nuts

BROWN SUGAR   The myth that it is unbleached natural sugar is untrue. White sugar is just as natural as brown sugar, which has been colored with molasses and processed with sugar cane syrup.

BUCHTELN   Sweet leavened rolls, usually filled

BUCKWHEAT FLOUR   The name buckwheat is misleading, because it is an Asian knotweed that is not related to wheat. Buckwheat is easy to digest, high in protein, and contains ingredients such as copper, lecithin, and unsaturated fats.

CANDIED ORANGE PEEL   Pieces of orange peel boiled in sugar

CANDY   Small sweets pressed into particular shapes made by boiling and cooling sugar solutions; also to boil fruit, citrus peels, and some flowers in sugar until they are infused

CARAMEL   Melted sugar colored from golden yellow to dark brown, depending on the heat

CASSEROLE   Similar to soufflés, also any dessert baked in a dish

CHARLOTTE   A dome shaped or cylindrical dessert from England, lined with ladyfingers and filled with cream and fruit

CHAUDEAU   Wine foam or sabayon

COCOA POWDER   An important ingredient of many flour-based desserts, with a minimum of 20 percent fat content. If more oil is removed, it loses flavor.

COCONUT FLAKES   Finely grated coconut

COMPOTE   Fruit purée or stewed fruit (see also p. 181)

CONFECTION   A general term for sugar based foods

COOKING CHOCOLATE   Unsweetened chocolate, used for chocolate glazes, sauces, etc.

COUVERTURE   A particularly high quality confectionary chocolate (see also p. 45)

CREAM   To beat fat with egg or sugar until it is creamy

CRÈME FRAÎCHE   Sour cream with a high fat content

CRÊPES   Small, thin pancakes that can be filled with fruit, marmalade, or chocolate sauce. A famous example are Crépes Suzettes , which are flambéd at the table with Grand Marnier.

CRESCENT ROLL   Called a Kipferl or Beugel in Austrian German, a Viennese baked good (see also p. 296)

CRUMBLE   Rub fat and flour between your fingers until it becomes a crumbly dough

DALKEN   A flour based dish that originates in Bohemia (see also p. 336)

DARIOLE MOLD   Small, flat, conical mold for flan, pudding, etc.

DECORATING SUGAR   Coarse sugar crystals used mostly for decorating

DOUBLE CREAM   Cream with a very high fat content. Can be replaced with crème fraîche mixed with heavy cream or equal parts mascarpone and heavy cream.

DRY   To let glaze and similar items set before further use

DUMPLING   A filled or unfilled ball made with flour

ÉCLAIR   A long pastry made of pâte à choux

EMULSIFY   To blend various ingredients to a homogenous mixture with an immersion blender

FLAMBÉ   To pour alcohol over a dish and light it (usually ice cream, fruit, or crepes)

FLOUR   In this book, flour refers to fine white pastry flour unless otherwise specified. If you don't have access to pastry flour, you can use 1 part cake flour to 2 parts all-purpose flour. (see also p. 94)

FLUMMERY   A milk based dish, also pudding (see also p. 258)

FOLD IN   Carefully mixing together liquids and creams with beaten egg whites so that they don't fall. To fold, lift the thicker substance and carefully mix in the lighter substance with a turning motion.

FONDANT   A thick glaze of reduced sugar

FRITTER   Fried dough filler with fruit or other filling

FRY   To cook something floating in hot oil

GANACHE   A glaze or filling where chocolate is melted in simmering cream

GELATIN   Scentless and odorless bone paste used to gel creams and liquids; also the finished product, a transparent mass that is chilled and set

GLAZE   To pour butter, sugar, glaze, or fondant over a food item; also the liquid to pour over, such as sugar mixed with egg white, water, or fruit juice (see also p. 43)

GLUCOSE SYRUP   Sugar syrup made from starch

GNOCCHI   Also Nocken, small, long dumplings

GRAND MARNIER   A French liqueur commonly used in sweet cuisine, made from cognac and bitter orange

GRANULATED SUGAR   The most common sugar used for baking

GRAPE SUGAR   Monosaccharide from grapes, fruit, and honey, also called glucose or dextrose

GRATINATE   To cook something so as to form a brown crust on top

GRENADINE   Syrup made with pomegranate and sugar

GUGELHUPF   The Austrian word for a bundt cake, also Kugelhopf (see p. 52)

HOMOGENIZE   Mix with an immersion blender for about 5 minutes without letting air bubbles inside

ICING   A mixture of milk, egg, and sugar that is spread over many cakes

KISSES   Usually round cookies

KNEAD   To work dough by folding and pressing

KOLACH   From Czech, originally a general term for small cakes, now a typical Viennese coffee shop item, usually filled with poppy or quark (see p. 54)

LACTOSE   Milk sugar

LEBKUCHEN SPICE   A spice mixture of anise, cloves, coriander, nutmeg, allspice, and cinnamon

LOAF PAN   A rectangular or square baking pan

MAPLE SYRUP   Sweetener made mostly in the USA and Canada from maple sap

MARGARINE   A vegetable based replacement for butter and animal fats

MARINATE   Soaking fruit, berries, etc. to achieve a particular flavor or to protect from spoiling

MARMALADE   Reduced fruit in which no fruit pieces are visible. In the UK, orange marmalade is understood.

MARZIPAN PASTE   Almond paste available in specialty food stores

MASCARPONE   A fresh cheese made from cow's milk. Contains almost 50% fat and is well suited to fine fillings and creams.

MERINGUE   Sweetened beaten egg whites that are more dried than baked (see also p. 132)

MILK   A basic ingredients. Makes dough smoother than water does.

MISE EN PLACE   Preparing the ingredients

MOLASSES   The syrup that remains after sugar crystallization

MUST   Fruit wine

NOUGAT   A mixture made with almonds or other nuts, sugar, and chocolate, which can be used in many ways

ORANGE BLOSSOM WATER   Very useful for flavoring dough and creams

PALATSCHINKEN   Austrian crepe

PARCHMENT PAPER   Paper used to line baking pans, which prevents baked goods from sticking

PARFAIT   Half frozen ice cream and heavy cream with various additional flavors

PASTEURIZE   Heat to 140–160 °F [60–70 °C] so that particular bacteria are killed

PASTRY CREAM   A basic cream, also called crème pâtissière, which can be flavored with poppy, cinnamon, etc.

PÂTISSERIE   General term for the manufacture of pastries and confections

PATISSERIE   Pastry bakery

PETITS FOURS   Classic small cakes covered in sugar or chocolate and garnished with candied fruit. In gastronomy, an expression for small snacks served at the end of a multicourse meal.

PIPE   To squeeze creams and batters through a piping bag (or pastry bag)

POACH   To simmer just at the boiling point

POPPY   The oily seeds of the poppy plant, which should be ground and used quickly because they spoil quickly.

PRESERVING SUGAR   Granulated sugar with added apple pectin citric acid, helps with the preparation of marmalade, jam, syrup, and compote

PUFF PASTRY   A basic pastry dough that can only be prepared with real butter

PUNCH DOWN   To hit a leavened dough strongly, so that it falls and becomes finer

QUARK   A fresh, white German cheese, also called Topfen in Austria. It is available in some U.S. stores, but can be substituted with ricotta, some types of yogurt, or cottage cheese.

RAW SUGAR   Sugar full of impurities and is hard to digest. The idea that raw sugar is healthier than white sugar comes from a comparison to bleached and whole wheat flours, and is false.

REDUCE   Boil until the liquid is the desired thickness

ROCK CANDY   White rock candy is made of sugar crystals that have been allowed to grow for a long time. Brown rock candy is colored with caramel.

ROLL OUT   To spread a dough out evenly with the help of a rolling pin

ROSE WATER   A mixture of rose oil and water (1 drop to 1 cup [250ml]) mostly used in marzipan. Also good for flavoring Christmas baked goods.

ROUX   A mixture of wheat flour and fat

ROYALE   Egg milk for gratinating

SABAYON   A warm whipped foam made from egg yolk, sugar, and white wine

SALAMANDER   A gratin oven in a professional kitchen. Can be substituted in the home kitchen by the broiler.

SAVARIN   A cake baked in a savarin pan (a ring pan with a hole, like a bundt pan)

SCHMARREN   Austrian pancakes that are torn into pieces (see also p. 289)

SET   When a mixture cools and becomes firm

SHOCK   To pour cold water over still hot pasta

SIEVE   To press through a sieve or strainer

SIMMER   To keep a liquid at a low enough temperature that it never boils (for example, when making dumplings)

SIMPLE SYRUP   Clear sugar syrup (see also p. 40)

SOUFFLÉ   A dish based on beaten egg whites and egg yolks, sugar, and various flavorings. It must be served immediately, otherwise it will fall.

SPATULA   Important tool for smoothing glazes and doughs

SPELT   An ancient form of wheat that is mostly used to make healthier foods. Its grains are larger and more colorful than wheat grains.

Because it has a high gluten content, it is great for preparing pastries.

SPUN SUGAR A sugar treat originally used as decoration for baked goods (see also p. 40)

STARCH FLOUR Binding agent for preparing dough and creams. Most commonly cornstarch or wheat starch.

STARCH SYRUP A substance that, among other things, can prevent sugar from browning too quickly

STARTER DOUGH The base of a leavened dough

STIPPLE Gently poking dough several times with a fork so that no bubbles form

SUGAR CUBE A kind of sugar invented by Jacob Christoph Rad in 1840 where sugar is dampened and pressed into a cube

SUGARCANE (Saccharum officinarum) This sweetgrass, which only grows in hot climates, was the only source of saccharine before the discovery of beet sugar. Sugar cane grows up to 13 feet tall. The sweet portion is in the pulp of the 1–3 inch thick stem and yields between 12 and 18% sugar.

SUGARLOAF For hundreds of years, the classic form of refined sugar, which is increasingly forgotten since the triumph of granulated sugar. In 1938 the last Austrian sugarloaf was produced by the Hohenauer sugar factory. It was recently rediscovered and produced in small amounts for nostalgic reasons.

SYRUP Fruit or herb extract which is made very thick by its high sugar content

TEMPER Cooling couverture chocolate by repeatedly spreading it on a marble stone with a spatula; also warming slowly at a low temperature

THREAD SUGAR Sugar solution used to make glazes. You can tell that it is the right consistency because it makes threads between your fingers (see also p. 40)

TO TASTE Season the amount that you like

TURN The folding and rolling out of puff pastry layers (see also p. 19)

VANILLA SUGAR Vanilla flavored sugar common in Austrian and German baking. If you can't find it in stores, you can make your own by mixing about 2 cups of sugar with the scraped out pulp of 1 vanilla bean or you can substitute vanilla extract where a liquid is appropriate.

YELLOW SUGAR Edible raw sugar

ZEST Very thinly cut or grated peel from citrus fruit

The Authors

Toni Mörwald, born 1967, is a prize winning chef and restaurant proprietor (Ambassador in Vienna, Zur Traube in Feuersbrunn, Schloss Grafenegg, Kloster Und in Krems, and Fontana in Oberwaltersdorf, among others). After hotel management school, he cooked with Reinhard Gerer, and then practiced with countless Grand Chefs from all over the world. From 1999–2001 he led the world famous Kurkonditorei OBER-LAA. He gives cooking seminars, shared cooking tips on TV and radio, and is the author of several successful cookbooks. He is married with three daughters.

Christoph Wagner, 1954–2010, was a restaurant critic, cookbook author, and crime novelist. He studied German, English, and Cultural Management. He wrote the bestselling cookbook Die gute Küche I + II *with Ewald Plachutta and a weekly gourmet column for* NEWS *Magazine in Austria, among others. In 2001 he was awarded the Decoration of Honour in Gold for Services to the Republic of Austria.*